THE SOCIAL RESPONSIBILITIES OF BUSINESS

THE SOCIAL RESPONSIBILITIES OF BUSINESS:

COMPANY AND COMMUNITY, 1900-1960

MORRELL HEALD

Transaction Books
New Brunswick (USA) and Oxford (UK)

Library of Congress Catalog Number: 88-4795
ISBN: 0-88738-231-2
Printed in the United States of America

Library of Congress Cataloging-in-Publication Data

Heald, Morrell.
    The social responsibilities of business, company, and community, 1900-
1960.

    Bibliography: p.
    Includes index.
    1. Industry--Social aspects--United States--History--20th century.   I.
Title.
HD60.5.U5H4 1988   306'.36   88-4795
ISBN 0-88738-231-2

For
David, Seth, and Sarah

PREFACE

Events of the 1960s have dramatized the extent to which supposedly private enterprises within the American economy affect the public interest in specific ways. No serious discussion of such problems as poverty and technological unemployment, the spread of air and water pollution, highway safety or beauty, mass transportation, and urban blight can overlook their direct relationship to important business activities and interests. Participants in the struggle for racial equality, the effort to enhance and enliven popular culture, or the protest against militarism and aggression necessarily confront the fact of business involvement in the conditions they deplore. At the same time, indices of business health and progress are nervously scrutinized for evidence that society, with all its present ills and inadequacies, may be heading for even greater difficulties brought on by either inflation or recession. Under such circumstances, the issue of what is private and what is public about private enterprise has become extremely difficult, and yet crucial, to resolve.

The growth of governmental participation in most of these areas of concern has reflected an emerging belief that private leadership and initiative alone are incapable of generating acceptable levels of social and economic welfare. Business has been widely criticized, sometimes from within its own ranks, for failing to respond in more enlightened and generous terms to the full range of needs of the society from which it draws its wealth. Critics of business have pointed to many instances of neglect of, or insensitivity to, considerations other than those offering short-term private advantage.

More recently, however, the worm has begun to turn again, as it has often before in the nation's experience. Government, it appears, has no magic answers to our problems. As President Johnson's Great

Society fades into memory, leaving its own tangle of failures and frustrations behind, voices can once again be heard arguing that only the full commitment of private, voluntary leadership and resources can reach the full dimensions of human need. Urban Coalitions and "Black Capitalism" must supplement, if not entirely replace, Offices of Economic Opportunity and Departments of Housing and Urban Development. Business leaders, quite naturally, have encouraged the movement away from primary reliance upon public programs as a solvent of the nation's ills. They have hailed, as did Gerald L. Phillippe, board chairman of the General Electric Company, "growing evidence that the private sector is in the process of breaking out of a long-standing system that insists that the social problems of our society are the exclusive province of the government—local, state, or federal." [1] In so doing, they have accepted responsibility for developing solutions to these problems; and, knowingly or otherwise, they have asserted their readiness to be judged on the adequacy of their performance in a difficult and not entirely familiar arena.

Such judgments cannot, and should not, be rendered prematurely. It will be some years before we can hope to evaluate fully and responsibly the significance, both for business and for society, of the growing participation of many companies in programs of remedial education and training, pollution control, community development, equal opportunity employment, and the like. Such programs are already under way on an unprecedented scale—often, to be sure, encouraged by substantial public subsidies. They deserve an opportunity for full testing and evaluation. More than that, they call for careful scrutiny of their assumptions and implications, since, whatever their specific outcome, it is unlikely that the men and institutions participating in them will ever again accept the relatively clear and simple distinctions between public and private interest which have guided so many of us in the past.

Unprecedented though the scale and scope of private business involvement in social problems and programs may be, the idea that business has a real interest in the condition of the community in which it operates is by no means new. On the contrary, it has developed over several decades, reaching earlier peaks in the assertion in the 1920s of the "trusteeship" of corporate management for the interests of all parties to the enterprise—including the community—and with the popularization in the 1950s of the idea of the socially responsible

[1] Gerald L. Phillippe, "Business and the Urban Crisis," General Electric Company, 1967.

enterprise, or corporate "good citizen." These ideas, which paralleled the development of large-scale industry and the rise of a semi-autonomous managerial elite, served in turn to justify a number of activities theoretically foreign to profit-oriented, private companies. The support of YMCAs and community chests, the development of civic welfare and public relations programs, contributions to institutions of higher education and culture, all helped to bring business resources and leadership into active participation in social life.

Such ideas and undertakings interpreted the social responsibility of business as a challenge to foster community health and stability by devoting a portion of its resources to social welfare programs. Seldom until recently has it been suggested, in business circles at least, that social responsibility might entail reevaluation of such "internal," and therefore supposedly private, matters as fair employment practices, advertising and pricing policies, disposal of production wastes, and the like. Yet, despite the limited application given it, the idea of social responsibility has at times been presented by its most enthusiastic spokesmen in terms which invited the broadest possible interpretation. Such representatives of the "managerial" version of the American business "Creed" have seemed on occasion almost to suggest that the business corporation had become a social service agency, with profit incidental to and merely indicative of its welfare functions.[2]

Such exaggerations might, of course, be discounted were it not for two considerations. The first is that they have sometimes led to quite uncritical identification of corporate policies and objectives with the general welfare, so that "What's good for business" becomes, *ipso facto*, "what's good for the country." The second, which only now we are beginning to be in a position to appreciate, is that the current expansion of our understanding both of business and of community welfare may reflect a rapidly shifting social and economic scene in which business (understood as our generalized system of production and distribution) and general social welfare are, indeed, becoming inseparable.

If it is too early to assess the full meaning and direction of the interpenetration of public and private, government and business, functions, it may be all the more helpful to review the steps and the phases through which this movement has passed. This book attempts to do

[2] The most thorough analysis of the ideological problems presented by the new thinking in business circles is Francis X. Sutton, Seymour E. Harris, Carl Kaysen, and James Tobin, *The American Business Creed* (Cambridge, Massachusetts, 1955).

just that with one important, if limited, aspect of the total process. It is a study of the ideas and activities through which American businessmen, in the course of the first sixty years of the twentieth century, have attempted to define and respond to the relationship of their firms to the surrounding community.

It should be clear at the outset that this amounts to far less than a full-fledged analysis of the extent to which American business has achieved the ideal of social responsibility which its admirers have claimed for it. Such an evaluation, if it were possible in a single volume, would be encyclopedic in scope. It would deal, among other things, with matters of production and distribution, pricing, labor-management relations, wages, advertising, and business-government relations. All these are aspects of the total social performance of business enterprise and all must be included in a complete analysis. My own objective is more modest, although crucial to an understanding of the total problem. It is to examine the ideas and viewpoints of businessmen themselves, their changing perceptions of their own social role and relations. Unless we recognize the premises, assumptions, and perspectives with which the leaders of American business have faced the issue of its community interests and obligations, we can neither properly assess its past performance nor anticipate future prospects and problems.

The attempt to maintain a distinction between those things which belong to business and those which belong to society has never been entirely convincing even to businessmen themselves. From the earliest days of industry in the United States, despite the stern injunctions of economists and other theoreticians attempting to isolate business from social and political pressures, many employers recognized that community conditions affected their ability to recruit workers. Many aspects of industrial relations—wages, working conditions, and strikes—had social consequences which companies could not in the long run ignore. Large-scale production and distribution added new points of contact with a broader community around which social and political, as well as economic, issues frequently arose. The crises of mass society in the twentieth century—wars, depressions, and international rivalries—have further emphasized the extent to which social climates and conditions can directly affect business security and success. Beneath the strongly moralistic and ideological overtones which discussions of the social responsibility of business have often assumed, therefore, there has usually been a solid base of practical realism. Businessmen have been aroused to community concerns by moral appeals, but their response has proved more pragmatic and cautious than the rhetoric of social responsibility may suggest.

I am concerned here with the idea of social responsibility as businessmen themselves have defined and experienced it. The evolution of their attitudes and policies has occurred in response to changes in the nature and structure of enterprise itself, as well as in the surrounding social environment. It has been an uneven development, reflecting varied and irregular pressures, rather than a continuous, steady movement. Yet its progression through war and peace, good times and bad, hostile and encouraging social climates, friendly and unfriendly administrations suggests a certain inexorability in the process. In the perspective of more than half a century, the drift toward broader conceptions of social responsibility is unmistakable. Indeed, in the 1960s business leaders have been finding it increasingly difficult to define the limits of the doctrine to which, over the years, they have largely committed themselves.

That the social policies of American business have often been limited in scope and inspired by defensive motives should not obscure their importance. Whatever their origins and limits, they produced significant changes in the allocation of business resources. They contributed to the development and strengthening of a nationwide network of community welfare, educational, and cultural activities. And they brought business leaders into contact with other community groups and interests, thus further broadening their social horizons and commitments.

The meaning of the concept of social responsibility for businessmen must finally be sought in the actual policies with which they were associated. For this reason I have examined those community-oriented programs which, at different stages in the development of business thought, commanded the broadest interest and support. I have chosen not to study each phase of business social involvement in depth. Instead, I have limited myself to the conditions and ideas which attracted business attention to a potential field of social action up to the point at which the new field became acceptable to substantial numbers of executives and firms. This has made it possible to explore the steps by which business commitments were extended without assuming responsibility for detailed analysis of continuing institutional relations and problems.

The chief exception to this approach has been the treatment of the community chest movement in the 1920s and 1930s. The role of business in the growth of the chests and that of the chests in the development of business philanthropy during the Twenties require more intensive examination. And the quite different circumstances of the 1930s made the community chest movement almost the only channel through which businessmen continued to confront the issue of social responsibility in an active and positive manner; the Great Depression left them too weak and defensive to undertake other social offensives.

I have deliberately stopped short of the 1960s, believing it better in a historical analysis not to press too closely upon contemporary events. Even within the limits established for this study, it has been necessary to impose still further restrictions on the scope of the materials consulted. In view of the wide variety of business types and situations which might have been considered, it can hardly be claimed that the findings derive from a representative cross-section of the American business community. Nor is it necessary that they should do so. In studying a social movement one naturally turns to those who have led, publicized, and popularized it most effectively. In the case of business social thought, the top managerial levels of the larger corporations have provided the most active and influential leaders. Although in specific communities small businessmen often have displayed initiative and insight, the public posture of large corporations and their managers has exercised a greater national impact. Furthermore, the fact that materials reflecting the interests of such leaders are more readily available has undoubtedly favored recognition of their role. To the extent that the men considered were actually pointing in directions in which others followed, this bias is not undesirable. Wherever possible, however, I have utilized available survey and other data to check the extent of support and agreement commanded by the leaders. Much more remains to be done on a community-by-community and company-by-company basis before a complete picture of business ideas and practices concerned with social responsibility can emerge. What is offered here can only be a first approximation.

An additional caution may be in order. In this analysis I have not always attempted to distinguish sharply between types of business enterprises and managerial roles While it is true that many businesses even today are not incorporated, the key position of the corporation in modern business is generally recognized. The size and character of the firms from which most of my material comes were such that by far the larger number of them were incorporated. With this general situation in mind, I have felt free to use terms such as "enterprise," "company," "firm," "corporation," and the like interchangeably. So also with terms describing the status and role of individual businessmen. I am aware of the problems involved in differentiating between "business leaders," "managers," "executives," "entrepreneurs," and others. The editors of *Fortune* in 1956 reported that ninety-nine different definitions of an executive had been uncovered in an opinion survey of some one thousand supposed members of that class.[3] A comparable number of meanings could be found for several of the other terms. For some purposes, of course, it is valid and important to distinguish between various business leaders and functions. Where this is true, notably in Chapter III, I have tried to do so.

[3] The editors of *Fortune, The Executive Life* (Garden City, 1956), 17–21.

ACKNOWLEDGMENTS

The sources of any scholarly work inevitably are diverse, although responsibility for their use and interpretation remains specific. I am grateful to a large number of individuals and organizations whose help, sometimes even without their realizing it, has been essential to this study.

Ralph Blanchard and the officials of the United Community Funds and Councils of America, Inc., generously gave permission to use and quote from their records. The Business History Foundation under the leadership of Professor Ralph H. Hidy offered a research fellowship at the George F. Baker Library of the Harvard Graduate School of Business Administration, as well as the stimulating company and counsel of the Business History Group itself. The John Price Jones Corporation kindly authorized use of and quotation from its papers deposited at the Baker Library at Harvard. Randall M. Ruhlman and the late Kenneth A. Sturges of the Cleveland Chamber of Commerce contributed their insights and experience at the local level of business-community relations. The public relations staff of the Ohio Bell Telephone Company gave additional help. Frank W. Abrams, Ralph Blanchard, and Whiting Williams offered their time most generously for extensive and invaluable interviews.

My academic colleagues also have contributed. In addition to members of the Division of Special Interdisciplinary Studies at Case Western Reserve University, association with whom has been always encouraging and stimulating, Ralph H. Hidy, David M. Potter, and Ralph A. Andreano made penetrating suggestions. Arthur M. Johnson, Associate Editor of the Harvard Studies in Business History, has saved me from more errors of fact and interpretation than I like to think of, even if he has not been able to prevent them all. Association with such a perceptive and friendly critic has been one of the unearned increments of this enterprise.

I should like to pay respect to two essential, if often anonymous, groups of collaborators in all scholarship, the librarians and typists. The efficient and knowledgeable staffs of the Case Western Reserve University, Cleveland Public, and George F. Baker libraries have eased my task in many ways; the university secretaries and those of the Kanpur Indo-American Program, Indian Institute of Technology, Kanpur, India, have been cheerful cooperators. Mr. Rick Lawrence, then a student at Case Western Reserve, was a diligent and intelligent assistant in the early stages of research.

It is a pleasure to acknowledge the support and encouragement of the Case Research Fund Committee in freeing me for several summers from the necessity of teaching, in order that the research and writing could go forward.

My wife, Barbara L. Heald, kept things in proper perspective by reminding me continually that there were important matters other than my book calling for attention and devotion; later she demonstrated her ability as a proofreader and indexer.

CONTENTS

Business and Social Responsibility Revisited, 1987

Seventeen years from the publication of the first edition of this book and twenty-seven from the point at which its treatment of the subject ended, this is a welcome opportunity to review the original work and to survey the ground we have travelled in the meantime.[1] Although the book was on the whole favorably received, the general response to what I then perceived as a timely subject was far from overwhelming. Possibly because its appearance occurred at a time when the social climate was more highly charged than in the years during which I had been working, my efforts to strike a balanced interpretation of business efforts to define and pursue socially responsible policies were dismissed by some as too bland and uncritical. Still, it has been gratifying over the years to observe a continuing, if not a steady, trickle of interest in the book. As the intellectual and institutional climate has once again shifted, the work can now be approached in the context of a burgeoning concern for the structures, interrelations, and internal workings of organizations–public, private, and non-profit–at the local, national, and international levels.

Certainly much has changed in the course of the intervening years, enough in fact so that it is difficult to cram the essential materials for a course on the period within the limits of a semester's syllabus. And this, equally certainly, is not the place to attempt an overview of all of these developments. Yet, one can hardly consider the meaning of changes in the practice of social responsibility without acknowledging the *conditions* which those changes have recognized and responded to. After so doing, I shall offer some observations on how business has appeared to be reacting as well as contributing to the emergence of a new balance of social and economic forces as we approach this century's final decade.

Toward the end of the 1970 edition I attempted to glean from my survey of corporate actions in pursuit of social responsibility some of the directions and developments that seemed likely to persist or grow still further. By then it was already clear that support for cultural and fine arts activities was a growing sphere of interest for business. This trend has continued so that now company contributions to museums, orchestras, community theatres, public television and the like have become virtually a prerequisite for any substantial cultural undertaking.2

A second area of potential growth in defining business responsibilities that I then identified, much more tentatively, involved the rights and freedoms of employees within the corporation itself. Here, suggestions were already being advanced by the late 1950s that, in view of the amount of life, work, commitment, and personal investment that companies expected of their workers, the guarantees of freedom and opportunity provided by the Constitution in the political sphere should logically be extended to the economic realm as well. Since then equal opportunity legislation has underwritten some basic rights, while more recent concerns over the quality of American output have impelled some companies to attempt more effective communication with and between their employees. Still, the notion of a "republic of work" then rather gingerly advanced seems little closer to achievement today—or likely to become so.

The key to an effective structure for corporate social responsibility seemed to me in 1970, as it does today, to lie in the creation of opportunitites for open exchange of views and needs between business and representatives of its various constituencies. At that time, two such opportunities seemed to stand out. Both were of relatively recent origin, experimental and uncertain as to their potential for expansion, yet each appeared to offer means for encouraging a "two-way street" approach to the problem: the company foundation and the corporate social audit. Neither has, in fact, moved appreciably in the directions I suggested they might. Company foundations have grown in number and expanded the range of their undertakings, to be sure; but for the most part they have concentrated on the distribution of funds rather than on fostering dialogue and discussion with the larger community. The social audit, an ambitious and perhaps somewhat naive effort to gauge in at least rough fashion the scope and consequences of a company's influence on a wide range of social conditions, has largely failed to thrive. Despite a number of imaginative efforts at measuring the social consequences of business policy and practice, the complexities of the problem proved such that relatively few companies have been persuaded of the social audit's workability and utility.3

In any event, the search for company-initiated forms through which effective two-way communication with the public might be fostered was soon swamped by the events of the late 1960s and 1970s. Dialogue and exchange were almost forcibly dragged from the polite precincts and conference tables of business to the rough-and-tumble arenas of the streets, the legislative halls, and the newspaper Op Ed pages. Before they fully realized what was happening to them the initiative seemingly passed from the business executives to their severest critics. In the wholesale onslaught against institutions that constituted one of the chief features of those years, business found itself high on the lists of the unpopular. Its philanthropy, its experiments and efforts to acknowledge the claims of a wider constituency apparently counted as nothing in the face of widespread dissatisfaction with "the establishment." A greatly enlarged agenda for corporate social action emerged from the pressing demands of a newly activated and discontented public.

That agenda placed greatest emphasis upon the internal performance of business itself, although it also extended the list of community-oriented policies for which companies were called to account. Equal opportunity for women and ethnic minorities headed the list of items for internal action, but job training or re-training for unskilled and displaced workers came to demand equal attention. Issues relating to occupational hazards and disease as well as sensitive questions of product safety and quality commanded widespread and usually critical attention. By the mid-1970s, job security in the face of a shrinking economy pre-empted the concern of many communities, while day care for the children of women workers presented a continuing concern. Beyond the company offices and factory walls issues involving the environmental effects of business activity came to the fore as questions of air, water, and noise pollution aroused disturbed citizens. Even visual pollution, as with anti-billboard campaigns and beautification programs, attracted the active intervention of high government officials and their spouses. As if this rapidly growing list of complaints was not enough, community protests at the consequences of unplanned, ill-prepared plant closings swelled, while public criticism of company involvement in military production and the development of nuclear energy became increasingly vocal and insistent.

In the face of such a comprehensive and critical assessment of virtually every aspect of their performance it was little wonder that many businessmen responded incredulously and defensively. When public regulation and restriction of matters previously left to their own initiative or discretion ensued, resentment and hostility grew. Another cycle of business fell from grace and dominance to public disrepute and contempt then seemed, as in the 1930s, to have come full circle. Public interest groups such as Ralph Nader's and other consumer agencies, regulatory bodies such as the Occupational Safety and Health Administration and the Nuclear Regulatory Commission, as well as environmental groups including the Sierra Club and the National Resources Defense Council dotted the nation's social and economic horizons and dominated many of its news columns. Journalists seemed eager to jettison any pretense of impartiality as they assumed an increasingly adversarial stance and sought out controversies for airing at every turn.

Business itself responded to the chorus of criticisms ambivalently. While many executives reacted negatively others recognized the justice of some of the complaints and attempted to meet them imaginatively. Individual companies moved effectively to deal with many of the new challenges. One influential business organization, the Conference Board, periodically sponsored discussions and reports on aspects of business social relations. Another, the Committee for Economic Development, which in the 1950s had provided a useful forum for dialogue and common problem solving between business leaders and representative of other communities, continued to do so but with special reference to issues of broad community interest such as international trade, taxation, public housing, and energy policy. Important as these matters were, they existed at a level somewhat remote from the hurly-burly of demands for immediate and direct action. New agencies, however, came into being in response to–even to profit from–the new conditions. A Journal, *The Business and Society Review*, appeared in 1972 and continued thereafter to offer a regular forum for the dissemination of information and ideas on corporate social behavior. Special investors' mutual funds were created to assist and solicit those wishing to place their money with companies whose policies with regard to equal opportunity, environmental safety, or similar matters, were considered socially responsible. The performance of such funds, while not uniformly successful, proved to be such as to suggest that sensitivity to social issues was no detriment and might even be conducive to sound economic performance as well.[4] However hesitantly and reactively, business thus began to join the ranks of those holding that higher standards of social accountability were both desirable and achievable.

By the mid-1970s, however, insistent economic problems were commanding the forefront of the business stage. The rise of the OPEC oil cartel, followed by a discouraging cycle of inflation, unemployment, and recession, served notice that American business and government had lost their vaunted ability to manage and dominate either the national or the international economy. Further, a growing influx of foreign manufactures, ranging from iron and steel to automobiles, household appliances, and computers–competitively priced and of superior quality–demonstrated beyond serious question that at its moment of seeming supremacy many elements of American business had in fact become slack and complacent, losing their competitive edge in the increasingly international marketplace.

These new problems rendered the pursuit of social responsibility even more difficult and complex. On the one hand, many companies moved to face overseas competition by transferring investment and production to other countries where cheaper and presumably more efficient or docile labor enhanced their ability to hold their own. A natural outcome of such policies was rising unemployment and community disaffection at home. The question inevitably arose whether business, despite its earlier professions, had truly incorporated into its councils a concern for the welfare of workers, and the perennial argument that social responsibility could only be pursued in the light of a prior commitment to profitability was sharply reasserted. At the same time there was evidence that companies in some other advanced industrial nations had achieved marked improvements in the quality and price of their products by encouraging employees to work together and with management in designing more cooperative, participatory work procedures and relationships. These accomplishments emphasized the value of careful attention to employee relations and motivations. Amid such concerns, however, public demands for the continuation and even for the extension of anti-pollution and community welfare programs eased surprisingly little; and calls for improved product quality and safety were, if anything, enhanced by international competition. Thus, despite pressures to economize, business found little respite from demands that the needs and expectations of others be served.

To the extent that relief from outside pressures did come, it arose most obviously in the political arena with the resurgence from the late 1970s onward of a more conservative ideology and leadership. The accompanying relaxation of federal regulatory and supervisory measures was matched by the Reagan Administration's generous taxation policies so that in significant respects some executives did regain a degree of economic leeway. Political leverage was regained, too, with the passage of the Electoral Reform Act of 1974, permitting corporations to organize and support political action committees (PACS) and with the rise to visibility and influence of a number of conservative public policy "think tanks," such as the American Enterprise Institute. Their support of such organizations offered hope to companies that a political climate friendlier to business interests could be fostered.[5]

Drastic reductions in government commitments to social welfare programs were accompanied by administration injunctions for private and business philanthropy to take up the slack in these areas. However, unrealistic, this appeal nevertheless seemed to authorize business leadership to resume a position of primacy in defining its social responsibilities. External pressures and criticisms, however, proved remarkably resistant to the new conservatism. And much as they welcomed the relaxation of government intervention, most businessmen by now recognized that the full range of society's welfare and cultural needs was far beyond their capacity to support unassisted. Twenty years of exposure to criticism and experimentation in these areas had left many corporations more modest about their accomplishment and capacities, more sensitive to the inevitable limitations of their efforts.

Through the ebb and flow of pressures and constraints affecting corporate social responsibility over twenty-five turbulent, eventful years the continuous, if irregular, growth of such policies is readily observable. As in the period covered by this book, good times and bad, liberal or conservative administrations, although they might stretch or contract the definition of socially responsible activities, seemed to do so without seriously diverting the direction of their development.

Statistics may be an unsatisfactory tool for assessing the needs, costs, and achievements of social responsibility, and the range of activities now encompassed under the rubric means that philanthropic contributions are an even less satisfactory measure than they had formerly been. Still, the available figures on company contributions at least provide a rough measure of the scope and direction of change. Although the total amount of company giving rose from about $1 billion in 1968 to $3.6 billion in 1983, as a percentage of profits, the increase was only from 1.14 percent to 1.48 percent.[6] Corporate philanthropy, thus, grew at a rate only slightly higher than that of the economy as a whole. Such slow growth gave little reason to believe that the increase in the legal limit of tax deductible company contributions from 5 percent to 10 percent made possible by the Economic Recovery Act of 1987 would encourage a significant advance. In the long run it appears to be society's knowledge and expectations of company performance that, together with fundamental considerations of profitability, set the limits of measurable business social performance.

Finally, although the issue of the legitimacy of corporate officials functioning as trustees for the public welfare is still debated, the debate now seems largely academic. Even in 1970 I felt confident in asserting that the question, regardless of its merits, seemed to have been settled in practice. Purists may carp and anxious liberals may deplore the assumption by executives of public functions and responsibilities for the exercise of which they have not been democratically selected and which may even at times conflict with their primary business duties. But public opinion, legal warrant, and even stockholder approval have, in effect, waived such technical objections aside. Management education and management theory have accepted and begun to incorporate the new functions into their field of concerns.

Still, the achievement of true mutuality in defining and fulfilling corporate social responsibilities remains an unresolved problem. Until appropriate institutions are developed to guide this process, future misunderstandings and confrontations are virtually inevitable. Nevertheless, social responsiblity is a fact of business life, obviously attracting greater interest and attention than ever.

Notes

[1]The new edition also provides an opportunity to re-emphasize my debt to Arthur M. Johnson, whose skillful editorial advice played a large part in enabling me to formulate and clarify my ideas. A rereading makes me more appreciative than ever of his generosity and confidence.

[2]A conference Board survey of the 800 largest American corporations in 1981 indicated that nearly 12 percent of their contributions were for the arts. *New York Times*, 20 February 1983, sec. 2, 1.

[3]Marc J. Epstein, Eric G. Flamholtz, and John J. McDonough, *Corporate Social Performance: The Measurement of Product and Service Contributions* (New York: National Association of Accountants, 1977).

[4]"Social Responsibility Funds Also The Most Profitable?" *Management Review* 73 (October 1984): 68; "Moral Mutual Funds," *Fortune* 111 (27 May 1985): 27-28.

[5]Ernest Lefever, Raymond English, and Robert L. Schwellinger, "Scholars, Dollars, and Public Policy. New Frontiers in Corporate Giving," (Washington, D.C.: Ethics and Public Policy Center, 1983).

[6]*Business and Society Review* 52 (Winter 1985): 7.

1 · RESPONSIBILITY AND PHILANTHROPY IN NINETEENTH-CENTURY BUSINESS

Philanthropy and fraternity were ideals doubly commended to nineteenth-century Americans. Both the humanitarianism of the Enlightenment and the precepts of Christianity reminded men of their mutual ties and obligations. The Industrial Revolution brought changes which challenged men to apply these values in new social contexts, but it failed to destroy the sources which fed them. Indeed, the conditions it created opened new perspectives on the relationship between economic growth and social welfare. It stimulated efforts to achieve deeper understanding of the nature of social relations, and it provoked many attempts to reform and strengthen them.

American businessmen fully shared the social concerns and preoccupations of their fellow citizens. Although they have often been depicted—indeed, caricatured—as single-minded pursuers of profit, the facts are quite otherwise. The nature of their activities often brought them into close contact with the harsher aspects of the life of a rapidly industrializing society. Like others, they were frequently troubled by the conditions they saw; and, also like others, they numbered in their ranks men who contributed both of their ideas and their resources to redress social imbalance and disorganization.

Businessmen, to be sure, had special reasons for desiring stable and healthy social conditions. To show that they were not guided by self-

1

interest alone is not to suggest that they were, at the opposite extreme, paragons of sympathy and understanding. When labor was in great demand, as was often true in America, it was practical good sense to show the workers some consideration. Where the masses were empowered with the right to vote, their circumstances and mood might be a matter of serious concern to even the staunchest conservative. From the outset, self-interest combined with idealism to foster sensitivity to social conditions on the part of the business community.

This mixture of practical and benevolent motives behind the thinking of businessmen in regard to social conditions often produced confusing results. If charity stimulated efforts to promote social welfare, on many occasions it encouraged unrealistic perceptions of the needs and wishes of others. Paternalism was a constant, usually unrecognized, source of distortion and disappointment. If self-interest stimulated attempts to improve social conditions, a narrow view of self-interest often limited the effectiveness of such measures.

Gradually, and in a variety of contexts, experience led to broader conceptions of self-interest. Even more slowly came the recognition that, for durable achievement, welfare must be defined by the community at large and not by business alone. Such understanding grew hand in hand with the lengthening time-horizons of business which, in turn, stemmed from the rise of large-scale enterprise. It has been further stimulated, in the course of the twentieth century, by the emergence of government as the ultimate guarantor of social and economic stability. Even so, the idea that business should strive to be socially responsible as well as economically profitable has many implications which remain to be fully explored.

Most of the controversies which have centered around this idea in recent years can, in fact, be found in embryo in the experience of nineteenth-century business. The development has been a continuous one which belies, on both counts, the popular contrast between the socially conscious businessman of today and his supposedly self-centered predecessor of a century ago. The well-documented philanthropic ventures of a number of early business leaders indicate a breadth of interests which should serve as a caution against such oversimplifications; but these philanthropies have ordinarily been seen as far removed, if not totally divorced, from the business pursuits which made them possible. A reexamination of the evidence, however, shows that businessmen confronted social conditions as part of their working —as well as their leisure—lives.

A close study of business involvement in nineteenth-century social problems would surely reveal a broad range of experiences and viewpoints. Even a review, in a number of different contexts, of selected situations and responses to them shows clearly that the foundations of much contemporary business social thought were laid in the practical needs of a swiftly developing economy. The moral climate, the language, and the institutional structure in which the social relations of business are considered have certainly changed. But the basic questions and the difficulties arising from efforts to resolve them seem on close inspection to be surprisingly familiar.

COMPANY AND COMMUNITY

Even had they wished to, businessmen could not avoid the fact that community conditions and economic interests were interwoven in the hundreds of company towns which sprang up in the isolated river valleys and mining areas of nineteenth-century America. Textile manufacturers, iron and steel makers, railroads anxious to promote settlement of their lands, as well as other enterprises, often found themselves the chief proprietors of such communities and, therefore, inescapably accountable for and dependent upon the social conditions which prevailed. The records of such company towns are too widely scattered for detailed analysis here, but the studies which have been made of them supply ample evidence of employer involvement in many aspects of community life.[1]

Perhaps the best-known early American enterprise organized on a considerable scale was that of a group of New England businessmen known as the Boston Associates. These mercantile capitalists, includ-

[1] For discussion of nineteenth-century company towns and business support of community services, see Samuel Eliot Morison, *The Ropemakers of Plymouth: A History of the Plymouth Cordage Company, 1824–1949* (Boston, 1950), 89–90, *passim;* Vera Shlakman, *The Economic History of a Factory Town, A Study of Chicopee, Massachusetts,* in Smith College Studies in History, XX, Nos. 1–4 (October, 1934–July, 1935), 14, 239; Thomas R. Navin, *The Whitin Machine Works Since 1931* (Cambridge, Massachusetts, 1950), 62–76, 361; Paul W. Gates, *The Illinois Central Railroad and Its Colonization Work* (Cambridge, Massachusetts, 1941), 370–79; W. H. Tolman, *Industrial Betterment* (Baltimore, 1900); G. W. W. Hanger, "Housing of the Working People in the United States," United States Bureau of Labor Statistics, Bulletin, No. 54 (Washington, 1904); Harriet L. Herring, *Welfare Work in Mill Villages; The Story of Extra-Mill Activities in North Carolina* (Chapel Hill, 1929); Edward C. Kirkland, *Industry Comes of Age, Business, Labor, and Public Policy, 1860–1897* (New York, 1961), 333–36; James B. Allen, *The Company Town in the American West* (Norman, Oklahoma, 1966).

ing such men as Francis Cabot Lowell, Nathan Appleton, and Patrick Tracy Jackson, turned to textile manufactures when the War of 1812 blocked commerce. In a very real sense, they were pioneers of modern industry in the United States. In addition to the factory system, first fully developed in their mills, they undertook the first substantial application of the corporate form of business organization to manufacturing. And, significantly, they displayed an active interest in the lives and living conditions of their employees.

Lowell, the leader in the early stages of the Associates' undertaking, may have imported his ideas regarding employee welfare, much as he copied his machinery, from British models. In 1811 he visited England and Scotland, where for over a decade Robert Owen at New Lanark had been demonstrating that good wages and healthy living conditions benefited employer and worker alike. There is no record that the two men ever met, although Lowell visited not far from New Lanark. But they shared a Nonconformist religious background, together with a shrewd appreciation of the value of a stable and efficient labor force. Waltham, Lowell, and other early mill towns developed by the Associates showed much the same concern for the needs of industrial workers as did Owen's own model community.[2]

[2] Robert Owen deserves far wider recognition than he has received as a forerunner of modern welfare capitalism. His role as a leader in the cooperative movement and as a socialist forerunner of Marx has obscured his earlier efforts to moderate the impact of industrialization on capitalist society through factory legislation and managerial benevolence. Owen stood at a fork in the road of modern economic thought. Down one path lay the rejection of laissez-faire capitalism for socialism or communism; down the other, the gradual modification of capitalism through a combination of public and private restraints. It was Owen's peculiar role to participate in the opening of both of these intellectual highways. In the United States he has been chiefly remembered for his part in the New Harmony experiment, an intriguing failure in utopian socialist reconstruction. But his more enduring monuments may be at New Lanark and at Lowell, showplaces and examples of welfare capitalism at the beginning of America's industrial history.

Owen recognized the employer's stake in the health and well-being of his workers and the manufacturer's interest in adequate wages for the laborer. Humane conditions within the factory, decent circumstances of housing and living, provision for the education of the community's children, all, in Owen's vision, were woven into the seamless web of a healthy and productive society. And his own experience seemed to offer proof that concern for the interests of the worker was profitable, as well as charitable. No wonder New Lanark attracted international attention and drew distinguished visitors from far and near! If he won few converts, it was perhaps because his restless mind moved too rapidly and erratically ahead of his contemporaries. Owen's conversion to socialism and free

Both a genuine wish to avoid the degenerate conditions of European factory towns and a practical need to attract reliable workers guided the policies of the Boston Associates. Their efforts to entice the deft and upright daughters of New England farm families into factory work included provision of decent working and housing conditions, as well as religious, social, and intellectual resources suited to the backgrounds and expectations of the prospective employees. During the 1820s and 1830s these Massachusetts mill towns became showplaces of the new industrial order. Drawing notable visitors from America and Europe, among them Andrew Jackson and Charles Dickens, they symbolized possibilities and hopes for a richer, more abundant life through the productivity of the new factory system. As a creative combination of benevolent and practical concerns, the city of Lowell stands as a landmark of early American business policy.

To be sure, the idyllic aspects of these model industrial towns proved short-lived. Not only did the independent-minded mill girls chafe under rigid management controls, but wages as well as working and living conditions deteriorated markedly after 1840. Depression and overproduction brought falling prices. The arrival of Irish immigrant labor, willing and able to work for lower pay, meant new competition for work and wages. As was to be the case again and again in the history of business benevolence, good intentions failed to outweigh the pressures of competition, the drive for profits, and, especially, the absence of mutual understanding between business leaders and their employees.[3]

The influences which led businessmen to concern themselves with the welfare of their employees were not limited to the textile industry or to the vicinity of Boston. As factory production spread along the coasts and valleys of New England, through the Middle States, and

---

love, as well as his atheism, soon alienated conservatives; the failure of his schemes for radical social reconstruction all too easily cast discredit on his achievement at New Lanark. G. D. H. Cole, *Robert Owen* (Boston, 1925), 127–29, *passim*.

[3] For a critical interpretation of the Boston Associates and their mill communities, see Hannah Josephson, *The Golden Threads: New England's Mill Girls and Magnates* (New York, 1949). Nathan Appleton, "Introduction of the Power Loom and Origin of Lowell" (Lowell, 1858), emphasizes the Associates' concern to protect the moral character of their employees. The most complete study of Lowell is John Coolidge, *Mill and Mansion, A Study of Architecture and Society in Lowell, Massachusetts, 1820–1865* (New York, 1942), 171–72, *passim*. See also Ferris Greenslet, *The Lowells and Their Seven Worlds* (Boston, 1946), 157–59.

gradually to the South and West, the company town was a recurring phenomenon of industrialization. Often located at sites remote from the centers of population, as available resources, cheap land, the accidents of discovery, or access to transportation might dictate, these nuclei of industrialism were frequently the creation of a single man or enterprise. Compelled to win and hold workers from the competing attractions of more varied communities, such isolated plants and towns were forced to offer supplementary facilities and services. Company housing and stores, libraries, schools, and similar institutions were often provided by employers to attract a stable and contented labor force. As the motives which inspired such undertakings were mixed, so, too, unfortunately, were their results. Power and paternalism, however well-intentioned, produced exploitation and bitterness more often than they managed to create harmony.

Modern methods of accounting and analysis attempt to specify relationships and responsibilities, often to the point of oversimplification. Such techniques were largely unknown, and scarcely feasible, in the nineteenth century. Just as distinctions between business and the community were not clear in the company town, so sharp lines were seldom drawn between contributions of the firm to community services and the individual benevolences of owners or managers. Especially in cases in which the enterprise was owned or managed by a single proprietor or family group, the question may not even have arisen. Similarly difficult to determine, in the simplicity of economic organization, is whether aid to the community was considered an aspect of employee relations or a separate and distinct sphere. Such issues awaited a less spontaneous era for their resolution. The assumption of social responsibility by American business preceded by many decades the emergence of theories which sought to justify it in economic terms or to locate it on organizational charts.

As industrial growth continued, the single-company town was superseded in many areas by urban centers of greater complexity. Here it was more difficult to assign to any given employer responsibility for conditions affecting the residents. The absence of standards or criteria for company participation in social welfare programs, coupled with the growing impersonality of the urban environment, discouraged business philanthropic activity in such communities. Consequently, individual rather than company contributions provided the chief support of urban charities.[4]

[4] For a summary and analysis of American philanthropy in the nineteenth century, see Robert H. Bremner, *American Philanthropy* (Chicago, 1960),

Still, occasional recorded instances of company expenditure for worthy community causes suggest that the practice was slowly developing. The activities of the R. H. Macy Company of New York City may have reflected an unusual social sensitivity on the part of its officers, or the special circumstances of a metropolitan center; but they can hardly have been unique. Whatever the personal philanthropies of its management, the firm's records show enough cases of assistance rendered to social agencies to indicate a sense of relationship to the community beyond the walls and hours of the business itself. Thus, in 1875 funds were contributed to an orphan asylum; and in 1885, in an action which anticipated modern fund-raising techniques, the firm sponsored a sale of miniature copies of the Statue of Liberty as part of a drive to pay for the pedestal upon which the original was to stand. In 1887, gifts to charities amounting to $1,084.91 were listed under Miscellaneous Expenses in the company's accounts. Apparently, the now-familiar device of company advertisements in the programs and publications of charitable organizations was not uncommon; in 1902 Macy's abandoned the practice, "preferring not to confuse business objectives with donations to community enterprises." That it was not easy to maintain such clear-cut distinctions can be seen in the fact that, a few years later, the company somewhat inconsistently undertook to provide floor space, fixtures, clerks, and related facilities for a department selling articles made by the blind.[5]

Thus, in larger cities as well as in small, company officials were a natural source from which assistance might be sought for a wide range of charitable and community purposes. Evidently, the temptations or pressures to respond to such requests were not eliminated by the anonymity of urban life.

PULLMAN, ILLINOIS

Visitors to Chicago's 1893 Columbian Exposition found another model industrial community at Pullman, on the southern rim of the

especially Chapters IV–VII. On the confusion of interests and loyalties characteristic of early corporate enterprise, see Robert A. Lively, "The American System," *Business History Review*, XXIX (March, 1955), 81–96. Lively's comments are based upon the experience of the early "mixed" corporations, in which both public and private investment contributed an additional element of ambiguity.

[5] Ralph M. Hower, *History of Macy's of New York: 1885–1919. Chapters in the Evolution of the Department Store* (Cambridge, Massachusetts, 1943), 119, 163, 178, 268.

young metropolis. According to its founder, George M. Pullman of the Pullman Palace Car Company, the new town was to have been "a bright and radiant little island in the midst of the great tumultuous sea of Chicago's population; a restful oasis in the wearying brick-and-mortar waste of an enormous city." Built in the 1880s, Pullman was a showplace widely heralded as an example of enlightened business policy; total company investment in the town was estimated at $8,-000,000. The community included tenements, parks, playgrounds, and a church. An arcade, a theatre, a casino, and a hotel named for Pullman's daughter, Florence, were provided for the use of inhabitants and guests. The Pullman Military Band entertained the public from the local bandstand and even went on nationwide tours, incidentally publicizing the "experiment" and the company. Standards of housing, lighting, maintenance, and appearance were far in advance of the time, winning for the town an award at the International Hygienic and Pharmaceutical Exposition at Prague in 1896 as "the most perfect in the world." Presumably, the prize jury was concerned only with the physical aspects of the community, for by then its social arrangements had been revealed as considerably less than perfect.

Jane Addams, who knew George M. Pullman and visited the town on many occasions, testified to the founder's well-intentioned interest in improving living conditions among his employees. It was said that his benevolence had endangered his reputation in more hard-headed business circles. Yet Pullman's motives were practical, too. Outstanding among them was the desire to attract skilled labor beyond the immediate vicinity of Chicago's trade unions and union organizers. His philanthropy was further tempered by a determination to realize a profit in good times or bad. Pullman saw no inconsistency or impropriety in permitting the company-built church on the town square to stand vacant when no group could raise the money to rent it at a rate which would assure six per cent return on investment.

Those who probed beneath the attractive surface of Pullman town found it riddled with suspicion and fear. Richard T. Ely, the economist, spent his honeymoon in Pullman in 1884 while preparing an article on the community for *Harper's Monthly*. Over glasses of buttermilk in a small shop, Ely and Simon Patten, another student of economic and social change, questioned the proprietor. Here and elsewhere they found a picture far less promising than official publicity suggested. Company spies pried for evidence of union infiltration or "dangerous" and disloyal views on the part of employees.

In 1894, depression exposed the inconsistencies of a management which laid off workers and cut wages nearly twenty-five per cent on the one hand, but refused to reduce rents on the other. A strike of Pullman employees spread rapidly to include the entire railroad network centering on Chicago. In a complex series of events, federal intervention to settle the Chicago railway strike was invoked by President Cleveland. Eugene V. Debs, president of the striking American Railway Union, was jailed for violation of a court injunction. Given leisure and opportunity to reflect upon the benefits which workers could expect from private benevolence and public justice, Debs later emerged from jail to lead the American Socialist Party for the remainder of his career.

Ely could hardly have been surprised at the outcome. A decade earlier he had written, "The idea of Pullman is un-American. It is a benevolent, well-wishing feudalism, which desires the happiness of the people but in such a way as shall please the authorities." And Jane Addams said of George M. Pullman's flawed experiment, "He cultivated the great and noble impulses of the benefactor until the power of attaining a simple human relationship with his employees was gone from him." [6] Yet Ely, too, acknowledged that Pullman's aims, and even his performance, were forward-looking in many respects.

Both in their recognition of the interest of business in social conditions and in the spirit of benevolent autocracy that guided them, Lowell and Pullman had much in common. A set of interrelated needs had been recognized, but the means relied upon to meet them had been one-sided and inadequate. The hierarchical structures of business, and particularly of the single-company town, encouraged employers to assume that the wealth and power at their command made them the

[6] The fullest treatment of Pullman is Almont Lindsey, *The Pullman Strike: The Story of a Unique Experiment and of a Great Labor Upheaval* (Chicago, 1942). George M. Pullman and the town itself are discussed in Graham Taylor, *Pioneering on Social Frontiers* (Chicago, 1930), 111–16; Jane Addams, *Twenty Years at Hull House* (New York, 1910), 214–18; Richard T. Ely, *The Ground Under Our Feet, An Autobiography* (New York, 1938), 166–71; Graham Romeyn Taylor, *Satellite Cities* (New York, 1915), 28–38, 70–76; Stanley Buder, *Pullman; An Experiment in Industrial Order and Community Planning, 1880–1930* (New York, 1962); and Richard T. Ely, "Pullman; A Social Study," *Harper's New Monthly Magazine,* LXX (February, 1888), 452–66.

The spirit of the showplace community, which the casual visitor might have missed, was captured in the words of one Pullman worker: "We are born in a Pullman house, fed from the Pullman shop, taught in the Pullman schools, catechized in the Pullman church [sic], and when we die we shall be buried in the Pullman cemetery and go to the Pullman hell." Quoted in Louise C. Wade, *Graham Taylor: Pioneer for Social Justice* (Chicago, 1964), 76.

best judges of the entire community's welfare needs. Wider business horizons and the emergence of more independent social institutions have since introduced checks upon such easy assumptions. Even so, the isolation of business leadership from community life and problems has continued to hamper the formulation of serviceable social policies.

WAR, RAILROADS, AND THE YMCA

Industrialization and social change, or fear of change, led some businessmen to consider their economic interests in a wider social context. Among the most drastic forms of change, especially in recent centuries, is war. The central crisis of nineteenth-century America, the Civil War, supplied an impetus—as have subsequent wars—for further experiments in the relief of social hardship. Extraordinary circumstances prompted Americans to develop new forms of cooperative assistance to serve the needs of soldiers and their families, Negro and white refugees, and others similarly deprived of normal sources of assistance.

Chief among the agencies which struggled with such problems were two war-spawned national organizations, the United States Sanitary Commission and the YMCA-sponsored United States Christian Commission. Both were private relief and welfare agencies, the first such to be organized and financed on a nationwide basis. Enjoying only minimal government sanction and support, they depended upon private contributions to sustain their work.

Contributions came largely from individual givers, yet such was the power of patriotism and the pull of need that business firms, too, appeared upon the lists of donors. The Baldwin Locomotive Company was certainly unusual in giving ten per cent of its annual earnings to the Christian Commission; in most instances gifts in kind—clothing, foodstuffs, or essential services—seem to have been involved. Railroads, express companies, and telegraph companies made their services available to both the Christian and the Sanitary Commissions without charge, while for a New York City Sanitary Fair the drygoods merchants contributed $9,000 worth of their wares. On the same occasion, gifts of money were also received from the mercantile community, $131,000 being reported from the drygoods companies and $20,000 apiece from the grocers and the fancy goods dealers.[7] Once again, the record fails to make clear the extent to which these contributions were

[7] Bremner, *American Philanthropy*, 76–88; Emerson D. Fite, *Social and Industrial Conditions in the North During the Civil War* (New York, 1910), 282; William Quentin Maxwell, *Lincoln's Fifth Wheel, The United States Sanitary Commission* (New York, 1956), 310.

company, as distinguished from individual, offerings; but it is reasonable to assume that they reflected a mixture of motives and sources similar to those already discussed.

There were, however, significant differences. In the company towns managers had direct responsibility for charitable and other welfare payments. Thus, they might well avoid or overlook sharp distinctions between business and community purposes. In donating to independent agencies such as the national commissions, businessmen faced conscious decisions about contributions policies, in this case about giving even to recipients in whom no direct business interest existed. Still further, the causes and agencies to which wartime contributions were made were national, not merely local, in scope. Such departures from past practice pointed in directions in which business policy was to move under the impetus of internal and external pressures as time went on. At the war's end it was scarcely imagined that a precedent for future, peacetime business giving had been created. Yet when such giving came it came through an organization, the YMCA, which had directly participated in the work of the Christian Commission.

If the Civil War had, for a time and under special circumstances, brought national problems and needs into the limelight, the industrial development of the postwar decades was equally national in its impact and consequences. The completion of a continental railroad network laid the foundation for the consolidation of a national economic and social order, in which large-scale production and urbanization brought new patterns of life and work to millions of Americans and immigrants within a few short years. That new social relationships should create problems of individual and community adjustment, as well as demands for public and private welfare measures, was inevitable. It was appropriate, therefore, that within a few years of the war's end the railroad companies—advance agents of social change—should join in a program of assistance to their employees, a group of people torn from their accustomed social moorings not by the circumstances of war but as a direct consequence of the nature of the railroad industry itself.

By the extent and nature of their operations, railroads created conditions for their workers and problems for their managements that local business leadership had not faced. By a series of unforeseen and even accidental steps, the rail companies forged an association with the Railroad Department of the YMCA for a joint venture in welfare organization for workers isolated by the nature of their work from home, family, and friendly associations.

The YMCA movement had begun in London in 1844 with the aim

of maintaining and applying Christian values within an urban, business-oriented society. Its founders had announced their purpose, that "in every house of business an altar shall be raised to God." Spreading quickly to the United States, the movement prospered and acquired a distinctly practical outlook. At a Detroit convention, in 1868, its delegates approved a statement proposing, in effect, that the relationship between the YMCA and business should be a two-way street, "that the manufacturers of our country can make no investment that will bring them greater dividends than that of contributing largely to aid in the formation and sustaining" of local YMCAs.[8] As this language suggested, the "Y" was strongly middle-class in outlook. The Railroad Department represented its most successful nineteenth-century effort to establish contact with the laboring classes; and even here its orientation seems to have been toward the aristocracy, the skilled mechanics and trainmen rather than the common workers.

After scattered, largely unsuccessful efforts along the line of the Union Pacific Railroad in the late 1860s, solid ground for the foundation of the Railroad Department appeared in Cleveland in 1872. There, out of the distress of an onlooker at the accidental death of an anonymous railroad worker came the provision of a room in the station of the Cleveland, Cincinnati, Columbus, and Indianapolis Railroad for employee rest, recreation, and prayer meetings. James H. Devereaux, the company's president, supported the effort; George W. Cobb, a local businessman, assumed a full-time job as secretary to the new "Y." Railroad officials showed a marked interest in the plan, and within a short time similar facilities had come into being in Chicago, Baltimore, Boston, and Detroit. When Cornelius Vanderbilt, Jr., became a director of the national YMCA and provided space in Grand Central Station for a New York branch, the movement was firmly launched. Vanderbilt's gift, in 1888, of $250,000 for a separate building equipped with baths, game rooms, and other comforts symbolized the combination of personal and company interests at work, at the same time that it set the stage for still further growth.[9]

As early as 1877 nineteen railroad branches had already come into being, and the Railroad Department acquired its own international

---

[8] Quoted in F. Emerson Andrews, *Corporation Giving* (New York, 1952), 24. See also Sherwood Eddy, *A Century with Youth: A History of the YMCA from 1844 to 1944* (New York, 1944), 4.

[9] C. Howard Hopkins, *History of the YMCA in North America* (New York, 1951), 227–29, 234–36; John F. Moore, *The Story of the Railroad "Y"* (New York, 1930), 16–37.

secretary. By 1903, there were 198 separate branches with over 60,000 members, and it was estimated that companies controlling 79 per cent of the total railroad mileage of the country were giving recognition and support to the activities of the Railroad "Y." Forty-two companies reported regular annual contributions totaling nearly $500,000; that of the Pennsylvania Railroad alone amounted in 1903 to more than $60,000.[10] In most instances the buildings which housed the YMCAs were company-owned. The better-equipped establishments provided housing and food, libraries, educational programs, and other recreational facilities, as well as the more traditional prayer meetings and Bible study groups; but many of the smaller branches, naturally, offered poorer accommodations. Members contributed their own funds to cover operating expenses.

By 1901 the railroad branches were "well on their way to becoming a YMCA-managed company welfare program," but their significance was greater than this statement shows. Most YMCA leaders came from middle-class backgrounds and took the side of management in the industrial disputes that erupted periodically in the 1880s and 1890s. Still, some were troubled by the paternal, autocratic attitudes displayed by company officials. They came to feel that questions of conscience were raised when the "Y" received funds from corporate treasuries. Their doubts revealed a growing sensitivity to the mixture of motives guiding business welfare policies and suggested the desirability of independent status for agencies working with the laborers.

Clarence Hicks, secretary of the Railroad Department from 1890 until 1911, was one of these thoughtful leaders. He had successfully solicited aid from such men as James J. Hill, Cyrus McCormick, Russell Sage, and even, after some difficulty, from George M. Pullman; but he had failed to persuade E. H. Harriman to support any agency over which Harriman himself did not have full control. Hicks noted a tendency on the part of the companies to think of the Railroad YMCA branches as philanthropy and "welfare work" rather than as an aspect of intelligent management and good business. Such thinking seemed short-sighted to Hicks, whose legal education had, perhaps, helped persuade him that the workers, too, should share in the support and leadership of a truly community-oriented YMCA program.[11]

Railroad officials accepted at least some of Hicks's ideas. A report to the national YMCA convention as early as 1882 stated, "The shrewd-

[10] Max Riebenack, *Railway Provident Institutions in English Speaking Countries* (Philadelphia, 1905), 258.

[11] Clarence J. Hicks, *My Life in Industrial Relations* (New York, 1941), 20–28.

est men, the most careful managers, are now ready to appropriate money for the purpose [support of the YMCA program] and the response they make to their stockholders is 'we are making money for you by it.'" [12] Association with, and support of, YMCA programs led some employers to see a closer relationship between business and community conditions than they had ordinarily recognized before.

As companies whose interests reached far beyond the limits of a single town or city and whose financial and organizational requirements placed them in the forefront of business growth, the railroads faced circumstances experienced in a growing number of industries. An Industrial Department was created by the YMCA in 1903 to extend the activities and influence of the association more generally among the workers in American factories. In the years before World War I, the growth of company giving for community-related welfare and social programs was closely associated with the work of the YMCAs.[13]

In this association, the spirit of the company town, of benevolent paternalism in employee and community relations, remained strong. Yet, increasing attention on the part of businessmen was paid to the idea that practical, as well as charitable, motives might justify company interest in social welfare. As business grew in scope and complexity, its impact upon those its interests touched became increasingly apparent. As industry and city life created a new social interdependence, agencies such as the YMCA, the settlement houses, and other charitable societies emerged to mediate between those who controlled property and those who struggled for it. The shortcomings of paternalism were becoming evident to a small number of community leaders, although this lesson was to prove particularly troublesome for businessmen. The new approaches to mutual understanding and assistance could find only limited expression in the novelty and turmoil of the late nineteenth century. Their significance as forerunners of a more socially minded business system as it emerged in the next half-century can now be properly recognized.

PHILANTHROPY AND BUSINESS THOUGHT

The cooperation which grew between the YMCA and industry underlines the continuing influence of religion on the thinking of American businessmen which other studies have already demonstrated. If worldly wealth and success were sometimes accorded a religious sanc-

[12] Hopkins, *History of the YMCA*, 234.

[13] Eddy, *A Century with Youth*, 59–60; Hopkins, *History of the YMCA*, 237, 475–78; Andrews, *Corporation Giving*, 23–26.

tion, religion by no means abdicated its right to influence the uses to which wealth should be devoted. The doctrine of the stewardship and responsibility of the successful for the unfortunate, stemming from centuries of Christian and Jewish teaching, continued to be preached to attentive ears.[14]

Trained in such ideas since their youth, businessmen did not succumb easily or entirely to the vogue of Social Darwinism, with its emphasis upon the relentless struggle for success and the survival of the fittest. Between competing ideologies individuals wavered or made their own private compromises. If some shared S. C. T. Dodd's belief that failure and misery stemmed from individual moral weakness and that "neither man nor God can do much for one who will do nothing for himself," there were others who could agree with Amos Lawrence that their wealth meant "increased responsibilities and duties, as agents who must at last render account" and who could have echoed Lawrence's prayer, "God grant that mine be found correct." [15] Toward the end of the century, the rising Social Gospel movement emphasized the application of Christian principles in everyday life, to the end that God's kingdom might come in this world. The Social Gospel preached the obligation to minister to men's needs within the realities of an industrial society: "Philanthropy is the dynamics of Christianity. That is to say, it is Christianity in action." [16] Thus, the obligation of the wealthy to the less fortunate was reaffirmed and the ideal of service to mankind vindicated.

[14] Irvin G. Wyllie, *The Self-Made Man in America, The Myth of Rags to Riches* (New Brunswick, 1954), 56–74, 83–87; Reinhard Bendix, *Work and Authority in Industry; Ideologies of Management in the Course of Industrialization* (New York, 1956), 257; Merle Curti, "American Philanthropy and the National Character," *American Quarterly,* X (Winter, 1958), 420–37; Ralph H. Gabriel, *The Course of American Democratic Thought,* 2nd edition (New York, 1956), 155–58. See Freeman Hunt, *Wealth and Worth* (New York, 1857), for many contemporary examples.

[15] Dodd was quoted in W. J. Ghent, *Our Benevolent Feudalism* (New York, 1902), 29; Lawrence, in Freeman Hunt, *Lives of American Merchants,* 2 vols. (New York, 1858), II, 270. See also Shlakman, *Economic History of a Factory Town,* 32–34; Hunt, *Wealth and Worth,* 282–89, 290, 382; Allan Nevins, *John D. Rockefeller, The Heroic Age of American Enterprise,* 2 vols. (New York, 1940), I, 642; Paul Goodman, "Ethics and Enterprise: The Values of the Boston Elite, 1800–1860," *American Quarterly,* XVIII (Fall, 1966), 452–76; and Edward A. Purcell, Jr., "Ideas and Interests: Businessmen and the Interstate Commerce Act," *Journal of American History,* LIV (December, 1967), 561–78.

[16] Richard T. Ely, *The Social Aspects of Christianity, and Other Essays* (New York, 1889), 85; Washington Gladden, *Social Facts and Forces* (New York, 1897), 99–104.

Religion and philanthropy, as we have seen, were not the only sources of business concern for the improvement of social conditions. Considerations such as the desire to attract workers, to resist the encroachment of unions, or to stem the appeal of other "radical" movements often pointed in the same direction. It was difficult to weigh such diverse objectives in economic terms. While some businessmen openly acknowledged them, others spoke of them only in the rhetoric of philanthropy. There is ample evidence in both cases, however, that substantial numbers of employers believed that healthy communities and plant conditions were economically, as well as morally, desirable.

The idea that business and the community shared mutual interests was a common theme of nineteenth-century discussions. Ordinarily, the idea was advanced as a warning against public interference with the freedom of enterprise. Occasionally, however, even businessmen reversed the emphasis to note their dependence upon a sound and satisfied society. They noted the "everlasting fact that there can be no permanent prosperity or good feeling in a community where benefits are not reciprocal." Or, more concretely, they recognized, with George F. Johnson of the Endicott-Johnson Company that "it is not entirely what happens inside of the factory, but also what happens outside, that affects working conditions." The confusion of motives which could be involved in such a position was evident in a statement issued by the Cleveland Hardware Company: "Although we believe that what we are doing [in plant and community improvement] is most practical and philanthropic, our company does not feel that it is a philanthropy, but a good business proposition." [17]

Personal, as well as practical and moral, considerations strengthened the interest of business in community welfare projects. The growth of large-scale enterprise and the spread of formal, institutional relationships did not eliminate the influence of the individual. Even some of the largest companies remained under the domination of their founders, owners, or chief executives. Only on a case-by-case basis is it possible to determine the specific combination of forces at work. Yet such personal ambitions as the desire to win social recognition, to demonstrate success, and to assert leadership could sometimes find sat-

[17] Tolman, *Industrial Betterment*, 81. Johnson is quoted in *Forbes*, VI (2 October 1920), 467; Bendix, *Work and Authority in Industry*, 266. See also Hunt, *Wealth and Worth*, 43; Homer J. Hagedorn, "A Note on the Motivations of Personnel Management: Industrial Betterment 1885–1910," *Explorations in Entrepreneurial History*, X, Nos. 3–4 (April, 1958), 134–139; Navin, *Whitin Machine Works*, 356.

isfaction through company participation in social service activities.[18]

In June, 1889, an article which has been called "the most famous document in the history of American philanthropy" appeared in the *North American Review*.[19] It bore the simple title, "Wealth," and its author, Andrew Carnegie, contributed as much as any single individual to popularize the idea that the successful business leader should consider himself a trustee for the interests of the community at large. Carnegie, an individualist and a follower of Herbert Spencer, was reluctant even to incorporate his vast steel properties. His philanthropies, like his business undertakings, bore the unmistakable stamp of his forceful personality. Yet his ideas and actions in distributing his fortune for social ends foreshadowed in many ways the later development of corporate philanthropic and community relations programs.

The "duty of the man of wealth," Carnegie held, was the administration of that wealth in the public interest. To this end, he ought

> ". . . to consider all surplus revenues . . . as trust funds, which he is called upon to administer . . . in the manner in which, in his judgment, is best calculated to produce the most beneficial results for the community—the man of wealth thus [would become] the mere trustee and agent for his poorer brethren, bringing to their service his superior wisdom, experience, and ability to administer, doing for them better than they would or could do for themselves." [20]

Despite Carnegie's rejection of religious orthodoxy, the continuing influence of the Christian doctrine of stewardship is clear in his words. It was not the originality of his views that was important (indeed, they were little more than a forceful statement of the beliefs which guided other concerned businessmen) but rather the prestige, breadth of interest, and commitment he brought to the task of putting those ideas into practice.

As a philanthropist on a large scale, Carnegie soon faced the inevitable problem confronting those who, however great their resources, must choose among a seemingly limitless number of social needs and

[18] Merle Curti, "The History of American Philanthropy as a Field of Research," *American Historical Review*, LXII (January, 1957), 359; Bremner, *American Philanthropy*, 246.

[19] *Ibid.*, 105.

[20] Andrew Carnegie, *The Gospel of Wealth*, ed. Edward C. Kirkland (Cambridge, Mass., 1962), 25.

worthy causes. The response to his initial article encouraged Carnegie, within six months' time, to prepare a second, setting forth his views on the principles which should guide the administration of philanthropy. Sharing with many of his contemporaries a fear of "indiscriminate giving," Carnegie cited with approval a statement that "nine hundred and fifty out of every thousand dollars bestowed to-day upon so-called charity had better be thrown into the sea." [21] To avoid supporting waste and sloth, he stressed giving to encourage self-help by the deserving. The famous Carnegie libraries perfectly exemplified this aspect of their donor's philosophy: not only did they provide aid and stimulation for those able to respond to it, but Carnegie expected the recipient communities to contribute to their maintenance and support.

Carnegie had a healthy respect for the experience of men more knowledgeable than he in the fields of his philanthropic interest. In giving for education and the advancement of knowledge, areas of special concern to him, he solicited the advice of men such as the presidents of Cornell and Johns Hopkins universities. He appreciated the value of informed, as well as systematic, philanthropy and in this instance was acknowledging a situation which the rise of large companies like his own had helped to create: the increasing isolation of business leaders from direct contact with many of the conditions which they hoped to alleviate.[22] Carnegie's recognition of the need for expert guidance and interpretation marked still another stage in the emergence of formalized business philanthropy.

The scope of philanthropy, as Carnegie conceived it, was not narrow. Although interested in "practical" giving, he did not rule out support for cultural institutions such as museums, parks, concert halls, and the arts in general. He strongly approved of contributions for municipal improvement and beautification.

> As with libraries and museums, so with these more distinctively artistic works: they perform their great use when they reach the best of the masses of the people. It is better to reach and touch the sentiment for beauty in the naturally bright minds of this class than to pander to those incapable of being so touched. . . . The man who erects in a city a conservatory or a truly artistic arch, statue, or fountain, makes a

[21] The second article, entitled "The Best Fields for Philanthropy," is reprinted in *ibid.*, 29–49.

[22] *Ibid.*, xvii–xix; Burton J. Hendrick, *The Life of Andrew Carnegie*, 2 vols. (New York, 1932), I, 340ff.

wise use of his surplus. "Man does not live by bread alone." [23]

In advocating such a conception of social giving, Carnegie exemplified the hope which Judge James Hall had expressed to the members of the Young Men's Mercantile Library Association of Cincinnati in 1846, that the successful business leader "should be a patron of the arts, a promoter of education, a friend to literature and science, an active agent in all public improvement. . . ." [24]

Judge Hall's dream, which anticipated to a remarkable degree the full scope of corporate philanthropy as it has developed in the twentieth century, won only a limited—and, primarily, an individual—response in the nineteenth. Yet by the end of the century businessmen were demonstrating a growing sense of involvement with the conditions of other social groups, such as workers, immigrants, and urban masses. They exhibited, to be sure, little inclination to question the extent to which business itself might have helped to create the very social needs they now sought to relieve. But company contributions to local and national welfare causes had become accepted, if not common, practice. Independent agencies of social welfare work, such as the YMCA and the Red Cross, had arisen on a national footing and had established a claim on business interest and support. The idea that the successful business leader was a trustee for the welfare of society had been impressively stated; and a broad cultural definition of that responsibility had been suggested and exemplified in the philanthropies of men such as Andrew Carnegie.

What the nineteenth century lacked, and what the twentieth was to supply, was a rationale—a concept of the the relationship of business to the community—in which social responsibility was clearly seen as a charge not merely upon individual conscience and concern but upon corporate resources as well.

[23] Carnegie, 41–45. In this article Carnegie further recommended hospitals, medical schools, and laboratories as appropriate recipients of gifts. In so doing he virtually completed the list of causes to which business leaders have subsequently devoted their own and their companies' funds. Hendrick, *Carnegie*, II, 220.

[24] Hunt, *Wealth and Worth*, 222. See also E. L. Godkin, "Idleness and Immorality," *Forum*, XIII (May, 1892), 335–43.

2 ▪ BUSINESS IN THE ERA OF REFORM, 1900–1920

The greatest contribution of nineteenth-century American business-men to the eventual emergence of a theory and practice of social responsibility may well have been not what they did in recognizing an obligation to their fellow citizens, but rather what they did not do. Clearly, as the old century merged into the new, the unhappy and disruptive consequences of industrialization were more widely apparent than were signs of evolving business statesmanship. Protests were leveled against the economic, social, and intellectual consequences flowing from the steady advance of large-scale production and business organization. The attack on big business came from many sources: from hard-pressed farmers and small businessmen struggling against the pressures of an increasingly interdependent economy; from union leaders and other spokesmen for groups of workers becoming aware of the relationship of organization to economic power; from the churches bestirring themselves under the influence of the Social Gospel movement to concern for the worldly welfare of mankind; from middle-class reformers, journalists, social workers, and intellectuals fearful for the survival of familiar values in the bewildering industrial cities of the land. Galvanized into an effective political force at every level of government by leaders such as Mayor Tom Johnson of Cleveland, Governor Robert M. LaFollette of Wisconsin, and Presidents Theodore Roosevelt and Woodrow Wilson, the Progressive movement made the years before the First World War a colorful and productive era in the history of American reform.

As criticism mounted, businessmen began to display a new sensitivity to public opinion—to social and political forces which they had hitherto dismissed, for the most part, with mild concern or contempt. As a climate of public disenchantment developed, the business community reacted in a variety of ways. In the case of the National Association of Manufacturers, for example, the response was one of aggressive attack upon issues and groups—notably labor unions—which threatened dominant positions. In other cases, it took the form of efforts to reconcile the interests of business and the community.

Such efforts centered around three broad categories of concern. Thoughtful businessmen noted, first, the disturbances and distress accompanying urbanization. They were, second, sensitive to the threats posed by economic concentration and large-scale enterprise to individual initiative and the laissez-faire tradition. And third, they responded slowly—but with gathering interest as international conflict after 1914 projected the struggle for democratic ideals on a wider stage—to the Progressive demand that freedom, equality, and responsibility be meaningfully established within the framework of an industrial society. Each of these concerns prodded business leaders to consider the social consequences of their positions and powers and, thus, to move toward new conceptions of opportunities and duties.

URBAN LIFE

Urbanization touched the interests and awareness of employers and merchants in many ways. It provided both a labor force and a market, thus offering an obvious motive for support of civic promotional activities. Experience further led some businessmen to see that qualitative, as well as quantitative, aspects of city life were important to them. Healthy workers and decent living conditions meant better business in the long run. Business leaders, too, could hardly escape the spur of local pride, especially when their own economic success and social status had risen side by side with the fortunes of the community.

Troublesome conditions in the cities—in employment, housing, and social and cultural development—had attracted the notice of a growing number of business leaders by the 1890s. Chicago was among the first of the large urban centers to develop a leadership group working for civic betterment.

Alarmed by the burgeoning social and industrial conflict of the late 1880s, a group of Chicago business leaders began efforts to promote harmony between industry and labor. Stimulated further by depression, the Pullman strike, and civic pride associated with the Columbian Exposition of 1893, the group organized itself as the Civic Federation of Chicago. Among its leaders was Lyman J. Gage, chairman of the board of directors of the exposition and later secretary of the treasury in the McKinley administration. Others included businessmen such as Cyrus McCormick, Marshall Field, Franklin MacVeagh (who followed Gage's path to Washington, becoming secretary of the treasury under President Taft), Charles Dyer Norton, and Charles Wacker. Also active in the Federation were such figures as C. L. Hutchinson, founder of the Chicago Art Institute, and Theodore Thomas, conductor of the Chicago Symphony Orchestra. Norton and Wacker, as well as Daniel Burnham, another Federation member, were prominent in the production of the Chicago Plan, a pioneer effort at urban reconstruction. With the creation of a department of philanthrophy, the Federation extended the range of its interests into the social welfare field.

Religious motives merged with economic interest and civic pride to inspire the Federation's leadership. William T. Stead, a British journalist visiting Chicago at the time of the 1893 exposition, played a leading role in effecting this merger. Impressed and depressed at the same time by the city's potential and its problems, Stead became an evangelist for civic purity. At mass meetings he exhorted Chicagoans to cleanse their community of crime, corruption, and poverty. Stead's book, *If Christ Came to Chicago*, measured the cruel realities of urban life against the standards of Christian humanitarianism; its influence upon the business community was electric.

The Federation's encouraging start in Chicago led to the idea of a similar approach to problems at a national level, and the National Civic Federation was formed in 1900. Mark Hanna, chairman of the Republican National Committee and an influential industrialist, was named president. Hanna's prominence and his record as an employer sympathetic to the needs of his workers, together with the fact that Samuel Gompers of the American Federation of Labor was named vice president, suggested a major effort on the part of business leadership to bridge the gulf of suspicion and misunderstanding separating it from labor and other reform leaders. A series of conferences between business and labor representatives, economists, educators, religious leaders, and others on subjects such as the trust problem and industrial relations was the National Civic Federation's chief contribution to mutual understanding. Although it produced few concrete results, the Federation did provide a forum for the exchange of views on important public issues. This approach proved to be compatible, however, with continued strong anti-union policies on the part of many employer members.[1]

Another Chicagoan, whose concern for workers and immigrants, their families, and their conditions of life drew her into association both with employers and employees and into the work of the Chicago Civic Federation, was Jane Addams. Pioneering in the social work movement, Miss Addams saw her role at the Hull House settlement, which she had founded, as mediating between the needs and pressures of conflicting social groups and interpreting the problems and prerequisites of an industrial democracy. By force of example and power of personality she illuminated the ideal of a humane social order encompassing the needs and interests of many groups. Nor were her ideas and influence limited to her generation alone. The college students who each year came to work at Hull House and who felt her dedication to human values in an impersonal world did not forget the experience. Among her apprentices, who later found in the business world opportunities for the expression of these values, were William Lyon MacKenzie King, Walter Gifford, and Gerard Swope.[2]

By direct contact with social workers, political reformers, and other Progressives, as well as by exposure to the growing volume of public criticism, businessmen began to face the social consequences of their

[1] Taylor, *Pioneering on Social Frontiers*, 18–34; Ray Ginger, *Altgeld's America, The Lincoln Idea Versus Changing Realities* (New York, 1958), 248–54; Marguerite Green, *The National Civic Federation and the American Labor Movement, 1900–1920* (Washington, 1956), 4. For Gage and MacVeagh, see *Dictionary of American Biography* (New York, 1943), VII, 85, and XXI (Supplement I), 535–36; for Stead, see *The Encyclopedia Americana* (New York, 1959), XXV, 539, and Joseph O. Baylen, "A Victorian's Crusade in Chicago, 1893–94," *Journal of American History*, LI (December, 1964), 418–34. See also Gordon M. Jensen, "The National Civic Federation: American Business in an Age of Social Change and Social Reform" (Ph.D. dissertation, Princeton University, 1956).

[2] James W. Linn, *Jane Addams, A Biography* (New York, 1935), 162–64, 186; Zona Gale, "Great Ladies of Chicago," *Survey*, LXVII (1 February 1932), 482; Paul U. Kellogg, "Twice Twenty Years at Hull House," *ibid.*, LXIV (15 June 1930), 266; David Loth, *Swope of G.E.* (New York, 1958), 153.

Jane Addams's own interpretation of her experience and its meaning is set forth in *Twenty Years at Hull House* (New York, 1910) and *Democracy and Social Ethics* (New York, 1905).

Settlement houses, like other social and charitable institutions, depend for financial support upon private contributions; Hull House was no exception. That Miss Addams's work in promoting mutual understanding and compromise between worker and employer did not compromise her own integrity was shown by her rejection of a $50,000 donation conditioned upon her withdrawal from the movement to secure passage of factory legislation. Linn, *Addams*, 121.

policies which they had previously neglected. And the Progressives' insistence upon a public interest to which all special interests were subordinate had a lasting influence on business thought, however much executives might on occasion resist specific Progressive policies. Owen D. Young, who was to be Gerard Swope's partner at the General Electric Company in enunciating in the 1920s a new concept of the position and obligations of corporate management, testified to the influence which Ida M. Tarbell and Lincoln Steffens had upon his own thinking.[3] The Progressives were preachers and teachers of moral values in a new and puzzling world; their lessons penetrated beyond their own time and ken, even beyond the conscious learning of their pupils.

The involvement of Chicago business leaders in social uplift, civic improvement, beautification, and cultural enrichment, as well as in a search for common ground between capital interests and labor interests, was not a unique instance of growing business concern for community life. In other cities, too, boards of trade and chambers of commerce, formed to advance the common economic and political interests of their members, were beginning to see the relevance of civic conditions to these interests. At a conference on "Community Education and Business Progress," sponsored by the University of Illinois in 1913, President Harry A. Wheeler of the United States Chamber of Commerce hailed this new understanding. "After all, only as civic conditions are ideal can commercial conditions be made ideal," Wheeler noted. He recognized, too, an educational function which enlistment in community affairs could supply: "Businessmen, through these organizations [chambers of commerce], have come to see their duty to the general public in an entirely different light." [4]

Kenneth A. Sturges of Cleveland, a leader among a new group of chamber of commerce officials specializing in civic affairs, asserted, "The progressive manufacturer has discovered that it is not enough to have a fine equipment; unless his employees are living in healthy and moral surroundings he cannot expect to get the highest efficiency." [5] Practical as well as altruistic motives mingled, clearly, in such an evaluation; but in their practicality businessmen were increasingly aware

[3] Loth, *Swope of G.E.*, 72, 153.

[4] University of Illinois, "Conference on Commercial Education and Business Progress," Urbana-Champaign, 1913.

[5] Kenneth A. Sturges, *American Chambers of Commerce*, Williams College, David A. Wells Prize Essays, No. 4 (New York, 1915), 215ff.

of a range of considerations extending beyond the traditional limits of business.

The Cleveland Chamber of Commerce worked actively on behalf of civic welfare and improvement after 1900. Its leaders included Ryerson Ritchie (President), Frank Scott (Secretary), Martin A. Marks, and Samuel Mather—all prominent Cleveland businessmen. Howard Strong, son of the popular Social Gospel leader Josiah Strong, served with Kenneth Sturges on the Chamber's staff. In 1899 the Cleveland Chamber organized a committee on industrial welfare, the first of its kind. The following year another precedent was set with the formation of the Committee on Benevolent Associations, whose purpose was to investigate and endorse worthy charities. In rapid succession, committees on housing conditions and education drew up model codes and worked to secure their enactment. City planning and industrial development similarly attracted the Chamber's active interest. Its efforts were also instrumental in the creation, in 1913, of the Cleveland Federation for Charity and Philanthropy, forerunner of the first modern community chest association.

The contributions of civic-minded business leadership to Cleveland in this period were outstanding. In addition to the work of the Chamber of Commerce, the administration of Mayor Tom L. Johnson (1901–10) brought a distinguished reform government to the city. Johnson, a successful industrialist who had turned reformer under the influence of Henry George's *Progress and Poverty*, led an urban renaissance whose influence was widely felt. Although the Cleveland business community fought many of Mayor Johnson's measures and Johnson himself considered the Chamber of Commerce a citadel of "Privilege," the rivalry between reformers and businessmen gave a strong lift to municipal spirit and institutions.

But business interest and reformist zeal were not the only sources of Cleveland's blossoming. Both Whiting Williams, executive director of the Federation for Charity and Philanthropy, and Allen T. Burns, director of the Cleveland Foundation, the first community foundation in the nation, through which Cleveland's citizens contributed to civic agencies, had studied for the ministry at the University of Chicago and participated in the settlement house movement under Graham Taylor at Chicago Commons. In Cleveland, as elsewhere, Social Gospel influences joined with political and economic incentives to arouse the interest of businessmen in urban conditions and problems. By no means were the religious influences exclusively Christian, however. Martin

Marks, chairman of the Chamber of Commerce Committee on Benevolent Associations, based his work for coordinated philanthropy on the
model of already-federated Jewish welfare agencies.[6]

A milder expression of business awareness of civic problems took
the form of "service" clubs, such as Rotary and Kiwanis. Rotary, the
earliest club of this kind, was founded in Chicago in 1905 and consciously emphasized friendship and service as against the materialism
and self-centeredness of economic life. Similar clubs followed in short
order. They acted chiefly as focuses for feelings of good fellowship
and identification, as symbols of status and recognition, and as channels
for regular, if limited, expressions of community feeling. They enlisted
aid, both personal and financial, for hospitals, youth work, and similar
social programs. Conservative and well-intentioned, providing a meeting-ground for business and professional people, their ideal—pursued
with enthusiasm if not always with discrimination—was perhaps best

[6] Interview with Kenneth A. Sturges, 11 February 1958; interview with
Whiting Williams, 31 August 1962; letter from Howard Strong to author, 20
May 1963. (Howard Strong served for several years as an official of the Cleveland
Chamber of Commerce and in 1907 and 1909 conducted surveys for the Chamber's
Committee on Benevolent Associations before the formation of the Federation for
Charity and Philanthropy.) *Cleveland Plain Dealer*, 4 July 1962, 32-A; "Allen T.
Burns, 1876–1953, Compiled by His Friends and Relatives" (Cleveland, 1954), 5;
Howard Strong, "The Relation of Commercial Bodies to Our Charitable and
Social Standards," *Proceedings of the National Conference on Charities and Cor-
rection* (1910), 247–52; Wade, *Graham Taylor*.

Federations of Jewish charities had begun in Boston and Cincinnati as early as
1896, then spread to other cities. An even earlier instance of federated fund-raising
took place in New York City, when ten hospitals joined to solicit contributions in
1879; see John R. Seeley and others, *Community Chest: A Case Study in
Philanthropy* (Toronto, 1957), 17–19. For Tom Johnson's relations with the
Cleveland Chamber of Commerce, see his *My Story*, edited by Elizabeth J.
Hauser (New York, 1913), xxii, 90, 113–14, 170, 267, and Scott M. Cutlip, *Fund
Raising in the United States* (New Brunswick, N.J., 1965), 65–68.

For parallel developments in Boston, see Alpheus T. Mason, *Brandeis; A
Free Man's Life* (New York, 1946), 109, 138, and the papers of the Boston
Chamber of Commerce at the Baker Library, Harvard University.

The latter half of the nineteenth century also saw the spread of the Charity
Organization Societies to many of the larger cities. These societies attempted to
bring a measure of cooperation and system to the rapidly proliferating urban
charity agencies. They were the forerunners of the twentieth century's welfare
federations and community chests. For a discussion of their efforts, see Amos G.
Warner, *American Charities: A Story in Philanthropy and Economics* (New York,
1894), 372–93. The Civic Federation of Chicago helped to organize a Central
Relief Association to act as a "charity clearing house" in 1894. Albion W. Small,
"The Civic Federation of Chicago; A Study in Social Dynamics," *American
Journal of Sociology*, I (July, 1895), 79–103.

summed up in the Rotary motto: "He profits most who serves the best." [7] Their popularity signified a deeply felt need, especially among small businessmen, for fellowship and idealism in an increasingly organized and impersonal world.

Across the nation a new civic consciousness was awakening. Businessmen were beginning to share with social workers, political reformers, and others a mutual sense of common interests and interdependence. From this new awareness would grow new forms of community organization, which, in time, would bind business closely into the web of urban welfare institutions.

BIG BUSINESS

The aspect of business which, during the Progressive years, attracted widest public attention was, of course, that of economic consolidation. Even more than urban living conditions, the spread of large-scale enterprise was a subject of immediate concern to many businessmen. In addition, rising public dissatisfaction with the "trusts" was producing a threat of political sanctions. The Granger Laws of the 1870s, the Interstate Commerce Act and the Sherman Act, and the "trust-busting" activities of the Roosevelt, Taft, and Wilson administrations were visible signs of government's responsiveness to groups threatened by big business. However vague their comprehension of the technological, economic, and social implications of industrialization, however ineffectual their efforts at control or reform, there was no mistaking the willingness of a growing number of Americans to favor measures to discipline and control business power. When, after the turn of the new century, muckraking journalists and sensitive politicians at every level of government successfully tapped these new sources of public interest, the Progressive movement surged rapidly to the crest of its popularity and influence.

That the Progressives, fearful of the implications of large-scale social and economic organization and outraged by clear evidence of abusive and undemocratic exercise of economic power, were still by no means totally "anti-business" in their outlook has been amply demonstrated.[8] Yet they were no longer so willing as they formerly

[7] Charles F. Marden, *Rotary and Its Brothers, An Analysis and Interpretation of the Men's Service Club* (Princeton, 1935), 6, 31, 123, *passim;* Frederic B. Greene, "Social Work and the Philistines," *Survey,* LXIX (December, 1933), 409.

[8] Among the studies of the Progressive period which illuminate the relations between reformers and businessmen, the following are particularly relevant:

had been to believe that the welfare and advancement of business or any other special interest group was automatically conducive to the public interest. In the bitter contest between organized power blocs, the weak and unorganized had too often felt the sting of deprivation. Simple observation recorded the obvious misery and inadequacy of large segments of society. The concept of a public interest distinct from and superior to the claims of local or special interests, and of government as the guardian of that interest, emerged as central to the creed of Progressive democracy.

Since business, especially big business, was the most visible interest group, it was most widely feared. Business was identified with the technological, economic, and organizational forces which were remolding American life. In its very successes it had often showed contempt or neglect for moral restraint, as well as for the broader social consequences of its actions. Yet American respect for the successful entrepreneur was not easily discarded. Indeed, the spectacular careers of business leaders in an era of rapid economic growth heightened the awe in which they were held. While Americans looked to government for protection from exploitation and predatory power, they looked also to established and respected business leadership for constructive efforts to overcome deficiencies.

Leading public figures urged businessmen to recognize the social consequences of business policies. Jane Addams noted at the time of the Pullman strike a growing belief that "a large manufacturing concern has ceased to be a private matter; that not only a number of workmen and stockholders are concerned in its management, but that the interests of the public are so involved that the officers of the company are in a real sense administering a public trust." [9] Many times in the course of his career Theodore Roosevelt expressed the hope that responsible conservative leadership would face constructively the needs of industrial society and the evidence of its inequities; and time and again Roosevelt received a negative response to even his moderate reform proposals.

President Arthur T. Hadley of Yale University felt it necessary in

---

Samuel P. Hays, *The Response to Industrialism, 1885–1914* (Chicago, 1957); Richard Hofstadter, *The Age of Reform, from Bryan to F.D.R.* (New York, 1955); John Chamberlain, *Farewell to Reform* (New York, 1932); and Robert H. Wiebe, *Businessmen and Reform: A Study of the Progressive Movement* (Cambridge, Massachusetts, 1962). See also Gabriel Kolko, *The Triumph of Conservatism; A Reinterpretation of American History, 1900–1916* (New York, 1963).

[9] Addams, *Democracy and Social Ethics*, 142–43.

1906 to warn businessmen that a short-sighted rejection of public criticism would encourage the spread of radicalism. Discussing "Ethics and Corporate Management," Hadley warned of the need for businessmen to guard against the abuse of economic power. "The president of a large corporation is in a place of public trust," Hadley asserted. "In an obvious sense he is a trustee for the stockholders and creditors of his corporation. In a less obvious but equally important sense he is a trustee on behalf of the public." Neither scrupulous fulfillment of strictly business obligations nor a conscientious sense of personal responsibility were adequate guides for men in such positions. Both on moral grounds and as a matter of practical significance, Hadley counseled against a narrow, legalistic interpretation of the rights and responsibilities of corporate officials.

> Industrial corporations grew up into power because they met the needs of the past. To stay in power, they must meet the needs of the present, and arrange their ethics accordingly. . . . Those who fear the effects of increased government activity must prove by their acceptance of ethical duties to the public that they are not blind devotees of an industrial past which has ceased to exist, but are preparing to accept the heavier burdens and obligations which the industrial present carries with it.[10]

Evidence that sensitivity to the issues raised by President Hadley was stirring in business circles can be found in the careers of individual business leaders. Executives of large companies, in particular, were beginning to recognize the value of public respect and confidence. It was scarcely a coincidence that E. H. Gary, chairman of the giant United States Steel Corporation, was among the first to concede the desirability of publishing information on company operations "to satisfy doubts and enlighten the ignorance of the public." Gary was a corporation lawyer with political experience and a strong religious background. An associate of J. P. Morgan, Gary had good reason to

[10] Arthur T. Hadley, *Standards of Public Morality* (New York, 1907), 79, 84–87, 95–96; Frank A. Vanderlip, "Business and Education," Address at the University of the State of New York, 29 June 1905. For another early statement of the trusteeship idea, see the remarks of Eugene E. Prussing, president of the Citizens' Association of Chicago, in the *Proceedings of the National Conference on Trusts and Combinations* (New York, 1908), 235. This conference was sponsored by the National Civic Federation. Samuel Gompers, another participant, warned, "Let the trusts remember that they will be required to give an account of their stewardship to the people." *Ibid.*, 254–55.

fear public opinion. As head of the nation's newest, largest, and most dramatically formed "trust" he saw the need to protect it from public criticism and possible governmental interference. His effort to present the company in a favorable light began in 1903 with U. S. Steel's first published annual report. Although Gary's concept of what the public should know would seem remarkably limited today, for its time it marked a significant recognition of public interest in the operations of a theoretically private enterprise. One disgruntled director of U.S. Steel resigned in protest over Gary's policies, which, he feared, were "turning business into a Sunday school." [11]

More directly involved in the daily life of the people than steel manufacture was the rapidly expanding telephone industry, which operated under near-monopoly conditions. As a national communications system was consolidated by the American Telephone and Telegraph Company, Theodore N. Vail, its chief executive, joined Gary as an advocate of public conciliation through a "policy of frankness." Recognizing that some governmental supervision and regulation of his company was inevitable, Vail set about assuring that such supervision would be friendly by cultivating cordial customer and public relations. Emphasizing courtesy, efficiency, and service throughout the organization, Vail and E. K. Hall, vice-president for public relations, combined conciliation and "education" with judicious acknowledgment of the ultimate authority of the people. Their purpose was to keep government supervision from becoming government control. In a series of annual reports, they argued that the alternative to public control lay in imaginative and unstinting efforts to win popular approval, to demonstrate that "we feel our obligations to the general public as strongly as to our investing public, or to our own personal interests." [12] The success of Vail and his associates in countering the

[11] Ida M. Tarbell, *The Life of Elbert H. Gary; The Story of Steel* (New York, 1925), 137–38, 144–45; Samuel Crowther, ed., *The Book of Business,* 5 vols. (New York, 1920), I, 11–19; A. H. Cole, *Business Enterprise in Its Social Setting* (Cambridge, Massachusetts, 1959), 66; B. C. Forbes, *Finance, Business and the Business of Life* (New York, 1915), 207–8. Cf. Samuel Gompers, "Preaching is Practice," *The American Federationist,* XXV (May, 1923), 402–4.

Twenty years later, Gary would still consider interference in his company's labor policies—by unions and even by the President of the United States—unwarranted.

[12] Albert Bigelow Paine, *In One Man's Life, Theodore N. Vail* (New York, 1921), 236–40, *passim.;* N. R. Danelian, *A. T. and T.: The Story of Industrial Conquest* (New York, 1939), 280; Norton E. Long, "Public Relations Policies of the Bell System," *Public Opinion Quarterly,* I (October, 1937), 6–19; Leila A. Sussman, "The Personnel and Ideology of Public Relations," *ibid.,* XII (Winter, 1948–49), 707; American Telephone and Telegraph Company, "Report of

stigma of monopoly and minimizing the danger of governmental interference was not lost upon other interested executives.[13]

A variety of backgrounds and experiences, religious, business, and political, encouraged executives of large corporations to consider the relationship of their firms to the public and its governmental representatives. Theodore Vail had served as a government official—general superintendent of the U. S. Post Office Department. Gary had been a judge and a corporation lawyer. George W. Perkins, outstanding among the younger generation of financiers and investment bankers for his perception of the changing social environment within which business was developing, was the son of a YMCA worker and Sunday school superintendent. After a career which included work in slum, railroad mission, and reform schools, the elder Perkins turned to the sale of life insurance with equal zeal. The son's career, in a sense, reversed that of the father, beginning with business and ending in an assortment of civic and humanitarian activities.

Throughout his life George Perkins demonstrated a strong need to associate himself with social and humanitarian causes. He felt an equally strong drive for power and leadership. Rising rapidly in the New York Life Insurance Company, where he applied his talents in a business which he attempted to identify with a new order of social security, Perkins attracted the attention of J. P. Morgan and joined the Morgan firm as a partner. Here his flair for organization was exerted both as a director of the new U. S. Steel Corporation and as promoter and director of another Morgan-sponsored combination, the International Harvester Company. Perkins's business experience thus involved him in some of the largest industrial and financial undertakings of his day.

Here, George Perkins found new outlets for his social impulses. Not only did he share E. H. Gary's attitudes toward public relations; he promoted efforts to improve working conditions and labor-management relations within the new steel empire. Perkins also developed an employees' stock ownership plan for U. S. Steel. By 1913 he was advocating the addition of a workers' representative to the corporation's board of directors.

Statements of the Structure of the Bell System and Some of Its Fundamental Principles . . . ," (New York, 192[?]), 38–45.

[13] Forbes, *Finance*, 34; Eugene E. Prussing, "Corporate Reforms," speech given at the National Civic Federation on Trusts and Combinations, Chicago, October 23, 1907; Forrest McDonald, "Samuel Insull and the Movement for State Utility Regulatory Commissions," *Business History Review*, XXXII (Autumn, 1958), 241–54.

Perkins's stock ownership plan was similar to others undertaken by moderately progressive companies in the years before and after the First World War. The altruistic elements of such plans were coupled with a desire to head off unionization while securing the benefits of a stable, efficient, and satisfied working force. They attempted to promote thrift among the workers, as well as a sense of partnership and participation in the enterprise. Although their results were not impressive, the continuing interest which such plans aroused among employers suggested a growing awareness in business circles of the need for management to develop stronger ties of understanding with its workers.

Despite the fact that U. S. Steel refused to deal with labor unions, Perkins, like Mark Hanna, maintained friendly personal ties with conservative labor leaders through his membership on the board of directors of the National Civic Federation. For a period of time Perkins paid out of his own pocket a portion of the salary of John Mitchell as head of the Federation's Trade Agreements Department. Thus, paternalistic and precautionary though his labor policies may have been, Perkins was probably ahead of prevailing business opinion in his sensitivity to the human and social dimensions of an industrial economy.[14]

Even the scope of the Morgan interests finally failed to quench Perkins's thirst for leadership. Familiarity with the affairs of some of the largest companies in the nation convinced Perkins of the semi-public character of such theoretically private property and power conglomerations. "The larger the corporation becomes, the greater become its responsibilities to the entire community," he stated in 1908. "The corporations of the future must be those that are semi-public servants, serving the public, with ownership widespread among the public, and with labor so fairly and equitably treated that it will look upon its corporation as its friend. . . ."[15] In this spirit, Perkins advocated government supervision of big business as an alternative to a program of trust-busting. The supervision he sought was preventive, rather than restrictive, intended to warn companies against untoward practices instead of penalizing them for violation of a law. As in his labor policies, Perkins's intention here was defensive: he aimed at preventing,

[14] John A. Garraty, *Right-Hand Man; The Life of George W. Perkins* (New York, 1957). "Giving the Corporation a Soul," *Current Literature,* LI (October, 1911), 460–62, summarizes Perkins's ideas on welfare capitalism.

[15] George W. Perkins, "The Modern Corporation" (New York, 1908). See also Perkins's "The Community Nature of Business," in Crowther, *Book of Business,* V, 148–50.

through a combination of managerial deference to public opinion and mild governmental supervision, more drastic interference with business freedom.

Such views, coupled with financial independence, unremitting energy, and a wide political acquaintance which included such men as Senator Albert J. Beveridge and President Roosevelt himself, gradually drew Perkins toward politics. As a progressive businessman Perkins was a natural leader of the right wing of Roosevelt's Bull Moose party in the 1912 election. Here he associated, not always harmoniously, with such social workers as Jane Addams, Frances Kellor, Paul U. Kellogg, and others who shared the party's leadership. After Roosevelt's defeat, Perkins struggled to keep the Progressive party alive; but internal dissension, lack of an adequate organizational and financial base, and Roosevelt's return to the Republican fold finally brought an end to the party and left Perkins without a cause. He ended, as his father had begun, with the YMCA, in whose Industrial Department he had maintained a steady interest and to whose overseas work during the First World War he made one of his final contributions.[16]

Perkins's career exemplified the impact of the varied forces which were moving American business toward new awareness of its social relations and responsibilities. As the visibility, and therefore the vulnerability, of large-scale business grew, its leaders faced the necessity of courting public favor and support. The personal backgrounds and motives of men such as Vail, Gary, and Perkins were probably less influential than were practical considerations of business strategy, yet it is worth noting that sensitivity to these considerations and to the general social situation which created them seems to have been particularly strong among business leaders with strong religious, humanitarian, or professional orientations. The combination of these factors was creating a new community consciousness in business circles.

When Arthur J. Eddy, in 1912, tried to justify large corporations and their efforts to eliminate "wasteful competition," he commended the public relations policies of companies such as A. T. & T. and U. S. Steel; and he stated the principle which men such as Perkins were beginning to apply to the circumstances of a mature economy: "The theory of the new competition is that no class can profit in the long run except as others prosper."[17] It was hardly a new idea; but in the context of an economy boasting its first billion-dollar corporation, it

[16] Garraty, Perkins, 159, 219–21, 296, 379.

[17] Arthur J. Eddy, The New Competition (New York, 1912), 227; Augustus Lynch Mason, "Corporations and Social Changes" (Indianapolis, 1908). For a more critical view see Ghent, Our Benevolent Feudalism, 11, 27–28ff.

pointed toward a broader concept of business interests and organization than even the most progressive business spokesmen had as yet envisioned.

INDUSTRIAL RELATIONS

Concern for the quality of urban life, sensitivity to growing political pressures, and a sharpening awareness of the need to bring order to the often chaotic procedures of large-scale production combined to focus employers' attention upon working conditions and labor-management relations. Industrial accidents, absenteeism, and labor turnover contributed to higher labor costs and provided practical arguments for reform. Under the leadership of Frederick Winslow Taylor, the scientific management movement had already begun careful studies of the physical aspects of worker efficiency; others extended the analysis into the field of worker morale. Both practical and altruistic considerations encouraged companies to add "social secretaries" and "social engineers" to their staffs. Limited though such undertakings might be in their understanding of worker motivation, they were a beginning; and significant improvements in working conditions were achieved. Employers who initiated industrial welfare programs were recognizing implicitly their stake in the conditions which affected the lives of their employees.[18]

[18] Homer J. Hagedorn, "Motivations of Personnel Management"; William H. Tolman, *Social Engineering, A Record of Things Done by American Industrialists Employing Upwards of One and One-Half Millions of People* (New York, 1909); Cleveland Chamber of Commerce, Committee on Industrial Welfare, "Industrial Profit Sharing and Welfare Work" (Cleveland, 1916); Hicks, *Industrial Relations,* 41–43; Mary L. Goss, *Welfare Work by Corporations* (Philadelphia, 1911); Arundel Cotter, *United States Steel, A Corporation with a Soul* (New York, 1921); *Golden Book of the Wanamaker Stores, Jubilee Year, 1861–1911* (Philadelphia, 1911), quoted in N. S. B. Gras, *Casebook in American Business History* (New York, 1939), 485–99. For the relationship of scientific management to interest in employee and community relations, see "Modern Manufacturing, a Partnership in Idealism and Common Sense," *Annals of the American Academy of Political and Social Science,* LXXXV (September, 1919) (hereafter cited as *Annals*).
   The most notorious expression of the idea of the identity of interest of employee and employer was that of George F. Baer, president of the Reading Railroad: "The rights and interests of the laboring man will be protected . . . not by the labor agitators, but by the Christian men to whom God in His infinite wisdom, has given control of the property interests of the country." Views such as Baer's inspired the rabid anti-unionism of many employers; but the same paternalism motivated others, more open-minded, to a genuine concern for working and living conditions. Baer is quoted in Arthur Link, with the collaboration of William S. Catton, *American Epoch,* 2nd edition (New York, 1963), 60.

Business organizations, as well as individual companies, took up the promotion of employee welfare schemes. Often the motive was fear of labor unions. The National Association of Manufacturers, which in 1903 embarked upon an active campaign of anti-unionism, offered a rallying point for hostile employers. It climaxed a decade of bitter anti-labor activity in 1914 with an "Industrial Betterment" program, which attempted to stimulate employer interest in plant safety, employee education, and the improvement of working conditions. A more conciliatory position was that represented by the National Civic Federation. Its members, including Mark Hanna and George Perkins, did not necessarily favor unionization; but they were willing to deal with representatives of the workers and to strive for mutual accommodation. The Federation had extended its early interest in the mediation of labor disputes to include the formation in 1904 of an Industrial Welfare Department, consisting entirely of employers.[19] Similar efforts had been launched even earlier by the Cleveland Chamber of Commerce and by the League for Social Service, which numbered among its members men such as George F. Peabody and George Westinghouse.[20]

Whichever path they chose, that of open warfare on unions or that of conciliation, employers were acknowledging the need to improve the physical and human conditions of labor. The same years which saw the enactment of legislation regulating the hours and conditions of work in American factories saw also the initiation of voluntary programs in accident prevention, profit-sharing, insurance, industrial recreation, education, counseling, and related areas on a level which sometimes considerably exceeded the still-meager requirements of the law.[21]

Sometimes employers chose to support employee welfare through independent agencies such as the YMCA. The "Y's" Industrial Department entered its second decade in 1916 with more than 200 secretaries, some 99 buildings valued at over $2,000,000 contributed by "industries," and annual maintenance contributions of $240,000. Such

[19] Green, *National Civic Federation,* 245–66. Albert K. Steigerwalt, *The National Association of Manufacturers, 1895–1914. A Study in Business Leadership* (Grand Rapids, 1964), 170–71.

[20] Homer J. Hagedorn, "Motivations of Personnel Management," 134–37.

[21] These programs are both summarized and idealized in Ida M. Tarbell, *New Ideals in Business, An Account of Their Effects upon Men and Profits* (New York, 1916). See also "Humanitarianism as a Business Investment," *Current Literature,* LIII (December, 1912), and "Enlightened Selfishness—The New Cue of Business," *Current Opinion,* LVI (February, 1914), 144ff.

impressive growth convinced the Department's Secretary, C. R. Towson, that "God had brought the Association into the industrial kingdom for such a time as this." [22]

New recognition of the central role of the worker in the total process of industrial production led to some reconsideration of the priorities which had customarily guided business policy. Albert R. Erskine, president of the Studebaker Motor Company in 1915, took the unorthodox position that his responsibility to his labor force *preceded* that to the company's owners:

> The first duty of an employer is to labor. . . . It is the duty of capital and management to compensate liberally, paying at least the current wage and probably a little more, and to give workers decent and healthful surroundings and treat them with the utmost consideration. If management cannot do this, then it is incompetent.[23]

Forbes magazine agreed that, in view of the power of workers to help or hinder their employer's plans, "one cannot but feel that the employer who does not do everything within his power to satisfy his men is not only shortsighted from his own point of view but is an enemy to national peace and harmony." [24]

As had been the case in the nineteenth-century company towns, employers who now tried to improve the situation of their workers found it hard to distinguish between conditions within the plant and those extending beyond its gates into the community. Absenteeism or inefficiency might result in any given instance from circumstances of home and family as easily as from those on the job. To provide healthful and attractive surroundings in the factory was to be reminded that housing and other facilities in the neighborhood might well need equal attention. Concern for education and morality as elements in labor productivity pointed to problems which outran formal employer authority and responsibility. The political value of a docile, if not a satisfied, community further stimulated interest in civic betterment.

[22] The "Y's" success in industry attracted the attention of President Theodore Roosevelt and resulted in its being assigned to provide for the crews working to construct the Panama Canal, "a big piece of Christian engineering." Hopkins, *History of the YMCA*, 478–79; Cutlip, *Fund Raising*, 38–44ff.

[23] *Forbes*, XIV (26 April 1924), 113. Erskine here described the ideas which had guided his earlier thinking.

[24] *Ibid.*, I (13 October 1917), 113; *ibid.*, I (15 September 1917), 36; Forbes, *Finance*, 236–38.

Under these circumstances, reports of company programs of civic uplift and beautification aroused growing interest among businessmen.

Dayton, Ohio, where Col. John H. Patterson of the National Cash Register Company actively intervened in municipal matters ranging from politics to landscaping, was often cited as an example of the new business outlook.[25] In Middletown, Ohio, George Matthew Verity of the American Rolling Mill Company developed a combined program of employee and community benefits. Its guiding principles were set forth in a 1920 policy statement:

> The American Rolling Mill Company was organized to pro-
> vide a permanently profitable investment through the manu-
> facture of special grades of iron and steel . . . to secure such
> a result in the largest measure, its organizers believed that it
> would be necessary to adopt and practice such policies as
> would bring about a condition of mutual confidence and cre-
> ate a spirit of sympathy and of real cooperation between the
> members of its working organization, its customers, its stock-
> holders, and the citizens of the communities in which its
> plants were located.[26]

Elsewhere, business support and assistance took still other forms. Peter Roberts's report on the Pennsylvania anthracite coal communities in 1904 noted contributions to community hospitals by coal companies, ranging from 25.5 per cent of the local hospital budget in Wilkes-Barre to 2.5 per cent in Carbondale.[27] Tom Girdler, moving to Aliquippa, Pennsylvania, in 1914 to manage the new Jones and Laughlin steel works, found himself part of a much more elaborate community program—"an unofficial caliph, an American Haroun-al-

[25] Samuel Crowther, *John H. Patterson—Pioneer in Industrial Welfare* (New York, 1926), 309–11, 341, *passim*.

[26] Christy Borth, *True Steel, The Story of George Matthew Verity and His Associates* (Indianapolis, 1941), 193–99, 216, 241–43. Similar considerations led Ernest T. Weir to build a new community for his company at Weirton, West Virginia, rather than remain in Pittsburgh: "In order to get harmony and good will we were entirely willing to undertake the double burden of building a new community at the same time as we were building our new plant and to undergo the growing pains that such a venture involved." Quoted in Ernest Dale, *The Great Organizers* (New York, 1960), 127–28.

[27] Peter Roberts, *Anthracite Coal Communities* (New York, 1904), 305. Hospitals in Pittston, Scranton, and Pottsville at this time received no such support. Roberts noted that little of the money granted came from individual owners, since they seldom lived in the community.

Raschid obliged by my office in a big corporation to consider a whole community as my personal responsibility." Girdler complained that the town fell into the habit of expecting the company to supply all its needs. Conceding the paternalistic quality of the relationship, he still took pride in what he felt was a generally satisfactory arrangement.[28]

Still another type of employee-community program which won business interest in the years surrounding the First World War was the Americanization movement. Spurred by civic leaders, patriotic societies, and social workers, Americanization aimed at fostering the assimilation of the millions of immigrants pouring into the country. Associations such as the North American Civic League for Immigrants made a special, and a largely successful, effort to win the cooperation of chambers of commerce and employers of immigrant labor in their educational programs. For businessmen, the effort to instill an understanding of American ways and a respect for law and order among the newcomers seemed eminently desirable. Fear of unionization and radicalism, which they associated with the uneducated masses of immigrants, led many employers to join the Americanization drive enthusiastically. The patriotic fervor of wartime only heightened what had already become a well-organized movement. Once again, efforts to assure a steady supply of docile labor had led employers to intervene in the educational and social adjustment of their employees.[29]

The outpouring of company and community welfare programs in the prewar years and the glowing colors with which they were usually portrayed in the business press make it easy to overemphasize both the content and the results of managerial "social consciousness." A corrective is supplied by the detailed findings of the Pittsburgh Survey, sponsored by the Russell Sage Foundation and published in 1910. The survey directed attention to working and living conditions at the heart of one of the nation's major industrial areas. In particular, Margaret Byington's study of Homestead described vividly and thoroughly the life of a town dominated by a single producer, the Carnegie Steel Company, a unit in the great U. S. Steel combination. Despite the

[28] Tom M. Girdler, *Bootstraps* (New York, 1943), 165–75, 178. See also Tarbell, *New Ideals,* 136–43; Tolman, *Social Engineering,* 234–56, 298–354; *Forbes,* III (11 January 1919), 697 and VI (2 October 1920), 467; Taylor, *Satellite Cities,* 506, *passim.;* "Interest in Employees Beyond the Works," *Iron Age,* XCI (3 April 1913), 834–35; "Developing the Community Interest," *ibid.,* CI (7 February 1918), 369–72; and J. C. Heckman, "The Community Relations of an Industrial Plant," *Annals,* LXXXV (September, 1919), 48–60.

[29] Edward G. Hartmann, *The Movement to Americanize the Immigrant* (New York, 1948).

company's profit-sharing plan, gifts of community facilities by high corporation officials, company housing, and a program of loans to enable workers to purchase homes, Miss Byington found generally unsatisfactory conditions, aggravated by political arrangements which helped the company minimize its taxes. Her summary of the corporation's role in the community was a strong indictment:

> The United States Steel Corporation operates in Homestead one of the largest mills in the country, provided with wonderful machines for producing steel; it has placed in charge a superintendent whose primary object is to produce steel perfectly and cheaply; it offers work on certain terms as to wages and hours which he who wills may accept. Its ignorant Slavic laborers, however, may be exploited by grasping landlords; the wives of many of its workers may find life merely a round of wearisome tasks in the attempt to make both ends meet; its men may be too worn by the stress of the twelve-hour shifts to care for their own individual development or too shorn of self-dependence to exert themselves to maintain a borough government that shall give them better living conditions. "Life, work and happiness,—these three are bound together." The mill offers the one, subject to no effective demand by society nor commercial necessity that the work be done under conditions which make the other two possible.[30]

Against such a background, the philanthropies of a Carnegie and the welfare programs of many companies might well seem trifling, if not irrelevant.

At the time of the Pittsburgh Survey, U. S. Steel was constructing a new plant and, indeed, a new community at Gary, Indiana. As the most recent and largest of the company towns built by America's biggest corporation, which was actively publicizing its supposedly progressive social policies, the town of Gary was closely watched. Praised in some quarters as a "model city" to which the company and its officers had contributed hospitals, a YMCA building, parks, and other com-

[30] Margaret F. Byington, *Homestead, The Households of a Mill Town* (New York, 1910), 46-62, 171-84. Graham Taylor stated that, after publication of the Pittsburgh Survey findings, Andrew Carnegie offered to contribute substantially to better housing for the steel workers. Taylor also claimed that the Steel Corporation took no action to improve conditions until a prominent stockholder forced the issue by threatening the company with a lawsuit. *Pioneering on Social Frontiers*, 148ff.

munity facilities, Gary did not escape sharp criticism. U. S. Steel officials had helped to finance city planning in Chicago. In Gary they failed, however, to consult planners, despite the fact that the city together with the plant required an investment of some $75,000,000. The company did try with some success to guard Gary's residents against the wiles of the land speculators, but the final verdict was unfavorable: "A great industrial power let slip [sic] its giant fingers a chance to work out a civic achievement the like of which the country has not known." [31]

Still another company venture in community welfare, productive at first of catastrophe but ultimately of substantial gains in managerial understanding, was that of the Colorado Fuel and Iron Company. Equipped with a "Sociological Department," a mission for migrant and unemployed workers at Bessemer, Colorado, and schools and libraries for the children of employees in out-of-the-way mining communities, the company announced that it was the ambitious "purpose of this corporation . . . to solve the social problem." [32] The inadequacy of these modest means to such an all-embracing end was tragically underlined by a strike of miners against the company in 1913, when bitter violence culminated in the deaths of innocent women and children. The resulting popular outcry forced the subject of industrial relations to the attention of John D. Rockefeller, Jr., whose family held a controlling interest in the company.

Although he resisted the workers' demand for unionization, Rockefeller's conscience was pricked. In an effort to overcome the obvious breakdown in understanding between management and labor, Rockefeller turned for guidance to the public relations counsel, Ivy L. Lee, and William Lyon MacKenzie King, a graduate of Jane Addams's Hull House. MacKenzie King, who had gone on to a career in Canadian industrial relations and politics, developed with Rockefeller's support an employee representation plan which was a significant step toward understanding of the workers' needs and point of view.[33]

[31] Taylor, *Satellite Cities,* 165–89, 224–29. Taylor's account was a balanced one, giving credit to another U. S. Steel subsidiary for a better job at Fairfield, Alabama; *ibid.,* 91ff., 237. For a friendlier view of Gary, see Cotter, *United States Steel,* 135, 161, 181; *Forbes,* VIII (23 July 1921), 271.

[32] Quoted in Ghent, *Our Benevolent Feudalism,* 61.

[33] Raymond B. Fosdick, *John D. Rockefeller, Jr., A Portrait* (New York, 1956), 130–31, 143ff.; Ben Selekman and May Van Kleck, *Employee Representation in the Coal Mines: A Study of the Colorado Fuel and Iron Company* (Philadelphia, 1924). Even before his association with MacKenzie King, the younger Rockefeller

MacKenzie King's plan did more than ease the immediate troubles of the Colorado Fuel and Iron Company. Through Rockefeller's influence, it was gradually extended to other Rockefeller-dominated companies. Clarence Hicks, who had served as International Secretary of the Railroad Department of the YMCA and later as industrial relations advisor to the International Harvester Company, was employed to supervise the new Colorado Fuel and Iron program. Hicks subsequently took a similar position with Standard Oil of New Jersey. Eventually he formed an industrial relations consulting agency which carried the enormous prestige of Rockefeller esteem and backing.[34]

MacKenzie King's ideas about the relationship of business to labor and to the public, distilled from his own strongly religious background, his association with Miss Addams and her fellow workers, and his industrial experience, struck a warm response in the younger Rockefeller, who became himself their most influential advocate. Thus, the man who was to become one of Canada's outstanding statesmen achieved an extraordinary position in American industrial relations. A thoughtful observer of the American scene, MacKenzie King was able to discern much of the central meaning of management's initial ventures into the welfare field.

Although his prime concern was with relations between employer and employee, MacKenzie King set these squarely in a context which stressed the over-arching interest of the public. There was a "party to Industry," he thought, whose interest was often overlooked, "a party which furnishes opportunity to all the others, and without whose implied sanction and cooperation the other parties could effect nothing. That party is the Community. . . ." Like the other participants, the community was entitled to a fair return on its contribution. This re-

had shown a certain sensitivity to the moral climate of business and a sympathy for the Social Gospel movement. It was in a talk to the Brown University YMCA on "Christianity in Business" that Rockefeller made the comparison of business to the American Beauty rose, which indicated how much he had still to learn. See also Roy E. Hiebert, *Courtier to the Crowd: The Story of Ivy Lee and the Development of Public Relations* (Ames, Iowa, 1966); John D. Rockefeller, Jr., *The Personal Relation in Industry* (New York, 1923), 46ff.; and Nevins, *Rockefeller*, II, 661, 667–73.

[34] Hicks, *Industrial Relations*, 51–59, 119–22; George S. Gibb and E. H. Knowlton, *The Resurgent Years, 1911–1927: History of the Standard Oil Company (New Jersey)*, Vol. 2 (New York, 1957), 572–74ff. Both Hicks and MacKenzie King knew Owen D. Young of the General Electric Company. Young asked King's help in resolving a strike at GE's Lynn, Massachusetts, plant in 1917. *Fortune*, III (February, 1931), 46; Hicks, *Industrial Relations*, 136.

turn included not only more and better products, but also "an orderly organization in the development and conduct of industry." [35]

MacKenzie King conceived of industry as a form of social service; the directors of business corporations were accountable for the social conditions to which their policies contributed. He called for recognition of the essential interdependence of company and community, guided by a spirit of justice. Good intentions, welfare work, "charity and philanthropy," he warned, "are no substitutes for justice." Without justice they were inevitably self-defeating. To insure the community's "right to representation in the control of Industry," he proposed a number of devices, including compulsory publicity and worker representation on corporate directorates. More significant than specific devices, however, was the general outlook to which he had alerted John D. Rockefeller, Jr., and which became, in effect, with Rockefeller's not inconsiderable support, a charter for progressive business thinking in the postwar decade.[36]

MacKenzie King realistically appraised the considerations which might urge businessmen to improve conditions of life for their employees. Without discounting paternalism, he attempted to base employee welfare programs on the solid ground of mutual benefit. Yet, most such programs failed to satisfy the critics of business, especially when, as was often the case, they were accompanied by refusal to accept and deal with labor unions. Louis Brandeis insisted that the welfare and profit-sharing plans of a company such as U. S. Steel amounted to little more than "pensioned peonage." Coupled with the continuation of the twelve-hour day, the seven-day week, and an elaborate system of espionage, they constituted, in Brandeis's view, simply "another of the chains to rivet employees to their employer and deprive them of the liberty of American citizens." [37]

The Socialist critic, W. J. Ghent, conceding that the new wealth and power of corporate management had brought glimmerings of conscience, remained dubious about motives. He noted that company benevolence was usually well-publicized, on the one hand, and yet directed toward easing the consequences rather than eliminating the causes of poverty on the other. A Progressive such as John R. Commons could find no prejudice against labor within the National Civic

[35] William Lyon MacKenzie King, *Industry and Humanity* (Boston and New York, 1918), 134ff.

[36] *Ibid.*, 178–79, 181–84, 204, 371–74.

[37] Mason, *Brandeis*, 357–59.

Federation; but *Forbes* magazine scarcely troubled to conceal the opposition to unionism in its unstinting praise of company welfare programs.[38] Contradicting MacKenzie King, *Forbes'* editor declared, "Generosity is a higher virtue than justice. Generosity is justice plus. Justice begets no gratitude; generosity does." Still, he acknowledged that "sentiment" was good business; and many of the welfare programs initiated in industry were justified by their authors not in paternalistic terms alone but also as measures intended to increase the efficiency of the labor force and the productive process.[39] Public and private interests, selfishness and altruism, hostility and friendliness toward workers and their organizations, justice and generosity, all joined in the beginnings of welfare capitalism; and, regardless of motives, a foundation of precedent and experience was laid upon which more enlightened corporate social policies could ultimately rest.

PUBLIC RELATIONS

In 1902, according to W. J. Ghent, Americans were generally favorable to big business, and opinion molders such as the schools, the press, and the church reinforced these pro-business views.[40] A decade of muckraking exposures and of Progressive agitation, however, made a difference. The election of 1912, in which both Theodore Roosevelt and Woodrow Wilson called for substantial federal regulation of business, suggested that public opinion, if not fundamentally hostile, was at any rate skeptical of the methods and objectives of business leadership. The popularity of attacks upon the trusts and of regulatory legislation indicated the potential vulnerability of concentrated wealth and power in a democratic society. To many businessmen they suggested, too, considerable public misunderstanding of economic issues. Hence,

---

[38] Ghent, *Our Benevolent Feudalism*, 9–11, 27, 38–39, 45–46; Edward T. Devine, "Philanthropy and Business," *Survey*, XXXII (6 June 1914), 263–65. Addressing the National Conference on Charities and Correction, Devine, a longtime leader in social work, argued that "business mitigated by philanthropy is better than business unalloyed, but it is no adequate safeguard for human interests."

Green, *National Civic Federation*, 68; *Forbes*, I (16 March 1918), 716; *ibid.*, III (14 December 1918), 617; *ibid.*, VII (23 July 1921), 271.

[39] Forbes, *Finance*, 299–300, 303–6, 331; Cotter, *United States Steel*, 195. Charles M. Ripley, *Life in a Large Manufacturing Plant* [General Electric Company] (Schenectady, 1919), 17.

[40] Ghent, *Our Benevolent Feudalism*, 122–53.

it appeared that extraordinary efforts might be needed to inform people of the "realities" and the constructive achievements of business enterprise. Public opinion was a power which business could no longer safely ignore.

One economic empire which had been slow and ineffective in defending its public image and which now paid a price for its failures was the Standard Oil Company. Standard Oil officials, criticized for ruthless suppression of competition, revealed as secret contributors to the expenses of public officials, and threatened with dissolution of their enterprise as an illegal monopoly, came to see that the cultivation of public favor might contribute to business success as much as did their avowed concern for economic performance alone.

An accidental opportunity gave Standard executives what has been called "an early lesson on the value of identifying the company with community welfare." At the time of the San Francisco earthquake of 1906, Standard's California subsidiary offered the stricken city assistance in the form of fuel, funds, and other company resources and, in doing so, earned much good will. Not only were California Standard's own resources thrown into the relief effort, but John D. Rockefeller made an additional $100,000 available for use at the discretion of local company officials. Iowa Standard sent $100,000 and officers of many of the companies in the Standard complex made personal contributions. Gifts totaling $70,000 were turned over to relief and Red Cross officials. Company tankers were opened to house refugees and, shortly, a relief camp, "Camp Rockefeller," of some thirty acres was set up to house a thousand homeless San Franciscans. Tools were distributed to the able-bodied, Bibles to elderly ladies and clergymen; help was offered to hundreds of individuals and families without regard to race or creed. Thus a dramatic response to community needs revealed the value of cultivating public favor to Standard Oil executives.[41]

Actually, Standard's policy toward publicity and public relations had been gradually shifting for some time. A more cooperative attitude toward public commissions and investigating committees, utilization of the services of advertising agencies, and, finally, the appointment in 1909 of the company's own publicity agent all showed that

[41] For the San Francisco story, see Gerald T. White, *Formative Years in the Far West. A History of Standard Oil Company of California and Its Predecessors Through 1919* (New York, 1962), 277–80, 379, 387. Other businessmen and organizations also came to the aid of the stricken city; the Board of Trade of Williamsport, Pennsylvania, sent $5,000, while the New York Chamber of Commerce contributed a princely $782,000. Wiebe, *Businessmen and Reform,* 186.

the costs of public disfavor were winning recognition in the corporation accounting processes.[42]

Other companies were moving along parallel lines. By 1917, many larger industrial and public utility corporations had publicity staffs. Under the chastening influence of antitrust action, the General Electric Company eased its tradition of secrecy in 1913. Owen D. Young and Gerard Swope urged that the company dispose of its stock in the Electric Bond and Share Company, which financed public utilities, arguing that it was unethical "to be in two businesses at the same time." Young further recommended that General Electric no longer conceal its ownership of a large number of supposedly competing lamp companies.

Effective public relations were coming to be understood as including more than just efforts to command popularity. It has been suggested that the dominant philosophy guiding early public relations was "the public be pleased (but fooled)." That is, at least in some cases, an unduly harsh characterization. The notion that good economic service, as well as satisfactory social policies, contributed to the overall public relations of business was already beginning to be heard.[43] Business leaders as a group were not yet willing to subscribe to B. C. Forbes's assertion that public opinion had become "the power omnipotent," but they had clearly begun to reckon with it as a power not to be ignored.[44] If better public relations seemed the answer to popular criticism and antibusiness pressures, there were those who already were coming to see that effective public relations involved persuasive actions as well as words.

[42] Nevins, Rockefeller, II, 501–4, 518, 547; Ralph W. Hidy and Muriel E. Hidy, Pioneering in Big Business, 1882–1911 (New York, 1955), 209–14, 654, 699–700.

[43] John A. R. Pimlott, Public Relations and American Democracy (Princeton, 1951), 5; Eric Goldman, Two-Way Street, The Emergence of the Public Relations Counsel (Boston, 1948), 9–10; Loth, Swope of G.E., 134; Crowther, Book of Business, IV, 78–81; N. S. B. Gras, "Shifts in Public Relations," Bulletin of the Business Historical Society, XIV (October, 1945), 120–21. Charles Coffin, the first president of General Electric, had argued even before the turn of the century that "the company should first consider the public it serves, second its own success." Herrymon Maurer, Great Enterprise: Growth and Behavior of the Big Corporation (New York, 1955), 46.

[44] Forbes, Finance, vii–ix, 45, 202, 233; Ghent, Our Benevolent Feudalism, 161. Col. George Pope, president of the National Association of Manufacturers, believed that too exclusive a concentration by businessmen on matters of production, to the neglect of social conditions, was a major source of the "dangerous legislation" he feared. George Pope, "The Betterment of Industrial Society," American Industries, XVII (December, 1916), 9–11.

"SERVICE"

A term which appeared with increasing frequency in discussions of business during the first three decades of the century, and which by implication summarized the growing perception of the interdependence between business and society, was the word "service." The idea that the pursuit of business involved a positive social value was, of course, not new. The assumption had been explicit in Adam Smith's concept of the "invisible hand" by virtue of which each man pursuing his own self-interest was led, even without intending it, to add to the common store of material goods. It had been an implicit article of American economic dogma throughout the nineteenth century not always stressed, perhaps, because widely taken for granted in a period of rapid economic growth and progress. Only as industrialization's seamier consequences became obvious was the assumption seriously called into question. The popularity of Henry George's *Progress and Poverty*, which directly challenged the customary and comfortable identification of private with public gain, was indicative of deepening doubts. So, of course, was the whole trend of Progressive legislation which assumed that governmental intervention was required to bring private and public interests into congruence.

Partly in self-defense and partly, no doubt, out of their own concern, businessmen were being forced to reconsider the relationship of their interests to society's welfare. Cyrus McCormick believed that a spirit of "service" had been fostered by the intense competition of the 1880s and 1890s, when the McCormick company and its rivals had contended for leadership in the farm machinery market. Service to the farmer had become the custom of the firm. After the International Harvester Corporation was formed, the tradition was institutionalized in its Agricultural Extension Department.[45] While the McCormicks found in competition the motive for service, Theodore Vail had found similar stimulus from the logic of monopoly in the telephone industry. When such different circumstances could produce common results, fundamental economic and social forces were clearly at work.

The service ideal had formed an element in the "uplift" morality of Progressivism, and businessmen were inevitably touched by it. B. C. Forbes, an ardent propagandist of service, asserted in 1915 that, while

[45] Cyrus McCormick, *The Century of the Reaper* (Boston, 1931), 100–10, 141–44, 276–79; William T. Hutchinson, *Cyrus Hall McCormick*, 2 vols. (New York and London, 1930 and 1935), II, 711–12.

"Success used to be spelt $UCCE$$—dollars," it was "now coming to be spelt SERVICE . . . . In order to gain and retain dollars under the incoming era it will be found necessary to render service, genuine, helpful service to the world, whether that service consists of sweeping streets, or organizing an international corporation or running a railroad." [46] Sensing the shifting winds of opinion, *Forbes* magazine warned, "The principle that business is war and that war is what Sherman called it must be dropped if the nation and other nations are to avoid out-and-out Socialism."

> The square deal is coming into vogue all round. Rivals are treated less savagely; employees are not treated as so many pieces of machinery; the public are treated with greater consideration. . . . The business of modern business is service. . . . If business cannot be conducted under the existing economic order cleanly, honorably, ethically and humanely, then it ought to be swept away, and something different established in its stead. . . . Capital must adapt itself thoroughgoingly to the democratic ideas which have taken possession of the civilized world.[47]

Clarence F. Birdseye offered still another example of Progressive moralism when he answered the question "Have Corporations Moral Natures?" with a resounding "Yes!" A corporation was "no more the repository of human wealth than of human lives and love and sacrifice and intelligence and service." Many corporations gave no evidence of possessing a conscience, Birdseye conceded; but,

> If corporate persons are to perform so many human functions, own so much human property, and employ so many human servants, they must also be capable of judging between right and wrong in conducting their lives and making

[46] Forbes, *Finance*, 218–20.

[47] *Forbes*, I (27 October 1917), 163; I (15 September 1917), 7, 19; I (29 September 1917), 59–60; II (27 July 1918), 260–61; II (1 June 1918), 114; II (15 June 1918), 148; III (14 December 1918), 620; III (28 December 1918), 667; III (25 January 1919), 724; and VII (16 October 1920), 4. These *Forbes* articles provide interesting insight into shifting tendencies of opinion at the war's end. *Forbes'* original idealism and effort to promote warmer, more human relations between labor and management gradually gave way to a growing fear of radicalism and Bolshevism. By 1920 it was attacking organized labor and calling for efforts to enlighten public opinion concerning "sound" economic principles. Although in greatly reduced degree, it continued to encourage managerial "statesmanship" and benevolence.

their choices. . . . More and more the president and other executive officers and the directors must be made to realize, and to take pleasure and pride in realizing, that they are largely the keepers of the corporate soul; and hence responsible, to the public first, and then to the others interested in the corporation. . . . [48]

Although *Forbes* was perhaps the foremost spokesman for the service *motif*, the theme was an increasingly popular one. Its advocates cited many examples of businessmen conscious of their social responsibilities, for the fact was that the reformist zeal which had inspired the Progressives had infected the business community as well. While men such as Samuel Milton ("Golden Rule") Jones and Tom L. Johnson had turned from successful business careers to active leadership in the movement for political reform, others had sought ways to build sounder relationships within and around their business lives.[49]

What such men felt even before World War I reached America, others came to feel as the war progressed. Patriotism, idealism, and a rising fear of radicalism all helped to popularize the notion of service as an integral aspect of the business function. The heights to which the spirit of service could soar in the wartime atmosphere were revealed in the words of one businessman who gave up his position to work for the Red Cross and who looked forward to a better, more harmonious economic order for the postwar world:

[48] Clarence F. Birdseye, "Have Corporations Moral Natures?" *The Outlook*, CIX (31 March 1915), 782–87.

[49] In a speech to the Bankers' Association of Indianapolis, George W. Perkins advocated a national incorporation law both to protect the public against such corporate abuses as stock-watering and to safeguard business against excessive government interference. Anticipating postwar problems, Perkins called for the same disinterested public spirit which had guided the nation through earlier military crises. "We Are as Unprepared for Peace as We Are for War," New York, n.d. [1915], 21. See also the statement of John D. Rockefeller, Jr., to the Industrial Relations Commission in 1915, republished in his *The Personal Relation in Industry*, 116. For other examples, see Wiebe, *Businessmen and Reform*, 185–86, 218.

Like Tom L. Johnson, "Golden Rule" Jones had been influenced by Henry George. Jones, however, had been even more strongly moved by the Social Gospel, with its emphasis upon social justice and the stewardship of wealth. Jones introduced the idea of a "living wage," together with benefits such as paid vacations and cooperative insurance programs into his own company, where, before 1900, the Golden Rule was promulgated as the guiding rule of the business. Jones had founded and helped to finance the Society for Applied Christianity. Hoyt Landon Warner, *Progressivism in Ohio, 1897–1917* (Columbus, 1964), 27–41, 54–61.

> Business hereafter will be conducted on a higher plane than
> that which prevailed in the carefree, money-making days be-
> fore the war. . . .
>
> We are to enter a new era; we are to face new ideas, new
> ideals, new situations; we are to see reformation and rebirth
> in the business world; we are to set a new value upon the
> things of the spirit, a new value upon helpfulness and cooper-
> ation, a new value upon things humanitarian, and also a new
> —but different—value upon mere money-making, mere accu-
> mulation of wealth on an inordinate scale.[50]

Even wartime zeal could bring such high hopes to only a few. For
many American businessmen, however, as well as for many others
whose concern for the role of business in the nation's life had been
aroused by years of controversy, the conviction was growing that business could achieve its full potential only through careful attention to
its social, as well as its economic, performance. The full implications
of this idea would take long to discover, but the postwar decade
would see the first considerable attempt to explore them.

THE FIRST WORLD WAR

The conditions which had stimulated business interest in social
problems during the reform years were augmented after 1914 by the
nation's growing involvement in the First World War. Years of political debate and experimentation had sharpened appreciation of the
latent power and authority of government. Now, even broader possibilities for governmental economic regulation were revealed by the experience of national mobilization. Fears of government coercion were
tempered for the time being by nationalistic feeling, which in turn
heightened business sensitivity to community needs. Employer attitudes toward industrial relations were shaped by similarly conflicting
forces. Reluctant concessions to organized labor, forced by manpower
shortages and other economic and governmental pressures, only

[50] Quoted in *Forbes*, III (30 November 1918), 588; see also *ibid.*, I (5 January 1918), 425, and VI (1 May 1920), 51. For additional evidence that *Forbes*
was not alone in promoting service, see Lucius E. Wilson, *Community Leadership,
the New Profession* (New York, 1919), 63–66; Robert D. Kohn, "The Significance
of the Professional Ideal," *Annals*, CI (May, 1922), 1; Robert A. Brady, *Business
as a System of Power* (New York, 1943), 194; and Glenn Frank, "Anonymous
Liberalism, A Study of the New Spirit in Business," *Century*, XCVII (April,
1919), 765–80.

strengthened managerial determination to maintain authority unimpaired. Yet employers were forced simultaneously to acknowledge the worker's role in increasing productivity. New incentives arose to improve working conditions and employee morale, while patriotism encouraged mutual cooperation and helped to smooth over past conflicts. Business prestige, tarnished by the years of conflict and muckraking, was refurbished by the remarkable record of wartime production. Extraordinary profits offered resources upon which society could register a claim. And, finally, heavy corporation taxes provided executives with practical reasons for channeling funds toward community needs at little cost to themselves. Thus, through the eddies and rapids of war flowed strong currents tending to unite business in interest and sympathy with the community.

Wartime needs created an extraordinary demand and opportunity for private philanthropy. The YMCA, which had pioneered in the promotion of company giving before the war, increased its efforts in order to finance its program among the armed forces. Its fund-raising experience enabled the "Y" to surpass its 1917 goal of $3,000,000 by an additional $2,000,000, aided by gifts of $500,000 from U. S. Steel and $250,000 from Standard Oil of New Jersey.[51]

Business gifts to war relief skyrocketed under the dual impetus of patriotism and profits. Widespread doubts as to the authority of officials to give away the shareholders' property spurred the adoption of a stockholder-approved Red Cross dividend contribution system. In 1917 over $18,000,000 was subscribed to the Red Cross by business corporations. In Pittsburgh, one per cent of net earnings was the goal

[51] After 1900, companies were called upon by, and gave financial aid to, a growing number of social agencies—hospitals, settlement houses, and similar institutions. Until 1910 the New York office of the Standard Oil complex, in theory at least, retained the authority to rule on all local "hospital donations, etc." In that year, discretion in the matter of such gifts, up to a limit of $50, was granted by New York to the executive committee of California Standard, operating on the West Coast. White, *Formative Years*, 382.

At least one company gift of $100,000 to the YMCA's building program was recorded in Chicago in 1910, and substantial though less astronomical gifts were reported elsewhere. In several major cities business donations to the annual operating expenses of the "Y" approached twenty per cent of total contributions. Andrews, *Corporation Giving*, 25–26.

Pierce Williams's and Frederick E. Croxton's *Corporate Contributions to Organized Community Welfare Services* (New York, 1930), 52–56, contains the most complete summary of business philanthropy during these years. Scott M. Cutlip, in *Fund Raising*, presents the fullest history of organized fund raising; see 38–44, *passim*.

for industrial corporations. The results of the national campaign support the conclusion of F. Emerson Andrews that 1917 was "the year in which corporation contributions first reached a substantial total in the history of American philanthropy."

Corporate giving increased with successive national wartime drives. Although detailed figures are lacking, it has been estimated that some $20,000,000 of corporate funds were received in the second YMCA drive, in November, 1917. Spurred by such successes, the Red Cross abandoned the complicated dividend plan in its second national appeal, yet managed to far surpass its goal.

The last great national drive of the war and the first national federated campaign, the United War Work Campaign, was almost as successful. For the first time quotas were set and employee-matching contributions were developed by some companies. The United States Steel Corporation gave $5,000,000. Legislation, meanwhile, had specifically authorized corporate contributions in several states; and Congress, in 1918, passed a bill permitting national banks to contribute to the Red Cross. To further allay legal doubts, Charles Evans Hughes offered the view that "the question is not one of permitting the use of corporate moneys for what are or may be called 'worthy objects' outside the corporate enterprise, but for the maintenance of the very foundation of corporate enterprise itself." [52] Hughes's argument that business had a stake in the maintenance of a social system friendly to its development foreshadowed a position which came to be widely held in the 1950s and 1960s.

At the local as well as the national level, wartime relief and charity appeals acquired a new urgency. Federations of charity and philanthropy, beginning with Cleveland in 1913, had spread to at least seventeen cities by 1917. Emphasizing coordinated fund-raising and allocation among agencies, they enlisted the interested participation of business executives. Following the example of the YMCA, they successfully solicited corporate contributions. In Cincinnati, company donations rose from $4,600 in one 1915 appeal to over $40,000 in 1917, with both the number of participating companies and the scale of giving showing marked increases.

The local counterparts of the national wartime drives were the War

[52] For the Hughes statement and additional data concerning the wartime fund-raising efforts, see Andrews, *Corporation Giving*, 26–32; Williams and Croxton, *Corporate Contributions*, 56–90; Cutlip, *Fund Raising*, 118–19, *passim*. Allen T. Burns of Cleveland and other Welfare Federation workers joined the United War Work Campaign effort. "Allen T. Burns," 20.

Chests, through which community leaders combined contributions to national appeals with the effort to meet increased local welfare needs. Again practices varied in the different communities, but intensive efforts to secure company donations were made in a number of cases. In Detroit, where War Chest officials specifically refused to approach corporations lest this encourage individuals to shirk their personal responsibility, a fund-raising drive nevertheless received $300,000 in unsolicited corporate gifts. Elsewhere, efforts were undertaken to work out quotas for business and industry by type or size.[53]

In response to wartime pressures, nearly every method utilized in the subsequent development of business philanthropy was tried: federated fund raising, quotas, employer-employee matching gifts, permissive legislation, and undoubtedly a good deal of high-pressure salesmanship. When peace came, the experience and ideas tested by war would remain. Out of them would emerge in time new conceptions of the role and responsibilities of corporate enterprise, to be tested, in their turn, in the still more intense fires of social and economic change.

POSTWAR ATTITUDES

The brief, if intensive, experience of the war failed to provide solid ground for uninterrupted progress toward closer business-community understanding. Although lessons were learned upon which future efforts could build, resentments and resistances were also created which were to distort subsequent relations between business and other interest groups.

A series of postwar strikes, in which organized labor's drive to consolidate and extend its gains confronted determined business resistance, signaled the opening of a new phase in industrial relations. In 1919 the steel industry turned back in bitter defeat an American Federation of Labor drive for union recognition. Elbert H. Gary of U. S. Steel, the industry's acknowledged leader, doggedly opposed both unionization and the eight-hour day—thus further defining the scope and orientation of his company's employee welfare program. In the unfolding of ideas and events, policies which at the beginning of the century had appeared progressive and social-minded now formed a bulwark for unbending conservatism.

A second indication of the strengthened will of management to resist encroachments upon its status and authority appeared in the fail-

[53] *Ibid.*, 78–79.

ure of the Industrial Conference, called by President Wilson, also in 1919. In an effort to resolve the accumulated differences between management and labor which had provoked a series of strikes, Wilson had resorted to a characteristically Progressive gesture. The Conference was composed of representatives of three groups: management, labor, and the general public. In wartime, and even under the sponsorship of private agencies such as the National Civic Federation before the war, similar meetings had been productive, if not always of agreement, at least of mutual tolerance and exchange. Now business was reluctant to participate, even when reassured by the naming of Gary and John D. Rockefeller, Jr., to the list of public members. The Conference collapsed when the employers' group refused to accept the principle of collective bargaining.[54] Business leadership, in effect, was insisting upon the right to define relations with its employees and with the public on its own terms.

Yet, it would be wrong to conclude that no lessons had been learned, that conditions had simply resumed their prewar basis. Both business and other groups had discovered new needs and interests. Behind conflict and confidence, a lively sense of the interdependence of business and the community remained and was to seek new outlets in the years ahead. This spirit was expressed in the words of Cyrus McCormick, whose business life had extended from the competitive wars of the late nineteenth century, through merger and the development of the giant corporation—the years of reform and regulation—to the end of the war itself:

> I believe that every company or organization of men doing business in any community, no matter where or how removed from the central office, is in duty bound to do something to help build that community, aside from the things required by law or the things beneficial to itself. The Harvester Company is a citizen of every community in which it sells a machine, and it is not a good citizen if it does not perform some service in that community, the same as any citizen who lives there would be expected to perform.[55]

Such a statement, however idealized a description of reality it may have been, was both a distillation of three decades of experience and an anticipation of the future.

[54] Fosdick, *John D. Rockefeller, Jr.*, 173–74.
[55] McCormick, *Century of the Reaper*, 277.

3 · MANAGERIAL LEADERSHIP

While many Americans during the Progressive years were searching for new definitions of the social implications and role of business, a smaller number of those directly concerned with the organization of large companies were pondering the meaning of changes taking place within the structure and leadership of business itself. Growth in the scale of operations, either by internal expansion or by consolidation of previously separate units, created many new problems. The expansive economic climate of the years between 1914 and 1929 forced top management to reexamine and define its relations with other groups involved in the total enterprise. Large corporations were rapidly lengthening their lists of stockholders and thus freeing many executives from close control by powerful owners. At the same time, the value of stable, mutually acceptable relations between management and labor was becoming increasingly clear, despite sharp differences about how best to secure such arrangements. The delineation of authority and responsibility within the burgeoning corporate bureaucracies was a major problem. Moreover, national corporations had been acquiring other kinds of dependents: a host of suppliers, distributors, and servicers whose interests both overlapped and conflicted with theirs. Big business was bringing its leaders into contact with many communities, interest groups, and governments. It heightened their visibility and, in some respects, their vulnerability. It brought them new power while, paradoxically, it increased their dependence upon others.

When the Great Depression struck, most Americans faced it with much the same fund of economic ideas and assumptions that the Progressive generation had held; within economic circles, however, both theory and practice had already begun to strike out sharply in new directions. The 1920s saw the first efforts on the part of business leadership to formulate what has since come to be called the "managerial" version of capitalism. Armed with a new sense of their position and powers, executives were beginning to explore new possibilities in the relationship of their firms to the communities in which they were located. In addition, a new type of business leadership was emerging, differing in education, experience, and style from its predecessors. The nature of this new management, the implications of its new roles, its preparation for its responsibilities, and the development of its social ideas and outlook will be the subject matter of this and the succeeding chapter.

THE ROLE OF MANAGEMENT

The publication in 1932 of *The Modern Corporation and Private Property* by two Columbia University faculty members, A. A. Berle, Jr., and Gardiner C. Means, climaxed several decades of growing interest in the evolution of the business corporation. It was an interest which academicians shared with political reformers and with the leaders of business itself. Berle and Means offered convincing evidence to document what was already a widely recognized trend in business organization, the diffusion of stock ownership in large national corporations, on the one hand, and the emergence of a distinct, largely autonomous managerial group on the other.

The separation of ownership from control in the big corporation, Berle and Means pointed out, meant the splitting of the "atom of property." Owners, to whom the enterprise legally belonged, were being deprived of effective control over its policies. Management, which actually exercised the policy-making power, had relatively little direct claim upon profits. The principle of division of labor had been extended from the sphere of production to that of administration.

The domination of the economy by a few large corporations and the emerging freedom of management from stockholder domination were the elements of Berle's and Means's analysis which attracted immediate attention; but their suggestions as to the probable future implications of these changes were equally significant. Large-scale enterprise, seen as a form of cooperation among a number of participants, Berle and Means suggested, had become a social as well as an economic system. Consequently, control could no longer be exercised in the interests of a single group, the owners. Nor could management be permitted to exercise its new power simply for its own benefit. Rather, "the claims of a group far wider than either the owners or the control group" had now to be taken into consideration. Given the extent to which corporate enterprise had penetrated the entire economy, that group could be nothing less than society as a whole. The changing character of the corporation, Berle and Means argued, made necessary "a wholly new concept of corporate activity. . . . The present claims of both contending parties now in the field have been weakened. It remains only for the claims of the community to be put forward with clarity and force." [1]

Berle and Means were not the first to note the changes occurring in business institutional relations. Woodrow Wilson and other Progressives had long feared the submergence of the individual in the organization, the small stockholder's loss of control over his property, and the aggregation of enormous power in the hands of a few magnates. Louis D. Brandeis, scorning the argument that size was the natural outcome of economic efficiency, had pointed to abuses of power on the part of those who managed "other people's money." Thorstein Veblen had attacked business managers as systematic saboteurs of the promise of technology, inefficient spokesmen for absentee ownership. The economist William Z. Ripley, noting the tendency of the corporation laws to reflect rather than to foster the enlargement of managerial discretion, pointed to instance after instance in which management actions had adversely affected shareholder interests. Ripley, like Berle and Means, concluded that the divorce of ownership from control in the large corporation spelled a fundamental change in the character of the institution of private property itself.[2]

[1] Adolf A. Berle, Jr., and Gardiner C. Means, *The Modern Corporation and Private Property* (New York, 1933), 2–9, 355–56. Later studies, while modifying details of the Berle and Means analysis, have supported its central thesis. See especially Robert A. Gordon, *Business Leadership in the Large Corporation* (Washington, D.C., 1947), 20–23; A. D. H. Kaplan, *Big Enterprise in a Competitive System* (Washington, D.C., 1954), 68–70, 117, 124, 132–55, 239–41, *passim.*; and Maurer, *Great Enterprise,* 6–8.

The conditions and consequences of large-scale organization have been brilliantly analyzed in Kenneth Boulding, *The Organizational Revolution: A Study in the Ethics of Economic Organization* (New York, 1953). Alfred D. Chandler, Jr., *Strategy and Structure: Chapters in the History of the Industrial Enterprise* (Cambridge, Massachusetts, 1962), emphasizes the later stages of organizational change, especially the forces and techniques fostering decentralization.

[2] For Wilson and Ripley, see William Z. Ripley, *Main Street and Wall Street* (Boston, 1927), 3–15, 38–40, 83, *passim.*; Louis D. Brandeis, *Other People's*

Businessmen, though they sharply rejected criticism from outside, were by no means insensitive to the changes taking place. Indeed, from the beginning of the corporate era dedicated individualists had doubted that hired management could be sufficiently motivated to handle the property of others with efficiency and profit. On this ground Adam Smith had questioned the capacity for survival of the corporate form of enterprise itself; and American defenders of individual enterprise in the early nineteenth century had argued along similar lines. Nathan Appleton, a leader among the Boston Associates who had effectively pioneered the application of the corporate form to American industry, doubted that managers who held little or no direct ownership in an enterprise could manage as effectively as those more deeply committed.

Despite such doubts and queries, the corporation had slowly proved its effectiveness—especially, in the nineteenth century, in the railroad industry, where extraordinary amounts of capital were called for. Yet, even here, Henry Varnum Poor, one of the most careful observers of railroad practices, felt that the corporate form encouraged irresponsibility and incompetence on the part of executives. He advocated publicity and public regulation as checks upon managerial discretion. Andrew Carnegie, individualist that he was, had likewise resisted incorporation long after his firm had begun to operate on a large-scale basis. Carnegie rewarded his collaborators with partnership shares in the business, believing that successful management required a share in the risks and the rewards.[3]

By the 1920s, of course, the competence of corporate management was seldom questioned in business circles; but those associated with the larger corporations were well aware that the relationship of man-

Money, and How the Bankers Use It (New York, 1913); Mason, *Brandeis*, 354–56; Thorstein Veblen, *The Theory of Business Enterprise* (New York, 1958), 29, 73–74; Thorstein Veblen, *Absentee Ownership, and Business Enterprise in Recent Times: The Case of America* (New York, 1923); John R. Commons, *The Legal Foundations of Capitalism* (New York, 1924), 321–28. See E. L. Godkin, "Idleness and Immorality," *Forum*, XIII (May, 1892), 334–43, for an earlier expression of concern about the plight of the "parasitic" stockholder.

[3] Adam Smith, *The Wealth of Nations* (New York: Modern Library edition, 1937), 700; Louis Hartz, *Economic Policy and Democratic Thought: Pennsylvania, 1776–1860* (Cambridge, Massachusetts, 1948), 57–62; Harold F. Williamson, ed., *The Growth of the American Economy* (New York, 1946), 308; Alfred Chandler, "Henry Varnum Poor," in William Miller, ed., *Men in Business: Essays in the History of Entrepreneurship* (Cambridge, Massachusetts, 1952), 270–71; Edward Kirkland, in Carnegie, *Gospel of Wealth*, viii.

agement both to stockholders and to the public was changing. Many shared the belief expressed by Sam A. Lewisohn, treasurer of the Maine Copper Company, that, "in view of the administrative position [managers] hold in industry, they are the natural leaders and have the corresponding responsibility of leadership."

Although business leaders might agree with other observers that the managers of large firms were rapidly achieving independence from stockholder domination, not all of them found the trend a desirable one. Alfred P. Sloan, Jr., generalizing from his experience with the DuPont-dominated General Motors company, upheld the desirability of preserving ownership interests sufficiently large to assure responsible administration. Strong ownership identification with management guaranteed personal commitment and responsibility, "the strongest possible safeguard of the public interest."

Sloan's position and that of General Motors was midway between that of the older, closely owned corporation and the emerging, publicly held enterprise. An outstanding example of the latter type by the 1920s was the American Telephone and Telegraph Company, which had sloughed off control both by owners and by bankers and developed an apparently thorough-going executive leadership by the time that Walter Gifford assumed the presidency in 1925.[4]

Next to the stockholders, the group best able to exercise an immediate claim upon the interest and authority of management was, of course, the workers. The postwar weakness of organized labor gave employers the initiative in industrial relations, but it did not permit them to neglect this crucial sector altogether. The Progressives' critique, the exigencies of war, and scientific management's study of the factors influencing productivity had all called attention to the problem of employee morale and to techniques for strengthening worker loy-

---

[4] Daniel Bloomfield, *The Modern Executive* (New York, 1924), 3–11, reprinted an article by Sam A. Lewisohn, entitled "Industrial Leadership and the Manager," from the *Atlantic Monthly,* CXXVI (September, 1920), 414–18. See also Alfred P. Sloan, Jr., "Modern Ideals of Business," *World's Work,* LII (September, 1926), 697–98; *Nation's Business,* XIV (July, 1926), 29. For A. T. & T., see Gordon, *Business Leadership in the Large Corporation,* 207–13; "World's Biggest Corporation," *Fortune,* II (September, 1930), 38–41ff.

Alfred Sloan reaffirmed his conviction that management should have a "real stake" in ownership in his *Adventures of a White Collar Man* (New York, 1941), 153–54, written in collaboration with Boyden Sparkes. The General Motors Bonus Plan, inaugurated in 1918, was, Sloan believed, a successful effort to provide executives with this direct personal interest.

Gerald T. White, in *Formative Years in the Far West,* 384, shows that effective stockholder control could be irksome to management. In this instance California Standard's executives chafed under domination from the "Trust's" New York office.

alty and sense of participation in the impersonal processes of large-scale enterprise. Consequently, employers looked with increasing favor upon a number of employee representation plans which seemed to offer a device less dangerous than labor unions for recognizing and dealing with problems affecting the workers. Employer reluctance to accept independent unions as representatives of their employees' interests was heightened in the postwar years by fears of radicalism and communism, shrewdly agitated by antilabor forces. With the assistance and counsel of a growing number of industrial relations "consultants," many companies launched employee representation plans; over four hundred such programs, claiming a membership of nearly one and one-half million, had come into existence by 1926.

A few of these company unions made a real contribution to the improvement of labor-management understanding and cooperation; the majority, however, were flimsy and pretentious affairs. They offered the appearance of consultation between employer and employee without the solid substance which only genuinely independent representative machinery could supply. They were a gesture in the direction of managerial acceptance of labor's claims for consideration of its interests; but the gesture was often a tactical device, aimed more at insuring employer supremacy than at achieving true mutual accommodation. Their inadequacy was exposed by the failure of most to survive the economic collapse which ended the decade. Yet, sincere and superficial alike, the plans testified to management's growing recognition that the interests of the workers should be formally acknowledged within the structure of enterprise itself.[5]

Employee representation was closely allied with the new interest of management in human relations. Insights into the conditions promoting worker productivity had been accumulating under the joint im-

[5] For discussion of the employee representation movement in the 1920s and before, see Tarbell, *New Ideals in Business,* and other sources cited in Chapter II. Also, John Leitch, *Man to Man: The Story of Industrial Democracy* (New York, 1919); James Myers, *Representative Government in Industry* (New York, 1924); Hicks, *Industrial Relations,* 80–94; Foster Rhea Dulles, *Labor in America* (New York, 1949), 255–58; and Henry L. Nunn, *The Whole Man Goes to Work: The Life Story of a Businessman* (New York, 1953), 56–63, 71–76.

The thinking of John D. Rockefeller, Jr., about labor-management relations moved, under the guidance of MacKenzie King, toward acceptance of true employee representation. Jarred into awareness of the problem through the Colorado tragedy, Rockefeller was slow to recognize the distinction between superficial and meaningful representation. MacKenzie King, however, opposed the use of company unions to fight organized labor. Through Rockefeller's influence, a number of companies undertook employee representation plans. Fosdick, *John D. Rockefeller, Jr.,* 143–44, 169–72, 182–84; Gibb and Knowlton, *The Resurgent Years,* 579.

petus of social science research and managerial efforts to promote efficiency. Scientific management and industrial psychology, developing side by side through the preceding two decades, commanded the attention of thoughtful business leadership in the 1920s. Careful studies of industrial workers, such as those at the Hawthorne plant of the Western Electric Company, were beginning to show the influence of noneconomic factors in performance. Management, it appeared, could no longer afford to neglect the social aspects of the workers' experience in considering its responsibilities toward them. One outcome of the broadening knowledge of the employee's needs, thus, was new sensitivity on the part of management to conditions in the communities from which it recruited its men, as well as to the environment it provided for them within the plant. Summing up the implications of these studies for business, B. Preston Clark, vice-president of the Plymouth Cordage Company, suggested that industry should no longer be thought of as a machine, but as an organism. Cooperation and coordination were its essence; responsibility for the health of these vital and intricate relationships was central to the managerial function.

Acceptance of the legitimacy of labor's claims for recognition had been growing for some years among thoughtful business leaders, especially those connected with large corporations. When Owen D. Young defended the workers' right to a voice in industry at the second National Industrial Conference in 1919, E. K. Hall of the American Telephone and Telegraph Company congratulated him. Gerard Swope, more sympathetic to organized labor than many employers, in 1926 proposed the formation of an independent national union of electrical workers. The employee representation plans, inadequate though they were, were straws in the same wind. Before the postwar labor-management struggles had soured *Forbes'* concern for industrial harmony, the magazine had proposed representation for labor on corporate boards of directors. "The truth which many employers need to digest," *Forbes* had asserted, "is that their most important partners are their workers, not their fellow capitalists." [6]

[6] For the seminal thinking of Frederick Winslow Taylor concerning the nature of the industrial process and the role of management, see his *The Principles of Scientific Management* (New York, 1911). Among Taylor's influential followers were Henry L. Gantt and Mary Parker Follett. See Henry C. Metcalf and L. Urwick, eds., *Dynamic Administration: The Collected Papers of Mary Parker Follett* (New York, 1941); William G. Scott, "The Social Ethic in Management Literature," Georgia State College of Business Administration, Bureau of Business and Economic Research, Studies in Business, Bulletin No. 4 (Atlanta, 1959),

In their shifting relations with stockholders and with employees, as well as with other groups outside the bounds of the corporation itself, managers were beginning to see themselves and their responsibilities in a new light. Instead of being mere agents for the owners, they had become coordinators, standing between and reconciling the claims of a variety of associated interests. A new conception of managerial powers and responsibilities was inherent in this view. Formulated as the idea of the trusteeship of management (to be discussed more fully in the next chapter), it was put forward by a small group of business leaders for the first time in the 1920s.

Those who advanced the trusteeship definition of the managerial role were clearly anticipating the conclusions of Berle and Means. Whiting Williams, a long-time student of business, noted that "certain of our huge commercial units are now generally regarded no longer as mere companies, but, instead, as institutions, nothing less!" Williams thought such changes meant a sure improvement in the quality of business performance. A large corporation was "expected by everybody to maintain unalterably through the years certain standards, ideals, and objectives, just as if it were for instance a university like Yale or Harvard!" While government intervention had helped to foster such expectations, Williams attributed them basically to the nature of large-scale enterprise itself. The life span and the interests of such a company extended far beyond an individual's, making necessary greater attention to long-range considerations. Under the circumstances, "far sight is fairly sure to become fair sight." [7]

Although events were shortly to prove that there was nothing automatic about the association between size and fair dealing, it was nevertheless true that, as the scope of enterprise increased, its social significance became clearer. Even as management in the 1920s attempted

22ff.; and B. Preston Clark, "On the Motives of Industrial Enterprise," *Annals,* LXXXV (September, 1919), 37–47. See also the remarks of Morris L. Cooke, entitled "Modern Manufacturing, a Partnership in Idealism and Common Sense," introducing this volume of the *Annals.* The Western Electric Company Hawthorne Studies, carried out by scholars of the Harvard Business School in the late 1920s and early 1930s, are discussed in Elton Mayo, *The Human Problems of an Industrial Civilization* (New York, 1933), and in F. J. Roethlisberger and William Dickson, with the assistance and collaboration of Harold A. Wright, *Management and the Worker* (Cambridge, Mass., 1939). For Young, Hall, and *Forbes,* see Clarence Hicks, 51; *Forbes,* I (30 March 1918), 737; I (27 October 1917), 165; II (20 April 1918), 6; II (18 May 1918), 94–95.

[7] Whiting Williams, "What Makes Business an Institution," *Magazine of Business,* LV (June, 1929), 658–59.

to formulate a new model of its relations with the other partners to enterprise, it was compelled to search for a new definition of its community responsibilities.

MANAGEMENT AS A PROFESSION

The counterpart of the idea of the manager as mediator was the concept of management as a profession. Popularized by a host of public relations and advertising men, it had strong roots in the changing character of large-scale enterprise, as understood by men such as Louis D. Brandeis and the leaders of the scientific management movement. A successful corporation lawyer, sufficiently familiar with business practices to criticize them knowledgeably, Brandeis had won national fame for his brief in Muller v. Oregon, which in 1908 helped persuade the Supreme Court to uphold state regulation of female labor. Together with E. A. Filene and other progressive Boston businessmen, Brandeis had led the fight for public control of municipal transportation and other utilities. He had helped to expose the mishandling of the New York, New Haven, and Hartford Railroad properties by the Morgan interests. Brandeis sharply challenged the belief of Theodore Roosevelt and George Perkins that bigness was the inevitable outcome of efficiency. Too often, he found, it was the result of dishonest manipulation and the shield of incompetence.

Yet, as Brandeis observed the changing character of American business in 1912, he found the elements of a new profession emerging. A profession required as essential characteristics the development of a body of knowledge, strict intellectual discipline, and an ethic which measured achievement in terms of service to mankind rather than individual advantage. Brandeis believed these conditions were being met through the growth of business and engineering education, the techniques of scientific management, and closer relations between business and government. Business success was coming to depend more than ever upon improvement of the product, the elimination of waste, "and the establishment of right relations with customers and with the community," Brandeis asserted. Recognition of the essential interdependence of business and society was spreading; men were coming to see that "with the conduct of business human happiness or misery is inextricably interwoven." [8]

In view of his own discouraging experiences with business altruism,

[8] Louis D. Brandeis, *Business—A Profession* (Boston, 1914), 1–12; Mason, *Brandeis*, 109, 138, 146–49. Brandeis, a strong believer in collective bargaining, served as vice president of the Civic Federation of New England.

whether in New England or in Oregon, it would seem that Brandeis's picture of a profession of business represented his hopes for the future at least as much as his objective evaluation of the present. The expansion of business in the nineteenth century had, indeed, increased its dependence upon professional disciplines and values. In banking and corporate finance, in transportation and industry as they called for the skills of an increasingly distinct set of engineering professions, and in the law, which was bound ever more closely to the needs of an intricate industrial order, professional standards had increasingly been called into the service of business. That the accession to economic power of lawyers and bankers in the wake of the captains of industry was no guarantee of professional, responsible business policies, Brandeis and his fellow Progressives could amply testify. Nevertheless, the traditions and outlook of the professions filtered into the ranks of business leadership as a new generation of executives took up the reins of power. Elbert H. Gary and Owen D. Young brought the lawyer's viewpoint to their conduct of the affairs of United States Steel and General Electric, respectively. Tom M. Girdler, whose career with the Republic Steel Company was not notable for sensitivity to human relations, still found in his professional background the rudiments of a social philosophy: "I knew that as certain obligations are fixed on the medical and legal professions," he reflected, "so there are obligations fixed on my kind of craftsmanship, on mechanical engineers; above all on any men who participate in management." [9]

Discussion of the professional qualities of business leadership was increasingly common after 1910 among executives themselves, as well as on the part of those who observed the business scene. Citing Young, Andrew Mellon, Dwight Morrow, and others, Charles Cason, vice-president of the Chemical National Bank of New York, was confident by 1927 that business had indeed become a profession. Its leaders were educated men, men of vision, men who knew that

> . . . real success in business is not attained at the expense of others. Business can succeed only in the long run by acquiring and holding the goodwill of the people. To do this it is necessary to render honest, intelligent service at a fair

[9] Cole, *Business Enterprise in its Social Setting*, 60–62, 81; Ida M. Tarbell, *Owen D. Young, A New Type of Industrial Leader* (New York, 1932), 62; Girdler, *Bootstraps*, 158. Arthur Pound, writing in the 1930s, attributed the "Public mindedness" of American business leaders largely to the influence of the legal profession. Lawyers are essentially public men, Pound argued. "It may be said that the legal influence introduced the idea of justice, the habit of compromise, and the institutional idea into American industry." *Industrial America: Its Way of Work and Thought* (Boston, 1936), 10–13.

price. . . . The best upper class men in business are really genuine in their belief in it [service] and are consistent in its practice. Most of them would not consider a policy which enriched them and their company and was at the same time against public interest.

E. A. Filene, a leading Boston merchant, found elements of professionalism even in "shopkeeping," which required careful study and, properly conducted, performed an essential public service. Filene, like Brandeis, saw in scientific management the intellectual discipline and standards required for a true profession. Systematic analysis of production and distribution clarified the essential interdependence of management, worker, and consumer and thus provided a solid foundation for the "social ethic" then being popularized through advertising and public relations programs.[10]

Interest in the idea of business professionalism expressed itself partly through the formation of new organizations. Groups such as the National Personnel Association and the Bureau of Personnel Administration, founded after World War I, held conferences, published journals, and worked with industry and educational agencies to promote a broader view of management's role. The American Management Association was created in 1923 through the combination of a number of such groups striving for professional recognition. Including among its members men whose interests lay in finance, sales, production, and personnel, the AMA was particularly cognizant of the coordinating, integrating aspect of the managerial function. Although its growth was slow in the 1920s, its journal, the *Management Review,* offered a forum for the discussion of management problems and interests. The close tie between the idea of management as a profession and the concept of managerial trusteeship appeared clearly in these exchanges:

> We are beginning to regard those who occupy executive positions in industry as having something in the nature of quasi-

[10] Cason was quoted in *The Commercial and Financial Chronicle* (hereafter cited as *Comm. Chron.*), CXXV (12 November 1927), 2625–26. Filene wrote that "our whole business philosophy needs an overhauling to the end that the creative spirit of the engineer may everywhere dominate our stores, our shops, our offices, our factories, and our banks." E. A. Filene, *The Way Out: A Forecast of Coming Changes in American Business and Industry* (Garden City, 1924), 9, 270–72. See also Bloomfield, *The Modern Executive,* 85–94; Sloan, *White Collar Man,* 144–45, 175; Edward D. Jones, *Industrial Leadership and Executive Ability* (New York, 1913), 11–14, 22; Glenn Frank, "Anonymous Liberalism"; William G. Scott, "The Social Ethic in Management Literature"; *Harvard Business Review* (hereinafter abbreviated *HBR*), V (July, 1927), 385–94.

public responsibility. The war merely emphasized a tendency to consider those in charge of various industries as trustees not merely for the owners of the particular industry but for the national community as well.[11]

The economist John Maurice Clark, then teaching at the University of Chicago, however, was among those who questioned whether professionalism had yet been achieved in business. Clark acknowledged that many individual businessmen had manifested the spirit of public service. He saw in the growing role of science and education in business the elements of a new discipline, and he recognized the potentialities of the codes of ethics which trade associations had begun to issue on virtually a mass production basis. Still, business training and ethics had scarcely developed beyond an elementary level, Clark held in 1926; and the weakness of personal ties between management, labor, and the consumer in large-scale operations seemed incompatible with true professionalism.

Clark's reservations may have been shared more widely than was publicized; they struck a somewhat discordant note in a rapidly swelling chorus of conviction that a new era of enlightened business leadership had begun. President A. Lawrence Lowell of Harvard, who had referred to business as "the oldest of the arts and the latest of the professions," emphasized the growth of formal training and of group endeavor on the part of management in the service of mankind. And the burgeoning of higher business education seemed to give substance to his assertions.[12]

SOURCES OF BUSINESS LEADERSHIP

Whether or not business had truly become a profession, it was increasingly clear by the 1920s that its top positions were being filled by men who could in some sense be considered "professionals." Already in the nineteenth century the railroads had begun to experience this "changing of the guard"; and, as industry after industry reached matu-

[11] Sam A. Lewisohn, "Managerial Achievement in Human Organization—Can It Be Measured?" *Management Review,* XII (November, 1923), 3–8. See also W. W. Kincaid, "Coordinating the Specialists: A Major Executive Function," *ibid.,* XII (October, 1923), 3–5, and "40 Years of Progress in Management," *New York Times,* 15 September 1962, Section 11, 14.

[12] John Maurice Clark, *The Social Control of Business* (Chicago, 1926), 226–40; A. Lawrence Lowell, "The Profession of Business," *HBR,* I (January, 1923), 129–31; James H. S. Bossard and J. Frederic Dewhurst, *University Education for Business* (Philadelphia, 1931), 12–15.

rity and faced new problems of finance, consolidation, or distribution, the older generation of founders and builders began to pass from the seats of power. No precise turning point can be set, as personnel and conditions varied with company and industry. The formation of the United States Steel Corporation in 1901, with Elbert H. Gary succeeding Andrew Carnegie as the leading figure in the industry, may be taken as symbolizing the change. And men such as Gary and Theodore Vail, who assumed the presidency of the American Telephone and Telegraph Company in 1907, had entered the ranks of business management after careers in public service which inevitably affected their outlook.

By the 1920s, however, a still younger generation of managers was assuming corporate leadership. Of this group, an even larger proportion had had formal professional training. Gerard Swope, Alfred P. Sloan, Jr., and Donaldson Brown of General Motors; Robert Wood and Theodore Houser of Sears, Roebuck and Company; and Paul Litchfield of the Goodyear Tire and Rubber Company were engineers. Owen D. Young, a major influence in business thought in the Twenties, like many other executives had had legal training. These men furthermore had risen through the ranks of business in a period of growth and reorganization, acquiring in the process an intimate knowledge of institutional problems and relations.[13]

Other changes, too, could be seen in the ranks of top executives of the larger corporations, who ordinarily provided the most influential and vocal business leadership. Fewer positions were being filled by men whose claims rested primarily on family ties and influence. As managers rather than owners, primarily, of the enterprises whose fortunes they directed, the new leaders reflected a different range of interests. A higher level of formal education may have made them somewhat more at home with the ideas which business specialists and consultants were deriving fom the social sciences. Of course, it did not necessarily follow that training for a particular professional specialty, whether engineering, accounting, or even the law, endowed a man with the qualities of vision and sensitivity to human relations that the new role of management called for. Yet it seemed clear that the younger leaders of business were bringing to their positions a set of

[13] Loth, *Swope of G.E.*, 19; Donaldson Brown, *Some Reminiscences of an Industrialist*, privately printed at Port Deposit, Maryland, 1957, 16; Chandler, *Strategy and Structure*, 316–17. Henry Ford, the best-known industrialist of the Twenties, represented traditional entrepreneurial leadership; this undoubtedly helps to explain his quite different point of view.

viewpoints about themselves, their institutions, and their society which would surely influence their behavior and expectations. The effect of these changes on management policies would take longer to assess.

Changes in the role of management and in the character of its members called attention to the recruitment of managerial talent. The first careful study of the backgrounds of American business leadership, by F. W. Taussig and C. S. Joslyn, appeared almost simultaneously with the Berle and Means interpretation of the new role which this leadership had achieved. Analyzing the family origins of the nearly 9,000 businessmen by age groups, Taussig and Joslyn concluded that leadership was "today being recruited, to a substantially greater extent than was the case thirty or forty years ago, from among the sons of major executives." Over fifty per cent of the men studied came from the independent business, big business, or professional classes; a marked decline was noted in the number of rural youths who made their way to the top of the business ladder. The study showed, too, that nearly thirty-two per cent were college graduates while almost forty-five per cent had had some college education.[14]

Subsequent studies have extended the analysis both forward and backward in time. They make possible a comparison of several generations of top business executives in terms of family background, career lines, and education. While such data are indicative only of general tendencies and by no means provide complete explanations for managerial attitudes and behavior, they do help in understanding the social and intellectual contexts in which American business policy has evolved. A summary of the family backgrounds of four generations of business leaders is presented in Table 1.

Efforts to define the career lines by which successive generations of business leaders have reached top executive positions have been fewer and even more difficult to compare. The estimates in Table 2, therefore, are only roughly indicative.

Finally, the rising educational level of business management is clearly indicated in a recent study (see Table 3).[15]

Other studies tend to corroborate the pattern revealed in the foregoing tables. There is little evidence that the proportion of top business

[14] F. W. Taussig and C. S. Joslyn, *American Business Leaders* (New York, 1932), 77–78, 106, 110–11, 161–64, *passim*.

[15] Mabel Newcomer, *The Big Business Executive* (New York, 1955), 68. Newcomer's data is based upon a study of presidents and board chairmen, primarily those of large corporations in industrials, railroads, and utilities.

Table 1—Family Origins of Business Executives
(Percentage distribution)

Generation of:	1870s [a]	1901–1910 [b]	1928 [c]	1952 [d]
Occupation of father:				
Business:	51.0	55.0	56.7	52.0 [e]
Minor executive			6.7	8.0
Owner, small business			19.4	18.0
Major executive			16.4	15.0
Owner, large business			14.2	8.0
Professional	13.0	22.0	13.4	14.0
Farmers	25.0	14.0	12.4	9.0
Workers—skilled and unskilled	8.0	2.0	10.8	15.0
White collar—clerical or sales			5.0	8.0
Other	3.0 (Public officials)	7.0 (Public officials)	1.7	2.0
	100.0	100.0	100.0	100.0

[a] From Frances W. Gregory and Irene D. Neu, "The American Industrial Elite in the 1870s," in William Miller, ed., *Men in Business: Essays in the History of Entrepreneurship* (Cambridge, Massachusetts, 1952), 193–211. This study reported on 303 top executives from 77 different large companies in the textile, steel, and railroad industries.

[b] William Miller, "The Business Elite in Business Bureaucracies," *ibid.*, 286–305. Miller's sample consisted of 185 men holding the position of president or board chairman in representative industries during the years 1901–10.

[c] F. W. Taussig and C. S. Joslyn, 77–78, based upon 8,749 replies to a questionnaire sent to 15,095 businessmen listed in the 1928 edition of Poor's Register of Directors and selected on the basis of the size and importance of the company with which they were associated.

[d] W. Lloyd Warner and James C. Abegglen, *Big Business Leaders in America* (New York, 1955), 14–33. This study, designed to be comparable to the Taussig and Joslyn data, utilized the replies of 8,562 top executives of the largest companies in a representative cross section of American industries. A total of 17,546 questionnaires were sent out.

[e] Includes three per cent whose fathers were classified as foremen.

Table 2—Career Lines of Business Executives
(Percentage distribution)

	Generation of: 1870 [a]	1901–1910 [b]	1950 [c]	1952 [d]
Basis of career:				
Family managers	32.0	27.0	11.0	
Entrepreneurial	36.0	14.0	6.0	
		("Independent entrepreneurs")		
Corporate hierarchies	18.0	47.0	68.0	8.2
		("Bureaucratic")		(lawyers)
Professionals (lawyers)	14.0	12.0	13.0	10.8
				(engineers)

[a] C. Wright Mills, *The Power Elite* (New York, 1956), 132. Mills's data is taken from Suzanne I. Keller, "Social Origins and Career Lines of Three Generations of American Business Leaders" (Columbia University, Ph.D. dissertation, 1954).

[b] William Miller, "The Business Elite in Business Bureaucracies," 290–93.

[c] C. Wright Mills, *The Power Elite*.

[d] The Editors of *Fortune, The Executive Life* (New York, 1956, Doubleday Dolphin edition), 26ff. *Fortune's* information was drawn from reports of the three highest-paid executives of the 300 largest companies (250 biggest industrials, 25 biggest railroads, and 25 biggest utilities).

executives recruited from middle-class backgrounds, either business or professional, has shifted greatly over the past century. There is even some evidence, notably that of the Warner and Abegglen study, that the opportunity to rise to leadership positions from the ranks of labor has increased. At the same time, it is clear that business backgrounds have supplied by far the most favorable opportunities for business success. There have, however, been dramatic changes in the preparation and experience of business leadership. Formal college and even postgraduate education has obviously become more important than in the past; the content of this business education will be considered shortly. The increasing dependence of business upon educated leadership, coupled with the American system of mass education, has kept access to the top ranks of management open to a broad segment of the community. At the same time, the emergence of a highly educated, specialized management has helped to create an environment in which

Table 3—Education of Corporation Executives [a]
(Percentage distribution)

Highest level of education reached [b]	1900		1925		1950	
	Older	Younger	Older	Younger	Older	Younger
Grammar school	25.3	22.7	26.0	19.8	6.5	2.5
High school	35.4	38.0	24.4	27.5	24.3	16.8
College: no degree	10.1	11.4	12.6	10.6	11.8	14.8
College: 1st degree	24.0	17.9	26.0	25.1	44.8	45.8
Graduate school	5.1	10.0	11.0	17.0	12.6	20.1
	100.0	100.0	100.0	100.0	100.0	100.0
Number of cases included	79	231	119	207	382	487
Education unknown	1	5	...	4	6	7

[a] The younger group for 1900 and 1950 are those who had been in office less than ten years as of the closing of the samples, 1903 and 1953 respectively. The younger group for 1925 are those who had been in office less than ten years as of the opening date of the sample, 1923. The longer period allowed for the middle period was chosen because of the smaller number of recent appointees in this period.

[b] Those attending business schools have been listed with the high school group.

the qualities of objectivity and sensitivity to the general welfare, which are the hallmarks of responsible professionalism, can grow.[16]

EDUCATION FOR BUSINESS

As higher education became increasingly important for business success, the necessity of education for business won growing recognition in American universities and colleges. The movement had to overcome the ingrained resistance of those men, of both the academic and the business realms, who clung to the ideal of the "self-made" man; but by the end of the nineteenth century the same circumstances which

[16] Seymour Martin Lipset and Reinhard Bendix, *Social Mobility and Industrial Society* (Berkeley, 1959), summarizes and analyzes the studies cited above. See also W. Lloyd Warner, "The Corporation Man," in Edward S. Mason, ed., *The Corporation in Modern Society* (Cambridge, Massachusetts, 1960), 106–61; W. Lloyd Warner and James C. Abegglen, *Big Business Leaders in America* (New York, 1955), 47–55ff.; and C. Wright Mills, *The Power Elite* (New York, 1956), 125–29.

were transforming the character of business itself were laying the foundations for the development of business education.

Robert E. Lee, who at the end of the Civil War had assumed the presidency of Washington College (later Washington and Lee University), is often credited with the first proposal for a collegiate school of business. Lee's idea failed to win the support of his trustees, thus permitting credit for founding the first such school to pass to the University of Pennsylvania, which, in 1881, created the Wharton School of Finance and Economy. A gift of $100,000 from Joseph Wharton, a Philadelphia merchant, made the new institution possible; and the motives of the donor foreshadowed a significant theme in the development of American business education. Wharton expressed a desire that emphasis be laid upon "the immorality and practical inexpediency of seeking to acquire wealth by winning it from another, rather than by earning it through some sort of service to one's fellow men"; and the school's curriculum included courses in philosophy, history, and the social sciences. In 1898 the universities of California and Chicago followed Pennsylvania in the establishment of schools of commerce. Two years later Wisconsin and Dartmouth followed suit, while seven other colleges had by this time founded departments of business education. By 1906 Washington and Lee's trustees had succeeded in breathing life into the long-dormant project of their distinguished past president, and in 1908 the Harvard Graduate School of Business Administration and the Northwestern School of Commerce came into being. Columbia's School of Business opened its doors in 1916.[17]

From the outset, academic tendencies to see business and business education in a broad social context seem to have been countered by pressures from the business community for a utilitarian, practical em-

---

[17] For business thought on many aspects of education in the nineteenth century, see Edward C. Kirkland, *Dream and Thought in the Business Community, 1860–1900* (Ithaca, 1956), Chap. III and IV. Upon the initiative of James D. B. DeBow, the University of Louisiana had organized a school of commerce as early as 1851; but this beginning did not survive the sectional crisis. Benjamin R. Haynes and Harry P. Jackson, *A History of Business Education in the United States* (Cincinnati, 1935), 84–87. See also Edmund J. James, *Education of Businessmen* (New York, 1891); N. S. B. Gras, *The Development of Business History up to 1950* (Ann Arbor, 1962), 123–30, 143; Northwestern University School of Commerce, "Training Business Executives," n.p., n.d. [1914]; Melvin T. Copeland, *And Mark an Era: The Story of the Harvard Business School* (Boston, 1958), 18; Thurman W. Van Metre, *A History of the Graduate School of Business, Columbia University* (New York, 1954), 3–11; and Fritz Redlich, "Academic Education for Business," *Business History Review*, XXVI (Spring, 1957), 35–91.

phasis. Joseph Wharton himself had balanced his statement of general objectives with quite specific instructions regarding what was to be taught concerning monetary and tariff policy; and emphasis upon specialized training soon dominated the Wharton curriculum. Specialization in finance, scientific management, and similar fields was the order of the day, although spokesmen for the universities continually stressed a broader interpretation of the social role of the business leader.

Edmund J. James of the Wharton School, later to become president of Northwestern and of the University of Illinois in turn, spoke as early as 1891 in favor of "an education which will broaden and liberalize [businessmen], enlarge their views, widen their outlook, quicken their sympathies, beget and increase a public spirit which shall find its greatest happiness in seeking out and utilizing means of promoting the common welfare." The role of scholarship in the education of businessmen with a broad social perspective was upheld by C. A. Henderson, a sociologist who rejected the view that business had nothing to learn from the ivory academic towers. It was important, Henderson thought, for businessmen to come into contact with views and interests other than their own. "It is of the essence of democracy that the interests of all should not be at the mercy of a few, but should be the care of representatives of the entire community." [18]

[18] American Bankers' Association, "The Education of Business Men" (New York, 1892), 13–14, 33; C. A. Henderson, "Business Men and Social Theories," *American Journal of Sociology,* I (January, 1896), 385–97. An indication of close cooperation between business groups and universities is the fact that the Northwestern School of Commerce was set up in association with the Chicago Association of Commerce and the Illinois Society of Certified Public Accountants. Northwestern University School of Commerce, "Training Business Executives." On pressures for specialization in business education, see Frank C. Pierson and others, *The Education of American Businessmen* (New York, 1959), 39–43; Leonard Silk, "The Education of Businessmen," Committee for Economic Development, Supplementary Paper No. 1, 1961, 18; and Haynes and Jackson, *History of Business Education,* 91.

The Harvard University catalogue for 1908–10, announcing the new Business School program, stated, "The School aims to give thorough and scientific instruction in the fundamental principles of business organization and administration. . . . A broad foundation may thus be laid for intelligently directed activity in commerce or manufacturing, or in those specialized branches of modern industry which now particularly call for professional training, such as accounting and auditing, railroading, banking and insurance." Harvard University, "Early History of the Business School," unpublished MSS., Baker Library, Harvard University, IV–A–3. A similar combination of objectives guided the founders of the University of Chicago business school; see University of Chicago Graduate School of Business, "The Challenge of Business Education" (Chicago, 1949), 33–45.

Henderson's words anticipated what has proved one of the most continuously challenging problems in the evolution of corporate social policies.

The importance of a "broad view" on the part of businessmen was emphasized by Albert Shaw, Arthur T. Hadley, Charles F. Thwing, and Harry Pratt Judson—the last three all university presidents. Yet, of the schools of business in operation by the time of the First World War, only two, Harvard's and Dartmouth's, were graduate institutions in which the study of business problems could begin to be carried on in a truly professional way. Northwestern University by this time was also seeking to found a bureau of business research, in keeping with its aim to "maintain an atmosphere in which large business problems will be regarded instinctively in a large and public-spirited way." Still another indication of growing interest in the study of business management was the fact that over 240 volumes on various aspects of the subject were published in the first decade of the new century.[19]

By the 1920s the idea of postgraduate education for business had won considerable acceptance, although the attainment of top managerial positions by the graduates of such educational programs was, of course, not yet common. Business leaders were increasingly conscious of the diverse issues and complex problems demanding their attention. Many, particularly those associated with large corporations, may have felt inadequately prepared for the constantly expanding responsibilities they faced. Increasingly aware of the potential contributions of the academic disciplines, they looked to the schools for help.

During the Twenties the Harvard Graduate School of Business Ad-

[19] Albert Shaw, *The Business Career in Its Public Relations* (San Francisco, 1904); Charles F. Thwing, *College Training and the Business Man* (New York, 1904); Harry Pratt Judson, *The Higher Education as a Training for Business* (Chicago, 1911); Hadley, *Standards of Public Morality;* Northwestern University School of Commerce, "Training Business Executives"; Gras, *Development of Business History up to 1950,* 143.

A report by the dean of the Harvard Business School asserted that success had been achieved "in giving to men not merely confidence in themselves as beginners in business, but a very potent consciousness of the dignity of business as a profession and one of the most honorable of professions, a reaction that would hardly be conclusively possible outside a strictly Graduate School." Harvard University, *Early History of the Business School,* IV–C–3; Copeland, *And Mark an Era,* 342; Harlow S. Person, "Education for Business," *Annals,* XXVIII (July–December, 1906), 101–10. This issue of the *Annals* was devoted to articles on "The Business Professions." See also the remarks of Edmund J. James, by this time president of the University of Illinois, printed in the *Proceedings of the University of Illinois Conference on Commercial Education and Business Progress* (Urbana-Champaign, 1913), 140–48; Thomas C. Cochran and William Miller, *The Age of Enterprise,* (Harper Torchbooks, 1961), 243.

ministration, with the blessing of President Lowell and the active direction of Dean Wallace B. Donham, played a leading part in the dissemination of the professional ideal for business management. The *Harvard Business Review,* which began publication in 1922, was eventually to become a major forum for expression of the new managerial philosophy. From the school's beginnings this concept of business professionalism had been central to the thinking of president and faculty. President Charles W. Eliot had spoken in 1908 of the universities' duty to "supply the leading men to all the professions, including business . . ."; and an almost unbroken line of courses on business policy, social factors in business enterprise, business ethics, and business history can be traced through the catalogues of the school from 1910 to the present. The business policy course soon brought to the Harvard campus thoughtful men such as Henry S. Dennison and Arch W. Shaw, who shared their business experiences and perspectives with the students. Shaw, in particular, stressed the legitimate interest of the public in the conduct of business affairs. Similar courses in other business schools were reinforcing awareness of the interdependence of business and society even before the advent of the First World War.[20]

After the war Willard E. Hotchkiss, Director of Business Education at the University of Minnesota, summarized two decades of experience in terms which foreshadowed much subsequent discussion of business education. The fact that business affected everyone's life was now generally understood, Hotchkiss thought; and consequently the public's right to question business policies and insist upon higher standards must be accepted. The public expected from business "a contribution to national welfare, and it has become convinced that, by taking thought, it can make the contribution more certain and more uniform than it has been in the past." Many businessmen agreed, and Hotchkiss expected that "with varying zeal they will try to work out

[20] Lowell, "The Profession of Business," 129–31; Business School courses were listed in the *Official Register of Harvard University, Graduate School of Business Administration* (Cambridge, Massachusetts), published yearly. See also Arthur Johnson, "Education for Business: The Harvard Business School, 1908–24," MSS, Baker Library, Harvard University, 30ff.; and Arch W. Shaw, "An Approach to Business Problems," *Harvard Business Studies* (Cambridge, Massachusetts, 1920), II, 322–32, lectures given by Shaw at Harvard. In 1915 a "Social Factors in Business" course was instituted, following the recommendations of a visiting committee headed by Howard Elliott, president of the Northern Pacific Railroad. Copeland, *And Mark an Era,* 18, 45, 78–79, 96, 342, *passim.* See also Edwin F. Gay, "The Founding of the Harvard Business School," HBR, V (July, 1927), 397–400. A course in business ethics was begun in 1913 by Frank C. Sharp at the University of Wisconsin. Frank C. Sharp and Philip G. Fox, *Business Ethics: Studies in Fair Competition* (New York, 1937).

standards of organization that will insure the kind of recognition for general welfare which the public has come to demand."

That education had a role to play in the working out of this "new ideal in business" Hotchkiss was confident. The two greatest contributions which the business schools could make were in scientific methods and human relations. Well-meaning paternalism in employer-employee relations would not suffice; there must be real understanding of the ideas and interests of workers and of the public. Professional education for business meant a search for underlying principles, and an effort to anticipate the kind of social environment in which executives would be working in the future.

Hotchkiss conceded that businessmen had been reluctant to acknowledge social pressures but felt that this attitude was waning. Developments affecting employment, sales, and advertising were all forcing business to turn outward. Furthermore, scientific analysis was demonstrating that good business and "good ethics" were often identical. It was the duty of business education to promote this understanding; it should make "constant reference to the fact that business is carried on in a community in which certain public policies are enforced and . . . that business should conform to these policies and help to make them effective in contributing to the public welfare." [21] Hotchkiss, who became dean of Stanford's Graduate School of Business in 1925, was one of a number of influential educators who carried the social ethic of the Progressive years forward into the business schools of the Twenties.

John Maurice Clark agreed in part with Hotchkiss. Clark defined business as "a pecuniarily organized scheme of gratifying human wants . . . [which], properly understood, falls little short of being as broad, as inclusive, as life itself in its motives, aspirations and social obligations." However, he was less confident than Hotchkiss that businessmen in very significant numbers were taking this broader view. Many still considered business an essentially private matter, rather than "an affair of community interest, in which individualism is tolerated only so far as it serves the common interest better, on the whole, than any other system."

What Clark was teaching at the University of Chicago, students of business were learning at a number of schools across the nation. At times the new glow of profits and prestige, coupled with the perennial need of educators for funds, tempted university spokesmen to identify the status quo with the ideal and to glorify business as having

[21] Willard E. Hotchkiss, *Higher Education and Business Standards*, Boston and New York, 1918, 3–4, 14, 24–25, 66, 81, 103.

achieved, rather than striving to acquire, the level of a profession. Thus President Josiah H. Penniman of the University of Pennsylvania, stressing the growth of close cooperation between business and higher learning, could boast in 1925 that "a university today is a glorified factory"; and others could hail uncritically the "self-generated improvement in business standards." But throughout the 1920s the better business school faculties and administrators maintained a steady emphasis upon the relevance of professional skills and attitudes to the business world.[22]

A study of the opinions of graduates of the Wharton School in 1929 seemed to confirm academic belief in the value of courses oriented toward the social relations and significance of business. More than sixteen hundred replies to a request for views regarding the most valuable courses for business training rated courses covering "the social setting of business life" third in importance, preceded only by English and "description and analysis of business activities" and ahead of

[22] Clark, *Social Control of Business*, x–xii, 45–50, 242–43. Clark taught in and prepared his book for use in the business administration program of the University of Chicago's School of Commerce and Administration. See also R. M. Binder, *Business and the Professions* (New York, 1922), a book which grew out of a similar course at New York University; *Proceedings of the Stanford Conference on Business Education*, Stanford Business Series, No. 1 (Palo Alto, 1926); *Proceedings of the Northwestern University Conference on Business Education* (Chicago, 1927), 46–49; and Glenn Frank, "Needed: A New Man of Business," *Magazine of Business*, LII (November, 1927), 565–67ff. More laudatory of existing standards were Josiah H. Penniman, "Business and Higher Learning," *Nation's Business*, XIII (November, 1925), 56ff., and Dean W. Malott, "Business Advancing as a Profession," *Iron Trade Review*, LXXIV (12 June 1924), 1564–65. Malott, later president of Cornell University, was at the time assistant dean of the Harvard Business School.

Commenting on the absence of checks upon managerial discretion provided for by the "professional" emphasis of business education, *The New Republic* in 1927 suggested, however, that without such checks talk of professionalism in management was "a sentimental smoke-screen thrown over the penetration of our universities by market values." LI (15 June 1927), 84–85.

A 1926 survey of course requirements in thirty-eight business schools and colleges revealed that courses in history, government, law, business policy, social control, and similar subjects were required in most institutions reporting. Since the majority of the programs were undergraduate curricula, however, many such courses were obviously related to the general education of the students. Comments by deans and faculty members of thirty-three schools affiliated with the American Association of Collegiate Schools of Business revealed strong, if not unanimous, support for a broad social emphasis in the curriculum. A question as to the desirability of preparing students for business careers with "a social point of view" brought a favorable response from 233 correspondents; 15 negative and 29 doubtful answers were received. Francis Ruml, "Collegiate Education for Business," *Journal of Business*, I (January, 1928), 1–59.

courses in administration. A growing conviction of the interdependence of business and the community was apparent.[23]

Yet Dean Donham of Harvard could not restrain a sense of foreboding. He saw business assuming the social leadership long held by religion, politics, or law at a time when rapid change was challenging established values and "discontent with the existing state of things [was] perhaps more widespread than ever before in history." As early as 1927 Donham had concluded that the "developing, strengthening, and multiplying of socially minded businessmen is the central problem of business," if not of civilization itself. "The business group, by accident of its position in control of the mechanisms of production, distribution, and finance, is in control of those results of science from which most of the discontent arises," he continued. The social responsibility of business leadership thus was "inescapable." But business lacked "broadly equipped" men to meet the times. "There are professional men of business, but business as a profession is developing rather than already in existence."

To be sure, Donham saw constructive forces at work in industry, among them a growing recognition that enlightened self-interest often coincided with the public welfare. Big business, too, he thought, was bringing an inevitable heightening of ethical standards, since trust among men was a necessary precondition of interdependence. Despite some indications of "dry rot," the larger corporations were "one of the strongest forces for steady ethical advancement in business." Donham found them ethically "in advance of their times." Education, he was convinced, had a role to play in building up "the intellectual basis for enlightened self-interest." Intellectual training could enable business students to think "broadly and soundly" on both social and moral is-

---

[23] Bossard and Dewhurst, *University Education for Business*, 153, 233–35, *passim*. This study reported that since the war "a veritable craze for business education has swept over the country." Between 1919 and 1924, 117 colleges and universities had undertaken organized instruction in the field of business.

An analysis of business books and articles appearing in the 1920s showed that a significant but not an overwhelming amount of attention was being given to the social aspects of business policy. The category of "Advertising and Public Relations" (which included topics in the fields of government and business, personnel and labor, general economic problems, advertising and publicity, cooperation and business ethics, as well as trade association activities) included 3,049 items, or 11.6 per cent of the total number listed, in the *Industrial Arts Index*, 1926–28; 428 items, or 7.4 per cent, in *Business Books*, 1920–26; 80 items, or 2.5 per cent, in *Nation's Business*, 1924–28; and 48 items, or 2.7 per cent, in *Magazine of Business*, 1927–28. Bossard and Dewhurst, *University Education for Business*, 132. Other categories included "Marketing," "Operating Management," and "Finance and Credit," each containing a larger number of items.

sues. "Without . . . a social point of view," Donham felt sure, "business education misses its maximum significance." [24]

POSTSCRIPT: BUSINESS EDUCATION AFTER 1930

To the "social point of view" which Dean Donham and others endeavored to build into the business curricula of the Twenties, the Depression subsequently lent new urgency. The social education of businessmen moved beyond the classroom into the larger world of politics and the life of a people mired in frustration. That much of this education took place in an atmosphere of disenchantment and suspicion was itself largely the result of business failure to achieve the ideal of professional competence which its apologists had prematurely claimed for it. The events of 1929–33 revealed all too clearly the inadequacies of economic understanding, insight into human relations, and ethical sensitivity which still characterized large numbers of executives.

The leaders of business education in the Thirties could scarcely deny that much remained to be done before the professional emphasis they desired to see in school curricula would become an actuality. Dean Leverett S. Lyon of Chicago asserted that those responsible for business training were awakening to the need for greater stress on the social implications of their subject. Yet, despite his and others' efforts, most business education continued its narrow focus on specialized topics and skills. Wallace B. Donham continued to complain of the gap between goals and performance: "The burden does lie heavy on universities to discover and give students a better understanding of the elements which bring social coherence and the conditions under which leadership may contribute to the stability and progress of a free people." Whatever its failings, however, business education was clearly winning increasing acceptance as preparation for business careers. By 1940 there were 110 "collegiate professional schools of business and public administration" in existence, with upwards of 100,000 students enrolled.[25]

[24] Wallace B. Donham, "The Social Significance of Business," HBR, V (July, 1927), 406–15.

[25] Haynes and Jackson, History of Business Education, 95; Wallace B. Donham, "Training for Leadership in a Democracy," HBR, XIV (September, 1936), 261–71. For statistics on business school enrollments, see University of Chicago Graduate School of Business, "The Challenge of Business Education" (Chicago, 1940), 1. The number of collegiate degrees in business had risen from 1,686 in the academic year 1919–20 to 55,404 in 1957–58; these figures include bachelor's, master's, and doctor's degrees. The 1919–20 business degrees represented 3.2 per

Events of the Second World War and of the postwar era left little doubt that business education would continue to stress the social framework within which economic institutions and policies operate. Many of the old controversies continued to smoulder, however—the issue of specialization versus breadth and that of the "social ethic" being outstanding examples. Although the professionalization of business had gained new meaning and new adherents over the years, there remained good reason for believing that achievement still fell far from the goal.[26]

The occasion of the fiftieth anniversary of the University of Chicago's school of business, in 1948, provided a useful point at which to review the achievements and shortcomings of a half-century's experience. Leslie Perrin, president of General Mills, Inc., and John L. McCaffery of International Harvester took the opportunity to argue for training which enabled the businessman to envisage the social implications of his policies; Robert E. Wilson, chairman of Standard Oil of Indiana, however, continued to uphold the advantages of specialized training for management. Still, the need for deeper understanding of the social sciences to help the student cope with the social dimensions of business could scarcely be denied.

Leverett S. Lyon, by now an official of the Chicago Association of Industry and Commerce, put the role of business education in a somewhat different perspective. The responsibilities of master craftsmen had formerly included both teaching apprentices the techniques of a trade and teaching them its social significance; more recently the two functions had been separated in business and business education. "It was when we put business education into the schools," Lyon suggested, "that we forgot what it meant." Business education now must assume the responsibility "to make crystal clear the role which business as an institution plays in modern society. . . . Every graduate student should know that business does not exist for itself but is a device which society uses and modifies for the accomplishment of social purposes."[27]

---

cent of the degrees earned in all fields, while business degrees in 1957–58 were 12.6 per cent of all earned degrees. Between 1947–48 and 1957–58 no significant change occurred in the percentage of degrees earned in business. See Robert A. Gordon and James E. Howell, *Higher Education for Business* (New York, 1959), 19–36, for further discussion.

[26] For an excellent evaluation of business in relationship to professionalism, see Gordon and Howell, *Higher Education for Business*, 69–73.

[27] University of Chicago, "The Challenge of Business Education," 20–29, 30–34, 49–52. For similar viewpoints see Robert J. Senkier, *Revising a Business Cur-*

Criticism of business education as inadequate to meet the complex demands of the postwar world continued, however. Studies sponsored by the Carnegie Corporation and the Ford Foundation pointed in 1959 to a variety of shortcomings in the pattern of business training. Overemphasis upon specialized courses at the expense of broad cultural studies in the preparation of businessmen was the most prominent complaint, even after a half-century of experience. Recommendations were advanced for still more consideration of the social responsibilities of management. Dean Donald K. David, summing up the drift of this thinking, in 1958 urged the 22,000 graduates of the Harvard Business School to fulfill their professional responsibilities through active community leadership. He reminded them that "the *prime necessity* for the businessman today is to weld to his economic prowess a similar drive, skill and creativity in his *dangerously neglected social and political function in society.*"

Small businessmen, faced with pressing problems and limited resources, were less able, perhaps, than others to accept this analysis. Many continued to call for "practical" business training and to resist the more ambitious definitions of responsibility as being too "big-business" or "liberal-arts" oriented. Yet for small enterprises, also, it was clear that social and political considerations were matters of ever-increasing importance and concern.[28]

---

riculum—The Columbia Experience (New York, 1961), 10–11, 18, 91; Indiana University, The School of Business, "Attitudes of Industrial Executives Regarding Education for Industry," Indiana Business Studies, No. 30 (Bloomington, 1948); Ralph Flanders, "The Function of Management in American Life" (Palo Alto, 1948) (lectures delivered at the Seventh Annual Conference for Business Executives, Stanford University); Thomas H. Carroll, ed., *Business Education for Competence and Responsibility* (Chapel Hill, 1954); Copeland, *And Mark an Era,* vi–x; and Harvard University, The Graduate School of Business Administration, "Education for Business Responsibility" (Cambridge, Massachusetts, 1947).

The fact that many of the discussions of the content and aims of business education were presented in the context of publications and conferences intended to enlist the support, financial or otherwise, of representative business leaders is significant. In such presentations business school spokesmen were at pains both to avoid offense to potential contributors and to indicate the advantages of advanced study in business problems.

[28] Donald K. David, "The New Relation of Business to Society" (Cambridge, Massachusetts, 1959), an address at the 50th annual conference of the Harvard Business School Association (italics David's). The studies referred to are Gordon and Howell, *Higher Education for Business,* and Pierson and others, *Education of American Businessmen.* These are summarized and analyzed in Silk, "The Education of Businessmen." For small business, see Raymond V. Lesikar, "Needs of

Perhaps the broadest vision of the future development of business education at mid-century was that offered by Robert D. Calkins, Director of the General Education Board. Calkins noted that society's need for enlightened economic leadership stretched further even than the domain of business. Labor, government, and international economic institutions were equally important. Schools of business administration, he argued, should seek to discover and teach the fundamental principles underlying *all* forms of economic organization. Problems of technological change, the business cycle, economic growth, underdeveloped countries, industrial relations, and the like were too sweeping to be treated from the business point of view alone. Nor were top business leaders likely to lack opportunities for public service. These

---

Education for Small Business, Based on a 1959 Survey of Louisiana Businessmen" (Baton Rouge, 1961).

Company interest in the further education of executives along social, professional, and cultural lines can be traced in the development of company-financed and, in some cases, company-operated "executive development" programs. These deserve a study of their own and can be referred to only in passing. In the 1920s trade associations and chambers of commerce served as the vehicles through which business representatives could be oriented to community problems. A two-week summer session course at Northwestern University, for instance, was sponsored jointly by the university, the Chicago Chamber of Commerce, the Northern Association of Commercial Organization Secretaries, and the American Trade Association Executives. It included courses on "Social Problems of a Community," "Civic Activities," and "Social Work—Solicitations—Community Chests." *Nation's Business*, XIV (April, 1926), 58–60. A variety of management training programs, of the specialized as well as the "broad-gauged" types, is discussed and some of the implications of the programs are noted in "The Crown Princes of Business," *Fortune*, XLVIII (October, 1953), 150–53ff.

Probably the most highly publicized of the management "mind-stretching," "horizon-broadening" programs were those sponsored by the American Telephone and Telegraph Company. The objective of the A. T. & T.–University of Pennsylvania program was that of helping future executives "to understand and interpret the social, political and economic changes—both nation and world wide—which will influence the problems of corporate management to an increasingly greater degree in the future. This might be defined as developing a breadth of outlook, looking toward future 'statesmanship' in the business." See Peter E. Siegle, "New Directions in Liberal Education for Executives," Center for the Study of Liberal Education for Adults, March, 1958.

A. A. Stambaugh, board chairman of Standard Oil of Ohio, put a cash value on liberal education for business executives: "Real leadership is compounded of the broadening culture influences of the liberal arts colleges. Industries have lots of men worth $10,000 a year, but can't find many worth $100,000." *Management Review*, XLIII (September, 1954), 563–64. This conviction on the part of many company officials accounted for their support of cultural programs for executives whose formal education had been more specialized.

facts suggested that education for business leadership as a separate field should yield to education for economic leadership in general.[29]

Here was a professional ideal for which probably little immediate business support could be mustered. But it was in many ways a logical outgrowth of the forces which, for over fifty years, had been lifting the eyes of business leadership beyond its account books and production schedules toward new shores, dimly seen.

[29] Robert D. Calkins, "Aims of Business Education," *Education for Professional Responsibility: A Report of the Proceedings of the Inter-Professional Conference on Education for Professional Responsibility Held at Buck Hill Falls, Pennsylvania, 1948* (Pittsburgh, 1948).

4 · BUSINESS AND SOCIETY IN THE TWENTIES

As executives of large corporations reviewed their responsibilities in the course of the 1920s, they showed growing awareness of the importance to their companies of social groups and conditions lying beyond the immediate circle of their authority. Sometimes, as we have already seen, this heightened social sensitivity stemmed from changing relationships within the corporation itself between owners, managers, and laborers. Sometimes it derived from systematic studies that brought new understanding of the social and psychological dimensions of business. The pressure to find markets for the economy's rapidly expanding productive capacities gave a growing sense of urgency to efforts to promote favorable public attitudes toward business. At the same time, the expansion of advertising and public relations fields and especially the new medium of radio strengthened the channels of communication between business and society. The leaders of some social groups, notably in the fields of education and social welfare, looked increasingly to business for both financial and organizational help; and postwar conservatism, heightened by fearful reactions to the specter of international communism, made many look to business rather than government for a significant social leadership. Under such a combination of pressures, top business officials could scarcely question the need to build closer relations between their companies and surrounding society.

The primary means by which business interacts with the community is, of course, through the production and distribution of goods and services. Rapid expansion in the 1920s in many lines of business brought widespread prosperity and encouraged even more extravagant hopes that the secret of permanent affluence was at last to be discovered. Economic collapse in 1929 showed how far business had fallen short of the expectations to which its achievements had given rise; but for most of the decade prosperity seemed to emphasize the right and duty of business leadership to assume broader social responsibilities.

The Twenties also saw a marked increase in the involvement of business in aspects of social life in which it had previously shown only limited interest. In addition to the employee representation and welfare plans previously discussed, advertising, public relations, and propaganda campaigns brought their sponsors squarely and consciously into the area of public opinion formation. Participation in the rapidly growing community chest movement consolidated and extended the limited experiments in corporation philanthropy undertaken earlier. Finally, in the realm of ideology, the concept of the trusteeship of business management, which had arisen from the internal relations between parties to the enterprise itself, was enlarged to bring within its scope a still greater circle of social interests.

As with the economic achievements of business, these ventures into the realm of social thought and action were seriously called into question by the impact of the Great Depression after 1929. Much that was flimsy or specious in the notion of a society enriched and dominated by business leadership was exposed in the searching tests of poverty. Still, a significant residue survived. Ten years of experience under rapidly changing social and economic conditions left business more fully committed to involvement in community life than it had ever been before.

MASS MARKETS AND PUBLIC RELATIONS

The power of public opinion in a society geared to the economies of large-scale production and mass consumption was increasingly clear to business leadership. The drive to woo and win consumers reached new levels of intensity in the 1920s. What was less clear—a source, indeed, of considerable confusion and disagreement throughout the decade—was the appropriateness of different means of courting public favor.

Broadly speaking, business thought divided into two schools. One, inspired by the capabilities of advertising and the rising public relations "profession," emphasized persuasion based upon psychological insights and the techniques of communication to win friends for business. The other, combining concepts of the nature and scope of business with recognition of the potentialities of the mass production system, stressed economic performance in the form of better products at lower prices as the chief path to the consumer's pocketbook and the public's favor. Neither of these views necessarily contradicted the other; each might, and in actual fact often did, imply or complement the other. Varying personal, business, or social influences produced a broad range of perspectives incorporating different combinations of values in the policies of different companies. Yet, for purposes of our analysis, it is necessary to stress divergence rather than interaction between the two approaches.

The cultivation of public relations attracted increasing attention in the 1920s, especially on the part of managers of large firms. Alfred P. Sloan, Jr., acknowledged that "the enormous scale upon which business is done had not only changed the methods of industrial management, but it has brought about an entirely new conception of the relation of business to the public." Samuel Insull asserted that public relations were "of more consequence to our properties than all the rest put together." When Col. Robert E. Stewart assumed the chairmanship of Standard Oil of Indiana in 1919, he took immediate steps to inaugurate a program of "frankness," publicity, and institutional advertising. "I am firm in my conviction," Stewart announced, "that the personnel of a business organization, as well as its policy, its purposes, its current activities, its volume of business, and its products all are matters of public interest, and that these matters should be given as wide publicity as possible." [1]

The idea that mass production under business leadership had ushered in a new era of virtually automatic prosperity and progress lent itself well to exploitation by those anxious to secure public acquiescence in business leadership. As guarantors of the nation's economic welfare, businessmen, in this view, could be trusted to know and to do what was necessary for the public's well-being. To question the wisdom of business policies under such circumstances was foolish, if not

[1] Sloan, "Modern Ideals of Business," 694–97; Samuel Insull, *Public Utilities in Modern Life* (privately printed in Chicago, 1924), 262; Paul H. Giddens, *Standard Oil Company (Indiana), Oil Pioneer of the Middle West* (New York, 1955), 330–33. See also J. H. Tregoe (Secretary-Treasurer of the National Association of Credit Men), "Canons of Commercial Ethics," *Annals*, CI (May, 1922), 208; and *Nation's Business*, XIV (July, 1926), 29.

actually dangerous. By no means were all businessmen so extravagant in the assertions they advanced in their own behalf, but there were enough who were to create an impression of business claims to infallibility. Their enthusiastic use of the new media of communication and persuasion gave them an influence over the tone of discussion about business in the Twenties which was perhaps disproportionate to their actual numbers.

The fact that men such as Insull and Stewart were later found to have been less than candid in their dealings with the public has fostered the conclusion that the public relations craze of the Jazz Age was only a tawdry attempt to fool the people into unquestioning acceptance of business ideas and products. Indeed, there is much to support this view. Institutional advertising, the promotion of customer stock ownership, particularly by public utilities, and the full panoply of propaganda techniques, including speeches, articles, and radio programs by such supposedly independent and objective citizens as clergymen and college professors were put to use to promote a favorable business image in the public mind. Books and pamphlets, films, writing, and speaking contests, all were called into service to spread the virtues of free enterprise, its products, or its stock offerings. Nor was the machinery of persuasion directed at adults alone. "Educational" materials were made available to schools and considerable pressure was exerted, particularly by representatives of the public utilities, to secure textbooks considered "safe" by self-appointed censors on behalf of conservatism, Americanism, or business enterprise.

So flagrant were some examples of intimidation and manipulation by those determined to achieve uncritical public acquiescence in their schemes for private advantage that suspicion fell upon the entire public relations industry almost from its beginning. Recurrent instances of exploitation of the means of mass persuasion for selfish purposes continued (and still continue) to raise questions regarding the morality and the social utility of the public relations function.[2]

[2] Advertising and public relations specialists had a direct interest in convincing troubled or naïve businessmen of the advantages of publicity campaigns. As a device for turning "public intrusion" into "public support," for counteracting radicalism, for promoting community harmony and good will, publicity could be made to seem the answer to many of the social conditions which more or less vaguely disturbed the minds of busy executives. See S. T. Scofield, "Business is Getting Public," *Advertising and Selling*, X (22 February 1928), 22ff.; *Forbes*, II (18 May 1918), 94–95, and XIV (10 May 1924), 178.

In 1924, *Forbes* sponsored an essay contest on the subject "How Sound Public Relations Between Public Utilities and Communities Can Be Best Developed and

The second approach to mass production stressed the possibilities the system offered for improving the performance of business itself. In this version, the emphasis was placed upon management's obligation to exploit and develop this potential to the fullest rather than on any supposition that it could automatically be relied upon to do so. Large-scale enterprise was seen as a challenge to managerial imagination and initiative, not as evidence of managerial infallibility. Properly administered, mass production might indeed contain the key to the reconciliation of private profit with public welfare; but administration rather than persuasion would provide the key to achievement. The position was argued most effectively by Henry Ford and Edward A. Filene, a Boston merchant whose reputation as a promoter of quantity sales at low prices approached that of Ford in the field of production. Both Ford and Filene had dedicated their business careers to the policies for which they spoke, and their success seemed to demonstrate the validity of their arguments. Although each was an able publicist for his point of view, they both emphasized that deeds rather than words must be the ultimate test of business claims to the public's patronage.

Ford's chief contributions to the development of large-scale production and consumption were already behind him by 1920, but statements of his views continued to be issued throughout the decade. He had become a folk hero of the new industrialism through his application of assembly-line methods in the automobile industry, his creation of the Model T, his persistent price-cutting, and his well-publicized announcement of the $5 day in 1914. There was something of the frustrated Populist reformer in Henry Ford. When sued by the Dodge brothers for his failure to pay larger dividends out of the company's profits, Ford was asked in 1916 for what purposes other than the max-

---

Maintained." The winning essay, by Paul C. Rawson, recommended worker education, use of newspapers, fuller explanations to the public of company activities, participation by company representatives in community social and civic groups, sponsoring of inspection trips, etc. Additional pointers were culled by *Forbes* from other entries and relayed to interested readers. *Forbes*, XIV (24 May 1924), 215, 226; *ibid.*, (21 June 1924), 368. Goldman, *Two-Way Street,* is a historical account. See also Hiebert, *Courtier to the Crowd;* Edward L. Bernays, *Biography of an Idea: Memoirs of a Public Relations Counsel* (New York, 1965); Otis A. Pease, *The Responsibilities of American Advertising; Private Control and Public Influence, 1920–1940* (New Haven, 1958); and Pimlott, *Public Relations and American Democracy.* Carl D. Thompson, *Confessions of the Power Trust* (New York, 1932), Part IV, summarizes hearings of the Federal Trade Commission on the propaganda activities of the public utilities affiliated with the National Electric Light Association.

imization of profits his company existed. His reply was startling: "Organized to do as much good as we can, everywhere, for everybody concerned." The money was ploughed back into still more efficient production techniques.

That such a viewpoint shocked orthodox corporation lawyers and stockholders is perhaps not surprising. But it did not really mean that Ford considered his enterprise an exercise in philanthropy. Rather, it was his curious way of putting the truth upon which he had already seized, that the greatest profits in the long run lay in the manufacture of quality products at the lowest possible prices for a mass market. To this end Ford did not hesitate to subordinate the short-term advantage of stockholders or to resist the temptation to seek outside capital and share control of his enterprise with the investment bankers.[3]

It was Ford's belief that proper organization of industry would produce both profits and social betterment. Through increased production at lower prices employment would grow and living standards rise. The logic of mass production thus reconciled the private interest of the manufacturer with the well-being of the consumer and, ultimately, of society at large. By doing his job as efficiently and intelligently as possible, the businessman became a social benefactor; the size of his profit indicated the scale of his service to the community. By the Twenties Ford's social idealism had soured. His unconventional views about profits and wages won him few friends in the business community. Still, the aura of remarkable success and the popularity attaching to one who had defied and confounded the experts assured a hearing for his views.

More articulate and sophisticated than Ford in preaching mass consumption as the key to economic progress was E. A. Filene. An enthu-

[3] The Ford story, including the development of the assembly line, the $5 day, the notorious, if well-intentioned, Ford Sociological Department, and the Dodge brothers' suit, is presented in Allan Nevins's two volumes, written in collaboration with Frank Ernest Hill, *Ford: the Times, the Man, the Company* (New York, 1954), and *Ford: Expansion and Challenge, 1915–33* (New York, 1957).

Ford's emphasis upon paying high wages and plowing profits back into better production methods raised the question of the rights of stockholders in relationship to management policies. The court's decision, upholding the stockholders' complaint, was an expression of then orthodox economic and legal thought, which was, however, already beginning to undergo modification: "It is not within the lawful powers of a corporation to shape and conduct a company's affairs for the merely incidental benefit of shareholders and for the primary purpose of benefitting others." Maurer, *Great Enterprise*, 65. Even at the time of this decision (1916) some managements were, in fact, exercising their discretion to dispose of corporate property for purposes even less directly beneficial to shareholders than were Ford's.

siastic liberal who in his personal life pursued the crusade for civic and social betterment as untiringly as he did the gospel of mass consumption in business, Filene was a long-time friend of Louis D. Brandeis. He shared Ford's belief that "businessmen can best serve the cause of social progress through activities in their own field—by advancing their own self-interest"; but Filene interpreted his own self-interest more broadly than did Ford. A convert to scientific management, he also supported progressive employee welfare and representation programs. No one better exemplified the Brandeis ideal of business professionalism.

Devoted to public causes, convinced of his special responsibilities to his employees, Filene nevertheless insisted that the chief duty of the businessman was to the consumer. It was his obligation to make better products available more cheaply and in this way to create a higher standard of living and a more productive society. For Filene, the path from producer to consumer, carefully cultivated by responsible management, became the highway of progress. "Real service in business," he argued, "consists in making and selling merchandise of reliable quality for the lowest practically possible price, provided that the merchandise is made and sold under just conditions."

Ford, Filene, and others who shared their views offered still another reason for executives to consider anew the relationship of their companies to the community. Not charity, not philanthropy, not paternalistic interest in a satisfied labor force, not the desire to maintain a free hand for business by cultivating public favor, but downright economic interest dictated concern for the condition of the consumer. Rising living standards meant better markets and expanding profits. Public acceptance would flow, not from efforts to manipulate opinion, but from what business did to demonstrate its continuing commitment to more efficient service of the public's needs.[4]

4 E. A. Filene, "A Simple Code of Business Ethics," *Annals*, CI (May, 1922), 223–38. See also his "I Believe in Working with Others," *Nation's Business*, XVII (April, 1929), 179ff. Filene's ideas are set forth more fully in two books, *The Way Out, A Forecast of Coming Changes in American Business and Industry* (New York, 1924), and *Successful Living in this Machine Age*, written in collaboration with Charles W. Wood (New York, 1931).

Eric Larrabee has written a thoughtful commentary entitled "The Doctrine of Mass Production," in Robert E. Spiller and Eric Larrabee, *American Perspectives: The National Self-Image in the Twentieth Century* (Cambridge, Massachusetts, 1961), 178–94.

Filene's philosophy has been perpetuated in the interests of the Twentieth Century Fund, which he created in 1919. The Fund has devoted a major share of its attention and support to studies of economic problems of the kind to which

A number of business leaders, including public relations specialists such as Ivy Lee and Edward Bernays, conceded that effective public relations must be a "two-way street," alerting management to public attitudes and needs as well as carrying the business story to the people. Alfred P. Sloan, Jr., noting that big business required public understanding, favored a policy of "frankness as one of the first characteristics of management." Such a policy implied, Sloan added, "That the corporation shall be of such a character that frankness cannot injure it." Joseph H. Defrees, in his presidential address to the United States Chamber of Commerce in 1922, concurred. "What is not for the public good is not for the good of business," Defrees asserted; and he explicitly acknowledged "the obvious fact that business alone cannot be the final judge of what is for the public good." Still, given these and other expressions of intent to earn, as well as to manufacture, public approval, the temptations remained strong to accept the word for the deed.[5]

Evaluation of the motives, performance, and achievements in the

Filene believed business leadership could make the most useful social contribution of its talents and resources. See *Survey*, LXVI (15 September 1931), 547, and LXXIII (October, 1937), 318–19; E. A. Filene, *Speaking of Change* (New York, 1939). Gerald W. Johnson, *Liberal's Progress* (New York, 1948), is a biography of Filene. For an earlier acknowledgement of the role of the consumer, see S. T. Henry, "Some Business Tendencies of the Day," *University of Illinois Conference on Commercial Education and Business Progress* (Urbana-Champaign, 1913), 18.

[5] Sloan, "Modern Ideals of Business," 696; *U. S. Chamber of Commerce Report of the Tenth Annual Meeting* (1922), 7–8; *U. S. Chamber of Commerce Report of the Twelfth Annual Meeting* (1924), 19. See also Goldman, *Two-Way Street;* A. H. Cole, *Business Enterprise in its Social Setting,* 66; Peter F. Drucker, *The Concept of the Corporation* (New York, 1946), 227; Thomas C. Cochran, *The American Business System* (New York, 1957), 154–57.

In 1923, Gerard Swope and Owen D. Young distributed to General Electric stockholders shares in the Electric Bond and Share Company long held by General Electric. Electric Bond and Share was a holding company formed by General Electric to promote the development of public utilities and, thus, customers for General Electric's products. Swope believed it to be both unethical and bad business to be involved in both enterprises. Loth, *Swope of G.E.,* 129–36. Similarly, *Nation's Business*, XVII (August, 1929), 13, reported that International Paper and Power Company had divested itself of its newspaper holdings in deference to public opinion. The 1926 annual report of the American Telephone and Telegraph Company contained a statement by President Walter Gifford that ". . . not only our stockholders, but the public generally, are entitled to know how we are carrying on our stewardship. . . . It is our further purpose to conduct the affairs of the Bell System in accordance with American ideals and traditions, so that it may continue to merit the confidence of the people of the country." Arthur Pound, *The Telephone Idea* (New York, 1926), 21.

field of public relations—in the Twenties or since—would surely produce an equivocal verdict. Apart from such considerations, the growth of business attention to public relations was an implicit acknowledgment that modern large-scale enterprise, in E. A. Filene's phrase, had indeed made "the whole world one." Giant business, especially, could no longer afford to ignore the ideas and conditions of other segments of society. Workers, investors, suppliers, dealers, customers, students, and voters were all affected by business practices for which corporate management had assumed primary responsibility. However inadequately the new techniques of advertising and public relations might recognize the needs of these groups, the fact that such functions had achieved their own distinctive places in corporate tables of organization marked another step in business recognition of its social ties.

BUSINESS ASSOCIATIONS

Company efforts to cultivate public acceptance were fostered, and to some extent paralleled, by the development of trade associations, through which many members of a given industry could cooperate in pursuit of their mutual interests. The trade association movement was part of the widespread revolt against conditions of intense competition which had characterized the early period of industrial development. Since they numbered among their members many small, as well as large, enterprises, these associations suffered relatively little from the onus attached to the trusts. Yet they offered similar advantages, since they could provide members with common information and services on matters ranging from production standards and pricing policy to industrial and public relations.

Trade associations long before the Twenties had undertaken a wide variety of community functions. They had lobbied and agitated on behalf of the interests of their membership on matters such as railroad legislation, banking legislation, and the tariff. In this capacity they had sometimes resisted and sometimes actively supported "reform" legislation. During World War I they served as coordinators of planning and production in a number of industries closely related to the national government's war production program. Also at the national level, the National Association of Manufacturers and the United States Chamber of Commerce had attempted even before the war to establish themselves as recognized spokesmen for the views and interests of the business community, transcending trade or regional lines.[6]

[6] The relationship of business to Progressivism and the part played by many business organizations is discussed in Wiebe, *Businessmen and Reform.*

When the war ended, businessmen were naturally anxious to speed the elimination of governmental restrictions and controls; but experience had shown the value of promoting and regulating common interests through the trade associations. The expansion of trade association services, freed of government supervision, became a major business objective. A 1918 United States Chamber of Commerce meeting on postwar problems accordingly resolved, "This conference heartily approves the plan of organizing each industry in the country in a representative national trade association and expresses the belief that every dealer, jobber, manufacturer, and producer of raw materials should be a member of the national organization in his trade and cordially support it in its work." Herbert Hoover, Secretary of Commerce after 1921, encouraged trade association efforts to achieve simplification and standardization of parts in order to reduce waste. The services of the Commerce Department in collecting statistics and promoting industrial conferences were placed at the disposal of the business community. Through distribution of information, standardized cost-accounting systems, and open-pricing systems by which companies publicized their schedules, some trade associations managed to infringe upon the spirit, if not the letter, of the antitrust laws and to minimize price competition. "Self-government" in industry thus moved a step in the direction of private economic planning.[7]

Public relations, especially the justification of industrial self-government, provided a major area of trade association activity in the 1920s. Spokesmen for the associations stressed efforts to raise standards of business leadership and integrity, much as they were improving and regularizing engineering standards. F. M. Feiker, vice president of the McGraw-Hill Company, saw the associations as one of the great "professionalizing forces" of the day; and others agreed. Sooner or later, Feiker stated, "Such associations become professionally conscious . . . [and] set up for the guidance of each member standards of practice or codes of ethics which, broadly speaking, constitute a great structure, with the service motive as the standard of conduct. . . ."[8]

Discussions of business ethics were common in the Twenties and the role of trade associations in promoting this ethical concern was

[7] Brady, *Business as a System of Power*, 195; George H. Soule, *Prosperity Decade: From War to Depression, 1917–1929* (New York, 1947), 140–41.

[8] F. M. Feiker, "The Profession of Commerce in the Making," *Annals*, CI (May, 1922), 203–7. Feiker found business education, industrial journalism, and the work of the Department of Commerce to be other factors contributing to professionalization.

widely hailed. Given the mood of the day, the trade association or chamber of commerce which did not at some time during the decade produce a code of ethics subscribed to by its membership was derelict in its duty. The idea that "good ethics" were good business, that "He profits most who serves best," helped reconcile those who were less morally minded to a veritable flood of inspirational business literature with a theme of uplift. The spirit of boosterism and "service" which Sinclair Lewis satirized in *Babbitt* filled innumerable business speeches and articles. It was seen, by men who took it seriously, as evidence of a growing sense of responsibility on the part of those best qualified to provide leadership for a permanently prosperous America.[9]

In 1924 the United States Chamber of Commerce adopted a statement of "Principles of Business Conduct" produced by its Committee on Business Ethics. The statement, in effect a kind of national code of ethics, summarized many of the current ideas concerning the relationship of business to society. Its first principle asserted, "The Foundation of business is confidence, which springs from integrity, fair dealing, efficient service, and mutual benefit." Profit was to be understood as the reward for such service. Principle Thirteen, on the role of management, stated the increasingly popular view that "the primary obligation of those who direct and manage a corporation is to its stockholders. Notwithstanding this, they act in a responsible capacity, and in such a capacity owe obligations to others—employees, to the public which they serve, and even to their competitors. . . ." Managers were reminded, too, that "the corporate nature of business did not absolve from or alter the moral obligations of individuals." Acknowledging that all forms of enterprise "are to some extent affected with a public interest," the statement warned, "Business should render restrictive legislation unnecessary through so conducting itself as to deserve and inspire public confidence." [10]

By 1925, this statement of principles had been approved by over 750 member organizations with some 300,000 members. President Rich-

[9] See *Nation's Business*, XV (March, 1927), 95–96, for an article by a Methodist minister, Dr. Roy L. Smith, "Business Becomes More Christian," which specifically challenged Sinclair Lewis. Also *ibid.*, XII (5 June 1924), 7–9; *ibid.*, XV (20 May 1927), 15; Caspar S. Yost, "Business Has a Spiritual Side," *ibid.*, XVII (March, 1929), 142–46; and *Forbes*, XXII (15 October 1928), 60, and XXII (1 December 1928), 9.

[10] Edwin B. Parker, "The Fifteen Commandments of Business," *Nation's Business*, XII (5 June 1924), 16ff. The original statement of principles appeared in the *U. S. Chamber of Commerce Report of the Twelfth Annual Meeting* (1924), 53.

ard F. Grant was able to boast, "I find no such recognition of obligation to the public among the other blocs or factions in this country." Grant continued, "Among businessmen generally there is a rising tide of conviction that business does not exist for itself alone, but is an institution which should serve the common lot and inspire men to give the best that is in them for the common good. This rising tide might properly be called the spiritual development in business." [11]

Others looked upon the proliferation of codes of business ethics from different vantage points. John Maurice Clark felt that the written codes set higher standards of conduct than the informal codes which actually governed most business behavior. He saw them as but one step in a generally desirable direction, vague and subject to abuse, emphasizing protection for the trade as much as obligations to the community, and needing to be backed up by law in order to become fully effective. Dean Donham of Harvard was also doubtful. The codes, he thought, dealt with serious problems but tended to dismiss them with "platitudes about morality and service, [just] as . . . most of the pressing problems of relationship with the public [are dismissed]." Henry S. Dennison rejected the codes of business ethics bluntly: "Compared with some notorious examples of business behavior, they are nuts for the scornful cynic." Nevertheless, Dennison accorded them some significance in the evolution of business as "first attempts of a great and powerful social group to gain its own self-respect and the respect of other members of society."

Owen D. Young saw the codes in quite a different light. He thought them an effort by business to find a substitute for outworn local community controls and standards, a search for new restraints upon rampant individualism. A national economy which suffered from a lack of agreed-upon standards invited external regulation and controls. Self-regulation, Young thought, was an alternative to intervention by "amateurs" and an effort to counter the impersonality of large-scale operations with professional standards of conduct.[12]

Whatever their disagreements, observers of the trade association

[11] Richard F. Grant, "The Case for Business," *Nation's Business*, XIII (January, 1925), 18–20; *U. S. Chamber of Commerce Report of the Thirteenth Annual Meeting* (1925), 16–17. The statement was reaffirmed by the national Chamber in 1928; see *U. S. Chamber of Commerce Report of the Sixteenth Annual Meeting* (1928), 3.

[12] Clark, *Social Control of Business*, 237–39; Wallace B. Donham, "Some Recent Books on Business Ethics," *HBR*, V (January, 1927), 244–50; Henry S.

movement accepted it as an important dimension of business organization. The compulsion felt by the associations to stress the responsiveness of their membership to public ethical standards was a further sign of the businessman's search for social identification and acceptance. Their codes and the publicity surrounding them represented still another form of commitment to the principle of social accountability. That the commitment was often more formal than real did not wholly negate its influence either on public expectations of business or on business attitudes toward society and its claims.

TRUSTEESHIP

The appeal of the new notions concerning the role of management and of business itself were perhaps best symbolized by the popularity of the terms "trusteeship" and "service." "Service" referred broadly to the ties relating business to society. It applied, therefore, to small businesses as well as to large ones, and it offered a particularly welcome rationale for the role of the often hard-pressed small entrepreneur. Subsequent events have led some to question whether, in fact, the ideal of service was anything but a pitchman's device for promoting his wares; and evidence of a mass conversion of business leaders from profit-seeking to enlightened professionalism was certainly lacking.

Nevertheless, it is impossible to doubt that the interest of many who sought to formulate new guidelines for business policy was sincere or that their concern for the broader consequences of business leadership was genuine. This was particularly true regarding the small number of executives of large corporations who were the chief spokesmen for "trusteeship." What such men said was listened to, what they did was observed. The ideas for which such influential individuals spoke, therefore, acquired a life independent of the motives and numbers behind them.

The idea of management as trustee had been clearly anticipated during the Progressive years by such students of business as Arthur T. Hadley and Edward D. Jones, professor of commerce and industry at the University of Michigan. Jones had seen management as becoming the mediator between stockholders and employees, "the central pivot

---

Dennison, *Ethics and Modern Business* (Boston and New York, 1932), 9, 15; Owen D. Young, "Dedication Address," *HBR*, V (July, 1927), 385–94. Donham expressed more confidence in the evolution of ethical standards within large corporations than in association codes.

upon which a vast number of human relationships will turn." "Upon these men," Jones had written in 1913, "will rest a sort of trusteeship to preserve the property intrusted to them, and a demand of leadership to guide and guard their employees. . . ." He foresaw an opportunity for "a new race of executives, which shall justly appreciate the various classes of responsibility resting upon it." [13]

Among the leading spokesmen for such a broad concept of managerial responsibilities in the Twenties were Owen D. Young and Gerard Swope, chairman and president, respectively, of the General Electric Company. Young, in particular, enjoyed a national reputation. Serving as chairman of a committee to study the business cycle for a conference on unemployment called by Secretary of Commerce Herbert Hoover in 1923, Young's attention was directed to the problem of economic stabilization. Later he served as an American representative in reparations negotiations with Germany. The Young Plan of 1929, which attempted a final settlement of the reparations problem, brought him international recognition and respect. As early as 1928 Young was being mentioned as a possible presidential candidate for the Democratic party.

Swope's attentions were confined somewhat more strictly to the internal affairs of General Electric, especially in the predepression decade; but he, too, was increasingly interested in broader economic and social problems. Long before the Great Crash, Swope had concerned himself with industrial relations and with the problem of economic instability and unemployment. By 1925 he had developed a contributory unemployment insurance program, which was rejected, however, by General Electric's employees. In 1931, when depression had nationalized the unemployment problem, Swope produced a plan for industrial stabilization through a federally supervised trade association, which included unemployment insurance and workmen's compensation. Although endorsed by the United States Chamber of Commerce, the Swope plan failed to win the support of the Hoover administra-

[13] D. M. Bates, "The Manager's Part," *Annals,* LXXXV (September, 1919), 152–65, quoted in Bloomfield, *The Modern Executive,* 85. Sloan (in *White Collar Man,* 202), comments on management's new recognition of dealers as "partners" in the General Motors enterprise. Edward D. Jones, *Industrial Leadership and Executive Ability,* 2nd edition (New York, 1920), 13–14; James D. Mooney and Alan C. Reilly, *Onward Industry! The Principles of Organization and Their Significance to Modern Industry* (New York, 1931), 475ff. For a more recent treatment of management's role as a coordinator of intra-corporation interest groups, see R. A. Gordon, 106.

tion. In some respects it anticipated provisions of the NRA and the Social Security Act of 1935.

Obviously, Swope and Young were not typical businessmen. Even among the rising generation of executives of large corporations they were unusual in the scope of their interests and their concept of their role. Each had been influenced by contacts outside the business community. Swope had known Jane Addams at Hull House and had encountered Louis D. Brandeis while a student at M.I.T. Young had been influenced by exposure to the ideas of Ida Tarbell and Lincoln Steffens.

Such men exemplified the type to which the term "industrial statesman" was beginning to be applied in the Twenties. They stood for a new view of the function of business management in its relationship to corporate enterprise and to society. As Young bluntly put it, "The old notion . . . that the heads of business are the paid attorneys of stockholders, to exploit labor and the public in the stockholders' interest is gone—I hope forever." [14] Swope held that management, in effect, was in a position to "define its own responsibilities"; and when he did so in a 1926 speech, he astonished his audience by putting the public and the employees ahead of the stockholders in the list of those to whom managerial obligations were due. Swope acknowledged that investors were entitled to a fair return on their money and a full reporting of company undertakings; but his emphasis almost suggested that he saw these as residual, rather than primary obligations. [15]

Swope and Young may have seemed visionary and radical to their staid business colleagues, but their belief that the relationship of management to stockholders in the large corporation called for reassessment was shared by others. An unnamed business executive, cited by *Nation's Business* in 1929, held that stockholders were to be thought of "primarily as investors," not as "participants in our business." It was

[14] Ida M. Tarbell, *Owen D. Young: A New Type of Industrial Leader* (New York, 1932), 124–28, 142–48, 183–205, 292, *passim*. Loth, *Swope of G. E.*, 167–72, says that Swope believed unionization inevitable and consulted with William Green of the American Federation of Labor. Swope's plan for a union failed because of trade union resistance to industrial unionism. An admirer of Samuel Gompers, Swope was the only business leader to attend Gompers's funeral. *Ibid.*, 20–21, 31–33, 120–21, 153, 196–215, *passim*.

[15] "The Responsibilities of Modern Industry," in *Selected Addresses of Owen D. Young and Gerard Swope* (General Electric Company, 1930), 35–43. Swope's was an address to the Associated Business Papers Convention in 1926. Owen D. Young, "What is Right in Business," in *ibid.*, 259–62.

management's duty so to conduct the business, he believed, "that the public who use our product shall be well served and that those who entrust to us their money shall be fairly rewarded for its use by dividends." [16] Such a viewpoint clearly left to management the chief responsibility for decision making but explicitly acknowledged that stockholders were not the only group to which it had obligations. From a slightly different angle George M. Verity of the American Rolling Mill Company argued that widespread stock ownership meant more exacting standards for corporate performance, "with the community so rapidly becoming the owner and also the one to be satisfactorily served."

A particularly influential proponent of the new managerial outlook was John D. Rockefeller, Jr. Not, strictly speaking, a businessman himself, Rockefeller's was nevertheless a name to be reckoned with in business circles. Shocked into awareness of industry's role in community conditions by the Colorado Fuel and Iron Company strike, Rockefeller subsequently resigned directorships of the companies in which his family held interests in order to avoid responsibility for managerial policies in which he could not participate intimately. He recognized, thus, the necessary and growing independence of corporate management; but he continued to urge policies responsive to the needs of workers and the public.

Rockefeller was impressed by the cooperation achieved between labor, capital, and government during the First World War. At the war's end he tried to formulate the lessons which he believed his own experience and that of the nation held for the future. The principle

[16] "The Unseen Business Revolution," *Iron Age*, CXVII (25 February 1926), 543–44; *Nation's Business* (17 March 1929), 11. Although American corporations since the Twenties have gone to considerable lengths to provide information for stockholders, to answer questions, and to invite support for management policies, such activities have become almost indistinguishable from general public relations. As Arthur Pound described the relationship, "The American way is to pay the stockholder well, to treat him honestly and gently, but to keep him in his place, so that he has neither the desire nor the extended opportunity to interfere with operations and policies." *Industrial America*, 16–17. Cf. John N. Sears, *The New Place of the Stockholder* (New York, 1929), 26–27.

More recently, Peter Drucker and other students of the contemporary business corporation have suggested formalizing the diminished status of the stockholder by relieving stock of even the "legal fiction" of ownership. Drucker points out that "the corporation is permanent, the shareholder is transitory," thus emphasizing the primacy of management's authority. *Concept of the Corporation*, 21; and *The New Society: The Anatomy of the Industrial Order* (New York, 1950), 339–43.

upon which he laid greatest stress was cooperation—between management and labor, producer and consumer, and business and the public.
Business no longer could be rightly conceived of, Rockefeller thought,
as simply a profit-making enterprise: "To cling to such a conception is
only to arouse antagonism and to court trouble." Instead, he argued,
"every thoughtful man must concede that the purpose of industry is
quite as much the advancement of social well-being as the production
of wealth."

Business was a partnership—or should be—between capital, labor,
management as a distinct group, and the community. The partners
shared a common interest in the enterprise and each should be represented in "the councils of industry." The rights of the community were
too often overlooked, Rockefeller held. The public supplied business
with many valuable commodities: law and order, transportation and
communication, money and credit, as well as other services. Quietly,
but persistently, Rockefeller stressed his point, that industry was "a
form of social service, quite as much as a revenue-producing process." [17]

Other influential leaders, of varying backgrounds, were similarly
concerned about the relations of business to the public. Howard J.
Heinz retained an active role in his family's company, but he shared
Rockefeller's sense of responsibility to "his" enterprise and "his" people. In such men, the ties between nineteenth-century paternalism and
the emerging trusteeship concept could be clearly traced. Heinz saw
his position and its obligations in personal terms:

> I learned from my father to look upon our business not
> merely as a source of profit and revenue. I was taught that a
> certain responsibility goes with it, and with any large busi-

---

[17] Rockefeller, *The Personal Relation in Industry,* 10–37. The influence of William
Lyon MacKenzie King on the development of Rockefeller's thinking is noted in
Chapter II and discussed in detail in Fosdick, *John D. Rockefeller, Jr.,* 181–84.
Fosdick also indicates Rockefeller's methods of bringing pressure to bear on the
managements of companies in which he was a large stockholder.

Skeptical businessmen may have permitted themselves the thought that only a
Rockefeller could afford to put social service before profits; but the U.S. Chamber
of Commerce, after listening to a Rockefeller speech in 1919, approved a resolution endorsing his position: "The purpose of industry is quite as much to advance
social well-being, as material well-being, and in the pursuit of this purpose the
interests of the community should be carefully considered, the well-being of the
employees as respects living and working conditions should be fully guarded,
management should be adequately recognized and compensated, and failure in
any of these particulars means loss to all." *U.S. Chamber of Commerce Report
of the Seventh Annual Meeting* (1919), 45.

ness affecting many people. I feel that, with due consideration to the owners who make the business possible, I am responsible to three groups of people affected by the Heinz business, and that it should be administered so that it is profitable, or satisfactory, or helpful to them, the three groups being the people who work for it, the grocers who distribute its products, and the customers who consume them.

George Eastman denied that sentiment or idealism had a place in business. Yet Eastman, an active philanthropist in his own right, told *Nation's Business:* "Anything for the betterment of humanity is good business. . . ." [18]

Rockefeller, Heinz, and Eastman all had strong personal or family ties with industry. More typical of the new managerial class were those career executives whose rise to power and leadership was attracting notice. Among such men Whiting Williams thought he saw by 1929 "a broader, higher, fairer attitude . . . toward their active, going, everyday business responsibilities." [19] For nearly three decades Elbert H. Gary of the United States Steel Company had exemplified some features of the managerial trusteeship concept. Gary had been among the first to include the general public along with the parties more directly connected with the corporation on the list of those for whom management served as trustee. In 1921 he attempted to define the role of management in this relationship. Gary saw the managerial group as occupying "a position of balance" among the other groups: the security holders represented by the board of directors; the general public "in which are included investors, employees, employers, consumers, or customers, competitors, and all others who may be interested in, or affected by, the actions or attitudes of the managers . . ."; and, finally, the workers. Recognizing fundamental obligations to the owners, Gary nevertheless justified the full exercise of managerial judgment and discretion: "The management of a corporation, for its own good and for the benefit of its stockholders, must have constantly and uppermost in mind the rights and interests of the general public, not only determined by the law of the land, but as ascertainable from public sentiment when the same is clear, well defined and settled." [20]

---

[18] Heinz was quoted in Earnest Elmo Caulkins, *Business the Civilizer* (Boston, 1928), 286. For Eastman, see Frederick Backmann, "Suppose You Gave Away $70,000,000," *Nation's Business,* XIII (May, 1925), 33ff.

[19] Whiting Williams, "Business Statesmanship, a New Force in Business," *Magazine of Business,* XVIII (April, 1929), 388–90ff.

[20] Elbert H. Gary, "Principles and Policies of the United States Steel Corpora-

Determination of what the public's interest might be was at least partially, in Gary's view, a responsibility of management.

Perhaps the fullest statement of the trusteeship concept was made by Owen D. Young who in the Twenties became the outstanding representative of the new corporate leadership. At the dedication of a group of buildings for the Harvard Graduate School of Business Administration, a symbol of the new management, Young spoke:

> We think of managers no longer as the partisan attorneys of either group [capitol or labor] against the other. Rather we have come to consider them trustees of the whole undertaking, whose responsibility is to see to it on the one side that the invested capital is safe and that its return is adequate and continuous; and on the other side that competent and conscientious men are found to do the work and that their job is safe and their earnings are adequate and continuous. Managers may not be able to realize that ideal either for capital or labor. It is a great advance, however, for us to have formulated that objective and to be striving for that goal.

Young was not fully satisfied with the gains already made. He foresaw a future when capital and labor might be made truly identical through some system of employee, or public, ownership. Meanwhile, he recognized that his position was ambiguous, involving a broad area of discretion and judgment.

Young's concept of the corporation extended beyond the relations of managers to stockholders and workers alone. Although the claims of other groups might be less clear, Young recognized that they could hardly be ignored. "It makes a great difference in my attitude toward my job as an executive officer of the General Electric Company whether I am a trustee of an institution or an attorney for the investor," Young held. "If I am a trustee of the institution, who are the beneficiaries of the trust? to whom do I owe my obligation?" [21]

tion," n.p., n.d. [1921]. For a 1915 statement by Gary expressing the view that management had not adequately recognized these responsibilities, see Gras, "Shifts in Public Relations," 120.

Samuel Gompers challenged Gary's words as a gesture, in response to public pressure and discontent, having little effect on actual company policy. "Preaching is Practice," *American Federationist*, XXX (May, 1923), 402–4.

[21] Young's Harvard address is quoted in Tarbell, *Owen D. Young*, 155–56; *Nation's Business*, XVII (April, 1929), 161–64. Similar statements can be found in *ibid.*, XVII (March, 1929), 9, 142–46, and (April, 1929), 90. The fact that so many articles emphasizing the social awareness and responsibility of business leadership appeared in 1929 is ironic.

What circumstances were causing men in positions such as Young's to recognize was that the large business corporation was inevitably a social creature with obligations to the community which sanctioned and depended upon it. External relations were beginning to be seen as essential characteristics—subsidiary, perhaps, but by no means irrelevant to its primary, internal purposes. Managerial trusteeship thus implied, as Berle and Means soon pointed out, social as well as economic obligations. Corporate enterprise and its management could no longer be considered entirely private affairs. Although few businessmen in the Twenties were prepared to push the analysis so far, the outlines of the future doctrine of corporate social responsibility were clearly discernible.

In its contemporary form, in the 1960s, the trusteeship concept has been still further elaborated and extended. As interpreted by Alfred P. Sloan, Jr., for example, it became an almost unlimited challenge to business leadership and initiative to "expand its horizon of responsibility." Management must recognize, Sloan asserted, "that it can no longer confine its activities to the mere production of goods and services. It must consider the impact of its operations on the economy as a whole in relation to the social and economic welfare of the entire community. . . . Those charged with great industrial responsibility must become industrial statesmen." [22] Either in this or in similar versions, the idea has attracted even more publicity and support than it commanded in Young's day. But, although often referred to as a "new" philosophy of management, its central features, including specific acknowledgement of the general public as among the beneficiaries of the corporation, had been clearly delineated by the leading "business statesmen" of the 1920s.

SOCIAL OR ECONOMIC RESPONSIBILITY?

Enlargement of the concept of managerial responsibility made possible a variety of interpretations of its scope. If profit alone were not the end in view, if a host of conflicting interests and objectives were to be weighed on the scale of executive discretion, then what guidelines could be found for striking a balance? Once a generalized social responsibility was accepted for the corporation, where could its limits be logically drawn? It was scarcely surprising, given the difficulties,

[22] Sloan, White Collar Man, 145. Sloan echoed Gary in his insistence upon the duty and competence of management to evaluate community interests.

that many businessmen hesitated to launch their enterprises upon the uncharted seas of trusteeship.

One group of business leaders who did accept the challenge to raise their sights to society's shifting needs nevertheless insisted upon concentrating their efforts on the improvement of the performance of business itself. Owen D. Young had posed the problem of corporate management as a question; his partner at General Electric, Gerard Swope, attempted to offer some concrete answers. Already on record as favoring labor unions, employment stabilization, and unemployment compensation, Swope tried to translate the principles of service and trusteeship into action. Service, as Swope understood it, meant concrete policies in the interests both of employees and of the consuming public:

> The responsibility of industry to the public is not only for comprehensive service, including quality of material furnished, but more important, that its attitude shall not be complacent but forward looking. Society, in testing the efficiency of any organization, is going to measure not only its service, but also its continual and progressive reduction in prices of its products to the public.[23]

Swope's argument, that the essence of service lay in enlightened economic leadership, resembled that of Ford and Filene. Of the three men, Ford had by now perhaps the narrowest outlook. As depression struck at the end of the decade, he criticized business leadership for having allowed prosperity to dull its thinking. Prosperity "took the brains out of business," Ford held. Men had forgotten their fundamental responsibility to insure economic stability and growth. For the future, "the degree to which business is intelligent and responsible may be determined by the degree of shame and better resolution with which it views its failure to function to the comfort and security of the whole people."[24] Ford spoke with the wisdom of hindsight; his age, as well as his intellectual and emotional ties to the agrarian past which he himself had done so much to make obsolete, prevented his making further positive contributions to the advancement of business thought.

Even before the collapse came, other business leaders had recog-

[23] Gerard Swope, "What Big Business Owes the Public," *World's Work*, LIII (March, 1927), 556–61.

[24] Henry Ford, in collaboration with Samuel Crowther, *Moving Forward* (Garden City, 1930), 143–45.

nized that instability of employment offered a major challenge to the business system. *Forbes* had spoken of a "solemn responsibility" to provide steady employment, warning that cost-cutting at the employees' expense would ultimately arouse public resentment. The Procter and Gamble Company, with a long history of family concern for employee welfare, faced this challenge with considerable success. It had evolved a program of profit-sharing, unemployment benefits, employment stabilization, and employee representation which commanded respect. One Cincinnati labor leader declared, "They've gone farther in civilizing industrial relations than any union today would ever dream of asking any employer to go." Col. William Cooper Procter, on the other hand, described the employment stabilization plan as "so simple it's really stupid. We went at unemployment, you know, from the worker's point of view. Sometimes it seems as though you get farther if you go at it that way than any other way." To Procter, "the big value is not having on our conscience the chap who wants to work and can't find a job. That is what no business can afford." [25]

While Procter and Gamble was attempting to translate into action the principles its leaders espoused, others were content to use talk of social responsibilities as a cover for irresponsible behavior. Such men troubled E. A. Filene, who continued to underline his conviction that management's broadening responsibilities could best be discharged in the economic sphere. Filene held that "a good ethical sense is no excuse for a bad business sense." Better to continue running one's business honestly in the old-fashioned way than to adopt social welfare policies as even an unconscious excuse for "doing business less well. Sincerity is no justification for sloppiness. . . . There is a lot of merely good impulse that is mistaken for that sound social thinking which is always straight business thinking." Time and again, Filene returned to the point that "the finest 'public work' is . . . the sort into which our own business planning leads us, and to which we give ourselves even more than we give our money." Student and disciple of Henry Ford though he was, Filene criticized some of Ford's social ventures as sentimental, rather than scientific. Some, such as the 1915 peace mission and Ford's Sociological Department, had failed to adhere to the strict economic doctrine which Ford and, even more consistently,

[25] *Forbes*, XXII (1 October 1928), 30, and XXII (15 November 1928), 26; Beulah Amidon, "Ivorydale, A Payroll that Floats," *Survey*, LXIV (1 April 1930), 18–20. See also Herman Feldman, *Regularization of Employment* (New York, 1925), published under the auspices of the American Management Association.

Filene espoused, that business itself provided ample scope for social improvement: "Nine-tenths of a businessman's best public service can be rendered by virtue of the way he conducts his business. . . ."

Such an approach, Filene admitted, was not always popular among socially minded executives. Many successful businessmen displayed "an astounding lack of vision in the larger matters of social and industrial policy that lie outside their immediate businesses." They lacked sufficient contact with members of groups other than their own and, thereby, became ready victims of the tendency to judge both business and social problems from a parochial point of view. E. A. Filene's brother, A. Lincoln Filene, summed up the family philosophy in a statement critical both of the older view of short-run profit as management's sole objective and of recent tendencies to see corporate officials as social servants and statesmen with a license to practice wherever they chose:

> Business cares about its obligations. . . . And yet business remains business. It has not gone into charity. . . . Business has proved to itself that the making of money and the making of citizens not only can, but must, go on together, for the simple reason that neither process can solvently function without the other. For too long a time the problem of human betterment was looked upon as a side issue, a charity, subsisting on the dole of philanthropists. Now it is being put where it belongs —on a business basis, in business itself.[26]

Men such as the Filenes, Swope, and Ford offered what may be considered a traditionalist interpretation of social responsibility. Although they accepted, in principle, the idea of managerial responsibility, they were suspicious of some of the broader interpretations given it by their business colleagues. By insisting that true responsibility lay in work efficiently and imaginatively executed, they were—in one

[26] Filene, *The Way Out*, 40–41, 278–82, 285, 292. Filene's criticism of Ford was directed particularly at his peace efforts. A. Lincoln Filene, *A Merchant's Horizon* (Boston, 1924), 257–58.

John M. Clark, however, questioned the adequacy of "enlightened self-interest" as a substitute for altruism. "Far-sighted shrewdness" was not enough, for, Clark argued, "one can be sure that at some point or other the shrewdness will not be farsighted enough and trouble will result." There was still a need for "genuinely ethical standards" in business and an understanding that, in the broadest sense, enlightened self-interest involved identification with the interests of others. *Economic Institutions and Human Welfare* (New York, 1957), 206–7.

sense—reiterating the old-fashioned slogan, "business is business." They were doing so, however, with a difference. Sensitive to many of the implications of the newly emerging mass production economy, they were asserting that abundance made possible a new concert of interests in which the prosperity of business and the welfare of society could still be seen as opposite sides of the same coin. Their strictures on charity and philanthropy stemmed not primarily from selfishness but from a faith that these activities were ultimately both undesirable and unnecessary. Although never wholly consistent in their applications of this faith, they seem to have been quite sincere in its assertion. To them, "charity begins at home" was to some degree a warning against paternalism but even more importantly a challenge to managerial talents for better economic planning.

If even Ford had difficulty adhering to such a doctrine, in less cautious hands the notion of managerial trusteeship and responsibility could all-too-readily lend itself to sweeping claims. Under the influence of prosperity, some business spokesmen were encouraged to assert management's ability to direct the course of social as well as economic development. Confidence had turned to arrogance when the president of the United States Chamber of Commerce wrote in 1929, "If America translates into the conduct of world enterprise the ethics and standards of American business today, it will more directly establish the welfare of uncounted millions than any crusade in history." And Merwin K. Hart, later to win notoriety for his services to a succession of reactionary causes, was happy to offer the example and services of business leadership for the solution of many of the problems of government, education, and justice. No social problem, Hart felt confident, could long remain unresolved once the leaders of business threw their minds and coordinating abilities into the effort.[27] Such claims were, of course, extreme; and their foolhardiness was shortly to be exposed by the collapse of business itself. Yet they sug-

[27] Julius H. Barnes, "Growing Responsibilities of Business," *Nation's Business,* XVI (25 May 1929), 15–16. Merwin K. Hart, "Next Jobs for Business Leadership," *Magazine of Business,* LV (January, 1929), 40ff. That a business dictatorship might be a means for improving social and economic conditions was an appealing notion to some businessmen. See "What a Business Mussolini Might Do in America," by Irving T. Bush, vice-president of the New York Chamber of Commerce, *Forbes,* XXII (15 October 1928), 11.

A new spokesman for an enlarged view of the managerial role appeared in February, 1930, with the first issue of *Fortune* magazine. From its beginning, *Fortune* gave particular attention to the professional, philosophical, social, and even esthetic, dimensions of business leadership.

gested some of the dangers management must be prepared to face if it were to accept a broader, social definition of its responsibilities.

THE CRITIQUE OF TRUSTEESHIP

Criticism of the performance of the American business system, and even of the socially minded attitudes which leading businessmen had begun to demonstrate, was not silenced during the Twenties, submerged though it may have been. Nor did criticism arise wholly from hostile sources. *Forbes,* ardent in its defense of business leadership, nevertheless pointed out that "the conditions in a deplorably large number of plants still tend to breed socialists, communists and other unwholesome agitators." And *Nation's Business* surveyed discussions of the service ideal with a critical eye. It flayed the rhetoric of service as little more than a sales device, a "glorified drone," dishonest, wasteful, and a symptom of moral decay, since it encouraged business to do things for people which they ought to be doing for themselves. The discoverer of the service motto, William Nelson Taft sarcastically observed, "should not be allowed longer to linger in the limbo of oblivion. . . . [He] is at least deserving of a place beside that of Columbus, for the Genoese located only half a world, while the man who brought to light the advantages of service uncovered an entire solar system in which there now blaze a myriad of star salesmen. . . ."[28]

From academic sources, too, came criticism of business, for its lack of response to economic change and challenge. John Maurice Clark, far from praising strides toward trusteeship and service on the part of industry, accused most businessmen of blind individualism which satisfied itself by concentrating on matters of production and took "all the complementary parts of the process for granted as having been satisfactorily attended to somewhere else behind the scenes where the economic student need not worry his head about them." Rather than rely upon business to police itself, Clark proposed a system of "social accounting" which would take cognizance of the social costs created by business and provide public self-protection: "industry is essentially a matter of public concern . . . the stake which the public has in its processes is not adequately protected by the safeguards which individualism affords." Society had ample grounds for interfering with business "whenever it sees its interests clearly and can devise appropriate

[28] Forbes, XXII (1 September 1928), 28; William Nelson Taft, "Shouting 'Service' as a Battlecry," *Nation's Business,* XIII (April, 1925), 37–39. See also *ibid.,* XIV (April, 1926), 104, and XIV (October, 1926), 120.

and effective means to safeguard or promote them. This last proviso remains perhaps the chief limit on the proper field of public action." [29]

Others also doubted that the necessary vision, understanding, and sense of group obligation for social welfare were developing rapidly enough. Business leaders were in command of the very tools of science which were in the process of overthrowing old values, Wallace B. Donham believed. Hence they had a particular obligation to exercise their power responsibly. Instead of realistic action, he heard pious platitudes:

> A sense of responsibility either to the community or for the standing of the profession is lacking. The Golden Rule meant much in the simple, pastoral society with reference to which it was framed. Its application to our complicated industrial civilization often presents an intellectual problem of greatest magnitude not solved by re-enacting it into a code. . . . Words about service too often are a smug cover for the desire to be left alone, rather than the expression of an intent to run one's business in socially sound ways, and no system of ethics can accomplish the desired result unless it can be defended on a hard-boiled business basis as sound institutionary policy for the permanency and efficacy of the profession.[30]

Berle and Means suggested that the motivation of the managers of large corporations could best be understood by comparison with "the motives of an Alexander the Great, seeking new worlds to conquer. . . ." And Aldous Huxley wrote, "For Jesus and St. Francis service connoted self-sacrifice, abnegation, humility. For the morticians and other American businessmen, Service means something else; it means doing profitable business efficiently, with just sufficient honesty to keep out of jail." [31]

[29] Clark, *Social Control of Business*, 45–48, 50, 84–85, 180–85. E. R. A. Seligman accused some businessmen of fostering "an old error . . . that an improved production will solve the problems of a more equal distribution" in his review of Julius H. Barnes's *The Genius of American Business*, in *Nation's Business*, XII (July, 1924), 36.

[30] Wallace B. Donham, "The Emerging Profession of Business," *HBR*, V (July, 1927), 401–5; *ibid.*, VII (July, 1929), 385–94.

[31] Berle and Means, *The Modern Corporation and Private Property*, 350; Huxley was quoted in Charles A. Beard, ed., *Toward Civilization* (London, New York, and Toronto, 1930), 8. Beard himself put the point more concisely: "Service without sacrifice is a fraud." Bruce Barton, however, in his immensely popular

If prosperity dammed up or deflected criticism, economic collapse and depression opened the flood gates. Not only did it become clear that business held no secret of permanent affluence, but there was accumulating evidence of carelessness, dishonesty, and simple graft on the part of numbers of supposedly respectable business leaders. John T. Flynn, summarizing in 1931 the findings of several governmental investigations, cited many instances in which company officers or directors had used their position and influence for personal profit. Far from producing higher standards of professional managerial behavior, Flynn found that the independence of corporate officials from close stockholder control had led them to "forget that they are trustees" for the owners and to a field day of self-aggrandizement. Much of the graft, Flynn concluded, "arises out of the notion which corporation rulers frequently get that the business belongs to them. . . ."[32]

One incident particularly damaging to the concept of responsible corporate leadership involved Owen D. Young. Investigations of the collapse of Samuel Insull's utility empire indicated that Young had approved loans by General Electric to Insull without adequate security and without careful scrutiny of Insull's financial position. Young's trusteeship was further called into question when he was shown to have been offered an opportunity to buy stock in Insull's enterprises at a special reduced price. The affair gave critics a golden opportunity to attack the claims which had been advanced on behalf of business statesmanship. Young's position as an outstanding spokesman for progressive business made his actions particularly vulnerable.[33]

For the time being, at least, "business statesmanship" had come under a cloud. Spokesmen for business who had reveled in assertions

---

The Man Nobody Knows (Indianapolis, 1925), 159–77, had presented Jesus as the prototype of the successful man of affairs, the first point of whose "business philosophy" had been "whoever will be great must render great service."

[32] John T. Flynn, Graft in Business (New York, 1931), 192–204, 246, passim. See also Ferdinand Pecora, Wall Street Under Oath (New York, 1931), and Thompson, Confessions of the Power Trust (New York, 1932).

[33] "The Loss of Owen D. Young," The Nation, CXXXVI (4 June 1933), 4; Norman Thomas, "Owen D. Young and Samuel Insull," ibid., CXXXVI (11 January 1933), 35–37. Even before the revelation of Young's relations with Insull, Stuart Chase, reviewing Ida Tarbell's biography of Young, conceded "occasional flashes of philosophical insight" in Young's thinking but found little evidence of basic understanding of fundamental economic conditions. Still, Chase gave Young credit for being "the last trump card in the deck of a doomed economic system." Stuart Chase, "Industrialist or Negotiator," The Saturday Review of Literature, VIII (25 June 1932), 801–2.

of enlightened business leadership now hastened to cut their losses and salvage what they could of their deflated prestige. *Fortune* tried to absolve management from responsibility for the depression. No one, it now appeared, had the authority or the ability to prevent overproduction. Nor did the social responsibility of corporate officials really extend beyond the obligation to the customer for value received. This primary responsibility to the consumer had been "obscured by the fact that the corporation manager has a tendency to talk . . . in terms of Service and the corporation critic has a tendency to talk . . . in terms of Materialism. (Both points of view are equally stupid. . . .)" Embarrassment, confusion, and uncertainty about what to claim and what to deny on behalf of business were apparent in *Fortune's* summary:

> Perhaps society itself is somewhat at fault . . . in emphasizing monetary returns too much. Possibly management should get Legion of Honor awards. Or perhaps there is nothing in any such theory, and the corporate system is rooted in the acquisitive instinct and not in the general good.[34]

Not for a decade after 1929 would the return of economic stability, and the blessed shortness of memory, revive claims of social responsibility on the part of business leadership. Subsequent discussion of the business emphasis upon service and trusteeship in the Twenties has, for the most part, continued to reflect the natural disillusionment of the depression years. The hyperbole and high pressure tactics of business propagandists, the failure of the business system to live up to the promises of permanent prosperity prematurely made in its name, and the high cost which the nation paid for its lesson in economic irresponsibility combined to leave behind a monolithic memory of a period characterized by jazz and gin, by speculation and mad pursuit of the almighty dollar, but seldom by serious efforts to come to grips with real problems. It has been customary to present the social and economic outlook of business in the Age of Coolidge as superficial, shortsighted, and selfish—even, on occasion, as fascist. To be sure, evidence to support each of these characterizations can be found—sometimes in ample supply. Yet the very real efforts and concerns of a significant portion of the business community cannot be dismissed so lightly, however far performance may have fallen short of hopes. Perhaps the fairest estimate of the position of these leaders was that given by Frederick Lewis Allen. "They were living by a code no longer ade-

[34] *Fortune,* VII (June, 1933), 51 ff.

quate for men whose decisions swung such colossal weight," he wrote. "They were able men, nearly all of them; wise men, many of them. They were not quite wise enough to realize what they and their like had done to revolutionize American life, and what new responsibilities to their fellow countrymen now rested upon their shoulders." [35]

CORPORATE PHILANTHROPY

The test of codes of business ethics, assertions of managerial trustee-ship, or company commitments to service—as their critics insisted—was the difference they actually made in business policies and proce-dures. Just as new understanding of their relationship and responsibil-ities to their employees challenged corporate officials to devise new programs in the field of industrial relations, so growing sensitivity to the social environment of business led them to seek new ways of identifying their companies with efforts at social improvement. Cham-bers of commerce, trade associations, and professional societies offered some channels for the expression of this interest. Responding to a ris-ing concern, several schools of business arranged courses dealing with civic affairs and community relations. Edward D. Jones's influential book on *Industrial Leadership,* among others, suggested concrete ways in which society might feel the impact of a manager's concern for his "function as a representative of public interests." "His neigh-borhood should be able to feel," Jones believed, "that any increase of his prosperity will not only mean a finer policy inaugurated in his es-

[35] Frederick Lewis Allen, *The Lords of Creation* (New York, 1935), 389–90. Robert A. Brady, *Business as a System of Power,* marshals arguments for consider-ing the trusteeship philosophy of the Twenties "the precise equivalent of authori-tarian leadership" in nations such as Germany and Japan. While much can be found in the decade that smacks of fascism—elitism, racism, nationalist funda-mentalism—what is significant is the fact that in the United States these forces failed to gain the upper hand. James Warren Prothro, *The Dollar Decade. Business Ideas in the 1920s* (Baton Rouge, 1954), analyzes the statements of Chamber of Commerce and NAM leaders and concludes, ". . . business leaders were unable to rise above the narrowest interpretation of the short-run advantage of the minority" (p. 239). But Prothro fails to recognize the complexity of the prob-lems with which some businessmen were wrestling and the difficulty of reconciling traditional economic creeds with rapidly changing reality.

Two popular books which survey the historical development of "welfare capital-ism," rather too favorably, are *U.S.A. The Permanent Revolution,* by the editors of *Fortune* with the collaboration of Russell W. Davenport (New York, 1951), and Frederick Lewis Allen, *The Big Change: America Transforms Itself, 1900–1950* (New York, 1952).

tablishment, but will benefit the town, strengthen the hands of good government, help the park and playground movement, and the public library, and all the general interests." [36]

The most significant effort to translate the new social consciousness of management into action in the 1920s was the emergence of organized corporate philanthropy. Demands upon business for contributions to social welfare agencies had been increasing steadily. Even before the First World War steps toward establishing systematic, federated fund raising for community services had begun. Spurred by the early success of the YMCA and the wartime chests, welfare federations, community chests, hospitals, colleges, and universities moved into the field of organized solicitation. Professional fund raisers, doctors, educators, and social workers all joined in efforts to promote more efficient financing of welfare work. Scientific management was invading the precincts of Lady Bountiful. Under the circumstances, the incentives for organized philanthropy to turn to business leadership for help were almost irresistible. No other group could offer so much, not only in terms of financial support but in prestige and administrative experience as well.

Business responded with growing interest to the opportunity for tangible contributions to community needs. At one extreme, a national enterprise such as the Bell telephone system with subsidiaries, branches, and offices in thousands of communities across the continent contributed to literally thousands of civic and social organizations. Between 1925 and 1934 a sum of nearly $5,000,000 was spent on dues for memberships in chambers of commerce, social and athletic clubs, professional societies, and the like; in the latter year alone payment was made by the Bell companies for 7,960 memberships in 5,178 noncommercial organizations. During roughly the same years a survey of the small mill towns of North Carolina revealed a degree of involvement by mill companies in the support of schools, housing, religious activities, and community welfare work at the local level which exceeded that of the most enthusiastic nineteenth-century paternalism. For small companies in the larger towns and cities, the chamber of commerce offered help in dealing with civic conditions, schools, and social services.

The justifications for business participation in community better-

[36] Jones, *Industrial Leadership and Executive Ability*, 270; Bates, "The Manager's Part," 152–65, quoted in Bloomfield, *The Modern Executive*, 85–94. See also Hotchkiss, *Higher Education and Business Standards*, 76ff.

ment were freely discussed. John Ihlder, head of the Civic Development Department created by the U. S. Chamber of Commerce in 1920 for the information and assistance of its membership, thought it necessary to demonstrate that "the business era having provided material wealth can and does use that wealth to provide even wider opportunities for all the people, to serve the needs of the mind and the spirit." "Not by domination," Ihlder warned, "but by opening the way to creators and builders; not by standing aloof, but by participating, will [business] win enthusiastic loyalty." Henry P. Kendall, president of the Lewis Manufacturing Company, felt business could not avoid responsibility for unhealthy social conditions. "There are industrial communities in my part of the country which one dislikes to go into; they are sorry, sad, sickening places, and they have been made so by the probably involuntary and unconscious attitude of a relatively small group of leaders of industry." Kendall believed business leadership capable of turning these communities into healthy, happy ones. "Industrial management must realize its responsibility for these things as well as for the excellence of technical management." [37]

The converging interests of business corporations and social welfare agencies thus brought the leaders of both into increasingly close association. Their meeting-ground was a joint interest in the financing of private social and charitable services; and their most impressive achievement in the 1920s was the creation of the national Community Chest movement (to be discussed in Chapter 5). But education and medicine, which after the Second World War were to attract the attention of the business community as prime objects of corporate philanthropy, managed also to win limited company assistance in the

[37] For the Bell system, see Danelian, *A. T. and T.*, 284–92. Harriet L. Herring's *Welfare Work in Mill Villages* was based on a survey of 322 companies. Herring reported that ninety per cent of the mill representatives interviewed supported some form of welfare work "as an expression not only of the business relation between employer and employee but of the personal relation as well" (p. 297). See also *Forbes*, XIV (26 April 1924), 87; *Nation's Business*, XV (December, 1927), 132; statements by Chamber of Commerce officials of Rochester, New York [*Nation's Business*, XV (December 1927), 78–79], and San Francisco [*Proceedings of the Stanford Conference on Business Education*, 182]; and Henrietta M. Larson and Kenneth W. Porter, *History of Humble Oil and Refining Company; a Study in Industrial Growth* (New York, 1959), 210–11. For the Chamber of Commerce, see *U.S. Chamber of Commerce Report of the Thirteenth Annual Meeting* (1925), 50, and other annual reports. John Ihlder, "The Business Man's Responsibility," *Nation's Business*, XIII (November, 1925), 52ff. Henry P. Kendall's address to the Taylor Society was reprinted in Bloomfield, *The Modern Executive*, 71.

Twenties. The beginnings of business giving in these fields well exemplified the means by which a social impulse in managerial thinking could be translated into support for nonbusiness institutions.

In 1919 Thomas Lamont, a trustee of Harvard University, persuaded another alumnus, John Price Jones, to assume the management of Harvard's $14,000,000 endowment fund drive. A Welsh miner's son, helped through Exeter Academy by a loan from a neighboring shopkeeper, Jones had supported himself in college as a newspaper correspondent. After graduation he continued in journalism, then switched to advertising until the First World War, when his employer contributed his services to the government's Liberty Loan campaigns. Here, Jones participated for two years in the largest national solicitation effort up to that time, a turning point in organized fund raising.

The postwar Harvard campaign was a success, and Jones was launched upon a career as a professional fund raiser. His services after the war were sought by a growing clientele of colleges, universities, hospitals, welfare federations, and even musical organizations. Jones saw in systematically organized solicitation the key to business support of philanthropic enterprises. He served, in effect, as a mediator and channel of communication between the converging interests of business and nonprofit institutions.[38]

As a number of fund-raising agencies similar to Jones's came into being in the 1920s, solicitations were slowly put on a businesslike basis. Gifts to educational institutions, for example, continued to come as they had in the past—primarily from individual alumni or friends of the school involved. College and university officials still carried much of the burden of solicitation, but Jones and fellow professional fund raisers helped to influence their methods. Careful analysis of an institution and its likely sources of support and painstaking scrutiny and interpretation of needs became the hallmarks of systematic fund raising. Institutions were taught to put their cases most persuasively, in terms congenial to business donors.

The practice of approaching corporations, as distinguished from individual businessmen, developed gradually in the 1920s and 1930s. A drive organized by Jones on behalf of the United Hospital Fund of New York City in 1920 raised nearly $130,000 from 1,258 donors through a Committee on Trades and Corporations; but the records fail

---

[38] For a summary of John Price Jones's career, see *Philanthropy*, LI (Fall, 1953), 11–13. "John Price Jones Corporation History," The John Price Jones Corporation Papers (hereafter cited as JPJC Papers), 1929, Baker Library, Harvard University; Cutlip, *Fund Raising*, 156ff., *passim*.

to show what proportion of these gifts, if any, actually came from companies, as opposed to individuals.[39] Princeton University, also with the assistance of the John Price Jones Corporation, carried out fund-raising drives in 1921 and again in 1925. The 1921 drive pressed into service a number of alumni prominent in business circles, among them Frank Vanderlip, Cyrus H. McCormick, and William C. Procter; but direct corporate solicitations seem not to have been attempted. In 1925, however, Princeton received a gift of $10,000 from the Public Service Corporation of New Jersey.[40]

Even more elaborate plans for corporate solicitations were laid in connection with a 1922 building fund drive for Pennsylvania State College. Cautious arrangements were made to secure the endorsement of chambers of commerce, the Central Pennsylvania Coal Producers' Association, and similar organizations. An appeal was directed to companies which employed graduates of the college, as well as to others supporting extension programs in mining and engineering. Campaign workers were told, "Pennsylvania's great industrial enterprises should, without exception, be expected to support the campaign for the Emergency Building Fund and for later legislative appropriations." Solicitors were cautioned to be discreet in asking for and publicizing company contributions, since "certain mine owners and operators have undertaken certain financial obligations in assisting extension work, but do not wish the matter to become generally known for obvious reasons."

Despite high hopes, results were disappointing. The final report on the campaign noted an interview with Joseph A. Grundy, of the Pennsylvania Manufacturers' Association, which produced the advice that, although "corporate contributions cannot be expected, leading industrialists . . . should be appealed to, but only when there is a contact with the college." The failure in Pennsylvania was followed, however,

[39] The JPJC Papers contain casebooks on all campaigns managed by the company. Client Casebook 9, "A Plan for Raising $1,500,000 for the United Hospital Fund. Synopsis." Reports indicated that business cooperation with the campaign was less than wholehearted. A 1923 campaign on behalf of the Middlesex General Hospital of New Brunswick, New Jersey, also included an approach to industrial and business concerns in the region; but again it is not clear whether corporate donations as such were solicited. Casebook 22.

[40] JPJC Papers, Casebook 10, Princeton Endowment Fund, 1920; Casebook 219, Princeton University Fund, 1935, contains references to earlier donors. A $14,000 gift from Pitney, Hardin, and Skinner, all of New York City, is also mentioned; but, again, it is not clear whether this was an individual or a company donation (p. 102).

by success in Illinois, when a Northwestern University fund drive the following year drew upon the services of "purse-string" men from four hundred Chicago firms with Commerce School graduates on their staffs. It received a number of company contributions, at least three of $5,000 or more.[41]

Confronted with such systematic tactics, it is little wonder that business resistance to philanthropic appeals eventually crumbled. It was not in education, however, that the most immediately successful appeals for business contributions were made. The field of community welfare offered a more obvious and immediate object for the expression of company social responsibility; and here wartime experience had already created a model. Through the collaboration of leaders in social work, fund raising, and business, a new institution—the community chest—came into being in the Twenties. The ideas of business trusteeship and service found expression in the growth of corporate support for community welfare services.

[41] JPJC Papers, Casebook 21, Pennsylvania State College, 1922, "Plan . . . ," 19; "Final Report," 3. Casebook 30, Northwestern University, 1923–24, "Final Report," 105, 122. A later Johns Hopkins University campaign was less successful. It failed to find a chairman for the committee on firms and corporations. Casebook 43, Johns Hopkins University, "Final Report," 29. E. H. Gary endorsed corporation contributions to higher education during a 1925 University of Pittsburgh campaign; Cutlip, *Fund Raising*, 260.

Business schools, naturally, had a particular appeal to business donors; and some of the corporate funds which went into this field were really public relations and propaganda expenditures rather than philanthropy. The National Electric Light Association gave Northwestern University $25,000 a year and Harvard $30,000 a year for a number of years, certainly in the expectation that the public utilities industry would receive sympathetic treatment in the curriculum. The American Telephone and Telegraph Company supported lectureships at Harvard and elsewhere. See Thompson, *Confessions of the Power Trust*, 332; Danelian, *A. T. and T.*, 297; Cutlip, *Fund Raising*, Chap. VI.

5 · THE COMMUNITY CHEST MOVEMENT, 1918–1929

At a time when company executives were impelled as seldom before to consider new forms of social participation, they found in the emerging community chest movement of the 1920s both ideas and patterns of action which helped to shape their philanthropic policies. The encounter of business with social work laid the foundations for organized corporate philanthropy. It brought businessmen into contact with segments of the community from which they were largely separated and thus helped to broaden their understanding and enlarge their interests. Within a short decade relationships were established which proved sufficiently strong to withstand the severe tests of depression and retrenchment.

The counterpart of the growing sensitivity of American businessmen to their social environment was the emergence of a businesslike approach to community welfare problems and a new interest in corporate contributions on the part of social agencies. The rise of professional consciousness among business leaders and educators was paralleled by the growth of the social work profession in the first two decades of the new century. The trade association movement, with its emphasis upon cooperation, the elimination of "unfair" competition, and the determination of common standards, was mirrored in the recognition among welfare organizations of the need to reduce duplication in solicitations and services. Scientific management's study of the elements of the production process was matched by philanthropy's search for causes, rather than symptoms, of social distress. Finally, the

117

formation in 1918 of the American Association for Community Organization and its subsequent development into an effective central coordinating body for local community chests were at least a pale reflection of the thrust for consolidation which had produced the large corporations dominating the American economic scene.

If organized charity in the United States modeled itself in some degree on the institutions and practices of business, the fact was not surprising. The problems which charitable and welfare agencies faced often grew directly from the conditions and characteristics of business, as the experience of the Railroad YMCAs had so clearly shown. Still further, welfare organizations had sought and received the assistance of business leadership in financing and publicizing their work. The promotion by the Cleveland Chamber of Commerce of federated fund raising by local charities before the First World War has already been noted. Denver, New Orleans, and Cincinnati were coordinating welfare solicitations in similar fashion by the end of 1915, as were some thirteen other cities. Experience with the War Chests spread the practice still further. Conversion to a peacetime basis brought community chests into being in many cities, with local chambers of commerce often supplying leadership and motivation.[1] With the creation of the American Association for Community Organization (AACO) came recognition that the community chest movement had become a national phenomenon. The AACO provided a clearinghouse for the exchange of information and experience between cities, as well as a means for extending the movement and increasing its effectiveness.

Not only did businessmen press for federated fund raising; companies supported the effort with their gifts as well. A study of corporate giving showed contributions of $2,539,819 by 2,652 firms in 13 cities in 1920, and $12,954,769 given by 33,977 firms in 129 cities in 1929. Much of the dollar increase, of course, was explained by the spread of the chest movement to additional cities. Corporate gifts during these years fluctuated between 19 per cent and 24 per cent of total contributions to the chests; but the highest figure was achieved at the beginning of

[1] Howard Strong, "The Relation of Commercial Bodies to our Charitable and Social Standards"; W. Frank Persons, "Central Financing of Social Agencies" (Columbus, Ohio, 1922); Williams and Croxton, *Corporate Contributions*, 76–90; Boston Chamber of Commerce Papers, Baker Library, Harvard University. For discussion of trends in the organization and philosophy of philanthropy, see Bremner, *American Philanthropy*, 117, 122–42; Cutlip, *Fund Raising, passim.*; and Roy Lubove, *The Professional Altruist. The Emergence of Social Work as a Career* (Cambridge, Massachusetts, 1965).

the decade in the aftermath of war. Depression in 1921 and 1922 reduced such gifts markedly; and, although an increase was shown thereafter, the earlier percentages were never quite regained. Nevertheless, corporate giving had become a well-established practice by the end of the decade. Despite variations and fluctuations which troubled chest officials, business contributions had come to constitute a significant element in the support of community welfare agencies.[2]

For many businessmen participation in community chest activities through the contribution of both their companies' funds and their own services was a new experience. For almost the first time in their external relations they encountered spokesmen for other groups in the community whose professional training and experience they were bound to respect and whose interpretation of the social role and responsibilities of business they could not lightly dismiss. Although such exchanges were sometimes controversial, they were nonetheless important. They encouraged the growth of a sense of corporate citizenship, which was a gain both to business and to the community and which compensated, in part at least, for the decline of traditional individual involvement in personal charity and philanthropy. They laid the foundations for the "two-way street" between business and the community which was so desirable but so often lacking in other public relations ventures.[3]

[2] Williams and Croxton, *Corporate Contributions*, 91–103. Reports of the Denver Charity Organization Society, available from the beginning of the century, showed contributions of $8,574 from 162 concerns in 1901 increasing to $15,652 from 249 firms in 1912. In these years Denver was unusual in the fact that it had a single appeal for a number of agencies. *Ibid.*, 76–77.

The President's Committee on Recent Social Trends concluded that "the lowering of tax rates and the increase of general prosperity which characterized the years from 1922 to 1929 inclusive, had little effect upon the [individual] contribution rate. The ratio between income and contributions is so consistent throughout the period as to suggest that giving is more definitely regulated by habit or tradition than by changes in income, tax, or any external circumstances." President's Research Committee on Social Trends, *Recent Social Trends*, 2 vols. (New York and London, 1933), II, 1219. Corporation giving, of course, represented a considerable departure from habit and tradition.

[3] Bremner, *American Philanthropy*, 140–41. Albert G. Milbank, "Socialized Capitalism," *Survey*, LXVIII (1 July 1932), 293ff., is a recognition by the chairman of the Borden Company that business could learn much from the social welfare movement. Interaction between business board members and professional staff of welfare agencies is considered in Harold L. Wilensky and Charles N. Lebeaux, *Industrial Society and Social Welfare* (New York, 1958), 272–82. Cutlip, *Fund Raising*, Chaps. VI and VII, contains the fullest treatment of organized philanthropy in the Twenties.

THE BEGINNINGS OF ORGANIZED SOLICITATION

The development of organized solicitation through the community chests was the result of growing need on the part of both businessmen and social welfare agencies for better management of fund-raising programs. The interest of businessmen in community chests is easily understood. Flooded with appeals for apparently worthy causes, even the most sympathetic company official hesitated. Not only did review of the many requests for assistance take valuable time, but the understanding and information required to evaluate them were often lacking. Suspicions of fraud, duplication, and inefficiency were widespread. One probably exaggerated estimate held that $10,000,000 a year was lost in New York City alone in stolen or misplaced charity funds and that the annual national loss was ten times greater still. The businessman's desire for system and order in his activities was affronted by the apparently disorderly ways of the welfare agencies. In desperation he turned to chambers of commerce or trade associations for help. It seemed elementary good sense to analyze one's philanthropic undertakings as carefully as one's business dealings. As one man put it, "the American businessman can be generous, but he doesn't have to be foolish." [4]

One answer was industrial solicitation—cooperation among the members of a single trade or industry to investigate requests for funds and consolidate giving into one campaign. By the mid-Twenties a number of such programs had come into being. *Nation's Business* in 1925 reported that trade associations were watching closely the plans of the New York fur industry to develop its own charity chest, as an investigation and distribution agency. A single drive would be conducted each year to meet the requests deemed necessary and legitimate; each contributor to the chest would vote for directors and designate the recipients of his gifts. The first fund-raising drive conducted by the chest was intended to reach "ten thousand persons identified with the industry, including firm members, salesmen, executives, clerks, designers and foremen." The appeal of such a plan was widespread. "It involves," wrote *Nation's Business*, "one of those why-didn't-we-think-of-it-before ideas which seem so simple and inevitable after someone has suggested them." [5]

[4] F. S. Tisdale, "Winning Ways of the Charity Fakers," *Nation's Business*, XIV (August, 1926), 26.

[5] *Nation's Business*, XIII (May, 1925), 120–21; *Minutes of the Corporation, Board of Directors, Executive Committees of the Community Chests and Councils*

The appeals of social agencies, however, were ordinarily to all the trades of a community rather than to a single industry. It was natural, therefore, that the chamber of commerce, in which many different companies and lines of trade were represented, should serve as the channel through which businessmen attempted to organize their response to solicitations. Chamber committees screened the applicants and issued endorsements and recommendations. The Chicago Association of Commerce urged its members not to succumb to appeals for advertising on behalf of a variety of "causes"; donations to worthy causes were appropriate, but advertising should be planned on a strictly business basis. The U. S. Chamber of Commerce Civic Development Department undertook a study of social agencies in the United States between 1920 and 1926 to help its members evaluate groups appealing for their gifts.

Still, a decade of efforts to systematize appeals, to explain needs, and to provide more adequate information about programs failed to achieve anything like full understanding between potential donors and hopeful recipients. Many businessmen remained uninformed about social needs and social agencies; some were downright hostile to solicitations. Even those favorably inclined were often uncertain as to how their giving should be planned. Helen B. Leavens, a social worker interviewing over a thousand businessmen for the New York Charity Organization Society in 1929, found the bankers courteous, the brokers busy, and the advertising men inaccessible. Businessmen expressed resentment at the red tape involved in charity and at the use of women solicitors. More than on any other single point, they agreed on the desirability of a federation or chest organization for fund raising.[6]

To meet the questions, objections, and confusions of the companies they approached, social agencies had little choice but to scrutinize their operations and attempt to put their own houses in order. Local welfare federations, councils of social agencies, and community chests provided a means for doing so. Some social workers feared business domination of federations and some agencies refused to participate,

of America, Inc., and Its Predecessor Organizations, Vol. 1 (12 January 1925), 5. The *Minutes* and other papers covering the activities of the community chest movement in the United States are housed in the archives of the United Community Funds and Councils of America, New York City (hereafter cited as UCFCA).

[6] For the Chicago Association of Commerce, see *Nation's Business,* XIV (February, 1926), 67. For the Civic Development Department, see *ibid.,* XV (January, 1927), 116. Helen B. Leavens, "A Social Worker in Prosperity Land," *Survey,* LXI (15 March 1929), 789–91.

but the spread of the community chests from 40 cities in 1919 to nearly 350 a decade later indicated the strength of the movement. Chest officials, at both the local and the national levels, were eager to increase business support and to overcome objections to appeals.

Business resistance was of two kinds. It came from those who challenged the validity and efficiency of welfare work; and it came, too, from others who, while not necessarily questioning the value of philanthropy, doubted the propriety, the necessity, or the legality of company—as opposed to individual—contributions. Spokesmen for the business community and representatives of the social work field carried on discussions covering these issues over many years, often through channels provided by the community chests.

A significant mutual exchange and education between two important community interests was, in fact, one of the major contributions of the chest movement of the Twenties. Welfare agency officials learned to coordinate and systematize their efforts, to prepare more effective and illuminating reports, to draw more heavily upon the leadership and interest of individual businessmen, and to see and present their work in terms of its relationship to industrial institutions and conditions. Businessmen drawn into active involvement with agency or chest affairs learned from direct contact with social workers something of the nature and the needs of a segment of the population with which they otherwise had little contact. They also broadened their understanding of and perspective on the place of business in the total community. Some even learned that not all community welfare activities could be run on a purely business basis.

Encouraged by the development of new contacts with the business world, welfare agency officials devoted their energies to building a case for corporate philanthropy. The Central Council of Social Agencies of New Bedford, Massachusetts, in 1920 issued a statement, "Why Corporations Should Contribute to Community Welfare Work," as part of its annual drive for funds. It argued that corporations had a civic duty to share the community's burden. It was not enough to rely upon the generosity of individual stockholders, the Council held. Many of them, after all, did not live in the community in which their company carried on its operations. Initiative on the part of management was as justified in philanthropy as it was in business:

> The individual stockholder throws upon the corporation management the responsibility for the conduct of the enterprise in which he is an owner. The same responsibility rests

upon the corporation management to assume the corporation's share of the support of the social agencies of the city. . . . Expenditures which would not now be questioned by anyone if made for the exclusive benefit of the worker in an individual plant should also be unquestioned if made for the common benefit of the workers in all the mills.[7]

New Bedford businessmen found this presentation persuasive. There had been no previous record of corporate charitable contributions, except for hospitals; but the 1920 appeal brought in some $47,000 of corporation gifts, out of a total of $125,000.

Other equally determined and imaginative approaches took place in other cities. The cold statistics concerning the number of community chests established, funds raised, and corporate contributions reported can only be interpreted as evidence of a revolution in welfare organization and fund raising. They do not reveal, however, the hours of effective work and communication which took place at the individual level, with welfare workers driving home to business executives the idea of the responsibility of their concerns for the very real costs to the community for the services upon which they and their employees depended.[8]

Local chests, under the pressure of local needs and limitations, could not have built a national movement by themselves. It was recognition of common problems and conditions shared by many agencies and communities which led to the formation of AACO. Experience with the War Chests had demonstrated the effectiveness of national publicity and coordination combined with local organization and solicitation. The lesson was one which welfare leaders now set out to apply on a peacetime basis. The Association's national office as the years progressed played an increasingly important and useful role. It received and compared reports from different localities, made ideas and information available to all, and, in general, served as a clearing-

[7] "Reaching the Corporations," *Survey*, XLV (25 December 1920), 458. Similar arguments were used by A. V. Cannon, chairman of the Corporations Committee of the Cleveland Community Fund, in a speech to the New York State Regional Conference of Community Chests, 11 January 1929. Cannon also stressed the point that business corporations had a direct financial stake in the social health of the communities in which they carried on their business. UCFCA File 106.

[8] For an example of such educational work on the part of one community chest official, see the letter of Ralph H. Blanchard, manager of the Niagara Falls Community Chest, to A. A. McLean of the U.S.L. Battery Corporation of Niagara Falls. Appendix I.

house and coordinating agency for the burgeoning community chest movement.

From the outset the chests were fortunate in the quality of their national leadership. Allen T. Burns, who had served the Cleveland Foundation and had helped establish the Cleveland Welfare Federation, became its secretary and chief executive officer in 1922; he served in that capacity until 1943. Ralph H. Blanchard came to the New York office from the Niagara Falls Community Chest in 1928. These men were professional social workers and administrators. They understood social problems and the needs of welfare agencies; at the same time, they were able to deal effectively with businessmen, understanding the interests and concerns of corporate officials, meeting their questions, and working with them as equals without servility or fear of domination.

The relationships which developed between representatives of business and of social work through joint enterprises, such as the community chests, is perhaps the most important single factor in the emergence of an informed sense of social responsibility on the part of American businessmen. With few exceptions, it has been only as business leadership has faced its relations with other social groups on a basis of equality that significant gains in understanding have been made. Under other circumstances, even the best of intentions have led in the end to benevolent, but ultimately unsatisfactory, paternalism. This was the lesson which George M. Pullman failed to learn. It was the lesson which the majority of employee representation plans of the Twenties failed to teach and which had to be taught again by the Wagner Act. It was the lesson, too, which the public relations industry then and since has too often overlooked, for all its talk of a "two-way street." The temptation for the businessman, especially for the successful and prestigious official of a large corporation, to believe that he knows the answers to society's social and political problems has often proved strong. The crash of 1929 revealed for a time how thin is the ice upon which such pretensions and illusions accumulate; but in a democratic society the lesson must be taught periodically, not to business alone but to any powerful social group.

Unlike the employee representation plans, publicity campaigns, and service slogans of the Twenties, which withered in the face of depression, the community chest movement survived and was stimulated to further action. Its survival suggests that here business leaders had begun to make meaningful contact with social problems. That they did so was in large part due to the strength, competence, and understanding of the social work professionals with whom they associated themselves.

PROBLEMS OF BUSINESS AND COMMUNITY CHEST COOPERATION

Despite the steady growth of corporate contributions to local welfare campaigns, word came regularly to the national association of questions and resistance encountered. The spread of the community chest itself had reduced complaints of duplication of effort and solicitation at the local level; but national corporations with offices and factories in several cities now began to be annoyed at the growing number of appeals they received. Comparison of reports from different cities, on the other hand, showed wide discrepancies in donation practices, even on the part of different local offices of a single corporation.

Lack of uniformity in company giving was documented by the Norfolk Community Fund in a 1924 study of bank contributions to the annual chest campaigns of forty cities, which the AACO distributed to its membership. According to the study, during the preceding year banks had contributed in all cities but Rochester, Roanoke, and Knoxville. In twenty-nine cities gifts came from individual banks; in six, quotas were first set by the local Clearing House Association. In three cities, the Clearing House Association itself contributed on behalf of its membership. The total subscription to the campaigns of the thirty-seven communities had been nearly $20,000,000, of which banks had given $471,993, or 2.4 per cent. Two years later, the Roanoke Community Chest, presumably in an attempt to stimulate bank participation there, surveyed 128 cities and reported that banks had contributed over $1,000,000 to their most recent campaigns. A study of the practices of railroad and steamship companies in 1926 and 1927 also revealed significant variations in practice between different communities.[9]

In 1928, Allen Burns's office examined practices of local chests and local and national companies in sixty cities, revealing a wide diversity in methods used to solicit funds as well as in response. In some places little effort was made to solicit corporations whose headquarters were in other cities; others tried but experienced difficulties. Auburn, New York, received contributions from nonlocal manufacturers, public utilities, and retail companies; the Schulte Cigar Company gave, but not

[9] UCFCA File 72: Corporation Giving—Standards—Banks, and Practices; and File 51: Washington Conference, 1928—Group 3.

the United Cigar Company. Cleveland reported gifts from most nonlocal companies, except for the railroads, Western Union, United Cigar stores, and the insurance companies. In Cleveland, too, chain stores such as Woolworth's, the A & P, Kresge, and Kroger companies contributed. Springfield, Illinois, successfully tapped its United Cigar stores. Hartford, which had previously solicited individuals rather than companies, was said to be planning to approach national corporations for gifts.

A perennial source of disagreement between company and chest officials concerned the basis upon which contributions to community services were determined. In towns where their factories employed substantial numbers of laborers, employers were more willing to support the chests than they were in towns where company personnel were primarily white collar workers, employed in service, sales, or other office installations. To chest officials, such a distinction between types of business operations seemed to neglect the issue of company responsibility for the overall health of the community upon which management depended. Community needs, not business organizational arrangements, should govern availability of corporate contributions.

Varying degrees of pressure or persuasion used by the chests to win company support were also shown in the AACO study. In a few instances, lists of subscribing or nonsubscribing companies were published; but this was unusual. The Los Angeles chest's Branch House Committee was heavily weighted with "Purchasing Agents, or other representatives of firms that are large buyers." In Youngstown, Ohio, the names of leading businessmen in the community appeared in a 1927 letter to corporations, with the statement that :

> These 108 trustees believe that every factory, firm, company, corporation, store or agent doing business in Youngstown has a direct obligation to help the city's destitute, unfortunate, sick, and handicapped.
>
> Many local branches with headquarters in other cities have been meeting their obligations by annual contributions for the past eight years.
>
> A Committee of businessmen well qualified to judge our resources finds, after careful analysis, that we are compelled to depend upon your good company for a contribution of not less than $——to enable us to reach our campaign quota.
>
> Their consideration takes into account the minimum needs

of the agencies, and assumes that all other contributors will likewise bear their fair share of this common responsibility.

Clearly, the age of high-pressure salesmanship had not bypassed the community chest.

In many cases, however, the appeal was more cautious. Chattanooga suggested to officials of nonlocal companies the unfairness of permitting local business to bear the burden alone, arguing that "absentee ownership or management gave no one immunity from his civil obligations." Lansing, Michigan, trying a positive approach, urged its prospects "to be numbered with progressive businessmen who recognize and accept their community responsibilities." Careful scrutiny of welfare agency budgets by businessmen was emphasized in Schenectady, and the damage to economic prosperity and civic pride from poverty and disease was pointed out. In Tampa, quotas were set and stress was laid upon sharing the city's burdens as well as its progress and prosperity. A letter from the mayor told nonlocal corporations, "Your firm's interests are as deeply involved in the successful outcome of this effort as those of any firm or industry in Tampa, and we do not hesitate to urge you to participate."

In Williamsport, Pennsylvania, chest officials suggested that contributions of local branches of national corporations in that community be planned as a percentage of total volume of business or of total corporate donations. Minneapolis, too, faced the problem of refusals by branch offices stating that their companies gave only at the home office. Harry Yeager, of the Committee on Foreign Corporations of the Minneapolis chest, found this argument unconvincing:

> Very few have excused themselves on the grounds that the branch office or plant is not producing profit. All seem to recognize the outlying [sic] principle of community service. . . . The branch, plant or agency operating for profit is subject to the state and local laws as to taxes and pay [sic] accordingly. There is no real difference between legal and moral obligations, and the profits . . . should be apportioned to take care of the local moral requirements the same as they are apportioned to take care of the legal tax requirements, and the head, or home office should not escape this obligation.[10]

[10] All letters and reports quoted are from UCFCA File 51, Washington Conference, 1928—Group 3. The survey was made in anticipation of this conference. For information on later inconsistencies in corporation giving practices, see the undated memorandum, "Variations and Inconsistencies within and between Individual Companies," UCFCA File 72: Corporation Giving—Practices, 1935–45.

Legal questions also plagued chest officials and troubled corporation executives and lawyers. Henry Ford had found his decision to reinvest the stockholders' profits in the business denied by the courts in 1916. The right of management to donate company funds to charity seemed even more questionable. Many local chests met refusals based upon the argument that the corporation had no legal right to contribute. Yet many corporations did, in fact, make contributions; so the issue was in doubt. To be sure, the legal powers of corporate officials were anything but clear. It seemed obvious that they must exercise some discretion in the expenditure of funds; and company donations to hospitals which treated their employees had, indeed, been upheld by the courts. Congress had enacted permissive legislation enabling national banks to contribute to the wartime Red Cross drive; and Texas, in 1917, also passed a permissive law, authorizing *all* corporations to give to the Red Cross. By 1925, New York, Illinois, Ohio, and Tennessee had followed suit; but still no clear and uniform policy had been achieved.[11]

Chest officials sometimes suspected that the legal reservations expressed by company spokesmen were simply an excuse to avoid giving. Thus, Ralph Reed, secretary of the Des Moines Public Welfare Bureau, asked the national chest office:

> Is there on record any case in which such contributions when not unreasonable in their amount, have been held by court to have been illegal under existing corporation laws? Is not this a technical evasion? Do not the corporations taking advantage of this evasion at the same time make certain other expenditures which are to an equal extent not specifically authorized by their charters or by the state statutes under which they are operating?[12]

In New York, Allen Burns and his staff saw that the legal queries coming in from around the country involved an issue vital to the future of corporation giving. They followed closely the current court decisions and ransacked old case books to find precedents and rulings which would support their cause. When particularly difficult or important questions arose, they turned to the lawyers who served as members of

[11] The legal issues, and the development of law and court decisions covering corporate contributions, are summarized in F. Emerson Andrews, *Corporation Giving*, 229–44.

[12] See UCFCA File 51: Washington Conference, 1928—Group 3, for this and other references to the legal question.

the national board of directors. Frederic R. Kellogg, of New York, was especially helpful in preparing letters and arguments to be used with recalcitrant prospects.

Still another question raised by businessmen concerned the tax status of corporate donations. Since 1917 the income tax laws had permitted individuals to deduct charitable contributions up to fifteen per cent of their income in calculating their returns. Now, with corporation gifts increasing, the question of a similar deduction for company contributions arose. In 1925, the Chamber of Commerce's Committee on Taxation argued, "Corporate gifts to worthy purposes under proper circumstances should be encouraged, not penalized by the tax laws." [13]

By 1927, local community chests were being urged by businessmen to ask Congress for suitable legislation. The reports the New York office began to receive from widely scattered communities amounted clearly to evidence of a nationwide campaign. The Indianapolis Community Chest forwarded a copy of a letter by W. B. Harding, head of the local branch of the U. S. Tire and Rubber Company. Harding asserted that the federal income tax laws did not permit charitable deductions and added:

> If you agree with us that the above named provision of the Federal Income Tax Law is unfair and that it will interfere with your securing necessary contributions from corporations, will you please communicate with your Senators and Congressmen, and also the Chamber of Commerce of the United States asking them to use their influence to secure an amendment to the law? [14]

Letters containing virtually the same request were received from the Omaha, Memphis, Shenango Valley, and San Francisco chests. Business leadership clearly expected something in return if it was to continue its growing support of the community chests. Again, a question had arisen which—like the number of appeals, the diversity of giving practices, and the legality of corporate donations—seemed to call for coordination of policy on a national level.

[13] Chamber of Commerce of the United States, "Federal Taxation. Report of the Chamber's Committee on Taxation" (Washington, 1925). A copy of this pamphlet is filed in UCFCA File 72: Corporation Giving—Tax Deductions—Rulings, Decisions, etc.

[14] UCFCA File 51: Washington Conference, 1928—Group 3; UCFCA *Minutes*, I, 381–389, 393, 398–99.

THE WASHINGTON CONFERENCE OF 1928

At the national association office, Allen Burns and his staff were already laying plans for a national conference on community chest problems. Late in 1926, the AACO's Executive Committee had approved a resolution calling for a meeting in Washington, D.C., early in 1928. In January, 1927, a bulletin had gone out to all local chests suggesting that the time had come to cooperate with the business community in reducing frictions arising out of the number of appeals received by national corporations. Since the situation was irritating many companies and sooner or later would force them to develop formal policies to deal with it, the community chest organization should take the initiative in facing the problem:

> Why not insure the formulation of a wise and generous policy on the part of national business concerns and incidentally cultivate good will by helping them to arrive at a policy which, while fair to their stockholders, will also enable the community chests to draw from nonlocally managed concerns, a reasonable measure of support for local charitable work?

Response to this bulletin demonstrated widespread interest and led to still further inquiries from New York about local practices. A central file was created with a record of each city in which national corporations were, or should be, contributing. Local chests were advised to gather data for the 1927 fund-raising campaigns showing the use of welfare services by company employees.

As information accumulated, it became apparent that early action was called for. Still, the limited facilities of Allen Burns's office were already strained by preparations for the forthcoming Washington conference. It was decided, therefore, to add the problem of national corporations to the Washington agenda. At the May, 1927, meeting of the AACO in Des Moines, formal approval was given for the calling of a "National Conference on Community Responsibility for Human Welfare," with the matter of "Local Responsibilities of National Business" high on its list of priorities.[15]

[15] UCFCA *Minutes*, I: Executive Committee, 2 October 1926; Board of Directors, 25 January 1927; Memorandum for the Advisory Committee, 11 March 1927; Recommendations of the Advisory Committee, 8 April 1927; "Proposal for a National Conference on Community Responsibility for Human Welfare," 251–53, 265, 285; UCFCA File 72: Tax Deductions; American Association for Community

Burns and the directors of the Association of Community Chests and Councils—as the AACO had been renamed at Des Moines—were anxious to encourage the interest and participation of influential businessmen in the conference. With the help of those already active in community chest work, they assembled a National Citizens Committee with Senator James Couzens, Harvey Firestone, Frederic R. Kellogg, William Cooper Procter, and other prominent business figures as members. The interest of Secretary of Commerce Herbert Hoover was enlisted and he agreed to serve as vice-chairman of the conference. It was hoped that President Coolidge would issue the invitations; but when this plan failed they went out in the name of Procter, chairman of the Citizens Committee.

The conference was to bring together leaders in the field of social work and philanthropy with representatives of the business community, but the planning was carefully designed to keep the social work professionals in the background. Business, political, and religious figures with a known interest in philanthropy were invited, and the community chest staff was instructed that the "program and meeting are to be arranged in such a way as to emphasize the primary responsibility of laymen [businessmen] for the success of community welfare work." Businessmen were asked to finance the conference.

At a December, 1927, meeting the National Citizens Committee set the dates of 20 and 21 February 1928 for what was now designated the "Citizens Conference on Community Responsibility for Human Welfare." Working committees were appointed to gather information upon which discussion would be based. The scope of the conference was broadly conceived. In addition to the role of national corporations, other topics for consideration included the relationship of tax-supported to voluntary welfare work, the welfare responsibilities of municipal governments, and a study of different types of welfare programs. In effect, Allen Burns and the community chest organization had planned an educational seminar through which they hoped to inform and instruct citizens and business leaders in the problems and needs of community welfare agencies.[16]

The conference convened in the nation's capital, with President W. H. P. Faunce of Brown University presiding. The roster of those attending included both little-known and well-known men, representa-

Organization, Bulletin No. 30, 8 January 1927. At the Des Moines meeting, the organization's name was officially changed to the Association of Community Chests and Councils (ACCC).

[16] UCFCA File 51: Washington Conference, 1928.

tives of cities and companies both small and large, delegates from the West as well as from the East.[17] President Faunce's opening remarks set the tenor of the meeting: "Where Shall Leadership and Responsibility for Community Welfare Be Found?" The answer, he asserted, lay in business, as well as in the churches, schools, and similar institutions. "A new conception of business as a public responsibility must be taught and learned. We talk of certain kinds of enterprise as 'public utilities.' The truth is every business, large or small, is either a public utility or a public detriment or damage." Businessmen were finding satisfaction, Faunce noted, in fostering the widespread distribution of wealth for the general welfare, as well as in its accumulation.[18]

As the meeting progressed, it became apparent that one of its aims was to win over those who remained dubious of the community chest approach. C. M. Bookman, president of the ACCC, stressed the organizational similarities between the chests and business: business principles of budgeting, rationalization, and cooperation were at work in private charity. Newton D. Baker further emphasized the movement toward national organization in the interest of efficiency but expressed fear that the trend might continue until all welfare agencies were consolidated into one, the government. The remedial welfare burden, he believed, should be borne by the state; but private philanthropy should concentrate on preventive work. William Cooper Procter pointed to the valuable training in community leadership which community chest work afforded business executives who participated in it. This experience alone, he asserted, was worth more than the monetary contributions involved.[19]

Formalities and introductory remarks concluded, the delegates turned to discussing the business at hand in smaller groups. Representatives of social agencies mingled with citizen and business delegates,

[17] A press release for February 20 listed the following businessmen in attendance, none of whom were members of the sponsoring committee: Charles A. Stillman, Goodyear Tire and Rubber Company; J. D. Robinson, Libby Glass Company; Edward Bausch, Bausch and Lomb; William D. McGregor, Pawtucket Chamber of Commerce; Alexander J. Porter, Shredded Wheat Biscuit Company; J. Byron Deacon, Tidewater Oil Company; George H. Bedell, Southern New England Telephone Company; Robert L. Cox, Metropolitan Life Insurance Company; A. C. Vander Vennet, Vander Vennet Clothing Company, Moline, Illinois; and J. Kindleberger, Kalamazoo Vegetable Parchment Company, among others. UCFCA File 51: Washington Conference, 1928.

[18] See UCFCA File 51: Washington Conference, 1928, for addresses delivered at the conference. *New York Times*, 21 February 1928, 27.

[19] *Ibid.;* UCFCA File 51: Washington Conference, 1928.

mindful still of their instructions to let the spotlight fall on the businessmen. Group Three, under the chairmanship of Paul A. Schoellkopf of the Niagara Falls Power Company, discussed "The Relationship of Local and National Business Corporations to Community Welfare." Strong leadership had been provided. Schoellkopf was an effective exponent of corporate contributions; and the group's secretary was Ralph H. Blanchard of the Niagara Falls Community Fund, who was soon to join the national office.[20]

Talk in this group ranged over by now familiar issues. Many corporate representatives underlined their primary obligation to maximum production and efficiency, consistent with their employees' welfare. Should not welfare services be supported by individuals? Would not corporate philanthropy tend to undermine business effectiveness? Was it, really, good for the community? In any case, were not sales offices on a different basis from factories, one which exempted them from any need to give? Was it legal to give company funds without a *quid pro quo;* must not a direct benefit be shown? Other business representatives, however, responded that "services financed through a Chest are believed to benefit living conditions, attract skilled labor and replace welfare provisions otherwise maintained by a corporation." [21]

Chest representatives, backing up the statements of friendly businessmen, put their case as forcefully as possible. The desirability of a community as a site for a plant or other company outlet often depended upon conditions directly related to the work of social agen-

[20] Interview with Ralph H. Blanchard, 30 December 1957. Participants in Group Three included, in addition to Schoellkopf, Procter, and Blanchard: A. W. Henshaw, General Electric Company; James L. Goodwin, Whitlock Coil Pipe Company, Hartford, Connecticut; Kenneth Sturges, Cleveland Community Chest; W. W. Head, Omaha National Bank; E. D. Duffield, Prudential Life Insurance Company; C. S. Woolworth; and E. R. Johnson, Virginia Supply Company. A number of other businessmen were listed as having been invited to participate in Group Three, but it is not clear whether or not they actually attended the meetings. Among these were Harvey S. Firestone; Charles L. Close, United States Steel Corporation; E. S. Stettinius, General Motors Company; Clarence J. Hicks, Standard Oil (New Jersey); C. B. Wigton, New York Central Railroad Company.

Those attending other group sessions of the conference included Henry D. Sharpe, Browne and Sharpe, Providence, Rhode Island; J. Herbert Case, Federal Reserve Bank of New York City; and Hugh M. Clarke, Armstrong Cork Company. UCFCA File 51: Washington Conference, 1928, "Personnel of Group Conference Committees," 25 December 1928.

[21] "Findings and Discussions of Group Conferences," Citizens Conference on Community Responsibility for Human Welfare. UCFCA File 51: Washington Conference, 1928.

cies. However elaborate company welfare programs might be, corporations usually depended upon the community for many more. Privately supported charities, too, offered an alternative to higher taxes for municipal welfare agencies. Corporate philanthropy was the logical and necessary successor to much individual charity, since modern corporate society often separated the owners of large enterprises from the needs and conditions of the employees. It was suggested that national corporations plan to allocate their contributions among branches, perhaps on the basis of the number of employees or the volume of business involved. Chest representatives, conceding a point on which they had been subject to business pressure, agreed that corporations should be permitted to treat donations as business expenses for tax purposes.

The formal report of Group Three recommended that both local and nonlocal companies share responsibility for support of community welfare services. It recognized that tangible benefits from company contributions could be demonstrated in services to employees, improved social and economic conditions, and community reputation. Business and chest officials joined in acknowledging that the basis for chest appeals and for company giving differed with the type of business activity involved, whether warehouse, factory, or sales office. The need for further study of the appropriate scale or standard for corporate gifts was recognized, and the ACCC was specifically requested to undertake such a study. Meanwhile, local chests were warned against bringing commercial pressures to bear upon prospective business donors. Where no legal basis for corporate contributions existed, the services of social agencies might be considered "a tangible return and value received in consideration of corporate payments to chests or individual agencies." Finally, recognizing that federal authorization to consider contributions as regular business expenses would "strengthen the position of corporate boards of directors in their desire to meet their corporation responsibilities through financial support of local chests," the report asked the ACCC to press for appropriate legislation.

Having achieved a considerable area of agreement, Group Three and, later, the Citizens Conference adjourned. William Cooper Procter and Francis Dykes of the Bethlehem Steel Company publicly subscribed to a statement by C. W. Pfeiffer of St. Paul: "Corporations should contribute to solve the social problems which they themselves create in the local communities." Dykes added, in a cryptic but apparently definitive way, "It is fundamentally the best thing for the community if large corporations contribute to welfare work." [22] The conference, in accordance with the hopes of its sponsors, had helped to win influential business understanding and support for the chests.

The work of the conference had ended, but that of Allen Burns and his staff had merely entered a new phase. Only a day after the delegates to Washington had concluded their discussions, the ACCC board of directors voted approval of Group Three's recommendations. At the same time, a committee of businessmen was requested to undertake the task of "getting the income tax law amended to permit corporations to deduct payments to charitable organizations as legitimate expenses of doing business." A report to local chests emphasized that a basis for mutual understanding and cooperation between business and social agency leaders had been laid at Washington.

In point of fact, however, representatives of several large, national corporations were continuing to discuss the formulation of a common donations policy that might well lead to reductions in their contributions. Sensitive to the threat which such an agreement would pose and working hard to prevent it, national chest leadership nevertheless chose to interpret these efforts in as friendly a fashion as possible. The large corporations were "waking up to the question of their community responsibilities," the member chests were told.

> Now it is up to the Chests to get over the Chest point of view that community welfare is a responsibility of every person or business benefited by being in a community. If these corporations should unite on a policy of giving, following the suggestions already quoted from one influential representative, what will be the situation? Such solidarity within big business would call for the strongest cooperative action by the Chests. We should welcome and must be ready for such a possibility, for consolidated policy is more desirable than a scatter-fire of indifference.

Announcement was made of the new committee which had been formed "for the peaceful penetration of this corporation situation." William Cooper Proctor of Cincinnati, Henry D. Sharpe of Providence, John Lord O'Brian of Buffalo, and Frederic R. Kellogg of New York had agreed to serve; other members would be added. Local chests were once again called upon for suggestions. At its May meeting the ACCC board of directors voted that the problem of national

22 *Ibid.; New York Times,* 22 February 1928, 14.

corporations be made "a major concern for the coming year." [23] It was essential that every possible step be taken to insure that corporate policy was made in full knowledge of community needs.

During the summer of 1928 Burns issued a statement on corporate responsibility for use by local chests in their fall campaigns. Paul Schoellkopf also prepared an article, "The Corporation and Its Community," for the September issue of *Survey*. To strengthen the arguments of local chests, Burns pointed out that, despite considerable variation in practice, there was little disposition among corporations maintaining factories in a community to deny an obligation to social agencies supplying direct benefits to employees and their families. The difficulty came in getting companies to acknowledge and support the community services which benefited them only indirectly. Companies should be reminded that they exercised great care in choosing the towns in which they located their plants. A "healthy" community was recognized as a desirable location, and sound welfare services were essential to community health.[24]

Schoellkopf's article dealt with two questions; what was the responsibility of a corporation to the community as a whole—"that is, what is its share in the common duty and desire to make that locality a good place in which to live and do business"; and to what extent did community betterment actually benefit the corporation itself? No valid distinction could be made, Schoellkopf believed, between local and national corporations. Both, in fact, were already supporting community welfare work through their taxes; and private agencies should be as readily supported as public. "Whether or not it is assumed, the responsibility is there, for the very conditions which make it possible for corporations to operate at a profit bring problems which must be met if our country is to achieve the full measure of its capabilities." Regarding benefits derived by business corporations, Schoellkopf mentioned the reduction of labor turnover as a consequence of sound community conditions. He repeated the idea advanced by Procter at Washington that the experience which corporation executives themselves gained from working on community problems "builds the corporation into the community as nothing else will." Corporate donations,

[23] UCFCA *Minutes*, I, Board of Directors, 22 February 1928; Memorandum of the Meeting of the Advisory Committee, 10 April 1928; Board of Directors, 2 May 1928. Association of Community Chests and Councils, "Big Business and Community Chests," 14 April 1928.

[24] UCFCA File 72: Corporation Giving—Rights, Laws; "Corporation Responsibility for Welfare Work in a Community Where It Does Business."

he argued, should be recognized as a regular business expense: "The returns which come to a corporation from better social conditions are so positive and unmistakable that there can be no question as to whether or not participation in community activities is profitable, from a purely selfish dollar-and-cent viewpoint." Furthermore, "the corporations which are recognizing the intangible values in their relationships with their staffs and their communities are the ones which are building soundly for the future of American industry." [25]

Anxious to get ammunition into the hands of chest campaigners as soon as possible, the New York office sent out copies of the Burns and Schoellkopf statements early in the fall, together with statements from other businessmen explaining the basis for their support of the community chests. The strategy of using businessmen who were friendly to the chest's interests to persuade their more doubtful colleagues was one which chest leaders had relied upon from the beginning. Thus, the president of a middle-western life insurance company was quoted as saying, "It strikes me as being so obvious that the public obligations of the community must be borne by the wealth-producing elements of the community that no business enterprise has the right to expect immunity." But not all business executives demonstrated such conviction and enthusiasm. For H. C. Atkins, president of the E. D. Atkins Company of Indianapolis, it was more a case of follow-the-leader:

> We operate ten branch houses in various parts of the country and naturally are in the same category that a lot of other people are. We are obliged to make our contributions from those branches where community funds are in vogue.[26]

Pressure, rather than persuasion, seems to have been the effective technique in this instance.

Other statements, emphasizing company benefits from social services, comparing voluntary gifts with contributions through taxes, suggesting that without private support governmental services and taxes would necessarily increase, stressing the efficiency and businesslike character of the community chest approach, and underlining the stake

[25] Paul A. Schoellkopf, "The Corporation and Its Community," *Survey*, LX (1 September 1928), 540ff.

[26] UCFCA, *Minutes*, I, Memorandum of the Meeting of the Advisory Committee, 11 June 1928; 8 October 1928; Meeting of the Special Corporations Committee, 17 October 1928. ACCC, "Corporation Support of Community Welfare," 26 September 1928.

of a corporation in the social conditions surrounding its properties, were issued from time to time. Every effort was being made to bring companies across the nation to accept a common policy.

Henry D. Sharpe of Brown and Sharpe, a Providence machine tool firm, addressed himself in 1929 to the problem of the large corporation or chain system with outlets in many communities. The management of such a concern found itself in a difficult relationship to the communities in which its branches were located. Corporate officers might feel a conflict between their obligation to the owners for dividends and their genuine desire to support the well-being of the towns in which they carried on their operations. "Directors may think of themselves merely as trustees of property interests and ignore the social conditions of the community from which their corporation draws its labor and its patronage," Sharpe conceded. But he insisted, "Not at all in an invidious sense, this is a narrow conception of corporate responsibility." The community chest's approach to regularized, efficient giving had encouraged management to find its proper role in relationship to society's needs. "For the modern corporation is really seeking to do its proper part in every community in which it operates." ACCC headquarters saw to it that such statements were called to the attention of local chests.[27]

BIG BUSINESS AND THE CHESTS: THE WILLIAMS-CROXTON REPORT

Such techniques, helpful though they might be in dealing with smaller companies, failed to persuade the corporate giants upon which, in the long run, the scope of business philanthropy rested. As early as April, 1928, Allen Burns had written to Paul H. Davis of the San Francisco Community Chest that the flow of form letters urging amendment of the income tax laws in behalf of corporate contributions had revealed a potentially dangerous situation. A number of large companies, among them General Motors, General Electric, Westinghouse, Western Electric, Tidewater Oil, DuPont, Union Carbide,

---

[27] "Corporations and the Community Chest," by Clarence B. Randall, then (1929) vice-president of the Tri-State Telephone Company of St. Paul, UCFCA Papers; Henry D. Sharpe, "What Business Owes to the Town," *Nation's Business,* XVII (October, 1929), 47ff. J. H. Case in a letter to Ralph Blanchard, 27 September 1928, wrote of getting "some interested corporate official" to appear as author of an article inspired by the ACCC. UCFCA File 72: NBER, 1930.

U. S. Rubber, and Remington Rand, had set up a committee to consider corporate donations. What had been in the background at the Washington Conference now came into the open. Burns warned,

> The chairman of this committee has stated to me that these corporations will fix some policy of giving that will be followed by corporations generally; and that then supplicant charities will take what corporations give them or leave it. You realize that this situation is loaded for Community Chests. We must either meet it constructively or suffer the consequences.

The directors and staff of the ACCC proposed to meet the situation constructively. The election of officers at the annual meeting in May was carried out with this new challenge very much in mind. J. Herbert Case of the New York City Federal Reserve Bank was named president, and the special committee appointed to deal with the national corporation problem was composed of businessmen who it was thought would have the strongest possible influence with the large companies. "This is as big a job as we have ever tackled," Burns wrote, "and we want you [local chest officials] to know that it is under way." [28]

A review of the legal situation showed that the Internal Revenue Bureau had disallowed charitable deductions as ordinary and neces-

---

[28] Burns to Paul H. Davis, 4 April 1928, UCFCA File 72: Tax Deductions: "Chronological Record of ACCC Activity in Connection with the Problem of Corporation Support of Community Welfare Organizations"; UCFCA File 72: Corporation Giving—Study—NBER—Minutes and Sponsors, 1930.

The corporate representatives were working in cooperation with the American Management Association, with Mark M. Jones gathering information for them. See "Proposal for a Fact-Finding Study of the Relationship Between Corporation and Community Welfare Services," UCFCA File 72: Corporation Giving to Studies—NBER, 1930. Jones, an advisor to John D. Rockefeller, Jr., believed that "less than fifteen per cent of the money donated [to welfare agencies] could stand the test of responsible giving." Businessmen, he said, simply met requests, charged their contributions to the cost of doing business, forgot about them, and then repeated the process the following year without further investigation. *New York Times*, 6 October 1929. Jones set forth his views on the inadequacies of existing thought and practice concerning corporation contributions in a paper presented at a conference of financial executives sponsored by the American Management Association on 9 May 1929. A copy of this paper, entitled "Corporate Contributions to Community Welfare Agencies," is in the UCFCA File 72: Corporation Giving—Tax Deductions.

sary expenses of business. Lawyers advising the ACCC recommended that the issue be taken to the courts in the hope of winning a favorable ruling there. An alternative possibility was to urge an amendment to the income tax laws; but it seemed doubtful that Congress would wish to seem to be favoring corporations in an election year. Furthermore, it was felt that Congress, in any event, was likely to follow the advice of administration income tax authorities.[29]

Uncertain which way to turn, Case and Burns laid their problem before Owen D. Young in July, 1928. They stressed the common desire of the corporations and the chests to work out a satisfactory formula for giving. Despite progress toward mutual understanding at the Washington conference, differences still existed over the status of chain stores and other wholesale or retail distributing agencies, and a general agreement on standards for apportioning contributions had not been reached. Some large corporations felt so beleaguered by requests that they were threatening to reduce or abandon their contributions; one company had reported over a thousand gifts to charities, chests, and similar agencies in the course of a single year. On the other hand, some branch offices and outlets derived as much benefit from community services as did local companies and it seemed only fair for them to share in the support of these services. Only a series of conferences between chest and corporate officials based upon the fullest knowledge of all the facts, Burns and Case thought, could resolve the different points of view.[30]

The meeting with Young produced agreement that further discussion was necessary and that a preliminary fact-finding study would be helpful. The subject was considered further by the ACCC directors in the course of the autumn. It was thought unwise for the community chest organization, as an interested party, to conduct the fact-finding study itself. Rather, an independent agency should assemble data "for a calm and dispassionate consideration of the matter by a conference made up of executives and directors of corporations and directors of community chests." Case and Burns thereupon requested the National Bureau of Economic Research to undertake such a study, to be completed in time for a second Washington conference in 1930. Case wrote to Wesley C. Mitchell, NBER director, setting the study in the perspective of changing economic institutions and relationships:

[29] Burns to Paul H. Davis, 4 April 1928, UCFCA File 72: Tax Deductions.

[30] UCFCA File 72: Corporation Giving—Tax Deductions, "Memorandum on Corporation Responsibility for Mr. Case," dated 24 July 1928, probably by Allen Burns. Case and Burns met with Young on July 25; "Chronological Record. . . ."

> As a bigger and bigger proportion of wealth, especially undis-
> tributed earnings, comes under corporate control, the urgency
> increases of inquiring whether wealth in its newer forms
> shares in meeting community welfare needs in proportion to
> . . . wealth in its more personal forms.[31]

Final approval came from the directors of the ACCC early in January, 1929. As defined in the formal proposal ratified by the board, the
project was to include data on corporation contribution practices, the
grounds upon which corporations based their support, comparisons of
amounts contributed by corporations to private welfare agencies and
taxes paid in support of governmental welfare services, and the "practice and results of deduction of payments to welfare agencies from
corporation income tax returns." [32]

Having accepted the proposal for an independent survey, Allen
Burns then surprisingly recommended that the study be directed by a
member of the ACCC's own staff, Pierce Williams. Williams was a
capable worker who had recently been loaned by the national office to
Washington, D.C., to help develop a federation of charities there; but
his assignment to the NBER study was certain to raise questions regarding its objectivity. Burns was aware of this possibility and left
the decision to the discretion of Wesley Mitchell and his NBER associates.[33] Whether for lack of other available researchers, out of respect for Williams's ability and integrity, or for other reasons, Mitchell
found the recommendation acceptable. Williams left the ACCC office
and joined the research staff of the National Bureau. Together with
Frederick E. Croxton, a staff economist for NBER, he directed the research which, published in 1930 under the title *Corporation Contributions to Organized Community Welfare Services,* was the first systematic study of the subject.

The ACCC had also agreed to raise funds to support the research
and to enlist a board of sponsors, which could secure access to infor-

---

[31] Case to W. C. Mitchell, Director, National Bureau of Economic Research,
20 November 1928; W. C. Mitchell to Burns, 21 November, 1928; Burns to E. F.
Gay, 4 December 1928, all in UCFCA File 72: Corporation Giving to Studies—
NBER 1930—Correspondence. Apparently the suggestion for study by an independent agency came from Young.

[32] "Proposal for a Fact-Finding Study of the Relationship Between Corporations
and Community Welfare Services." UCFCA File 72: Corporation Giving to Studies
—NBER, 1930.

[33] Burns to Wesley C. Mitchell, 20 November 1928. UCFCA File 72: NBER,
1930.

mation corporations might otherwise to be reluctant to disclose. Interested national corporations, those which had already led in pushing for answers to the problem of contributions, agreed to provide a major share of the funds. They were thus offered a substitute for their own projected study of the contributions problem. They were also, to a degree, committed to act upon the findings of the ACCC–NBER study. Local community chests and welfare federations and companies working with them also contributed—making it a joint, rather than a purely business-financed, undertaking. The money seems to have been raised without great difficulty.[34]

The problems of selecting sponsors and of securing corporate acceptance of them were more difficult. Sponsors were chosen largely from among those executives who either already were active in community chest affairs or whose companies were among those toward which the study was directed. Among the former group were J. Herbert Case, president of the ACCC, Frederic R. Kellogg, William Cooper Procter, Paul A. Schoellkopf, and Henry D. Sharpe. Among the latter were A. J. Byles, president of Tidewater Oil Company; Lammot DuPont of General Motors; Walter Gifford of AT & T; Clarence J. Hicks of Standard Oil (New Jersey); Julius Rosenwald of Sears, Roebuck; Gerard Swope of General Electric; and Paul D. Cravath of Westinghouse.[35]

Even with such a star-studded group of business sponsors, the study encountered some difficulty in gaining access to company records. Pierce Williams, reporting to Allen Burns in March, 1929, on a number of interviews with top corporation executives, said that Walter Gifford had been friendly and cooperative, but discouraging. "He believes that the facts disclosed will lead corporations to decrease their payments to welfare organizations because of the large totals such a study will reveal." H. T. Parsons of the F. W. Woolworth Company had agreed to give Williams the information he desired but not to support the study financially. The Woolworth company had developed its own policy and did not feel the need of a study; nevertheless, C. S.

34 UCFCA File 72: Corporation Giving to Studies—NBER, 1930, memorandum dated 1 May 1929. Major contributors listed include: American Telephone and Telegraph Company ($2500), General Electric ($2500), General Motors ($750), John D. Rockefeller, Jr. ($5000), Sears, Roebuck and Company ($2500), Standard Oil of New Jersey ($1000), Tidewater Oil Company ($1000), and five Cincinnati corporations listed as giving a total of $5000.

35 The full list of sponsors appears in Williams and Croxton, *Corporate Contributions*, 10.

Woolworth became a sponsor. Paul Cravath of Westinghouse, chairman of the sponsoring board, had agreed to cooperate fully. He felt the need of a basis in economic principle, Williams reported, to justify the large sums which his company was contributing to welfare work. A lawyer, Cravath apparently regarded the issue of the legal status of corporate donations as little more than a ruse—"excuses with no substantial validity." Williams found Thomas Lamont of J. P. Morgan and Company noncommittal toward the whole enterprise. On the other hand, W. F. Merrill of Remington Rand had favored the study despite the fact his company did not contribute to philanthropic causes. Merrill hoped that a basis could be found on which to justify corporate giving in the future.[36]

Williams sensed an "attitude of suspicion" in certain quarters, he told Burns:

> They pretend to believe that the whole study is a set up job on the part of the community chests, aiming at getting information from corporations as to how much they are giving, and where, in order to make out a case for more generous giving on their part.

A *Saturday Evening Post* article, quoting Paul Cravath in terms which suggested that his position favoring corporate contributions had already become solidified, had further aroused suspicions. Williams recognized the importance of conducting the study in a fashion which would leave no doubt as to its validity and objectivity. *"From tomor-*

---

[36] Pierce Williams, "Progress Report," 17 March 1929, in UCFCA File 72: Study—Progress Reports. At an April meeting of the Board of Sponsors, Julius Rosenwald said that Sears, Roebuck was "non-plussed" by the number of appeals it received and hoped that a "scientific" basis for giving might result from the study. Gifford explained corporation giving primarily as "a defence against bad will and a result of pressure." C. S. Williams of New Orleans also referred to the public relations value of corporate giving. He stated that Standard Oil (Louisiana) "was being popularly supported as against the present Government's attacks because of the company's liberality in participating in community affairs, particularly welfare services." UCFCA File 71: Corporation Giving—Study, NBER—Minutes and Sponsors, 1930.

S. I. Whitestone of General Electric wrote to Paul Cravath to complain that some community chests were pressuring companies to contribute simply by virtue of the fact that the company's products were used in the community. Whitestone questioned the justice of approaching corporations which did not "maintain a factory, warehouse or service shop, or even a large sales office" in a community. S. I. Whitestone to Paul Cravath, 22 January 1929, UCFCA File 72: Corporation Giving—Tax Deductions.

row on," he wrote, *"I want to be in a position to say that the ACCC, after taking the initiative in launching the study and getting it financed, is withdrawing from the study itself, and leaving it entirely to the Bureau to carry on."* Burns, meanwhile, had encountered difficulty in securing the sponsorship of some businessmen whom he had hoped to interest in the project. Recognizing the dangers to which Williams had referred, he told Wesley Mitchell that some of the community chest representatives would withdraw from the board of sponsors in order that community chest interests might not appear to be overrepresented.[37]

When it appeared in 1930, the first year of the Great Depression, the Williams-Croxton report seemed to have overcome many of the obstacles and resistances encountered at its inception. Not only did it reveal the very considerable growth in the number of community chests and in the contributions of business corporations to the support of chest agencies, but significant variations in practice and experience were thoroughly documented. Differences between cities, between industries, and between chest and nonchest fund-raising drives were recorded. Variations between cities corresponded, roughly, with the degree to which industrial enterprises dominated the community. Thus in 1929, Pontiac, Michigan, showed the highest proportion of chest funds coming from corporations, 58.2 per cent, while Morristown, New Jersey, had the lowest proportion, only 1.9 per cent. The 1929 chest returns showed manufacturing corporations contributing the largest share of corporation funds, 47.2 per cent. Wholesale and retail trade, banks and trust companies, public utilities other than transportation, insurance companies, and railroads followed in that order, with 22.4 per cent, 10.7 per cent, 6.1 per cent, 1.5 per cent, and 0.3 per cent, respectively. Significantly, Williams and Croxton also found that the trend toward large-scale enterprise, which underlay the whole movement toward corporate giving and similar expressions of the new social role of business, was manifest in the pattern of corporate contributions. Thus, of 119 chests studied, half of the total amount of corporate contributions had come from 16 per cent or less of the total number of firms giving. Finally, less complete information indicated that community chests had, on the whole, been more successful in securing corporate support than had nonchest charitable agencies.[38]

[37] Williams to Burns, 10 March 1929 (Williams's italics). UCFCA File 72: NBER, 1930. Memorandum of conference between Mitchell and Burns, 25 March 1929, UCFCA File 72: Corporate Giving—Progress Reports.

[38] Williams and Croxton, *Corporation Contributions*, 91–92, 137–38, 228–29, *passim.*

As might have been expected, Allen Burns and the ACCC staff had prepared to put the Williams-Croxton study to good use as soon as it became available. In the spring of 1930, J. Herbert Case reported to the ACCC Advisory Committee that copies of the study would be distributed by June. Paul Cravath wrote to influential business leaders in July, sending copies of the report "in the hope that it may help in solving some of your own corporation's problems. The purpose of the report," Cravath reminded them, "is to discover a basis in existing facts for developing fundamental principles to guide corporations in their relation to community welfare work." Data and suggestions based on the report were sent from New York to local chests during the summer and fall for use in the annual fund-raising drives. Suggestions of ways to use the report for comparing local performance with national averages and the records of other cities were forwarded, and local chest officials were also advised that the material could be used to demonstrate to the dubious that individual givers were not shifting the burden from their pocketbooks to corporate treasuries.[39]

At the local level, too, chest officials were eager to put the new ammunition to use. In Cleveland, Kenneth Sturges prepared a series of bulletins interpreting the NBER data for campaign workers. Railroads and insurance companies in particular had hitherto resisted chest appeals; they should now be made to recognize that they were out of step:

> Fund-supported welfare organizations in Cleveland are required to provide various services for railroad employees located here. It is a fair estimate that not less than 12,000 Cleveland residents are in the local employ of the principal railroads entering this city. We can make no logical differentiation between the obligation of railroads as employers and the obligation of manufacturers.[40]

[39] UCFCA *Minutes*, II, Advisory Committee, 27 May 1930; UCFCA File 72: Corporation Giving to Studies—NBER—1930; Use of Report; ACCC *News Bulletin*, 1 July 1930, and Bulletin No. 55, 15 October 1930.

[40] UCFCA File 72: Use of Report, "Bulletins to the Committee on Company Support," Cleveland Community Fund. In November, 1930, Mason City, Iowa, reported to national headquarters that the Williams-Croxton report had been useful in approaching local banks. ". . . With the corporation study plus the statement you sent out a number of months ago quoting the Comptroller of the Treasury with regard to Washington, D.C., banks, we were enabled to get a subscription of $750 from the principal bank and raised the other to $100, or a total of $850 from banks, where we had $50 last year. . . . This new bank

Plans for the projected 1930 Washington conference also had been laid by Burns. The Williams-Croxton study was to be used for detailed discussions with business delegates, grouped by trades or industries. Paul Cravath and Walter Gifford would be asked to speak on the central question, "Should Corporations Support Community Welfare Services?" A discussion of legal and tax aspects of corporate contributions would be led, it was hoped, by Frederic R. Kellogg, A. V. Cannon of the Cleveland Community Fund's Corporate Gifts Committee, and Secretary of the Treasury Ogden Mills. An address by Herbert Hoover would place the authority and prestige of the presidency behind the deliberations of the conference.

Ambitious plans these were, but their realization depended upon circumstances beyond the control of the ACCC. By December, 1930, it had become clear that most American business corporations confronted problems more serious and pressing than how to dispose of their surplus funds. The board of sponsors, meeting to discuss prospects for the conference, agreed that it could not be held until "more optimistic viewpoints could prevail." Six months later Allen Burns bowed to the obvious in his annual report, acknowledging that plans for action based upon the corporation study had been brought to a standstill by the Depression. With characteristic determination, however, he refused to admit defeat. "Experience and problems are accumulating," he wrote, "that will force further cooperative efforts for developing fundamental principles when business conditions are more auspicious." [41]

To a degree, Burns's confidence was justifiable. The progress which had been made in understanding and cooperation between business and community welfare agencies within a single decade was, indeed, remarkable. Some of the most effective advocates of corporate giving were by now being recruited from the ranks of business itself. In every chest city businessmen were actively participating in the planning and execution of fund raising. The sources of business resistance, as well as of acceptance, were being discovered; and effective mea-

---

subscription this year made up the other shrinkages which we had in corporate gifts due to consolidations and a few business failures." UCFCA File 72: Corporation Giving—Study, NBER—Minutes and Sponsors.

[41] UCFCA File 72: Corporation Giving—Study, NBER—Minutes and Sponsors, 1930, "Proposed Program for National Conference on Corporate Relations to Community Welfare," and "Minutes of Meeting of Program Committee of the Board of Sponsors, 16 December 1930." *Minutes,* II, Annual Report of the Executive Director, 13 June 1931, 197.

sures—again involving both business and chest officials—were being aimed at overcoming them. To be sure, there were many problems— conflicts of power, point of view, understanding, and interest—between businessmen and social workers. Evidence of such differences at the local level reached the national community chest office from time to time; only careful scrutiny of local chest records can reveal the full range of differences. Some social work leaders feared the intrusion of business values into their field and a consequent weighing of considerations of efficiency against those of humanity. If business domination of social agencies was by no means as complete as some have suspected, business influence probably did moderate and make "respectable" some of the less conservative tendencies of social work. The evidence is impressive, however, that influence or domination ran in two directions. Agency leaders could be at least equally ingenious in influencing and manipulating their business board members.[42]

Acceptable guidelines for policy and practice had not yet been agreed upon, but the issues were beginning to be definable. Mutual understanding was growing and leading to mutual accommodation. The future would show that community chests alone could not supply a full answer to the problem of business social responsibility; but the chest movement did provide a model for the type of relationship between business and other community interests which was to develop after the Second World War.

[42] Wilensky and Lebeaux, *Industrial Society and Social Welfare*, 272–82; Floyd Hunter, *Community Power Structure. A Study of Decision Making* (Chapel Hill, 1953).

6 · THE FIVE PER CENT AMENDMENT: 1929–1935

Depression converted the hopes of welfare leaders for increased support from business corporations into concern for a host of problems which they confronted with limited preparation and even fewer resources. Falling wages and rising unemployment created difficulties and tensions for individuals, families, and communities on a scale America had not previously known. The first lines of defense, local governments and voluntary agencies, crumbled rapidly under the attack. Private philanthropy had long emphasized preventive and "character-building" services rather than almsgiving. Thus, it was not equipped to deal with the circumstances of mass unemployment. The resources which local governments could mobilize for relief purposes, meanwhile, shriveled almost as fast as the demands upon them grew. President Hoover's insistence upon voluntary and local responsibility for relief of the needy virtually eliminated federal sources of assistance until the closing months of his term. The times called for heroic efforts to mobilize aid; but the best endeavors of thousands of social workers, businessmen, and other concerned citizens failed to keep pace with the unprecedented needs.

At the same time that business executives gave generously themselves and contributed through their companies to relief and welfare agencies, they succumbed to market pressures, often cutting back employment and wages and thus undoing with their left hands what they had done with their right.[1] Believing with President Hoover in

[1] For an overview of the relief situation, see Bremner, *American Philanthrophy*, 143–50. See also Beulah Amidon, "Toledo: A City the Auto Ran Over," *Survey*

the principles of self-help and limited government, many opposed federal relief expenditures. Yet few could be insensitive to the plight of their unfortunate fellow citizens. Strong motives, then, existed to maintain or, if possible, increase individual and corporate contributions to charitable agencies. "Either we must give generously and voluntarily to our social agencies," wrote Louis E. Kirstein, "or we must stop whining when government is forced to impose the added taxes required for succor until jobs appear." The striking of a new balance between private and public responsibility for social welfare had become a central problem for the American people. Neither businessmen nor welfare officials, however their perspectives might differ, could remain insensitive to the issue.

The effort to maintain company contributions to relief and welfare agencies may have been further stimulated by recognition that business leadership could not avoid responsibility for its role in creating the conditions which had unexpectedly culminated in depression. As Kirstein saw it,

> Insofar as responsibility can be assigned to any group for such a complex phenomenon as the present world-wide economic collapse, it seems to me that the business and financial group is plainly indicated. Insofar as an individualist society has any leadership, it is made up of business and financial men. . . . It is we who extol a system of free enterprise and individual initiative; it is we who have asked a mandate from the people for its continuance in the future.[2]

Graphic, LXIII (March, 1930), 656–57; *Survey*, LXIV (15 July 1930), 348; Paul U. Kellogg, "Security Next," *ibid.*, LXVII (1 December 1931), 349–50. Commenting on the discharge of large numbers of employees by Willys-Overland in Toledo in 1929, Kellogg noted, "The company could not have treated its real estate or its bonds or its taxes or its machinery that way."

The U. S. Chamber of Commerce opposed federal relief assistance and through its Civic Development Department attempted to help local organizations plan more effectively for local relief and reemployment. See *U. S. Chamber of Commerce Annual Report* (1932), 10.

2 Louis E. Kirstein, "The Challenge to Business Men," *Survey*, LXVIII (15 October 1932), 501–3. Kirstein, president of the Associated Jewish Philanthropies of Boston, was also a none-too-cordial partner of E. A. Filene. See Gerald W. Johnson, *Liberal's Progress*, for Kirstein's role in the displacement of Filene from the leadership of the Filene Company.

Harvard's Dean Wallace B. Donham observed a failure on the part of business leadership in the face of economic catastrophe, in sharp contrast to its social contributions. "Churches, universities, hospitals, charities and similar public institu-

Not many businessmen, of course, put the idea so plainly; many strongly repudiated it. Still, it is hard to avoid the conclusion that a sense of guilt must have mingled with sympathy in the minds of more than a few of those who struggled to cushion the impact of depression and unemployment on those more vulnerable than they.

For a brief period it seemed to the hopeful that those employers who in the bright yesterdays of the Twenties had tried to build security for their employees into their welfare programs through unemployment compensation or work stabilization plans might offer the leadership and example the country so badly needed. Thus, Gerard Swope's unemployment benefit plan for General Electric workers attracted particular attention and was seen by Frances Perkins as evidence of "industrial statesmanship of the first order." And the much-discussed Swope Plan for national economic stabilization through private economic planning was hailed in some quarters as a step forward by American business leadership, although it met with criticism elsewhere for concentrating too much power in private hands. *Survey* welcomed the Swope Plan as "the first public evidence . . . that an American industrial leader . . . was willing to identify himself with the slowly evolving idea that all business enterprise is affected with a public interest"; yet it warned that the plan was based upon "the common fallacy that public action and private initiative are antagonistic." [3]

For the most part, however, such efforts were destined to fail, the best of them turning out to be little more than valiant straws in the economic gale. "Nobody bothers much in these days about whether a corporation has a soul or not," wrote Arthur J. Todd.[4] The impo-

---

tions testify to the idealism, high standards of service, and generous support both in time and money of great numbers of businessmen. The war service of American business was outstanding in history. Yet this group now fails to rise to a great emergency in its own general field." "The Failure of Business Leadership and the Responsibility of the Universities," *HBR,* XI (July, 1933), 418–35. See also "Business Implications of Recent Social Trends," *Management Review,* XXII (May, 1933), 131–35; Cutlip, *Fund Raising,* 301.

[3] Robert W. Bruere, "The Swope Plan and After," *Survey,* LXVII (1 March 1932), 583–84ff. See also *ibid.,* LXIV (15 July 1930), 340, for Frances Perkins's evaluation; Beulah Amidon, "Out of the House of Magic," *ibid.,* LXV (1 December 1930), 245–46ff.; Beulah Amidon, "Fourteen Firms Go Pioneering," *ibid.,* LXV (15 March 1931), 654; and *Nation,* CXXXVII (15 November 1933), 554, for another critique of the Swope Plan as one which "would remove the last vestige of social control over business and let business run itself."

[4] Arthur J. Todd, "Corporations as Givers," *Survey,* LXIV (15 August 1930), 424–25. Albert G. Milbank, on the other hand, thought that one of the lessons taught by depression was that business *should* pay more attention to the state

tence of business leadership in the face of economic catastrophe discredited for the time being its claims to statesmanship. Yet, while such grandiose notions as the corporate soul and statesmanship were abandoned, the solid effort to build effective business-community relations through the community chest movement nevertheless went forward. Depression conditions served to remove many doubts as to the value of the association and provided new incentives to establish it on the firmest possible footing.

BUSINESS AND THE CHESTS IN THE DEPRESSION

Faced with an impossible task, the community chests performed the unlikely feat of raising the total contributions received during the early depression years from $73 million in 1929 to $101 million in 1932. But the pace could not be sustained, and in 1933 the figure dropped back to the $78 million level. Only after 1935 did contributions slowly begin to climb once more. Information showing the overall pattern of corporate contributions during these years is lacking; but there is evidence of a substantial, if uneven, increase to meet emergency appeals. A number of cities reported rises in total corporate giving or in gifts from designated trades or groups. Pittsburgh showed an increase in total corporation contributions from $147,000 in 1929 to $600,000 in 1935. A study of six national chain stores and ten large manufacturing companies showed overall increases, with some individual company decreases, between 1929 and 1934. Contributions from the chain stores rose from $149,000 to $189,000, while those of the manufacturing companies surveyed rose from $653,000 to $683,000.[5] Newton D. Baker announced to the National Conference

---

of its "soul." The achievements of the social welfare movement suggested to Milbank that business might better serve both its own ends and those of society "by broadening its purposes to include social objectives as well as profits." The profit motive was essential, to be sure, but overemphasis upon "maximum profits within a minimum time" had created "the feast-or-famine experiences of business which are noticeably finding less favor." Milbank, "Socialized Capitalism," 293–97.

[5] Andrews, *Corporation Giving*, 35–37. The fund-raising experience of the Salvation Army followed a pattern similar to that of the community chests. In 1929, $148,000 was contributed by the Trade and Industries Division. This figure was raised slightly to $149,000 in 1930, then fell off sharply to $106,000 in 1931. A strong recovery was made in 1933, however, when the Trade and Industries Division, headed by Thomas J. Watson, managed to raise $142,500. The Salvation Army included gifts from individual executives and employee groups as well as

on Welfare and Relief Mobilization, organized by the ACCC in 1932, that "known increases in individual corporation support have been so notable that undoubtedly an even larger proportion of community welfare finance has come from this source" than in the past.

Nevertheless, returns were spotty. The results of the 1933 chest campaigns were disappointing to Allen Burns, who revealed that large individual gifts had "shrunk painfully, particularly from what is described as the bankers and brokers division." At times, the discontinuance of the chests and the elimination or reorganization of agency programs seemed inevitable. Scanning each year's returns closely, Burns clutched at such encouragement as he could find. When the 1934 campaigns attained 88.5 per cent of their goal, as compared with 82.4 per cent the preceding year, he bravely announced that the chests had "stemmed the tide of retreat"; but the total amount collected was still less than in 1933.[6]

---

from companies under this division. JPJC Casebook 168: The Salvation Army.

The fund-raising effort of the Commerce and Industry Committee of the New York Emergency Unemployment Relief Committee was reported in 1931 as "rapidly running down, despite the work of U. S. Steel's Myron C. Taylor who headed the appeal to business and industry." JPJC Casebook 149: New York Emergency Unemployment Relief Committee.

At least one depression-born study of business leadership and its interests paid plaintive tribute to the sincerity of business motives. "It has been a sort of fad to abuse the American businessman, with his homely habits, his Main Street prejudices, his Rotarian playfulness, etc., but as one moves about the length and breadth of this country, there isn't a town, a city, a college, a scholarship fund, a community chest, a home for tubercular children, but what evidences concretely his communal interests." Bossard and Dewhurst, *University Education for Business*, 320.

[6] Baker's report is in UCFCA File 51: Washington Conference, 1932. Burns is quoted in *Survey*, LXXI (January, 1935), 18. See also JPJC Papers, "Community Fund of Baltimore—Daily Report, November 17–28, 1931"; *New York Times*, 7 June 1933, 19, and 19 June 1934, 23; Gertrude Springer, "The Chests in a Recovery Year," *Survey*, LXIX (October, 1933), 339–41; and *ibid.*, LXX (1 January 1934), 15; Cutlip, *Fund Raising*, 301ff.

A comparison of gifts to eight community chests in 1932 and 1933 by the John Price Jones Corporation showed small but significant decreases in the percentages contributed both by banks and by "firms and corporations." JPJC Papers, Case 4: "Giving . . . Corporations." A 1935 community chest report showed an overall decline of thirteen per cent in the volume of giving to chests between 1929 and 1935, while charity contributions reported on income tax returns were said to have decreased fifty-three per cent in the same period. *New York Times*, 4 August 1935, Section II, 6.

Depression conditions seem to have further stimulated the extension of the community chest approach to community welfare fund raising. From 353 in 1930

To "stem the tide" the officers and staff of the Association of Community Chests and Councils applied the same diligence and ingenuity which, in more prosperous years, they had devoted to promoting closer ties between business leadership and welfare work. Local chests took advantage of the new sensitivity to community needs and problems to make more information available to the public and to teach some of the ideas and principles guiding the activities of social agencies. New York headquarters continued to keep in touch both with local chest problems and with national conditions and organizations capable of strengthening the cause. Discouraging reports and requests for help from the field were met with whatever assistance or guidance the New York office could offer, and public statements of ACCC officials urged corporate and other donors not to relax their efforts. At its 1932 annual meeting the ACCC renewed its efforts to educate businessmen in their social responsibilities. In a session on "Corporations and Community Welfare," Percival Dodge of the Detroit Community Fund discussed company welfare programs for employees and "former employees," pointing out that even the best of them could not possibly meet the crisis posed by the depression.[7]

---

the number of chests in operation rose to 561 in 1940. Seeley and others, *Community Chest*, 27.

[7] *Comm. Chron.*, CXXXI (27 September 1930), 2004; Jeanette Gerson, "Industry Tours Social Work," LXVII (15 October 1931), 99–100; UCFCA Papers: Mobilization 1932—Corporation Committee; File 106: Speeches; ACCC News Bulletin, 21 April 1932.

A letter to Paul Schoellkopf from M. M. Paine, executive secretary of the Community Chest of Brunswick, New Jersey, and Vicinity, reported on 24 October 1932 a variety of responses to the current campaign. Insurance companies stated that they could not legally contribute although, Paine pointed out, they would have no choice but to pay the taxes which would be assessed if private resources failed to meet the need. The Western Union and Postal Telegraph companies had conceded the legality of contributions for the first time; but this was cold comfort, as they now said they were losing money and thus could not contribute. The Pennsylvania Railroad, said to be particularly anxious to avoid higher taxes, nevertheless refused a donation; and the American Express Company stated that it would be covered by any gift which the Pennsylvania Railroad might make— if any.

Paine urged efforts to secure a ruling from the Comptroller General which would deprive banks of the argument that contributions were illegal, an argument some continued to use despite the fact that many banks were in fact contributing to chests. "The stimulation you are giving to national corporations is of vital importance to us," Paine wrote, "and we are very grateful for all you are doing." See also Lester Milligan, of the Mason City Community Chest, to Allen Burns, 25 July 1935, UCFCA File 72: Services to Employees.

Anxious to support voluntary agencies, President Hoover in 1931 announced the creation of an Organization for Unemployment Relief, to carry on national promotion and coordination of charitable fund-raising activities. Its head was Walter S. Gifford, president of the American Telephone and Telegraph Company. Other business and social work leaders were invited to serve with Gifford. The ACCC, uniting the interests of a large number of social agencies, contributed strongly to the effort and shared whatever benefits the new organization's elaborate, nationwide campaign produced. Unfortunately, the opening of the campaign coincided with the announcement of ten per cent wage cuts by United States Steel, Ford, General Motors, and a number of other large corporations. Faced with such grim realities, the campaign had, at best, mixed results. It provided, however, the model for an annual national publicity program, tied to the fund-raising efforts of community chests, which came to be known as the Mobilization for Human Needs.[8]

For the 1932 Mobilization drive, Newton D. Baker and Paul Cravath, chairmen of the Committee on Business Corporations, which had been formed by the ACCC, prepared a letter "To National Corporations from the National Citizens Committee." Their appeal for funds was coupled with the suggestion that national corporations apportion their gifts among the various communities in which they maintained branches, another reference to a by-now familiar problem. Baker and Cravath urged that gifts by national corporations to local welfare and relief organizations might serve to forestall public criticism. To reinforce the pragmatic emphasis, they enclosed copies of a recent Internal Revenue Service ruling which broadened the right of corporations to deduct such contributions from taxable income.

This letter and a subsequent one from Baker alone were sent to a long list of companies including both past subscribers and nonsubscribers to community chest drives. Replies showed a large number of corporations in agreement with the position stated in the letter. Yet, insurance companies in particular denied their legal authority to contribute, and the Western Union and Postal Telegraph companies termed the Baker-Cravath proposal "inexpedient . . . impracticable." Lewis H. Brown, president of the Johns-Manville Corporation, on the other hand, replied, "Even though our corporation is showing losses instead of profits this year, we are increasing our total budgets for relief work." The board of directors of the P. Lorillard Company wrote

[8] Bremner, *American Philanthropy*, 145–50. For an interpretation of reaction to Gifford's appointment, see Norton E. Long, "Public Relations Policies of the Bell System," 19.

that $10,000 had been appropriated for relief in response to the appeal and asked to what agencies the money should be sent.[9]

With the coming of the New Deal in the spring of 1933, the federal government was at last participating actively in the administration of relief. Businessmen, private social agencies, and even government officials were anxious, for varying reasons, that the entire welfare burden not be relinquished to Washington. Accordingly, the Mobilization appeals in 1933, 1934, and 1935 laid particular stress upon individual responsibility, private philanthropy, and local agencies. The specter of federal domination was repeatedly called up to arouse Americans to even greater private effort. In the spring of 1934, John Stewart Bryan, who in 1933 had succeeded J. Herbert Case as president of the once again renamed Community Chests and Councils, Incorporated, warned against the temptation to relax private efforts in the face of expanding government activity: "If we take the easy way out, something deadening will happen to everyone that no efficiency can make up for." Later in the year, Newton D. Baker inaugurated the Mobilization drive by asserting, "Pressure has been brought to bear on the Federal Government to take over the support of all welfare work, but so far it has successfully resisted these efforts."

Managers of large corporations were beginning to see corporate philanthropy as a possible counterweight to the expanding role of government. Donaldson Brown, vice president of General Motors, stressed this point in the appeal he issued on behalf of the 1935 Mobilization campaign. Business must rally to the defense of private philanthropy, Brown urged. "We have abdicated much to the authority of government but not until human sympathy is bankrupt will men allow any government to deny it to them to render assistance to those afflicted by the misery and misfortune which society relentlessly grinds out for so many of its members."

Corporate, rather than individual, contributions now seemed the likeliest source of increased giving. Conditions were driving home the lesson of the interdependence of business and the community. It would, Brown argued,

> . . . be incongruous for a corporation to divorce itself from that common life in which it is a participant when its business and profit are directly concerned. There is a justifiable

[9] UCFCA Papers: Mobilization for Human Needs, 1932—Corporation Committee. The 1933 Mobilization for Human Needs had Newton D. Baker as its chairman, with Gifford, R. K. Mellon, Edward L. Ryerson, and other prominent businessmen on its Citizens Committee. Myron C. Taylor of United States Steel was chairman of the Commerce and Industry Division.

corporate reason for its maintaining a lively interest in social welfare. It, as in the case of an individual, can not hope to thrive if it is surrounded by degeneracy and squalor. There is no magic in a charter and the fiction of its corporate existence will avail it nothing if the community on which it and its employees so vitally depend should decay.[10]

This being true, it seemed to Brown "inconceivable" that stockholders should object to corporate assumption of a "just share of social obligation" and "the ordinary incidents of citizenship." "No one has ever seriously contended," he continued, "that a corporation should be exempt from the common burden of taxation—quite the contrary. With no greater force may one urge that it should be free from the duty of contributing to voluntary philanthropic objects which hold such constructive benefits to its employees."

Concerning the primacy of private and local responsibility for assistance to the needy, Brown found himself in agreement with President Franklin D. Roosevelt. Speaking for the Mobilization drives each year, the President, too, deplored the tendency to assume that the federal government was now prepared to accept total responsibility. He criticized the "buck-passers" who encouraged the shirking of responsibility by state and local governments. He spoke warmly of the personal touch associated with private charitable work. In 1935, although he had already demonstrated misgivings about tax deductions for corporate contributions, Roosevelt emphasized the obligation of industry to support private social welfare services, since "industrial life creates new problems of community living." Other New Deal spokesmen, too, underlined the continuing role of private welfare work.[11] Yet, inexorably, the circle of governmental responsibility continued to expand.

CORPORATE PHILANTHROPY AND THE LAW

Two legal issues hampered expansion of corporate donations to welfare agencies. The fundamental principle of management's right to

[10] New York Times, 12 June 1933, 4 August 1933, 20 August 1933, 7 December 1933, 14 April 1934 (Bryan), 10 September 1934 (Baker), 24 August 1935, 25 August 1935, 24 September 1935. For Donaldson Brown's letter, see UCFCA File 72: Standards. The 1933 meeting which named Bryan as president also appointed Allen T. Burns as executive director and Ralph H. Blanchard as assistant director of Community Chest and Councils, Inc. Newton D. Baker, "Can Uncle Sam Do Our Good Neighboring?" Saturday Evening Post, CCVII (13 October 1934), 23.

[11] New York Times, 9 September 1933, 7; 12 September 1934, 25; 23 October 1934, 1; 24 August 1935, 1; 21 October 1935, 5.

give away property technically belonging to corporate shareholders had never been fully clarified by legislation, despite the special emergency acts of the state legislatures during the First World War. Even the enactment of permanent legislation in many states in the course of the 1920s failed to satisfy leaders of national corporations. Judicial precedents did exist for the exercise of such managerial discretion; but the point remained a controversial one and, from the viewpoint of the chests, afforded an excuse behind which reluctant company officials and their lawyers could hide. Many executives who were willing to assume responsibility for corporate philanthropic contributions, however, argued that such gifts should be accorded tax deductible status like that allowed individual contributions by the Internal Revenue Act of 1917. It was obvious that such favored status could greatly encourage company giving.

Business spokesmen had been emphasizing this point for some years, while community chest officials had been attempting to solidify the legal basis for corporate giving. Immediately after the Washington conference of 1928, the ACCC board of directors had appointed a committee to work for an income tax amendment authorizing corporate deductions for contributions to charity. Pierce Williams, still a member of the ACCC staff, had met with representatives of the United States Chamber of Commerce in March, 1928, to discuss the problems involved. Williams learned that an amendment would probably be necessary, as tax officials felt there must be some indication in law "as to the maximum percentage any such payments shall bear to total expenses." He had further been advised to go directly to the tax officials to get their views and, if possible, persuade them to draft "the right kind of an amendment." The U.S. Chamber of Commerce had offered still more suggestions: it would be helpful to take along "an executive of some big corporation" and to be prepared to discuss specific examples of past disallowances. A conference with Senator Reed Smoot might then be in order, for discussion of general principles, not of specific provisions. If Smoot showed interest, however, it would be advisable to offer to draft a specific amendment.[12]

Following this program Williams, in October, 1928, conferred with an Internal Revenue Service official in Wichita. Administration officials were inclined to interpret the law quite literally, he found. A corporation could not legally give away its stockholders' money without any material consideration. "The object of the corporation is to

[12] Pierce Williams, "Memorandum of conversation with Mr. O'Connor of the U.S. Chamber of Commerce, 23 and 24 March 1928," UCFCA File 72: Corporation Giving—Tax Deductions.

add to the money its stockholders have given it." And if it were argued that corporate contributions were made with the expectation of benefit, then they could not be considered charitable. Payments to welfare services which helped sustain purchasing power or promote employee efficiency might, however, be considered advantageous to stockholders. Since it might be difficult to demonstrate conclusively the direct benefits required by this interpretation of the law, the situation remained obscure.

In view of this uncertainty, companies had resorted to a variety of devices to account for their contributions, Williams discovered. Some included charitable gifts under miscellaneous expenses, but this the government did not allow. Others were reportedly paying the money directly to a company official as salary; he then made the contributions and deducted them, together with his individual donations, for tax purposes. As the New York office continued to receive reports of company pressure on local chests to work for an income tax deduction, Allen Burns searched in every possible direction for a solution. Lawyers had advised, he wrote to a San Francisco chest leader, that "we need some corporation that is willing to be the 'goat' and take its case for such deductions before a United States Court in an appeal from the Internal Revenue authorities' decision." [13]

Bank officials were experiencing particular difficulty in justifying their charitable contributions. Williams had attended an informal conference between bank representatives and the Comptroller of the Currency in January, 1929, at which the problem was discussed. Both sides preferred to avoid a formal ruling on the subject, since it appeared that such a ruling would necessarily be unfavorable to the right of managers to "give away" the owners' money. Some banks were proposing to consider community chest payments as an item of advertising expense.

The chests, Williams had concluded, would do well to ask not for "charitable contributions" but instead for "payments" on the basis of benefits received. To strengthen this position, in the face of possible government or stockholder criticism, community chests

[13] "Notes of Conference Between Pierce Williams and Mr. North, Auditor in the Internal Revenue Office, Wichita, Kansas, October 30, 1928," UCFCA File 72: Corporation Giving—Tax Deductions; Burns to R. W. Smith, 20 September 1928, UCFCA File 72: Tax Deductions. Burns's characteristic probing for a solution to every new problem was revealed when he added, ". . . corporations have so much bigger questions with the income tax authorities that they doubtless will be slow to make this kind of a sacrifice hit. Perhaps the aggressive West can dig us up one."

were already gathering data which would demonstrate the extent to which company employees relied upon the various community services which the chests represented.[14]

The legality of corporate donations to charity was a crucial problem both for business and the chests. Chest leaders believed that there was more flexibility in the law than government officials had been willing to concede. Frederic R. Kellogg, therefore, prepared for distribution to local offices in 1929 a summary of the relevant court cases which placed the authority of management in a more favorable light. Stressing a gradual expansion of managerial powers by the courts—the ultimate interpreters of law—Kellogg wrote:

> If the act [of giving] is one . . . done for the purpose of serving corporate ends and is reasonably tributary to the promotion of those ends in a substantial and not a remote and fanciful sense, it may fairly be considered within the charter powers. The field of corporate action in respect to the exercise of incidental powers is thus, I think, an expanding one. As industrial conditions change, business methods must change with them and acts become permissible which at an earlier period would not have been considered to be within corporate power.[15]

Kellogg's position seemed to be upheld by a succession of administrative and court decisions during the early depression years. Cases involving the Corning Glass Company, the American Rolling Mill Company, and others found the courts ruling in 1930 in favor of company-built hospitals and corporate gifts to community agencies, provided an objective demonstration of benefit to the business could be made.[16]

At the same time, the ACCC continued its efforts to secure favorable administrative rulings, offering Kellogg's services without charge to the *Washington Star*, which, as the largest contributor to the Washington Community Chest, was pressing the Internal Revenue Bureau

[14] Pierce Williams's memorandum, 28 January 1929, UCFCA File 72: Corporation Giving—Standards—Banks; UCFCA File 72: Service to Employees, 1928.

[15] Frederic R. Kellogg's memorandum, 8 March 1929, UCFCA File 72: Standards—Banks.

[16] UCFCA File 72: Corporation Giving—Tax Deductions; A. V. Cannon to Kenneth Sturges, 14 January 1930; Allen T. Burns to Frederic R. Kellogg, 5 February 1930; ACCC Bulletin, 15 October 1930, UCFCA File 72: Use of Report Tables.

for approval of its practice of charging donations to the good will account. The *Star's* case was closely watched in New York, and Allen Burns even traveled to Washington to attend the hearings. Headquarters followed reports of other cases, too, noting with satisfaction reversals of earlier disallowances.[17]

Meanwhile, determined to overlook no possibility, chest leaders prepared to ask Congress for changes in the income tax law. In June, 1930, Kellogg and A. V. Cannon of Cleveland drafted an amendment authorizing corporate contributions under the same terms as those provided for individuals, who were already permitted to deduct donations up to fifteen per cent of their income. Kellogg saw this proposal essentially as a basis for bargaining. He questioned "whether the authorities . . . will approve such a broad amendment" and hoped that, "if the Bureau does not approve it, it will lead to the discussion and possible formulation of something else which they are willing to support." Shortly thereafter, Burns and J. Herbert Case, president of the ACCC, seized an opportunity to discuss the tax problem with Ogden Mills, under secretary of the Treasury, "almost as though," Burns gloated, "ripe fruit were falling into our laps." Mills proved sympathetic and recommended that a brief be prepared explaining the amendment proposed, the reasons for it, and providing additional background information; then a formal conference could be sought with Treasury officials. Kellogg continued to scrutinize recent court decisions for indications that a clear policy was emerging.[18]

Hoping for a clearer statement of government policy at the highest administrative levels, Case appealed to Secretary of the Treasury Andrew Mellon in the fall of 1930. Mellon, who strongly favored privately supported charities, agreed to back an amendment to the Revenue Act of 1928 that would permit corporations to deduct for tax purposes amounts up to fifteen per cent of net income that were granted for unemployment relief. Bills to accomplish this end were introduced in both houses of Congress in 1930 and again in 1932 but without success. These bills were intended as emergency measures, limited in the time period and in the type of assistance which they recognized as a basis for deductions. Efforts by Kellogg and Case to win Treasury support for a broader range of philanthropies than simply aid to the unemployed and for the removal of the restriction which limited gifts to

[17] UCFCA File 72: Tax Deductions; Frederic R. Kellogg to Allen Burns, 15 November 1932; UCFCA File 72: Corporation Giving—Study, NBER—1930.

[18] Kellogg to Burns, 19 June 1930; Burns to Kellogg, 27 August 1930; Kellogg to A. V. Cannon, 26 November 1930; UCFCA File 72: Tax Deductions.

the period of economic emergency proved fruitless. The ACCC board of directors accepted the Treasury's terms, obviously hoping to improve upon them at a later date; but no further legislative action occurred.[19]

Then, when the Internal Revenue Bureau in 1932 issued a ruling which upheld contributions "if the taxpayer corporation can show it reasonably contemplated a financial return commensurate with the payment and was motivated by such expectation of a financial return in making the payment," success for a moment seemed within grasp. Compared with the Bureau's previous insistence upon a showing of "direct benefits," this was a considerable liberalization. But it was not enough. A number of important company executives continued to insist upon an amendment. Responses to the 1932 Mobilization for Human Needs brought evidence of unremitting corporate pressure. C. B. Tuttle, treasurer of the S. S. Kresge Company, wrote Cravath that tax officials could always find "a loophole through which to argue every contribution made and when we exercise every care in filing correct returns, they in turn seemingly attempt to make it continuously hard for us." Jesse Straus of R. H. Macy and Company agreed: "The rule of the Bureau of Internal Revenue enclosed in your letter is not sufficiently definite to encourage liberality in corporate gifts. . . . The statute should be changed . . . and your National Committee should have the influence to bring about that change." [20]

Rulings favorable and unfavorable to community chest interests meanwhile continued to issue from courts and administrative agencies as companies tried to account for their gifts most advantageously. In September, 1932, the Interstate Commerce Commission held that the

[19] See ACCC News Bulletin, 20 December 1930, UCFCA File 72: Tax Deductions—Rulings, for the background of House Joint Resolution 443, 71 Congress, 3rd Session. Kellogg to Case, 4 February 1932; Case to A. A. Ballantine, under secretary of the Treasury, 10 February 1932; Ballantine to Case, 18 February 1932; Ballantine to Kellogg, 24 March 1932, all in UCFCA File 72: Tax Deductions; UCFCA Minutes, VII, Board of Directors, 3 March 1932. See also Survey, LXVI (15 January 1932), 406.

As early as 1921 a provision authorizing deductions for corporate donations was included in a revenue bill which passed the House of Representatives. It was rejected by the Senate. Similar attempts to win congressional support had occurred from time to time in the course of the decade. Beardsley Ruml, with the collaboration of Theodore Geiger, The Manual of Corporate Giving (Kingsport, Tennessee, 1952), 35.

[20] See Survey, LXVIII (15 November 1932), 579–80, for a discussion of the Bureau's ruling. See UCFCA File 72: Tax Deductions; Mobilization for Human Needs, 1932—Corporations Committee, for replies to the MHN appeal.

New York Telephone Company had acted improperly in charging to operating expenses its $75,000 contribution to the Unemployment Relief Fund of New York City. The ACCC had joined the telephone company in arguing this case, hoping for a reversal of a previous ruling by the New York Public Service Commission. In August, 1934, the Public Service Commission approved gifts by five public utility companies. In December of the same year word was received that the Deputy Comptroller General had ruled "that directors of a national bank have no authority to use the profits of the bank for any purpose except to provide for losses, expenses, and the payment of dividends." Such differences and discrepancies in official policy fostered confusion and uncertainty in both business and chest circles.

The United States Supreme Court further threatened the status of corporate contributions when it held, in a 1934 case, that the Old Mission Portland Cement Company had erred in deducting charitable contributions where no evidence was submitted to show direct benefit to the company other than good will. Burns and Newton D. Baker feared this new decision would end efforts to win more favorable consideration from the Internal Revenue authorities. At about the same time Kellogg received word from Minneapolis that General Mills was considering an appeal of a disallowance. But the company's lawyer feared, wrote O. F. Bradley of the Minneapolis Community Fund, "that the company would not wish to place on the printed record the information about the number of employees and their families served because of the possible implication that it was the result of a low wage policy." Bradley reported that General Mills was paying reasonable wages, but the company feared that "inference to the contrary might be drawn from these facts." [21]

[21] *New York Times*, 30 September 1932; see *Business Week*, 12 October 1932, 6–7, for New York Telephone Company; see *New York Herald Tribune*, 1 August 1935, for utility companies ruling. Welfare officials had their own qualms about the New York Telephone Company's practice of "hiding" charitable contributions in the operating budget. Critics had already suggested that this might be a device used to pad expenses as a basis for requesting a rate increase. *Business Week*, 8 June 1932, 14.

The Deputy Comptroller General, George Lyon, discussed the bank directors' powers in a letter to A. T. Gibbs, President, First National Bank and Trust Company, Montclair, New Jersey, 24 October 1934. This letter and additional correspondence concerning it is in UCFCA File 72: Corporation Giving— Standards—Banks. For Old Mission Portland Cement Company v. Helvering (79 U.S. Reports 1934, p. 70), see Allen Burns to Ray Smith, San Francisco Community Chest, 13 June 1935, File 72: Tax Deductions. For General Mills, see O. F. Bradley to Frederic R. Kellogg, in the same file.

Another 1934 Supreme Court decision, dealing with price fixing in the milk

ACCC leaders had originally preferred to secure clarification of the legal status of company giving by administrative or judicial interpretation, rather than through legislation. They had believed that this approach would produce the desired result more quickly. Now the premise was proving difficult to defend. Four years' efforts had produced some progress but still no clear and satisfactory definition of corporate powers. Events moved more rapidly elsewhere: during 1933 and 1934, as the depression deepened and the new Roosevelt administration launched a series of dramatic programs aimed at reversing the economic tides and relieving social distress, chest leaders grew increasingly impatient at their inabilty to resolve their problem. If the long-desired goal were to be reached, a new approach seemed to be called for.

In 1934 Frederic R. Kellogg assumed the presidency of the Community Chests and Councils, Inc. Exploring the possibilities for legislative relief, Kellogg and Burns prepared a brief which Burns presented to the Senate Finance Committee in March, 1934. Returning to the original "broad" proposal, which put corporations on the same footing as individuals in deducting charitable contributions, Burns told the senators that 415 community chests had unanimously agreed that such a measure would be the most effective means of strengthening private welfare agencies. He cited President Roosevelt's support of private charity in his speech to Mobilization for Human Needs leaders the previous fall. "Adoption of the proposal now made," Burns argued, "would be the best concrete evidence that the administration means to promote charitable contributions to its utmost." [22]

Having presented their case to Congress, Kellogg and Burns proceeded to press it upon the executive branch as well. Kellogg, who still believed that a satisfactory adjustment could be reached on the basis of existing law, approached Secretary of the Treasury Henry Morgenthau in the fall of 1934 but received no encouragement. Preparing for President Roosevelt's inauguration of the 1934 Mobilization

industry, affirmed the broad principle that any form of enterprise, under appropriate circumstances, might be "affected with a public interest" and thus subject to regulation. Nebbia v. New York, 291 U.S. Reports 502 (1934), discussed in Richard Eells, *The Meaning of Modern Business* (New York, 1960), 390. Thus, extension of governmental powers to regulate corporations paralleled corporate assertions of social responsibility.

[22] Kellogg to Burns, 21 December 1933; Burns to Kellogg, 9 March 1934, enclosing a brief and a proposed draft of an amendment "Submitted to the Finance Committee of the U.S. Senate, March, 1934, by Community Chests and Councils, Inc.," in CCC News Bulletin, March, 1934, UCFCA File 72: Revenue Act of 1935.

for Human Needs campaign, Burns wrote to Raymond Moley, the President's close advisor. A presidential endorsement of tax deductions for corporate giving, Burns urged, would be most helpful:

> I would do anything in my power, you know, to help the administration, but here is a possible act of the administration itself that would go far to make smoother sailing with the business world by a declaration of equity that business would understand. . . . As Owen Young has told us such [charitable] contributions are the most effective, economic, and non-paternalistic method for an employer to do welfare work.[23]

The suggestion was not accepted.

By the spring of 1935 chest leaders were desperate. In the light of the Supreme Court's adverse decision in the Old Mission Portland Cement Company case, administrative action alone to define the basis for corporate philanthropy no longer seemed adequate. Yet, the decision may have been the turning point. Burns wrote a San Francisco chest leader that it was "a blessing in disguise." It had adversely affected the General Electric Company's method of securing tax deductions and had "resulted in Gerard Swope's becoming militant to have something done about it." Swope's energy and influence, Burns hoped, would add new strength for the struggle. "He is to be our Mobilization chairman and is also the closest of the big businessmen to the President. . . ." [24]

Determined now to press for legislation, Burns once again wrote to Raymond Moley. It was of the utmost importance, he argued, that President Roosevelt support legislation putting corporations on the same basis as individuals in regard to charitable donations. Corporations contributed almost twenty-five per cent of community chest funds, Burns pointed out.

> As corporations possess more and more of the reserve wealth of the country their support and good-will is increasingly important. The main chance of private charity regaining its losses is to secure larger contributions from corporations. . . . Will you be good enough to throw any possible light on the

23 Burns to Moley, 15 October 1934, UCFCA File 72: Corporation Giving—Revenue Act of 1935.

24 Burns to John B. Dawson, New Haven Community Chest, 20 December 1933; Burns to Ray Smith, San Francisco Community Chest, 13 June 1935, UCFCA File 72: Tax Deductions. Burns to George W. Cobb, Montclair Community Chest, 10 December 1934; and "bb" to Cobb, 20 November 1934, File 72: Corporation Giving—Standards—Banks.

best course for us to follow in solving a problem which must be very small to the administration but of permanent importance to the private philanthropy of the country?

Without waiting for a reply, Burns proposed an alternative strategy to Moley three days later. Would it be possible, he asked, to join the income tax deduction proposal to the pending social security legislation? "Why would it not be logical, in view of what corporations will feel is a new additional burden, to exempt from taxation the amount of money they give to private charities?" [25]

Burns had struck upon a formula remarkably close to the solution eventually hammered out. In the meantime, however, the tax deduction issue had been projected into the midst of a bitter struggle between the President and the business community. For the moment, at least, the administration was in no mood for compromise.

THE DRIVE FOR THE FIVE PER CENT AMENDMENT

In the spring of 1935 what historians have characterized as the "Second New Deal" was rapidly emerging from the wreckage of the first. On May 27 the Supreme Court declared the NIRA unconstitutional, thus officially bringing to an end the already discredited experiment in joint government-business economic planning. A disillusioned President and an embittered business leadership had, in any event, begun to cross swords even earlier. The Wagner Act, Social Security Act, and the Public Utilities Holding Company Act were signed into law in July and August. Under growing pressure from disgruntled liberals and others, Roosevelt was casting off his ties with big business and steering his ship on a port tack. Raymond Moley, Allen Burns's connection with the President's official family, had already begun to lose favor and influence. Few, if any, of the events of the summer offered hope that a tax adjustment favoring corporation gifts to private philanthropies was in the making. Only the fact that President Roosevelt was insisting on major tax reforms opened the door the slightest crack to the amendment for which the community chests and their business backers had so long been contending. It was a very slight crack, indeed, but through it Allen Burns and his well-disciplined forces now pushed to their goal.[26]

[25] Burns to Moley, 2 April 1935 and 5 April 1935, UCFCA File 72: Corporation Giving—Revenue Act of 1935.

[26] The political situation in 1935 and the emergence of the Second New Deal are brilliantly described in Arthur M. Schlesinger, Jr., *The Politics of Upheaval,*

The Revenue Act of 1935 in spirit and intent was hostile to big business. It included a graduated corporate income tax and a tax on intercorporate dividends, aimed at holding companies. An undistributed profits tax and an inheritance tax had been part of the original proposal but were dropped along the way and replaced by an excess profits tax. Attacked as a "soak-the-rich" measure by businessmen, the package was defended by New Dealers as an effort to build justice and equality into the nation's tax structure. Such a measure was surely an unlikely host upon which to graft concessions to corporate benevolence.[27] Unpromising as it was, it was all that was available; and community chest officials were now convinced that their difficulties could no longer be allowed to continue unresolved. What might be the last chance to join government and business in support of private philanthropy could not be allowed to slip away.

From Allen Burns's New York office the word went out to local chests urging a massive letter-writing campaign. Burns himself, together with Kellogg, Swope, and John Stewart Bryan, traveled to Washington, seeing Treasury Department officials and congressmen. Invited to testify on behalf of the tax deduction feature before the House Ways and Means Committee, Kellogg reduced the requested exemption from fifteen to five per cent of taxable income. He stressed the growing dependence of private philanthropy upon corporate support. "Private charity cannot carry on without the help of the corporations to which it has become accustomed," he argued. The loss of funds to the government which the deduction would entail would be slight in comparison with the costs involved if private charity should fail. Ironically, while the chests pressed their effort to secure the tax deduction business had long demanded, the U. S. Chamber of Commerce, National Association of Manufacturers, and the other business organizations were loudly attacking the entire tax measure, while largely ignoring the deduction proposal.[28] Only chest leaders at the

Vol. III of his *The Age of Roosevelt* (Cambridge, Massachusetts, 1960). See also William Leuchtenburg, *Franklin D. Roosevelt and the New Deal, 1932–1940* (New York, 1963).

[27] Schlesinger, *Politics of Upheaval*, 325–34.

[28] Letters from Allen Burns to Community Chest executives, 13 July, 20 July, 25 July, and 28 July 1935, UCFCA File 72: Corporation Giving—Revenue Law. *New York Times*, 11 July 1935, 6; 12 July 1935, 8; 13 July 1935, 1; 14 July, 1935, 2. "Proposed Taxation of Individual and Corporate Income, Inheritances and Gifts. Hearings Before the Committee on Ways and Means," House of Representatives, 74 Congress, 1st Session, 10 July 1935; "Memorandum Submitted by Community Chests and Councils, Inc.," UCFCA File 72: Revenue Act, 1935.

moment of crisis, remained steadfast in pursuit of the original goal—
the building of a solid base for corporate philanthropy and, thus, for
private charity.

In a July report to his forces in the field, Allen Burns urged them to
maintain "all possible pressure" on Washington and noted that Harry
Hopkins, a former social worker now in charge of the New Deal's relief program, had promised to use his influence in behalf of the deduction measure. Bills incorporating the proposal, but limiting the corporate contributions which might be deducted to five per cent of total
annual income, had been introduced into both houses of Congress.
Soon, however, a new and formidable obstacle appeared. At a press
conference, President Roosevelt himself sharply opposed the five per
cent exemption. Saying that he "did not believe any company had a
right to buy good will . . . ," the President further questioned the
right of corporate officials to dispose of property legally belonging to
stockholders. Individuals should have the right to determine for themselves how their money should be distributed.[29]

Roosevelt's stand can not have come as a complete surprise to the
friends of the measure. In their discussions with administration
officials, after all, they had encountered a noticeably cooler reception
from the New Deal than from the preceding Hoover regime. Still, the
difference might have been accounted for by the great preoccupation
of the new administration with governmental relief and recovery programs. F.D.R. himself had seemed sympathetic in the past. As governor of New York, he had approved laws permitting corporations to
contribute to emergency relief. He had urged upon business the need
for a broader concept of its economic and social responsibilities. As
President, he had spoken repeatedly in favor of private and local initiative in the welfare field. Already plans were being laid for the annual Washington meeting of the community chests' Mobilization for

---

The minority report of the House Ways and Means Committee favored the
amendment. *Congressional Record,* 74 Congress, 1st Session, 12307.

In the course of discussion of the deductions amendment in the House, Representative Samuel B. Hill observed that corporate officials sometimes used the
trusteeship concept as an excuse to avoid actions they did not wish to take,
arguing that their responsibility to their shareholders inhibited their freedom.
On the other hand, when it suited their purposes they continued to fall back
upon the legal fiction of the corporation as a person. Pragmatic considerations
might well govern which set of symbols a businessman chose to use in considering his corporate role. *Ibid.,* 12302.

[29] Burns to local Community Chest officials, 20 July 1935, UCFCA File 72:
Corporation Giving—Revenue Law, 1935; *New York Times,* 25 July 1935, 27.

Human Needs, at which the President would welcome representatives of private social agencies from all over the nation and give his blessing and encouragement to their annual fund-raising effort.

Still, the mood of the White House was far from friendly to big business. Roosevelt may have seen the proposed amendment as an attempt to water down his wealth-equalization program, or he may have seized upon it as a bargaining device. More likely, however, his outburst expressed resentment at what he considered the lack of understanding and concern for the common good demonstrated by business opposition to his regime. Interestingly, the argument upon which the President leaned most heavily, defense of the rights of the individual stockholder, was an essentially conservative one. It ignored the collectivizing tendencies of the corporate economy and came down squarely on the side of rugged individualism in philanthropy.

In any event, the President's objection posed a serious threat to the tax deduction amendment. Allen Burns later admitted that it had created "havoc" among his forces. The *New York Times* reported that "inquiry at the Capital indicated . . . that no serious consideration has been given to the exemption proposal." Burns, Newton D. Baker, and Gerard Swope immediately conferred on measures to counteract the new danger. Swope, who remained on good terms with the President and who was chairman of the forthcoming Mobilization campaign, arranged a White House appointment for July 29. His mission was to persuade the President that his statement had damaged the outlook for the Mobilization and, if possible, to win a reversal of the position taken. Faced with the growing indifference, or distraction, of the business community, chest leaders could not allow government, too, to turn its back on their cause.

All the publicity resources and experience of the national community chest network were pressed into service. Chest personnel were once again urged to write their congressmen and attend the hearings. A statement was quickly released to the press, deploring the presidential position. Corporations were giving some $20 million annually to community chests in over four hundred cities, it was pointed out. With corporation support, chest contributions had decreased only thirteen per cent during the past five years, while net taxable income had shrunk fifty-seven per cent in the same period. To discriminate against corporate gifts would be "discrimination against the keystone of support for private social agencies." If corporate giving were discouraged, the burden upon the government would increase: "Preventive programs now undertaken only by private agencies, if abandoned, would eventually place on public agencies enormous institutional bills for the care of delinquency and disease which might have been prevented." [30]

Thereafter, events moved swiftly. On July 27 the President reiterated his opposition to a tax exemption for corporate gifts, while expressing approval in principle of the practice of corporate contributions. But other pressures were building up. The *New York Times* foresaw a major battle on the floor of Congress over the tax exemption issue, for "scores of Congress members continued to receive letters from individuals and charitable organizations urging the exemptions." Howard Cullman, president of New York's Beekman Street Hospital, wrote an open letter to President Roosevelt arguing that opposition to the measure "would undoubtedly result in the closing of many voluntary institutions." Many companies depended upon private hospitals to care for their employees, Cullman noted, and had perfectly valid business reasons, therefore, for contributing to the support of these agencies. "Unless the Federal, State, and municipal governments are ready to supplant this service, I can see no reason why contributions by the industrial concerns in this town are not a perfectly legitimate and necessary business expense," Cullman wrote.[31] He brushed over the President's distinction between the propriety of corporate giving and the necessity of a tax deduction.

On July 29 Gerard Swope emerged from his conference with President Roosevelt with the rallying cry, "Don't let up on the pressure for one moment. You have brought a great victory within reach." At Swope's request, Newton D. Baker went before the Senate Finance Committee to testify again on behalf of tax exemption. Couching his plea in somewhat different terms than those previously used, Baker argued that corporations should be encouraged in their duty to support the services necessary to deal with the social problems industry itself created:

> I deeply believe that the corporation has not only a right but a duty to be a good neighbor in the town in which its own employees live, and that there are obvious and direct benefits going to a corporation which makes a subscription to [the community chest]. . . .

[30] Burns to Community Chest officials, 29 July 1935, UCFCA File 72: Corporation Giving—Revenue Law, 1935; *New York Times*, 25 July 1935, 27.

[31] *New York Times*, 27 July 1935, 4; 28 July 1935, Section II, 2. See also a similar statement by David H. M. Pyle, president of the United Hospital Fund, *ibid.*, 16 July 1935, 9.

> I am not representing any corporations. . . . What I am
> trying to do is to get the help of the Senate to make corpora-
> tions contribute. I think they ought to contribute. I want
> them induced to contribute more by giving them the same op-
> portunity you give the private individual.

Baker's emphasis upon community benefits rather than corporate
privilege, added to a flood of mail supporting the tax deduction feature, was apparently persuasive. On August 2, another Burns report to
the local chests announced that the House committee had united behind the proposal and urged that fire now be concentrated on the Senate Finance Committee.[32]

Following Swope's advice to keep up the pressure, Burns issued a
public statement on August 4, charging that "President Roosevelt
deals a staggering blow when he not only disapproves of tax exempt
corporation giving, but denies the very obligation of corporations to
make gifts to private social work." But the battle, in reality, had already been won; only mopping-up operations remained. On that very
day the House passed the tax exemption amendment with "an overwhelming chorus of 'ayes.'" On August 6, the entire measure passed

[32] Burns to Community Chest officials, 2 August 1935, UCFCA File 72:
Corporation Giving—Revenue Act, 1935; "Newton D. Baker Argues the Case for
Exemption from Taxable Income of Corporate Gifts to Community Chests,"
excerpts from Baker testimony, 1 August 1935, UCFCA File 72: Revenue Law,
1935. Burns later stated that following Swope's meeting with the President there
was no further evidence of administration opposition to the tax exemption amendment. He described the controversy with Roosevelt as "one of those accidental
happenings which are part and parcel of the working of our democratic institutions." Allen T. Burns, "Tax Exemption of Corporate Gifts," *Survey*, LXI (September, 1935), 261–63. One can only speculate as to Roosevelt's motives for
relaxing his opposition. He may have been impressed by Swope's arguments, or
he may have been willing to concede the point in order to reduce opposition to
features he considered more vital. See *Business Week*, 10 August 1935, 7.
Kellogg's testimony before the House Ways and Means Committee had not
been particularly effective. Baker's appearance was more successful. He spoke as
representative not only for the Mobilization for Human Needs and the Community Chests and Councils, Inc., but also for a number of cooperating Catholic
and Jewish agencies. For this stand, the private welfare and philanthropic organizations had achieved a truly national front. See "Revenue Act of 1935,
Hearings before the Committee on Finance, United States Senate, 74th Congress,
1st Session, on H.R. 8974; An Act to Provide Revenue, Equalize Taxation and for
Other Purposes" (Washington, D.C.: U.S. Government Printing Office, 1935),
111–20.

the House. Anticipating Senate opposition, chest officials arranged a conference with Senator Edward P. Costigan of the Senate Finance Committee and Treasury Department representatives. Here, the case for privately supported philanthropy was again set forth and the importance of corporate contributions was documented. A showing was made, Burns reported, that the

> . . . community-wide nature of the chests' appeal and their representative structure has to an increasing extent influenced corporations to support these services . . . that these corporate gifts now represent about 25 per cent of the total contributions to chests and have played a very important part in stabilizing the financial structure of private social work. . . .[33]

On August 14 the Senate Finance Committee reported the bill favorably with the tax exemption feature intact. The following day the bill passed the Senate; and, after modifications in Conference which nevertheless left the five per cent deduction untouched, final congressional approval was reached on August 24.

Only one event marred the satisfaction with which the community chest leaders could enjoy their triumph. Frederic R. Kellogg had suffered a stroke the day after his appearance before Congress. On August 18, with victory in sight, he died. In a formal eulogy presented to the CCC annual meeting in September, Allen Burns reviewed the many contributions Kellogg had made to the success of the community chest movement. He had prepared pleas which had won favorable decisions in twenty-five cases involving both individual and corporate deductions, a service which, Burns flatly stated, "really made the community chest movement possible in this country." Although in declining health, Kellogg had continued in the work to the end. More than any individual except Burns himself, Kellogg had earned the tribute which Burns paid him: "Wherever the gospel of corporate responsibility for social ills is preached, this law shall be spoken of as a memorial to Frederic Kellogg." [34]

[33] Burns's statement is from the *New York Times,* 4 August 1935, Section II, 6; Burns, "Tax Exemption of Corporate Gifts." J. Prentice Murphy, "The Question of a Federal Tax on Company Gifts to Private Charities," 18 September 1935, is a summary of the actions leading to passage of the five per cent amendment. It includes a statement of issues discussed at the August 13 meeting. UCFCA File 72: Revenue Act, 1935.

[34] UCFCA *Minutes,* III, 47–50; cf. Cutlip, *Fund Raising,* 318–29.

FIRST FRUITS OF THE AMENDMENT

There was scarcely time for celebration or mourning. The fall Mobilization campaign was launched the day Congress completed its deliberations on the tax bill. President Roosevelt, concealing any embarrassment he may have felt toward the Mobilization leaders—many of whom had come to Washington to lobby for the amendment he had opposed—spoke of the "obligation of industry above all other elements of the community to support social welfare services," since, as Baker had emphasized to the congressmen, "industrial life creates new problems of community living." Roosevelt made no mention of the tax bill, but other speakers did. Swope now could assert that Congress had removed the last doubt concerning the legality of corporate donations; improving business conditions, too, he thought, offered encouragement for a successful campaign. A National Citizens Committee, including the usual group of prominent business leaders, was announced; and a conference of leaders in Washington was set for 23 and 24 September.[35]

New problems presented themselves to chest officials for the new campaign. Although the five per cent exemption had been achieved, business was smarting under the new tax law. Furthermore, the passage of the Social Security Act, it was feared, might lead some to believe that the need for private charities was diminished. Despite confident talk of the new selling point provided by the tax exemption, chest leaders privately did not expect greatly increased giving. As reports began to come in, it appeared that contributions were running slightly ahead of the previous year. In February, 1936, *Survey* reported an overall increase of 4 per cent, bringing the national campaign to 91.2 per cent of its goal. This was less than the 12 per cent increase which had been hoped for, however, and left total chest collections still 5 per cent below the level achieved in 1929. Nonetheless, for the first time in three years an increase in total giving had been recorded, and a goal long-sought through seven years of effort had been achieved.[36]

[35] *New York Times,* 24 August 1935, 1, 3; *ibid.,* 26 August 1935, 17.

[36] *New York Times,* 23 September, 25 and 28 October, 8 December 1935; *Survey,* LXXI (October, 1935), 298, and LXII (February, 1936), 49. Memoranda advising local chests on the relationship of the new income tax law to corporate deductions were sent from national CCC headquarters, 8 and 25 October 1935, UCFCA File 72: Revenue Act, 1935.

Both before and after passage of the 1935 Revenue Act, community chest

What did passage of the five per cent amendment actually mean, to corporations, to community chests, to the American people? Was it a triumph for private philanthropy, a windfall for corporate treasuries, an alternative to socialism? In fact, it was all, and none, of these. Certainly it brought no immediate flood of treasure into philanthropic coffers. Corporate contributions hovered between $30 million and $33 million yearly from 1936 to 1939, and fluctuations mirrored shifting economic conditions more than any steady growth in business giving. Not until 1940 did the return of favorable business conditions foster significant increases in corporate donations.[37]

The five per cent amendment, long sought by business and chest leaders, passed in conjunction with some of the most sweeping and fundamental New Deal reform legislation. Much as President Roosevelt's tax bill and the Social Security Act of 1935 tapped corporate surpluses for the general welfare, so the tax exemption for corporate contributions directed some of those same funds into private philanthropic channels. A mixed economy was thus strengthened in welfare as well as in production and distribution. And those who controlled the fortunes of large business enterprises were further encouraged to play active roles in allocating those resources to social ends.

---

officials worked diligently at the state level for complementary legislation. Corporate contributions were authorized by New York in 1918 and by Illinois and Ohio in successive years. By 1935, Tennessee, New Jersey, Massachusetts, and Michigan had joined the list. Passage of the federal law encouraged still more states to act. By 1951, twenty-six states and the Territory of Hawaii had permissive statutes. Andrews, *Corporation Giving*, 233–35.

[37] *Ibid.*, 42–44. With wartime and postwar prosperity, total corporate contributions increased strikingly, from $38 million in 1940 to $223 million in 1949. Such generosity, to be sure, was encouraged by a severe excess profits tax. When the tax was repealed at the end of the war, corporate giving dropped noticeably yet remained significantly above prewar levels. At no time, however, have corporate contributions approached the five per cent level officially encouraged by statute. In this respect, corporate generosity may have been overestimated by enthusiastic welfare workers. On the other hand, corporate gifts, while not constituting an extraordinary share of corporate profits, have become a major source of support for private educational and cultural, as well as welfare, institutions in America.

7 ▪ BUSINESS AND SOCIETY: THE YEARS OF DEPRESSION AND WAR, 1935–1945

The achievement of the five per cent amendment was a bright spot in what from the perspective of business-community relations was a dark decade. The strains of continuing depression, the challenge of the New Deal to business freedom and power, and other evidences of popular disenchantment with managerial leadership combined to foster a touchy defensiveness among businessmen. The times did not encourage ambitious schemes of social amelioration promoted by enlightened and socially responsible corporations. Rather, they seemed to call for determined business efforts to retain a beachhead from which, eventually, economic initiative and public acceptance might be regained. Even the legal sanction for corporate philanthropy, upon which community chest leaders had counted so heavily, opened no magic doors. Instead, it transferred attention to a host of details concerning the proper scope for company giving—each containing its own potential for disagreement.

Gradually, however, experience, coupled with slowly improving economic conditions, laid the foundations for future growth. With the approach of the Second World War, business confidence and a more optimistic view of social prospects grew side by side. Only the return of peace and domestic stability would reveal what business had learned from the depression about its social role and relations.

174

STANDARDS FOR COMPANY GIVING

In 1935, community chest leaders, flushed with their hard-won victory, turned with new hope to the 1935 Mobilization for Human Needs. Gerard Swope, chairman of the campaign, appealed to corporations to increase their support of chest agencies—now urging augmented giving because of the tax advantage, as well as the benefit to communities, employees, and companies. He encountered a response which was far from cheering. At a meeting with Detroit businessmen, Swope was photographed with Henry Ford; but the cordial atmosphere which the pictures suggested was less than complete. The Detroiters, it soon appeared, had their own ideas of the proper scope of corporate giving. Ford himself had never been a proponent of company philanthropy. Now in his declining years, he was faced with social and economic problems he did not comprehend. Others were not lacking for ideas, but their notions of the corporate share in private philanthropy proved more modest than Swope and chest officials had anticipated.[1]

Although the reports coming into Allen Burns's office from local chests were mixed, their overall tenor was disappointing. Little change was perceptible in the pattern of business giving. From Kansas City, C. W. Pfeiffer wrote that the largest corporate contributors seemed to have "got their support definitely pegged. Out of a certain feeling of loyalty they don't want to cut, but on the other hand, in spite of increased earnings and other factors, they are unwilling to increase it." The Los Angeles chest actually suffered a $31,000 decrease from the previous year's corporate total; a single large decrease had

---

[1] Gerard Swope to the heads of a number of large corporations, 16 September 1935, UCFCA File 73: Corporation Giving and Tax Deductions; Community Chests and Councils News Bulletin, November, 1935.

Swope's biographer reports the following conversation with Ford and Swope at their Detroit meeting:

"Swope, you know I don't agree with this thing you are doing."

"Well, Mr. Ford, how would you do it?" Swope asked.

"That's the worst of it. I don't know."

Loth, Swope of G.E., 253.

In 1931, the New York Times had noted a report that twenty per cent of Detroit's welfare costs could be attributed to employees laid off by the Ford Motor Company. Even then, Henry Ford had clung to his rule against welfare and charitable contributions. See Charles R. Walker, "Down and Out in Detroit," in Charles A. Beard, ed., America Faces the Future (Cambridge, Massachusetts, 1932), 82.

canceled the effect of several small gains. A number of companies doing business in the millions of dollars annually continued to make donations averaging $100 each. Straining to be optimistic, the Los Angeles report speculated that losses might have been greater without the tax deduction.

Similar gloomy news came from Omaha, St. Louis, Denver, Dayton, Washington, D. C., Pittsburgh, Newark, Detroit, and elsewhere. From Cleveland the word was only slightly less discouraging. Twenty-five per cent of the leading firms had, indeed, increased their contributions; but the tax deduction privilege seemed to have been only a minor consideration. In the thinking of most businessmen, higher taxes loomed larger than did the untested five per cent deduction. St. Paul, however, noted an increase of twelve and one-half per cent in total corporate gifts, "directly due to the deductibility of corporate gifts as well as to a 10 per cent increase in our goal." Some encouragement came, too, from Richmond, Columbus, and Indianapolis. Scanning the pattern of returns, however, Allen Burns knew, if he had not already suspected, that his work was not completed.[2]

The impression of unity and harmony which chest and business leaders had cultivated for the sake of the five per cent amendment was, in part, illusory. Despite the insistence of business spokesmen upon a supposed identity of interests uniting the objectives of management with those of labor, stockholders, customers, or the community at large, day-by-day experience revealed innumerable points of difference and dispute. The community chest movement itself had come into existence in the 1920s in large part to cope with such differences between actual and potential business donors on the one hand and hopeful, hard-pressed charitable agencies on the other. The success of the chests, in turn, had caused company officials to reconsider the implications of their philanthropic interests and to attempt the formulation of donations policies or guidelines. Some social workers, on the other hand, had long questioned the entry of business into the welfare field. Assertions that business representatives favored economy and an almsgiving approach at the expense of a professionally oriented welfare program aimed at the prevention of social distress were heard periodically.[3] Participation by businessmen on the boards of chests

[2] UCFCA File 73: Corporation Giving—Tax Deductions, contains reports answering a letter of inquiry written by Burns.

[3] Interview with Whiting Williams, 31 August 1962, concerning formation of the Cleveland Welfare Federation; Robert W. Kelso, "Banker Control of Community Chests," Survey, LXVIII (1 March 1932), 117ff. See also Seeley and others, Community Chest, 109.

and charitable agencies provided many opportunities for disagreement over agency budgets and procedures, anticipated financial needs, the establishment of chest goals, and the allocation of quotas between different industries and companies.

The association of business and welfare leaders included learning as well as conflict. Stillman F. Westbrook, vice-president of the Aetna Life Insurance Company and 1936 Community Chests and Councils president, had begun as a fund raiser; but he came to see his participation in a broader perspective. "I feel that I am a representative of a growing number of business and professional people who have become more familiar with . . . the true nature of our social problems than are the great bulk," Westbrook wrote. "I feel that this chest movement, which perhaps is unfortunately named for the purpose, offers in embryo the most potent medium through which the intelligent layman . . . can learn about the problems and through which he can make his influence felt." [4] Other business leaders vouched for the value of community chest work in the training of executives for more responsible business positions. Uneasy as the relationship between members of the two quite different fields of business and welfare may at times have been, it clearly was not without both its individual and its social compensations.

Passage of the five per cent amendment, however, left fundamental questions about the standards by which companies should guide their donations policies largely unsettled. Few companies could be expected to match the level permitted by law; and within whatever limits were accepted there still remained the troublesome problem of allocation among competing agencies and causes. Still further, trades and industries varied so greatly in their financial and other circumstances that a contributions formula satisfactory for one was unacceptable to members of another. As the Williams-Croxton study had shown, the financial, employee, and tax status of retail companies often differed markedly from those of manufacturers. Public utilities were in a unique position. Railroads were understandably, but from the point of view of local chests discouragingly, reluctant to acknowledge an obligation to contribute in every town through which their locomotives ran.

National corporations continued to press for a standard suited to their needs. Gerard Swope, who had participated in discussions concerning this matter in the Twenties, reviewed the problem with Allen

[4] S. F. Westbrook to Donaldson Brown, 5 June 1936; S. F. Westbrook, "Memorandum in reply to Mr. Donaldson Brown's statement of June 23, 1936"; UCFCA File 72: Corporation Giving—Standards.

Burns in 1936. Swope listed several alternative formulas: donations might be based upon a calculation of the value of services rendered by community agencies to a company's employees, upon the ratio of company taxes to total taxes in a community, upon the ratio of company employees to total population, or upon the amount contributed by employees. Still another possible standard might be a percentage of the total community chest goal, not to exceed the amount contributed by employees. Most of these guidelines had been previously suggested or applied; none had won anything like general acceptance. Now, with the five per cent amendment accepted, it seemed time for another effort to achieve agreement.[5]

Among those pressing for firmer standards was Donaldson Brown, vice-president for finance of the General Motors Company. Brown, an engineer who had studied at Virginia Polytechnic Institute and at Cornell, had been employed by the DuPont Company. When the DuPonts acquired a controlling interest in William Durant's struggling General Motors firm in the early Twenties, Brown had transferred to the automobile industry. Taking corporate finance as his specialty, he associated himself closely with the decentralization policies of Alfred P. Sloan, Jr. He developed a system of "target pricing" by which operations could be planned on a unit-by-unit basis and production geared to an anticipated rate of return. Brown was obviously a business leader of stature. Any donations policy adopted by General Motors would command the respectful attention of the entire business community.[6]

Unsystematic giving troubled Donaldson Brown almost as much as unsystematic pricing. He arranged for a survey of General Motors plants which had shown a variety of contributions practices, as well as of a number of considerations upon which giving policies were—or might be—based.[7] Brown agreed that the discretion of the local manager should, within limits, determine the assistance given to social

[5] Swope to Burns, 27 April 1936, UCFCA File 72: Corporation Giving—Standards.

[6] Memorandum to local community chests, 15 May 1936, UCFCA File 72: Corporation Giving—Standards. Brown, Some Reminiscences of an Industrialist, passim. The target pricing system is discussed critically, insofar as its contribution to price stability in large-scale operations is concerned, in Gardiner C. Means, The Corporate Revolution in America; Economic Reality vs. Economic Theory (New York, 1962), 161–68.

[7] One example of community differences in standards brought to Brown's attention indicated both the strength and the subtlety of the ties by which business was bound to the surrounding society. It concerned the issue of racial segre-

agencies. His basic concern, however, was to distinguish between types of agencies, some of which he felt were more logically entitled to corporate support than were others. Like Swope, Brown hoped to develop a formula which would establish an overall quota for industrial giving and provide a basis upon which allocations within the total could be made between individual companies or plants. By June of 1936, Brown had worked out a proposal on behalf of General Motors which he presented to Burns, Swope, and other national chest officials. Brown's plan was to provide the basis for an extended discussion of the standards problem during the summer and fall.[8]

As it emerged from these conferences, the Brown plan rested on two basic principles. First, it accepted private philanthropy in principle as more economical and efficient than public welfare services. From this standpoint, and in the interest of limiting the expansion of governmental functions, corporations could well justify support of some private welfare agencies in the communities where their plants were located. Second, the Brown plan acknowledged the obligation of the corporation to support basic community health and welfare services in the name of "simple justice" and in recognition of the dependence of company employees upon the existence and quality of such services.

Brown noted that his ideas derived from the experience of an industrial corporation, conceding that the problems of other types of enterprise, such as public utilities and chain retail stores, might support a different analysis. To guide the giving practices of industrial employers, however, Brown suggested that an overall quota be established for that group in each community, based upon the proportion

---

gation, which was to confront the business community with inescapable force in the 1950s and 1960s:

> Is a corporation justified in appraising its obligations to Southern towns on the same basis upon which it would appraise its obligations in a Northern industrial community? A too rapid increase in social measures for the benefit of Southern negro workers probably would dislocate the whole social structure in that community and result in antagonism. To a large degree a corporation must be bound by the rule that "when in Rome do as the Romans do" whenever there is no universally accepted standard to apply.

S. M. DuBrul to Donaldson Brown, 22 May 1936, UCFCA File 72: Corporation Giving—Standards. The United States Steel Corporation faced the same question in Birmingham, Alabama, in 1963. See Chapter VIII.

[8] Stillman to Brown, 5 June 1936, UCFCA File 72: Corporation Giving—Standards.

of total taxes paid by such employers to the total community tax bill. Within this factory quota, Brown then proposed allocation between individual employers on the basis of the ratio of their average number of employees to total factory employment.

Having laid down a general formula for industrial contributions, Brown next raised a crucial question: "Can employers justifiably extend the same degree of support, relatively, to each of the various activities supported by a particular Chest?" His own conviction was that they could not. Referring to management's position of trusteeship and accountability to stockholders, Brown underlined the need to justify contributions in terms of "legitimate corporate purposes." He distinguished between the fundamental services which community agencies offered to those actually in need and "character-building" services which, admirable though they might be, seemed to him less clearly entitled to a claim on corporate, as opposed to individual, contributions. Brown held that "a corporation is fully justified, from the viewpoint of enlightened self-interest, in assuming its fair share of the support of those activities which fulfill the community's responsibility to those actually in need." To other causes, Brown felt a less compelling responsibility; to these "management is justified in contributing to whatever degree it concludes, after careful appraisal, that it may enjoy benefits which will balance the costs so assumed." [9]

In the light of his conclusions, Brown announced that General Motors was adopting an experimental contributions policy for the coming community chest campaign. Chest budgets would be separated, according to the nature of the agencies involved, into two categories: those existing "for the relief of human suffering, misery and destitution," which included "hospitals, free clinics, milk fund, day nurseries, orphan asylums, the Red Cross, family relief and welfare"; and those which could be classified as "recreational, character building and miscellaneous services." [10]

Activities in the first group would receive full recognition and support based upon the quota assigned to General Motors under the overall formula previously derived. Contributions to the second group of activities would be left to the discretion of management and its judgment of the value and relevance of the work of the agency in question. General Motors' local plant managers were authorized to contribute between twenty and fifty per cent of the firm's quota of the chest

[9] Donaldson Brown, "Corporation Community Chest Contributions," unpublished, September, 1936, UCFCA File 72: Corporation Giving—Standards.
[10] *Ibid.*

budget attributable to such agencies. In cases in which they felt extraordinary justification, local managers could apply to the corporation's Executive Committee for approval of donations beyond the fifty per cent level for these activities. Brown proposed that a similar formula be adopted by other manufacturers and accepted by community chests, although he emphasized the need for managerial discretion and volition rather than purely automatic procedures.

Brown's proposed program, especially its plan for reducing corporate commitments to "character-building agencies," aroused immediate concern on the part of chest officials. Allen Burns at once pressed Brown on this point. Given the inevitable differences in judgment and outlook of different individuals, Burns foresaw endless discussion of the relative merits of specific agencies and programs under the Brown plan. Corporations would do better, he believed, to accept the evaluation already made by welfare and business representatives cooperating through the local chest organization.

Burns took sharp issue with Brown's distinction between basic and incidental community services. "The real question," Burns argued, "is whether corporations have a responsibility for the problems they indirectly and incidentally help to create as well as for the direct services to their employees." Leisure-time and character-building agencies, he suggested, might well be of more direct value and interest to business than was the provision of relief. The history of corporate philanthropy showed that the YMCA, a leisure-time agency, had been the first to win large-scale business support; similar character-building activities had also won substantial corporate backing over the years. The growth of leisure time through the shortening of the work day, as well as through forced unemployment, was a direct outgrowth of industrialization. To Burns it seemed unrealistic for management to deny both interest in and responsibility for this fact of industrial life. To Stillman F. Westbrook, Burns urged opposition to Brown's scheme of weighting agencies by their presumed importance to industry. "Really what we are up against is the old argument against having character-building agencies in the chest," he wrote. "It seems to me we just have to stand adamant on that. I really fear that to have a discrimination in the legitimacy of their support would disrupt chests. We could get plenty of corporation people to stand with us on this argument." [11]

[11] Burns to Donaldson Brown, 25 June 1936; Burns to S. F. Westbrook, 25 June 1936; Westbrook to Burns, 26 June 1936; Westbrook, "Memorandum in reply to Mr. Donaldson Brown's statement of June 23, 1935," UCFCA File 72: Corporation Giving—Standards.

Donaldson Brown was not, however, easily discouraged. Without some "purification" of the list of chest agencies, he insisted, company officials as trustees for the interests of their stockholders could hardly help looking askance at chest requests. Brown's views commanded a respect which Allen Burns and his community chest associates fully recognized. When a revised draft of the Brown proposal, more conciliatory in tone but with no fundamental change in principle, reached chest headquarters late in July, 1936, Westbrook suggested that it be placed on the agenda of the forthcoming Washington conference of the Mobilization for Human Needs. Further suggestions and criticisms from chest people, Westbrook felt, would only serve to alienate Brown. Meanwhile, Brown had submitted a study of General Motors chest contributions in seven communities. This showed, as Burns had suspected, that the actual gift in most cases greatly exceeded what would have been contributed under the Brown formula. A full and open discussion of the issues Brown had raised now seemed imperative.[12]

The 1936 Mobilization conference met in Washington, D.C., in September under the chairmanship of Gerard Swope. Representative business leaders from the public utilities and the railroad, retail, and industrial trades were in attendance. These men were much interested in comparing notes on their respective companies' donation policies; Donaldson Brown's plan, therefore, provided a useful basis for discussion.

As Allen Burns had anticipated, the Brown formula failed to command general approval. Gerard Swope restated the General Electric policy which based the company's giving upon its share of community taxes and accepted the budget prepared by chest officials. This standard might not be better than Brown's, Swope conceded; but it had the advantage of simplicity and it minimized controversy. Albert H. Morrill, board chairman of the Kroger Grocery and Bakery Company and spokesman for the chain store group, rejected the Brown formula for his associates; but Morrill acknowledged the need for a more suitable plan. Representatives of the railroad and utility companies agreed; they proposed further conferences between businessmen and chest leaders, but showed little enthusiasm for Donaldson Brown's brainchild. Howard Bruce, president of the Baltimore National Bank, ob-

[12] Brown to Burns, 8 June 1936, UCFCA File 72: Corporation Giving—Correspondence; Brown to Burns, 29 July 1936, Burns to Westbrook, 30 July 1936, Westbrook to Burns, 1 August 1936, Brown to Burns, 13 August 1936, File 72: Corporation Giving—Standards.

jected to rigid formulas as a straitjacket for charity and found fault with the tax base as a standard for philanthropy.

Welfare officials, too, voiced their reactions to the proposed formula. C. M. Bookman of Cincinnati argued for effectiveness of services rendered as a yardstick for giving. A representative of the New York Catholic Charities termed the Brown plan "shockingly reactionary." Welfare agency and chest leaders obviously feared the judgment of influential businessmen who might not be familiar with agency circumstances. The question, as they saw it, was simple: "Is an employer or a local plant manager better qualified to determine the value of social services than a group of men of tried judgment and experience in community concerns?" They thought they knew the answer.[13]

Despite disagreements between representatives of different industries and between business and chest participants, the conference increased understanding among those present. Recommendations were accepted favoring greater decentralization of management's authority for giving, stressing the need for company guidelines to assist branch managers in making their decisions, and approving a campaign of "education" to be undertaken by the chests, aimed in particular at chain store home offices. Recognition was given by both business and chest representatives to the diversity of conditions faced by companies in different lines of trade, different communities, and different types of local offices. In view of this diversity it was further agreed that no single standard, or "yardstick," could win general acceptance.

Yet the placing of company contributions on some level higher than sheer managerial caprice was as important to welfare leaders as it was to business executives; and the principle that local managers should be more familiar with the work of the agencies to which they granted, or denied, support was one which few could deny. After further analysis and criticism from both chest and business sources, the Brown formula was officially withdrawn in the spring of 1937. Donaldson Brown informed Stillman Westbrook that the plan's failure to win broad support had made it "inoperative so far as the General Motors

---

[13] *Business Week*, 26 September 1936, 26; "Proceedings of the 1936 Mobilization for Human Needs Conference," UCFCA File 51: Washington Conference, 1936. Gertrude Springer, "Youth and Yardsticks," *Survey*, LXXII (October 1936), 291–94, is a summary of the conference. The attitudes revealed by the "hardheaded" business representatives to the conference, according to Miss Springer, "made the hardest-boiled social worker feel, in comparison, like a gentle old Lady Bountiful." *Business Week*, 26 September 1936, 26, reported that Wendell Willkie, fresh from his controversies with the TVA, felt the conference was spoiled by recurrent use of "that damn word 'yardstick.'"

Corporation is concerned. . . ." He expressed willingness to look at other proposals as they might appear. The problem of standards which had troubled Brown remained unresolved, a continuing source of difficulty and disagreement between the chests and the business community.[14]

[14] Brown to S. F. Westbrook, 26 May 1937, UCFCA File 72: Standards—Manufacturing. Dudley S. Blossom, Elwood H. Fisher, and Kenneth A. Sturges of the Cleveland Community Fund prepared a detailed critique of the Brown formula for the Washington conference. They argued that the plan might encourage some chests to inflate their budgets in order to compensate for expected reduced weightings by business executives, that chests differed widely in the scope and number of community agencies they included, that the plan left no flexibility to provide for loss of subscribers due to business difficulties in any particular year, that the tax data upon which Brown's plan rested was not always readily attainable, and that many taxes besides those on property entered into the total community tax situation. The Clevelanders also questioned the allocation of giving on the basis of factory employment. This standard made little provision for the varied employment situations of companies in different lines of production and failed to deal with seasonal employment differentials.

Cleveland reported its own plan, based upon a ratio of company gifts to number of employees. Companies in related lines were classified on this basis and encouraged to match the ratios set by their more generous competitors. Simplicity and comparability were pleaded as advantages of this plan; but variations in the circumstances of companies were recognized here, too. "Notes on Mr. Donaldson Brown's Plan for a Standard of Manufacturers' Contributions to Community Chests," File 72: Corporation Giving—Standards—Manufacturing. For another critique, see Bradley Buell to Burns, undated memorandum, in same file.

Allen Burns kept Donaldson Brown's idea and its possible applications under close scrutiny until Brown himself abandoned it. A. W. Robertson, board chairman of the Westinghouse Electric Company, had suggested to Burns that the General Motors plan was aimed particularly at the Ford and Chrysler companies. Comparison of chest contributions by the three companies in the Detroit area during the 1936 campaign showed a basis for such a charge. Under the Brown plan, General Motors' contributions would have been reduced some $56,000 from its actual pledge, Chrysler would have given only about $2,000 less, while the Ford Company would have had to increase its giving by nearly $70,000. Since, however, the Ford Motor Company—apparently in keeping with Henry Ford's long-standing strictures against philanthropy—actually pledged no contribution to the 1936 chest fund, this was clearly an extraordinary situation. A further comparison of the contributions policies of the automobile industry's Big Three was made in the spring of 1937, using the Cleveland formula of company contributions per employee. This showed that, in order for Ford and Chrysler to match the General Motors record of $2.93 per worker, their contributions would have had to increase $148,000 and $74,000 respectively. Burns to W. F. Maxwell, Pittsburgh Community Fund, 2 October 1936; "Estimated Pledges to Fund by Various Corporations . . . ," memorandum dated 9 October 1936; memorandum dated 19 May 1937, UCFCA File 72: Standards—Manufacturing.

INDUSTRYWIDE COMMITTEES

As a consequence, then, of views exchanged and issues discussed at the 1936 MHN conference, further consideration of the standards problem seemed necessary. Under CCC sponsorship joint business-chest committees were set up for several of the most important, or most difficult, lines of business. Periodic meetings of these committees were held between 1937 and 1941, but little progress was made toward resolution of the difficulties involved in finding acceptable yardsticks. In 1937, economic recession once again diverted business attention from concern for fixing standards. Chest officials, fearing that standards set in bad times might prove hard to change when business improved, were not unhappy to let the matter drop.

Meanwhile, the committee formed to discuss contributions by industrial corporations had met in July, 1937, in New York City. Percival Dodge of Detroit reported to Allen Burns that a formula based upon the ratio of company employees to total population in a community had been agreed upon, which would produce severe reductions in corporation giving. In Kansas City, Los Angeles, and Washington, D.C., which were not primarily industrial cities, no serious effect would be felt; but in Detroit, the gifts of the fifteen largest firms would be reduced by $60,000, a "disastrous" result. Once again, the welfare agencies' stake in flexible and discretionary, rather than standardized, giving had been demonstrated.[15]

According to Allen Burns, the biggest surprise of the 1936 conference had been the interest shown by spokesmen for the railroads in a joint effort to work out a giving standard suited to their peculiar position. "You don't need to be told," Burns wrote C. M. Bookman, "what slackers the railroads have been. We were astonished to have them go as far as they did. . . ." While not all railroad representatives were ready to consider a fixed formula, some were willing to acknowledge the same responsibilities and relationships to the community which other industries had accepted and acknowledged.

Evidently at Burns's request, Bookman prepared a statement to meet the claim of some railroad companies that they provided adequately

[15] For the effect of the 1937 recession, see the remarks of Ralph Blanchard in a discussion of "Corporation Support of Chests," led by Lester Adams of Oakland, California, at the Pacific Coast Conference of Community Chests and Councils, Inc., 11–13 May 1938; UCFCA File 106: Speeches. Percival Dodge to Burns, 21 July 1937; UCFCA File 72: Corporation Giving—Correspondence.

for their own employees. The Pennsylvania and the Baltimore and Ohio companies made no chest contribution in Cincinnati, Bookman noted, yet a spot check revealed that a substantial number of their employees had been served by chest agencies. At an October, 1936, meeting between members of the executive committee of the Association of American Railroads and Burns, S. F. Westbrook, and J. H. Case, representing the CCC, possible standards were explored and an agreement reached that the railroads would attempt to develop a standard of their own. Within a month, the railroad association's general counsel reported that an Interstate Commerce Commission decision, which forbade charging contributions to operating expense and required that they be paid out of profits, made further consideration of railroad contributions unlikely.[16] Allen Burns's pleasant surprise had been short-lived.

Little further progress in the systematic development of railroad support for community chests occurred until the Second World War. With few exceptions, the major railroads remained aloof. Wartime pressures subsequently led, however, to a gradual breakdown in their resistance. In 1945–46, trunk line railroads donated over $500,000 to the National War Fund, while Ralph Blanchard estimated that another $500,000 may have been given directly to local community chests for the work of the United Services Organization. When the war emergency passed, such gifts from the railroad companies dwindled sharply; but their solid front had been pierced.[17]

Chest officials experienced similar lack of success in winning the backing of insurance companies. It seemed to those in the welfare field that the contribution of social agencies to the health and well-being of individuals and communities was a matter of direct economic benefit to insurance interests. Most insurance companies gave to the chest drives in the towns where their home offices were located, but seldom elsewhere. Stillman Westbrook, an insurance company execu-

[16] Allen Burns to C. M. Bookman, undated, UCFCA File 72: Corporation Giving—Chain Stores; "Memorandum of round table discussion on contributions by railroads . . . September 18, 1936 . . . ," UCFCA File 72: Standards—Railroads; C. M. Bookman, "A Fact Finding Inquiry into the Extent of Social Service Aid Given to Railroad Employees," 28 October 1936; UCFCA File 72: Standards—Railroads. J. H. Case, "Report of Committee on Railroad Contributions," 4 March 1937, UCFCA File 72: Standards—Railroads.

[17] Ralph Blanchard to P. Josephson, 17 September 1940; Blanchard to all chests, 5 March 1948, UCFCA File 72: Corporation Giving—Correspondence; interview with Ralph Blanchard, 30 December 1957.

tive himself, testified in 1938 that he had long been waging a losing battle with the mutual companies, which refused, on the basis of their trusteeship status, to contribute to chest and similar cooperative activities. He had given up hope, Westbrook wrote, "of ever seeing them enlightened in a far-reaching activity of this kind." The approach of war brought a different outlook, however. Ralph Blanchard noted in 1941 the first gifts by the large life insurance companies to the Greater New York Fund.[18]

Leaders in the public utilities industry proved more sympathetic toward efforts to broaden the base of corporate giving, undoubtedly because they had an obvious stake in the economic and social climate of their communities. But they, too, faced special problems. Wendell Willkie, president of the Commonwealth and Southern Corporation, noted at the 1936 Washington conference a widespread suspicion that gifts by public utilities were chiefly aimed at the purchase of public favor; he recognized also considerable local resentment at absentee ownership of public utilities, similar to that experienced by the retail chain stores. The acceptance of a standard contributions policy, Willkie believed, would alleviate these problems. Other utilities executives agreed, but found the formulation of a standard difficult. An Edison Electric Institute study of 84 companies serving communities of over 100,000 people showed a range in contributions from one to five cents per capita.

An additional problem for the utilities was the peculiar relation in which they stood to government. On the basis of past experience, they feared that utilities commissions might oppose philanthropic activities. Efforts were made to sound out the authorities, stresssing the widespread agreement of utilities representatives concerning their interest in community life. The results of this "fishing" expedition were not encouraging. Commissioner Edwin L. Taylor, of the Connecticut Public Utilities Commission, wrote Stillman Westbrook that the utilities companies should charge any contributions made against their stockholders, not their customers. Gifts could not be considered business expenses. Taylor further made clear his suspicion that utility companies were maneuvering to pass their responsibilities on to the commissions.

[18] See Stuart C. Rand, Community Federation of Boston, to A. E. Tuck, Equitable Mutual Life Assurance Society, 26 November 1938, for a criticism of insurance company contributions policies. Stillman F. Westbrook to Stuart C. Rand, 2 December 1938; Ralph Blanchard to Alex D. Hardie, 25 September 1941; UCFCA File 72: Standards—Insurance Companies.

Again it seemed that general agreement on policies and standards was not to be achieved on short notice.[19]

The position of local branches of national chain store systems had long been troublesome both to chest and to company executives. Discontent by each party with the policies and expectations of the other had been evident even before the 1928 Washington conference, and a decade of experience had not removed all the sources of disagreement. There had, however, been growing recognition among chain store managements of the value of cultivating local good will. Popular resentment against absentee ownership was heightened during the depression by the inability of many local branch managers of some chains to join fully in community welfare and civic undertakings.

Although the 1936 conference produced no startling new approaches to long-standing issues, the threat of legislation regulating and taxing national chain stores in the late Thirties aroused new interest among chain store executives in winning public acceptance through greater participation by branch managers in community affairs. *Advertising Age* acknowledged in 1939 that some national chain systems had been "notorious" for their failure to interest themselves in, and support, local community welfare. General Robert E. Wood of Sears, Roebuck and Company raised an influential voice for chain store giving: "The impersonal large national corporation, with branch factories, branch offices and stores scattered all over the nation, must do its part as a citizen, and must contribute its share in the upbuilding of each community in which it is located, as well as any individual citizen of that community." Paul Mooney, in charge of public relations

---

[19] L. G. Tighe, of the Ohio Edison Company, to Wendell L. Willkie 19 October 1936; Stillman F. Westbrook to C. S. Bailey, National Association of Railroad and Utility Commissioners, 21 October 1936; Edwin L. Taylor to Westbrook, 3 November 1936; UCFCA File 72: Corporation Giving—Utilities, 1936; "Notes on Public Utilities Meeting," Washington, D.C., 18 September 1936, UCFCA File 72: Corporation Giving—Utilities, 1942.

President P. S. Arkwright of the Georgia Power Company wrote to Gerard Swope strongly favoring the effort to win support of local welfare programs by national corporations. Arkwright took a rather relaxed position toward both the matter of standards and that of charging gifts to operating expenses or against surplus. He left it up to solicitors to set what they considered a fair contribution in relationship to his company's situation, Arkwright wrote; and he had not found that they took advantage of him. The issue of accounting for company donations he found not particularly significant, since the amounts involved were too small to make a great difference in the company's financial picture. Arkwright to Swope, 20 October 1936, File 72: Corporation Giving—Utilities, 1936.

for the Kroger chain, stated that the industry needed help in arriving at a standard and would welcome the cooperation of community chest representatives in working out a fair formula for contributions.[20]

At a meeting of chain store and community chest leaders in Detroit in May, 1940, a tentative policy offered by the chests was considered. Agreement was reached in principle as to the desirability of chain store participation in chest campaigns, of local branch managers' having discretion to participate quickly and effectively, and of recognition by local chests of the distinctive problems of the chains. Subsequent meetings held to discuss agreement upon a specific donations policy produced no national formula. Formulas worked out by local chest and company officials within a broad policy laid down by corporate headquarters appeared to offer the best solution. Many chains still resisted community chest appeals, while in other cases decisions continued to be arrived at on a company-by-company and community-by-community basis.[21]

By 1942, Allen Burns was openly criticizing the idea of national "yardsticks." Consultations between community chest and corporation representatives since 1942 have produced greater mutual understanding of problems but have not resulted—nor do they seem likely to result—in the development of any universal, or even widely accepted, "yardstick." The diversity of industry, company, and community conditions is too great. Even if some workable overall formula were agreed upon, continuing rapid changes in social and economic conditions as well as in public attitudes would soon outmode any rigid standard. Individual companies and communities, out of their own experiences and preferences, have evolved a great variety of approaches

---

[20] For articles discussing the role of company contributions in winning community support, see "How Chain-Store Managers Can Remove the 'Foreign' Taint," *Printers' Ink*, CLI (1 May 1930), 110ff.; *ibid.*, CLXXVI (20 August 1936), 77–80; John Arthur Reynolds, "How One Chain Builds Good Will," *Barrons*, 15 August 1938, 8. Woods was quoted in *Advertising Age*, 27 March 1939, 12. For Mooney's statement, "Memorandum on Round-Table Discussion of 'Relations Between Community Chests and Retail Chain Stores,'" Detroit, 24 May 1940, UCFCA File 72: Corporation Giving—Standards—Chains.

[21] *Ibid.*; "Minutes of Joint National Committee of Chain Store and Community Chest Representatives . . . ," 20 September 1940; "Food Chains and Community Welfare, A Statement of Principles of the Executive Committee, National Association of Food Chains," 1941; Iowa Chain Store Council, Inc., *Bulletin*, 1941; Allen Burns to Lionel Wachs, 20 May 1942; UCFCA File 72: Corporation Giving—Standards—Chain Stores and Joint National Committee.

and policies and will continue to modify and adapt them to new circumstances. The search for standards thus continues, but it seems destined to prove a search without an end.[22]

BUSINESS AND SOCIETY

Significant as the effort to establish corporate philanthropy on a regular and legal basis ultimately proved, the depression years raised far more urgent questions concerning the role of business in American society. The New Deal posed a fundamental challenge to the primacy of business leadership and initiative. Businessmen viewed the expansion of government with feelings which ranged from hesitant acceptance to apoplectic antagonism. Yet they could hardly argue convincingly that business had proved itself equal to the task of securing the general welfare. Throughout the Thirties business found itself faced by a resentful, if not hostile, public. Every group for which business leadership in the 1920s had somewhat prematurely appointed itself trustee seemed to turn upon its erstwhile benefactor. The assertion of responsibility for the welfare of others now unavoidably entailed the acceptance of blame when failure became obvious. Limited though their capacity for action may have been by prevailing economic conditions, businessmen confronted with private criticism and public regulation could scarcely avoid thinking about the social responsibilities of their firms.

Even before the depression Dean Wallace B. Donham of Harvard had questioned the adequacy of business response to changing conditions. He had acknowledged the groping effort toward a wider understanding of social relationships implicit in the codes of business ethics and the practice of corporate philanthropy but believed that these were only surface reactions; a more fundamental examination of the very character and scope of business itself was called for: "No amount of support of hospitals and charities, of fine arts and universities, will serve to remove the stigma of materialism from our civilization. The idealism of our business leaders must be focused on business itself, on the great task of adjusting business progress to community happiness."

[22] Companies, trade associations, the community chest organization, and other organizations have made periodic surveys of the standards problem from varying perspectives. A number of these have been summarized in Kenneth A. Sturges, "Yardsticks for Corporation Gifts to Community Chests, a Survey of Past and Present Plans," Community Chests and Councils of America, Inc., Bulletin 160, January, 1952.

External regulation alone could not, Donham had held, enforce the kind of social responsibility the times required. Law could establish general standards; but only direct and intimate knowledge on the part of businessmen regarding the relation of business to social conditions could effectively adapt economic institutions to social needs.

Donham now saw the reaction of business to the depression as largely defensive and ineffectual:

> We build great industrial corporations which introduce amazing novelties into life. Their executives behave first, last, and nearly all the time as if their companies had no function except to manufacture and sell. They have a fine understanding of their own business, too little grasp of their industries as a whole, almost none of the relation between their particular interests and our general social and economic structure, and far too little grip on the social consequences of their activities.

Only when business leadership faced the full scope of its social and economic involvement could realistic ethical standards prevail.[23]

Other academic voices similarly challenged the adequacy of business understanding in this area. Did executives truly recognize the intimate connection of their policies with social conditions? Did their training and outlook equip them to appreciate these relationships? Were they, for that matter, really alert to the internal problems and potentialities of business itself as they affected social conditions? Did they understand the causes of the business cycle, the relationship of wages to consumption and production, the implications of technological unemployment, the problem of social security? More than this, did they *want* to understand, to support fact-finding studies, to reexamine company policies and modify them in the light of clearer knowledge of their social consequences? Did they think too much in short-range terms of simple economies of production which might, in the end, entail unrecognized social and economic costs? Did they attempt to counter external criticism too simply, through resort to high-pressure propaganda campaigns and gestures of benevolence, feeding their own egos and ignoring the true needs and wants of society?

"The true indictment against business is one of not knowing rather than not caring" about society's real needs, wrote J. David Houser in the *Harvard Business Review*. Businessmen had managed to convince

---

[23] Wallace B. Donham, "Business Ethics," *HBR*, VII (July, 1929), 385–94; Donham, "The Failure of Business Leadership and the Responsibility of the Universities," 418–35.

themselves by their own public relations campaigns that they knew best what was good for others, but they had signally failed to come to grips with actual social conditions and attitudes toward them. Priding themselves on their practicality, they had lost touch with the real world around them.[24]

Academic critics were not alone in their refusal to be impressed by the spread of corporate philanthropy. At the time of his controversy with the community chests over the five per cent amendment for corporate contributions, President Roosevelt clearly showed his suspicion that corporate giving was aimed at influencing public opinion rather than meeting fundamental public needs. John T. Flynn during the Thirties charged that corporate gifts were really paid by the consumers if charged against business expenses and by the stockholders if taken out of profits. In either event, management derived public credit and prestige by spending other people's money. And Thurman Arnold wryly noted that businessmen approved those types of private charity which reflected credit on their own generosity, while attacking governmental welfare measures, the necessity for which stemmed in large part from business negligence and irresponsibility. "Therefore one never hears a community chest spoken of as a necessary evil as the dole is." William O. Douglas, chairman of the Securities and Exchange Commission, advocated the addition of a paid public director to the board of business corporations to insure that adequate attention be given to the external implications of management policies.[25]

Unlike their critics, businessmen themselves tended to react to their loss of prestige and influence by stressing shortcomings in the public's understanding of economic forces rather than in the economy's performance. At the depths of the depression this was an argument difficult to maintain, difficult in all probability even for the most ardent defenders of business fully to believe. As the sense of crisis waned, how-

[24] John W. Riegel, "Some Basic Management Responsibilities," *HBR*, XII (September, 1935), 286–308; Ellsworth Faris, Ferris Laune, and Arthur J. Todd, eds., *Intelligent Philanthropy* (Chicago, 1930), 188, 204; J. David Houser, "Method or Results: Profit Motive or Ego?" *HBR*, XVI (Spring, 1938), 290–98. Morris E. Leeds, president of Leeds and Northrop, similarly stressed the tendency of many businessmen to debate issues without having first made serious efforts to collect and study the relevant facts. See "Political Economy and the Industrialist," *Annals*, CCIV (July, 1939), 72–79.

[25] Flynn's comment appeared in the New York *World Telegram*, 26 July 1935. Thurman Arnold, *The Folklore of Capitalism* (New Haven, 1938), 36; William O. Douglas, *Democracy and Finance* (New Haven, 1940), 53, quoted in Mason, ed., *The Corporation in Modern Society*, 60.

ever, past failings were more easily obscured by present perplexities and future prospects, and it became increasingly possible for company officials to propound the view that the chief failure of business lay in its lack of good public relations.

Whatever the range of opinions at business meetings over the merits of whichever New Deal measure happened for the moment to dominate the news, there was one point around which all could rally. This was the need for more effective interpretation to the American people of the positive contributions of their economic system and its business leadership. In this conviction the public relations industry was, of course, quick to concur. Individual businessmen, to be sure, recognized the emergence of new economic and political relationships in the course of a decade of unprecedented change and experimentation; but the importance of greater sensitivity to public opinion was the lesson most effectively taught by the depression and the New Deal to business leadership as a whole.

As early as 1931, Ralph E. Flanders observed that the depression experience demonstrated the last thing business could afford to lose was the customer's good will. Alfred P. Sloan, Jr., in the General Motors annual report for 1932–33, reiterated the point, adding that all company policies would, to the fullest possible extent, be subjected to the test of the public interest. Paul W. Litchfield of the Goodyear Tire and Rubber Company was also aware that business practices must meet public scrutiny. "Lasting success in any industry depends upon public support and confidence," he believed. "More and more the attitude of the public toward business is going to be influenced by the attitude of business toward its social responsibilities." [26]

As it had in the 1920s, business opinion wavered between recognition of the need to adjust business policies to the requirements of the general welfare and the temptation to settle for public relations campaigns in which the emphasis was more upon words than deeds. Raymond Moley, speaking at business conferences in 1936, encouraged his listeners to "set up a counter-current of understanding" to offset the widespread criticism of business. He urged a group of advertising men to "make the public look upon business as a good servant rather than

[26] Ralph E. Flanders, "What Industrial Management Has Learned in the Last Two Years," *Iron Age*, CXXVIII (24 September 1931), 803–8. Sloan's statement in the General Motors annual report is quoted in Samuel Crowther, *Public Opinion, Private Business, and Public Relations* (New York, 1934), 2. Paul Litchfield, "The Trend in Industry," *Vital Speeches of the Day*, III (15 December 1936), 146–49.

a selfish master," so that business might be defended against the hostile "prophets of politics." As the 1936 election approached, Colby M. Chester of General Mills, president of the NAM, urged corporations to "sell themselves," especially to their stockholders. Reaffirming the idea of management as the mediator between associated interests, Chester insisted that it approached this role with humility and deserved public understanding and tolerance. He argued, however, that managerial responsibility to employees must be voluntary, not coerced; and his language displayed little of the humility of which he spoke.[27]

The outcome of the 1936 election sobered and chastened some of those who believed that public favor could be regained simply by insisting upon the need for it. Within a month after Maine and Vermont had registered their historic dissent from the Roosevelt "revolution," Chester was displaying a notably greater degree of the humility he had called for earlier. Business must demonstrate its willingness to *win* public approbation, Chester now acknowledged. Listing the obligations of business leadership, he began with the sweeping assertion, "Industry must accept its responsibility for the national welfare as being an even higher duty than the successful operation of private business." Raymond Moley, too, appeared ready to concede that "the function of management has in fact and in practice become quasipublic." Management had already accepted this fact, Moley believed; but the public had not recognized management's new understanding.

---

[27] Raymond Moley, "The Future of Corporate Prophets," *ibid.*, II (15 July 1936), 636–38; Colby M. Chester, "Money Is Not Enough," *ibid.*, II (1 August 1936), 682–85. In 1936, the NAM had undertaken a national billboard campaign built on the theme "What is Good for Industry is Good for You." See "The Public is Not Damned," *Fortune*, XIX (March, 1939), 83–88ff. See also H. Walker and R. Sklar, *Business Finds Its Voice: Management's Effort to Sell the Business Idea to the Public* (New York, 1938). The *New York Times* (5 December 1935, 9ff.) reported that the national convention of the NAM had set as its aim to rid the country of the New Deal. Alfred P. Sloan, Jr., speaking at the convention, had stressed industry's responsibility to "enlighten" the public.

Harold Coonley, NAM president in 1939, also stressed the necessity for business leadership to show the public that its policies were "in tune with social and economic trends," that industry was doing "everything possible" for the public good. Having reviewed its own practices and put its house in order, business, according to Coonley, was now ready for wider responsibilities: "Business—big or small—is responsible for the welfare of every citizen in the nation." Harold Coonley, "Business Must State Its Case," *Dun's Review*, XXVII (August, 1939), 5–8. For other comments, more critical of business policy, see Morris E. Leeds, "Political Economy and the Industrialist," *Annals*, CCIV (July, 1939), 72–79, and Alpheus T. Mason, "Business Organized as Power: The New Imperium in Imperio," *American Political Science Review*, XLIV (June, 1940), 323–42.

Nevertheless, he stressed the need for "words and deeds" which would remove the cause of misunderstanding.[28]

Joseph P. Kennedy, one businessman who had found it possible to accept and even to join the New Deal, interpreted the 1936 election as "a most decisive factor in our economic history." Business had been given clear instructions by the electorate to cooperate with the Roosevelt reforms. Too often management had run the large corporations in accordance with its own ideas and objectives, neglecting the true interests of the stockholders, wrote Kennedy, whose interests were primarily those of an investor rather than an administrator. It was President Roosevelt himself who had had to remind business leaders, in the midst of the economic wreckage their policies had produced, that they were trustees for the interests of others and must act accordingly, he pointed out. Business had not yet put its house in order; it must stop resisting needed reforms. "Business and finance must henceforth deal with . . . [the American people] as partners, not as minor wards." [29]

Others, less critical of their fellow executives, still recognized that a change in business posture was called for. Ralph E. Flanders insisted that business had done much to provide economic opportunity for Americans, although it had failed in certain important respects—notably in raising wage levels and promoting economic stability. Now, management should accept sincerely "the social ideals which the election has indicated are the evident purposes of the American people" and work in statesmanlike cooperation with government and organized labor.[30]

A slowly returning self-confidence characterized most business pronouncements of the later New Deal years. There remained, however, a strong awareness, as *Fortune* put it, that the public could no longer be "damned" openly or with impunity. Both individual companies and business associations such as the NAM extended their advertising and public relations programs during these years, establishing full-fledged

[28] Colby M. Chester, "Better Living," *Vital Speeches,* III (1 January 1937), 166–67; Raymond Moley, "Industrial Leadership—1937 Model," *ibid.,* III (1 January 1937), 184–86.

[29] Joseph P. Kennedy, "Big Business, What Now?" *The Saturday Evening Post,* CCIX (16 January 1937), 10–11.

[30] Ralph E. Flanders, "Business Faces a New Year—and a New World," *Dun's Review,* XLV (February, 1937), 7–9; George E. Sokolsky, "The Bewilderment of Business," *Nation's Business,* XXV (September, 1937), 38–40ff. A more positive argument for business leadership was that of T. N. Whitehead, "Social and Political Tendencies of the Present Day," *HBR,* XV (Spring, 1937), 275–82.

institutional advertising programs, news services, and similar means of winning public sympathy.[31]

For an industrial complex as large as the General Motors Corporation, adjustment to the new social and political climate involved structural changes as well as new sensitivity to issues previously considered of secondary importance. The corporation's 1937 annual report announced that a careful review of its social relations was under way:

> More recently a further responsibility has claimed an increasing amount of attention from management, and that is the relationship of industry to the community as a whole. For many years the chief and absorbing problems of industry lay in the fields of engineering, production and distribution. Out of these endeavors came new products, new comforts and better ways of living. Today there is a greater necessity than ever before for improving the relationships of industry as affecting human progress and for new interpretations of the fundamental place of industry in our social and economic structure.

The following year saw the formation, at General Motors' top managerial level, of its policy group, to consider economic and social trends. Donaldson Brown, the group's chairman, later conceded, however, that its chief interest lay with what it discerned as the interference of government with the "fundamental principles essential to the maintenance of a free and competitive economy." [32]

Brown, whose experience in working with the community chest

[31] Thomas C. Borshall, "The Responsibility of Private Enterprise," *Vital Speeches*, IV (15 September 1938), 725–27; William Allen White, "Thoughts after the Election," *Yale Review*, New Series, XXX (December, 1940), 217–27; "The Public is Not Damned," *Fortune*, XIX (March, 1939), 83–88ff. Marshall E. Dimock and Howard K. Hyde, "Bureaucracy and Trusteeship in Large Corporations," Monograph No. 11, Temporary National Economic Committee (Washington, D.C., 1940), 83–84. See also Daniel Starch, "The New Social Consciousness of Industry," in Leigh S. Plummer, *Getting Along with Labor* (New York, 1941), ixff.

James T. Adams, scanning the future of capitalism for *Barron's*, believed that it was moving toward "Greater Realization of Its Social Responsibilities without the Destruction of Freedom." The freedom it offered to the individual "to express his own personality" and to work for the correction of abuses made capitalism worth saving, Adams was sure. Men were learning, too, that property was "tinged with a public interest and that society, which protects our property, has a right to see that it shall not be used in an anti-social way." James T. Adams, "Where is Capitalism Heading?" *Barron's*, 15 August 1938, 3–4.

[32] General Motors Corporation, Annual Report, 1937; Brown, *Some Reminiscences of an Industrialist*, 101–2.

movement had alerted him to industry's stake in social conditions and pressures, was also concerned with the public posture manifested by the National Association of Manufacturers. He thought that the NAM too often spoke in bellicose terms which made it appear little more than a selfish spokesman for a special-interest group. It was futile, Brown felt, to expect the public to accept business leadership or to remain loyal to sound economic principles unless management itself made clear its adherence to the same principles and its acceptance of its social responsibilities. Only when convinced of management's own good faith would the people feel "that they can rely upon the force of enlightened self-interest to accomplish the essentials of industrial control in the broad interests of the public." As chairman of a committee for the 1939 Congress of American Industry sponsored by the NAM, Brown played a leading part in the drafting of a declaration of principles, which, not unlike the Chamber of Commerce's code of ethics of the Twenties, pledged industry to help itself by "serving the interests of the nation as a whole." [33]

Another view of corporate social responsibilities, differing in emphasis from Brown's, was expressed by Paul G. Hoffman, president of the Studebaker Corporation. Hoffman agreed with Brown that "it goes without saying that American business can never discharge its present great responsibilities on the basis of being suspect, or of being constantly policed and coerced." He stressed, however, a functional approach to managerial obligations and criticized "the assumption that corporate management is under obligation to act as the guardian of its employees and the mentor of the communities in which it operates. Some of the most disastrous failures in the social relations of corporations," Hoffman noted, "have broken over the heads of kindly gentlemen who held such views." Rejecting paternalism, Hoffman nevertheless found a basis for arguing that management's social contribution could be a constructive one. Like E. A. Filene, he insisted that "enlightened self-interest rather than benevolence should be the impelling motive in every relationship between the corporation, on the one hand, and its employees, neighbors, and customers, on the other. After all, it is the job of the corporation to make money for its stockholders. And it so happens that it is good business to be humane and that decency pays in dividends." [34] Thus, intelligent management could pre-

[33] *Ibid.*, 99–101. For an aggressive and pointed response to criticism of American business, see the NAM's *Fact and Fancy in the T.N.E.C. Monographs* (New York, 1942).

[34] Hoffman is quoted in Bronson Batchelor, ed., *The New Outlook in Business* (New York, 1940), 105–12, a symposium of business points of view.

vent undue government infringement upon a still free and essentially private economy.

Such discussions of the public relations and responsibilities of business did not advance thinking on the subject much beyond the level already achieved in the 1920s. The failure of most businessmen to consider seriously the relationship of social responsibility to such key issues of the Thirties as social security and industrial relations makes clear the limits—and may even raise questions as to the seriousness— of their thinking. That they were seldom able to go beyond, or even to match, the degree of concern for these problems which had been shown by some companies in the preceding decade indicates the extent to which defensive postures had frozen attitudes and blocked experimentation. Only in connection with community chest and similar welfare agencies were they able to find outlets for specific application of notions of responsibility. Still, the survival of the chest movement through these difficult years, coupled with the emphasis which the depression gave to the stake of business in community health and favor, offered a basis for further development in their thinking during and after the Second World War.

THE ROLE OF MANAGEMENT

Much as the changing climate of opinion in the late Thirties encouraged business executives to renew efforts for public approval and to emphasize their concern for the general welfare, so also it fostered new attempts to interpret the role of management itself. Ironically, the revitalization of agencies representing the interests of workers, consumers, and the general public served to focus attention upon management's role as an economic mediator. The very fact that business leadership now found itself forced to deal formally with governmental and union officials as well as with stockholders underlined its status as a distinctive group with crucial powers and coordinating functions. What Owen D. Young and a few other officers of large corporations had sensed as the trusteeship status of management in the Twenties was now ready for wider acceptance. The fact of a managerial interest group pressed by, responsible to, and mediating between an assortment of social groups which included stockholders, workers, suppliers, customers, government, and the general public was increasingly evident in discussions of business by insiders and outsiders alike. The understanding that the large business corporation had become a key social institution, inextricably involved in the lives and fortunes of all the American people, was a lesson which depression taught even more effectively than prosperity.[35]

The Harvard Business School, with its journal, *The Harvard Business Review*, continued to serve in the Thirties as a training ground and—occasionally—a critic for the trusteeship concept of management. Reporting on the Seventh International Management Congress, held in Washington in 1938, one business school faculty member noted that nine of the sixteen papers delivered at the congress's general sessions had dealt with social and economic responsibilities. He found the assembled industrialists "fully aware, painfully so," of their interests in this field; but many of them were "regrettably vague on the subject." What was particularly significant and unfortunate, they still tended in their thinking to draw a sharp line between operational matters and social and human problems. "To bring the two into daily operating harmony is the task which this and the succeeding generation must accomplish or such ground as has been gained will be lost, probably irretrievably." [36]

The *Review* chided business leadership for its failure to understand and accept some New Deal legislation as an expression of public dissatisfaction with its performance. Too much time was spent resenting and resisting governmental intrusions, and not enough was devoted to searching for their causes and attempting to eliminate them. "Business statesmanship" presented the obligation, not of opposition for opposition's sake, but rather of constructive analysis of society's needs, by means of which private enterprise and the public interest could be reconciled.[37]

A book which strongly reflected some aspects of the Harvard influ-

[35] For a variety of expressions of this view of business management, see the following: Arthur Pound, *Industrial America*, 26; Hicks, *Industrial Relations*, 167; A. P. Young, "Social Responsibilities of Business: A Manager's View," *Annals*, CCIV (July, 1939), 86–92; Robert S. Watt, "Social Responsibilities of Business: A Labor View," *ibid.*, 80–85; Dimock and Hyde, *Bureaucracy and Trusteeship in Large Corporations*, 107–22; Gordon, *Business Leadership in the Large Corporation*, 147, 222ff.

[36] F. E. Felts, "The Recent Literature of Business Management," *HBR*, XVII (Autumn, 1938), 117–24. The books reviewed by Professor Felts in this article, however, deal for the most part with technical rather than human aspects of management.

[37] Charles I. Gragg, "Reform Law and Business Statesmanship," *HBR*, XVII (Summer, 1939), 414–33. Gragg, also a business school faculty member, had formerly served as director of marketing research for the Manufacturers' Research Association.

ence in business thought was Chester I. Barnard's *The Functions of the Executive*, which appeared in 1938. Barnard was president of the New Jersey Bell Telephone Company. His interest in the philosophical, structural, and moral dimensions of business organization had been strengthened by association with a number of Harvard Business School faculty members, including Wallace B. Donham, Elton Mayo, and T. N. Whitehead. Barnard's book, based upon his Lowell Institute lectures in 1937, attempted to formulate a theory of the executive function suited to the conditions of large, complex social organizations. As an analysis of the theory of management, *The Functions of the Executive* marked the growing recognition on the part of the academic community of the social significance of business and its institutional relations. It signified, too, the emergence in managerial circles of a new sense of the intellectual aspects of business organization and administration.

Barnard concerned himself primarily with the structural elements in formal organizations and the way these elements molded, and were in turn modified by, human relationships and motivations. Although his treatment dealt almost exclusively with the internal dimensions of business, or other, organizations, it had obvious applications to their external affairs as well. Barnard's view of the executive or administrator as one whose responsibility it was to reconcile divergent interests and motives and build cooperation among diverse groups and specialties was a more sophisticated version of the idea of managerial trusteeship.[38]

A more flamboyant interpretation of management's role was offered, against the uncertain background of a menacing second world war, by James Burnham. Drawing upon a Veblenesque faith in the primacy and integrity of technological processes, on Berle's and Means's conception of the separation of ownership from control in the business system, on a depression-fostered disillusionment with the capitalist economy, and on an appropriate awe at the mushrooming powers of the state in both its democratic and its totalitarian forms, Burnham projected a "Managerial Revolution" underlying and hastening the collapse of traditional societies. Behind the apparent conflict of democracy with totalitarianism, of laissez faire capitalism with "New Dealism," Burnham thought he saw the emerging outlines of a new order. It would be an order in which the managers, the organizers and

[38] Chester I. Barnard, *The Functions of the Executive* (Cambridge, Massachusetts, 1938). See also M. F. Copeland, "The Job of an Executive," *HBR*, XVIII (Winter, 1940), 148–60.

administrators of society's productive machinery, would take the lead. Already they were assuming the reins of power from the owners of property and the finance capitalists. Ultimately, with the state as the characteristic instrument of their control, they would achieve a position of recognized and unrivaled dominance based upon their mastery of the forces of production.[39]

Burnham's vision, although shrouded in the trappings of objective and neutral analysis, was apocalyptic. It was scarcely encouraging to business leaders to learn that the system under which they had risen to leadership was doomed, and it was possibly even less satisfactory to be told that they and their supposed arch-enemy, the New Deal, were together the advance agents of such a social transformation. Still, Burnham offered a not-implausible interpretation of an era marked by disillusionments and doubts. And the heroes of his drama, even if not fully cognizant of their heroic role, were the managers—already leaders and destined to be arbiters of the future. This was consolation and encouragement, indeed.

Burnham had singled out the administrators, the " 'production managers,' operating executives, superintendents, administrative engineers, land supervisory technicians," as the managerial models for his new order. It is therefore of more than incidental interest that the participants in the 1938 International Management Congress included relatively few such men. Although the Congress roster listed many of the top executive officers of important American business corporations, legal and sales experience loomed largest in their backgrounds. The discrepancy between Burnham's theory and this reality, however, may have been less than it appeared, since the thinking of the delegates reflected what one observer described as a "painful sense of responsibility." Some appeared to be "oppressed by the burdens of Atlas"; and yet as a group they recognized that they must indicate their acceptance of responsibility for "industrial statesmanship." The major New Deal regulatory legislation had by now been upheld in the courts, and business faced a choice between acknowledging obligations to the public only under the threat of compulsion or on a broader, more voluntary basis. Under such circumstances some felt they could discern the emergence of a new, if not yet clearly defined, social philosophy,

[39] James Burnham, *The Managerial Revolution. What is Happening in the World* (New York, 1941). For comment, see *Business Week*, 24 May 1941, 68, and "Coming Rulers of the United States," *Fortune*, XXIV (November, 1941) 100ff. Paul M. Sweezy, "The Illusion of 'The Managerial Revolution,'" *Science and Society*, VI (Winter, 1942), 1–23, offers a Marxist critique.

one which recognized that "the major problem of industrial management lies outside the factory gates in industry's closer integration to
the social whole and the communities of which it is so vitally a
part." [40]

As they had in the face of the Progressive attacks of an earlier era,
businessmen responded to the New Deal reforms with a renewed emphasis upon the professional character and responsibilities of management. Lewis H. Brown, president of the Johns-Manville Corporation,
used the occasion of the 1938 International Management Congress to
underline the high qualifications of "a whole new generation of executives who occupy a strictly professional status. . . ." Acknowledging
that the full implications of managerial trusteeship had not yet been
fully grasped, he accepted social consequences, as well as private
profits, as an appropriate test of performance.

The argument for managerial professionalism, better justified by the
patterns of managerial recruitment in the Thirties than it had been a
decade earlier, was still difficult to sustain at a time when memories of
the depression remained vivid. Like other businessmen, Lewis Brown
was tempted to fall back on familiar calls for acceptance of a "new
concept of mutuality of interest" between business and the community
or for the framing of a new industrial "creed." Nor did his demand for
professional status fully accord with his suggestion that business court
public favor by staying "as simple and unpretentious as an old
shoe." [41] The defensive tone of such phrases was clear. Not until conditions changed and confidence returned could businessmen move toward a more comprehensive view of their relationship to society and
its needs.

THE SECOND WORLD WAR

Doubts and disagreements about the position of management, the
relationship of business to society, and the proper scope of corporate
philanthropy all characterized business thought in the 1930s. Yet such
were the dimensions of economic crisis and social need that even the
uncertainties of the time failed to block entirely the development of
new ideas and practices. As the "depression decade" drew to a close
and international problems superseded domestic issues in the head-

[40] Bronson Batchelor, *The New Outlook in Business*, 10. The book contains
summaries and excerpts of the views expressed at the congress. See also Beardsley
Ruml, *Tomorrow's Business* (New York, 1945).

[41] *Ibid.*, 91–100.

lines, new circumstances accelerated the pace of change. The return of prosperity and the approach of war altered business prospects. As had been true in the First World War, ideas and policies binding business closer to the community, which had developed slowly under peacetime conditions, now were forged into strong ties with remarkable speed.

Under the uneven impact of economic conditions in the late Thirties, corporation giving grew uncertainly but perceptibly. Recession, war "jitters," and other explanations were offered by community chest officials to explain fluctuations in their yearly returns. Yet, beneath the surface of events indications could be found of growing corporate interest and support for a variety of community needs. After 1939, defense orders offered a new stimulus to industry and employment, and funds were pumped into circulation through the by now accepted channels of philanthropy as well as through the market. A comparison of corporate gifts to the Atlanta Community Fund, for example, showed nearly a one hundred per cent increase in dollars contributed in the 1941 campaign over the figures for 1929. During the same years, the number of contributors had increased by one-third, from 332 to 433. Comparing corporate gifts to community chests in 1941 with the annual average for the decade 1920–29, a National Industrial Conference Board study indicated that such gifts had risen from 22 per cent of total contributions to 27 per cent. Still another study of the "top ten" corporate community chest donors in 53 cities showed that they had increased their gifts by 13½ per cent between 1929 and 1939. Company gifts to the Salvation Army had increased from 9.67 per cent of total gifts in 1934 to 21.63 per cent by 1937, according to the same report; but the United Hospital Fund of New York City had suffered a decline in corporate giving from over 31 per cent of total receipts in 1935 to less than 7 per cent by 1938.[42]

Education, as well as health and welfare, mirrored the uneven effects of fluctuating interest and support. Fund raisers for the Univer-

[42] "Company Policy on Donations," NICB, Studies in Business Policy, No. 7, 1945. The data in this report were drawn from a varying number of community chests and are therefore not statistically comparable. Survey, LXXIII (January, 1937), 21–22; Survey Midmonthly, LXXV (January, 1939), 16; Madeline Berry, "Corporations Set Giving Pace," Community Chests and Councils, Inc., June, 1939, UCFCA File 72: Corporation Giving—Pamphlets; Boyce M. Edens, "Corporation Giving," speech at the Southeast Conference, 1941, UCFCA File 106: Speeches, for Atlanta. "Staff Letter of John Price Jones Corporation," XX, No. 37, 5 August 1939, JPJC Papers, cites the Community Chests and Councils "top ten" report.

sity of Chicago had secured $57,000 in 1934–35 through a separate division for solicitation of business firms. Riding the business cycle, company contributions rose to $63,000 in 1936–37, then fell below $40,000 the following year, only to struggle upward again. The University of Pennsylvania achieved later but even greater success in winning the ear of company executives. The files of the John Price Jones Corporation, which handled solicitations for the university, showed a single company gift of $25 in 1938 and only four gifts totalling $75 in 1939, but corporate subscriptions to the University's Bi-Centennial Fund in 1940 and 1941 reached $113,000.[43]

If the approach of war loosened company pursestrings and quickened corporate consciences, war itself intensified the process. A 1945 survey of 578 manufacturing corporations found only one which made no charitable contributions whatever; gifts to community chests by these companies had risen from 27 per cent of total community chest receipts in 1941 to 33 per cent by 1944. Patriotic motives, the extraordinary social needs of wartime, the equally extraordinary profits enjoyed by an economy strained to the limits of its productive capacity, a tax structure making philanthropy an attractive alternative to governmental expropriation of excess profits—all these factors combined to stimulate new ventures in corporate giving.

In 1941 and 1942 the International Business Machines and DuPont companies gave $50,000 and $40,000, respectively, to the United Services Organization campaign, while other large corporations also made substantial contributions. General Motors and the United States Steel Corporation in 1942 were reported as giving $75,000 each to the United China Relief Fund. By 1943, with a ninety per cent excess profits tax in effect, gifts by large corporations reached unprecedented levels. The New York Committee of the National War Fund in that year received from U. S. Steel $750,000 and from General Electric and Bethlehem Steel $300,000 each. As the war ended and another Victory Campaign and War Fund was launched in September of 1945, fifteen large corporations pledged $1,372,000 even before the formal drive began.[44]

[43] For the University of Chicago, see JPJC Papers, Casebook 265: University of Chicago. For the University of Pennsylvania, Casebook 245: The University of Pennsylvania, "University of Pennsylania Bi-Centennial Fund." One Jones Corporation estimate put total corporate contributions at $29 million in 1936, compared with $58 million in 1941. Memorandum entitled "More About Corporate Giving," 29 September 1945, JPJC Papers, Case 4: "Giving . . . Corporations."

[44] "Company Policies on Donations," NICB, Studies in Business Policy, No. 7, 1945; JPJC Papers, Casebook 334: United Services Organization, Inc., 1941 and

The National War Fund, established by business and welfare agency leaders in 1943 to coordinate fund raising for the host of war-related appeals which flooded the nation, carried business commitments to relief and other welfare programs to unprecedented levels. Relying heavily on the community chests for leadership and techniques, the fund brought into the orbit of philanthropic giving more companies and more executives than had ever participated before. In three annual nationwide campaigns sponsored by the fund between 1943 and 1945, over $321,000,000 were raised and distributed. Businessmen such as Winthrop W. Aldrich, Gerard Swope, Irving S. Olds, and Edward T. Ryerson gave their names and services in an attempt to bring order out of a potentially chaotic situation. In addition to promoting contributions, fund leaders scrutinized budgets, evaluated competing or overlapping agencies, and attempted to steer funds to areas of greatest need.

In its role as mobilizer of voluntary support for wartime relief and service programs, the National War Fund made an impressive contribution. Its effect upon the growth of business relations and expectations in the philanthropic fields was equally important. In every community, it drew into the planning and practice of giving, companies and executives hitherto unaffected. It played a vital role in the development of corporate philanthropy by helping to convert the extraordinary into the expected.[45]

Still, with due regard for such spectacular, if substantially tax-induced, philanthropy, it was also true that corporate giving barely kept pace with the overall rate of economic expansion. Not until 1945 did it reach the level of one per cent of company profits, despite the five per cent exemption provided by law since 1936. Furthermore, it was the smaller corporations which gave more generously in relation to their resources. Nevertheless, a significant spreading of the habit of corporate giving did entail a substantial increase in its volume.

What wartime problems and prosperity did for corporate philanthropy in consolidating and extending the experience gained in the

1942; "A Memorandum to the Officers and Directors of New York Corporations," JPJC Papers, Casebook 4, "Giving . . . Corporations." See *New York Times,* 12 April 1942, for gifts to United China Relief. See *Chicago Tribune,* 7 September 1945, for gifts to the 1945 Victory campaign and War Fund. Between 1939 and 1951 eighteen states passed laws authorizing corporations to make charitable contributions. Beardsley Ruml, *Manual of Corporate Giving,* 45.

[45] Harold J. Seymour, *Design for Giving. The Story of the National War Fund, Inc., 1943–47* (New York, 1947), 64–67, *passim.* Giving by corporations constituted between thirty-five and forty per cent of wartime contributions, compared with a pre-war average of less than twenty per cent.

Thirties, it did also for ideas concerning the role of business in society. The doubt and defensiveness which had characterized business
thought during the depression rapidly faded. Business emerged from
the war triumphant, its capacity to perform economic miracles—under the forced draft of military orders, to be sure—no longer in doubt.
The renewal of confidence and leadership provided a climate of business opinion in which initiative in exploring the social dimensions of
corporate enterprise was encouraged. No one expressed better than
Henry J. Kaiser this spirit of renewed opportunity and adventure. "We
have fulfilled ourselves," Kaiser rejoiced before the 1942 annual meeting of the NAM. "We can dare and we can face, unafraid, *now, to-
night,* whatever is to come." [46] In such a mood, with determination to
recapture lost prestige and freedom of action, yet prodded continually
by external pressures both at home and abroad, businessmen were
prepared to undertake new explorations of the idea of social responsibility.

[46] For the psychology of wartime and post-war business leadership, see Boyce F.
Martin, "What Business Learns from the War," *HBR*, XXI (Spring, 1943), 358–
68; Edgar M. Queezy, *The Spirit of Enterprise* (New York, 1943). Henry J.
Kaiser's speech, "Management Looks at the Post-War World," was published by
the Newcomen Society of England, American Branch, 1943.

8 · NEW HORIZONS OF CORPORATE RESPONSIBILITY, 1945–1960

Chastened by the experiences of the Thirties, yet encouraged by post-war prosperity, American business in the 1950s extended its social interests in new directions. Even less than at the close of the First World War did it prove possible after 1945 to return to the conditions which had defined the social horizons of business during the prewar years. The business literature of the Fifties was crowded with discussions of social problems and of management's responsibilities for dealing with them. Although in principle there was little that went beyond the trusteeship concept enunciated nearly a quarter of a century earlier, the elaboration of the concept and the new areas of application opened to it did signify an important advance. A second major phase had emerged in the development of the idea of the social responsibility of business. As the trials of peace and plenty replaced those of war and depression, business leadership was drawn into participation in a range of social interests and institutions extending well beyond what was hitherto considered appropriate. Education, recreation, the arts, and even politics discovered claims upon business which executives were willing to acknowledge.

At the end of the war, however, concern for the immediate problem of conversion to a peacetime economy temporarily delayed the exploration of new social interests. Purely patriotic motives for corporate philanthropy ended with the war; and the repeal of the excess profits tax in November, 1945, removed another incentive for giving. As problems of reconversion and adjustment demanded the attention of top management, interest in the social responsibilities of business temporarily waned. *Business Week* in 1946 noted what it called a "Pause for Inquiry" on the part of many companies—a reexamination of motives and interests in the context of peace and, in part, an expression of doubt at the many "causes" which wartime enthusiasm and prosperity had spawned. Company officials were warned to consult their chambers of commerce and other recognized evaluation agencies before making contributions. Surveys of company policies and practices were undertaken as guides in developing more orderly and consistent procedures for the future.[1] By 1948 business had completed with unexpected smoothness its conversion to peacetime production. Prosperity continued, although with some uncertainty as to its probable duration.

External conditions, therefore, assumed a higher priority in business thinking; and on this front the prospects appeared to many businessmen considerably less promising than did those for purely economic progress. Despite the achievements and resurgent prestige of business leadership, dangers seemed to hover on both the domestic and the international horizons, calling for efforts to define and defend in newer, more imaginative terms what had come to be called the private enterprise system. At home, business still confronted a national government which many felt lacked understanding of the conditions basic to a free and private economy. The "Fair Deal" policies of the Truman administration were often alarming; and even the self-proclaimed "businessman's government" offered by President Eisenhower after 1953 proved less willing to undo the work of the New Deal than many conservatives had expected.

Overseas, the situation seemed even more alarming. The spread of communism among peoples and nations released from the bonds of empire and war troubled most Americans. During the 1950s, preoccupation with the specter of a worldwide Communist conspiracy had reached its peak; but even earlier businessmen as well as many others had become uncomfortably aware that democracy and the private enterprise economy faced formidable challenges in an era of internation-

---

[1] *Business Week,* "Pause for Inquiry," 6 July 1946, 17–18; Paul H. Davis, "Will Gifts to Universities Continue?" *School and Society,* LXI (10 March 1945), 145; NICB Studies in Business Policy, No. 7, 1945, "Company Policy on Donations." See also "Survey of Business Practices: Postwar Trends in Corporation Giving," JPJC Papers, Case 4: Giving—Corporations.

al upheaval. Uncertainty and concern for the future prevailed as businessmen in the late Forties examined their posture and prospects. The belief that they and the firms whose fortunes they directed had a positive role to play in the strengthening of democratic society was manifest in both their words and actions.

Changes in the internal composition of business leadership were also having important effects upon managerial social horizons. The elder business statesmen, mellowed by survival and success, were passing from the scene in a climate of confidence and accommodation. Their successors, a third generation of corporate leaders, constituted even more clearly a professional management schooled in the theory and practice of large-scale operations. The business school students of the Twenties and Thirties, after rigorous postgraduate training in the classrooms of depression and war, were scaling the heights of the corporate pyramids.

From the new perspectives of management, new approaches to the social relations of business emerged. One analysis of business participation in community affairs distinguished three phases through which attitudes and policies had passed: "the isolation stage with its company police," the "philanthropic stage with its public relations men," and the "cooperative stage with its community relations studies." [2] Such a classification was obviously too simple. It overlooked the fact that a given company or business organization might find itself in two or more of these stages simultaneously with regard to its policies toward different community interests. In some respects, the Cleveland Chamber of Commerce had placed itself in the "cooperative" stage as early as the first decade of the century, while the supposedly progressive General Electric Company, for example, had not clearly emerged from the "philanthropic" stage as late as the 1950s.

Still, over the years business executives on the whole had learned the lesson that "businesses can fight or cooperate with local agencies, but they cannot ignore them." John L. McCaffery, president of the International Harvester Company, put this understanding straightforwardly: "We can't expect the community to be interested in our problems unless we are interested in it and its problems." [3] It was against such a background of circumstances and commitments that the officers

[2] Ralph B. Spence, "Some Needed Research on Industry Within the Community," *Journal of Educational Sociology*, XXVII (December, 1953), 147–51.

[3] Quoted in Robert G. Dyment, "The Contributions Problem. How International Harvester Handles It," *American Business*, LVII (August, 1957), 28–30ff. For the preceding quotation, see William H. Form and Delbert C. Miller, *Industry, Labor, and Community* (Bloomington, 1960), 8.

of many companies in the course of the 1950s reviewed the nature and extent of corporate interest in community problems and resources which previously had received only casual attention.

BUSINESS AND EDUCATION

Most successful of the new claimants upon corporate time and treasure in the postwar era were the institutions of American higher education. Business and the colleges and universities had long recognized common interests. Leaders of education had been prominent among those calling for closer attention to the ethical and social implications of business. The development of business education had paralleled the economy's growing need for specialists in all the lines of activity required for planning and supervising intricate production and distribution processes. During the 1920s new business courses had begun to emphasize the role of managers as leaders and mediators, as economic "statesmen" with broad social perspectives. Business and education thus shared a concern for the training of the nation's economic leadership. It was widely assumed that corporation executives, recognizing their dependence upon the nation's colleges and universities for the production of such leadership, would support them financially.[4]

Between 1929 and 1945, the attention of most businessmen was focused on other matters than their stake in the fortunes of higher education; but even before the end of the Second World War there were signs of growing awareness of the dependence of the American economy on scholarship and learning. The scientific and engineering research which had assured America's victory in the battle of production inevitably impressed those who directed the effort. The dependence of American business upon industrial research had long been recognized in principle; the war erased the last doubt as to the absolutely essential character of that relationship. It also demonstrated the equally important role of organizational and administrative knowledge in adjusting to rapidly changing demands. As business officials looked ahead, they saw the value of maintaining the close relations which war had fostered between their firms and leaders in science and education. This feeling was no doubt strengthened by recollections of the mutual suspicion which had separated the groups during the depres-

---

[4] Subscriptions to the *Harvard Business Review*, long a focal point for discussions of business professional and social problems, increased markedly in the 1950s.

sion years. It was reinforced in some quarters by a desire to minimize, if not wholly silence, the "radicalism" conservatives often associated with the nation's intellectual centers. A variety of motives, then, underlay consideration of the interdependence of business and education as the Second World War ended and a new and uncertain peace emerged.

In the summer of 1944 the Los Angeles Chamber of Commerce and the NAM jointly sponsored a conference on education and industry which revealed several of these concerns. Speakers underlined the desirability of continued partnership between the two fields; they noted the relationship of living standards to general educational levels. "The best barometer of business is the cultural level of the masses of people in a community. . . . The volume of business is in direct proportion to the level of education of the people, their wants, and their abilities to purchase. . . ." A common stake in the preservation of freedom, both academic and economic, was stressed; and references were made to the need to weed out "subversive elements" in industry, labor, and education.[5] Some businessmen made clear their beliefs that the schools bore primary responsibility for maintaining cordial relations with industry and that criticism of business should therefore be muted. "The making of a life and the making of a living should be done under auspices that have sympathetic understanding," insisted Dwayne Orton, director of education for the International Business Machines Corporation.[6]

The needs of American universities and colleges themselves did as much as any overarching interest on the part of businessmen to draw attention to education as an area of interest for corporate enterprise. The rush of veterans to the nation's colleges after the war, as well as the general increase in college enrollments, brought unprecedented demands upon budgets and facilities. As high taxes and the diffusion of corporate ownership foreshadowed the end of large private fortunes, educators looked elsewhere for new sources of financial sup-

[5] W. C. Bagley, "The Interdependence of Business and Education," *School and Society*, LX (2 September 1944), 148–49.

[6] Dwayne Orton, "The Interdependence of Business and Education," *School and Society*, LXII (22 September 1945), 178–80. See also *ibid.*, LXII (10 November 1945), 304. For subsequent discussions of difficulties encountered in building understanding between business leadership and educational circles, see J. Austin Burkhart, "Big Business and the Schools," *Nation*, CLXXIII (10 November 1951), 400–402; *Newsweek*, 17 September 1951, 58; and *Business Week*, 22 September 1951, 64. These articles point to the continuing difficulty some businessmen faced in distinguishing between true education and propaganda pure and simple.

port. As had the community chests in the Twenties, college and university presidents turned hopeful eyes upon the business corporation. Out of the financial needs of education on the one hand and a growing awareness by corporate executives of the world outside their offices on the other, was forged a new alliance. One outcome was to be a significant strengthening of the financial foundations of private education in the United States. Another, equally important, was a further broadening of the conception of private business enterprise as a social institution.[7]

Among the first to urge the plight of the nation's overstrained educational institutions upon the attention of the business community was Laird Bell, a lawyer and director of several large corporations who served also as vice-chairman of the board of trustees of the University of Chicago. Writing in The Atlantic Monthly in May, 1948, Bell called upon corporate managers, as the custodians of wealth belonging in point of law to a widely distributed and diversified ownership, to exercise their discretionary powers in the light of the social obligations inherent in such control. These obligations, already acknowledged through gifts to charity and community chests, should be extended to include education, Bell argued. The tradition of independent scholarship was maintained with difficulty by private colleges and universities in the face of rising economic pressures. The freedom to study and learn, Bell felt, was the counterpart of economic freedom. Business had a stake in efforts to prevent academic "dry rot and mediocrity," to support pure research and untrammeled thought and experimentation.

Noting the pleasure which corporate officers might derive from the avoidance of taxes through increased philanthropic giving, Bell recognized the difficulty they faced in justifying to themselves and their

[7] Frank W. Abrams, board chairman of Standard Oil of New Jersey in the 1950s and one of the leaders in the drive to promote corporate support for higher education, stated that his interest in this field stemmed from two considerations. One, highly personal, was his appreciation of what a college education had meant in his own life in equipping him for a career in business. The second was his interest in improving public attitudes toward his company, following criticisms made by Congressman Jerry Voorhis of Standard's part in the wartime production of synthetic rubber. Interview with Frank W. Abrams, 27 December 1963. Further influences noted by Abrams upon his personal conception of management's role were the examples of Owen D. Young in relationship to community affairs and of Clarence Hicks in the field of industrial and human relations. See also "Colleges Turn to Industry," Business Week, 10 September 1949, 97ff., for recognition of the economic problems of higher education.

shareholders gifts to institutions which, at first glance, seemed remote from the direct interests of profit-making concerns. Yet he felt that ways could be found to make giving both effective and practical. Some companies were already donating to scholarship programs, to regional college associations, to the United Negro College Fund, to specific industrial-oriented programs and schools. A few of the "advanced corporations" had already recognized that "it is good business to promote higher education in its research aspects." Bell believed that the "logical next step is to recognize an obligation to promote both theoretical research at the university level and the production of good citizens at the college level." [8]

Laird Bell's concern for the future of American colleges and universities had been stimulated, as was that of others, by a 1947 report of the Commission on Higher Education created by President Truman. Surveying past patterns and future prospects the commission members, most of them educators, marked out an ambitious role for educational institutions. Their contributions to individual fulfillment and responsibility, to international understanding and cooperation, to economic opportunity and political freedom were of fundamental importance. The goal of equal educational opportunity for all, according to needs and capabilities, set new tasks and standards for the nation's colleges and universities. Opportunity for more people to pursue knowledge at higher levels and in more diverse forms was central to the development of a "democratic dynamic" suited to the times.

The commission carefully considered the financial pressures its recommendations entailed for American higher education. It reviewed in some detail the possible sources of future support, both for private and for public institutions of higher learning. Attention was called specifically to the fund-raising models provided by relief and welfare agencies: well-coordinated, carefully planned group appeals. The United Negro College Fund, through which in 1944 twenty-seven Negro colleges had organized a nationwide solicitation effort, was cited as an example of an "educational community chest" already in operation. Possibilities for increasing individual gifts to education through better-organized appeals appeared substantial, but the commission laid even greater stress upon corporation giving as a resource heretofore only slightly tapped. Both educational and business leaders were urged to undertake new efforts to the end that private support might be increased to meet unprecedented needs.

[8] Laird Bell, "If Corporations Will Give," *The Atlantic Monthly*, CLXXXI (May, 1948), 68–72.

Even assuming that private colleges and universities could double their support by 1960, bringing it to the level of $200,000,000 per year, the commission concluded that this sum would still fall short of the need. Nor would anticipated increases in existing types of public expenditure for higher education simplify the problem. The expansion of state and local institutions might be expected to drain some funds from private schools, while the unequal resources of different states and communities would make it impossible for public colleges and universities to offer equal educational opportunities to all students. On these and other counts the commission based its final recommendation: that federal funds underwrite the elimination of inequalities and assure the unhampered development of a total educational system for the unprecedented challenges facing the American people.[9]

If the commission's suggestions for organized appeals by colleges and universities for corporate financial aid stimulated interest among both educators and business leaders, its proposal for the expansion of federal aid to higher education aroused outright alarm. Coming at a time when many Americans were eagerly anticipating a reduction of government's role in the life of the nation, these recommendations jarred the business community. It is in this context that the sudden and surprisingly fervent interest of American business leaders in the problems of private higher education must be understood. Reactions to the suggestion that business now undertake to support higher education and obviate the pressures for governmental initiative varied among them. Some arguments for corporate assistance to the colleges and universities were thoughtfully couched in terms of educational needs and their importance for business. Others emphasized ideological considerations, stressing that private education and private enterprise must join in resistance to socialistic encroachments. For both business and educational leaders, however, the issue of federal aid raised the question of the status of private education in a free society.

Laird Bell's appeal to the corporate conscience on behalf of higher education caused a series of discussions and exhortations to issue from the press, the conference table, speakers' platforms, and other forums of business opinion. Between 1948 and 1952 leaders of the business community swung into line, affirming the justice and propriety of corporate support for the colleges and universities. Arguments for the inclusion of education within the circle of corporate philanthropies ranged from the crass and obviously self-serving to the sophisticated and en-

[9] The President's Commission on Higher Education, *Higher Education for American Democracy* (6 vols., New York, 1948), I, 101–3, *passim.*, and V, 45–49, *passim.*

lightened. Among those who saw in education a "most fertile field of protection against creeping socialism," the desire to avoid federal aid to education was obviously influential. Laird Bell's emphasis upon the issue of academic freedom, which put the question of public versus private education in a more positive context, was echoed by Beardsley A. Ruml and others. Other common themes were the premium upon corporate contributions arising from the five per cent income tax deduction and the additional economic incentive provided by the revival of the excess profits tax during the Korean war.[10]

Among the most effective advocates of corporate contributions to education were Frank W. Abrams of Standard Oil (New Jersey), Irving S. Olds of United States Steel, and Alfred P. Sloan, Jr., of General Motors—a trio whose combined powers of persuasion among their business colleagues would have been difficult to match. Their efforts paved the way for rapid and general acceptance of corporate support for higher education in the 1950s. Although their companies had long contributed to community welfare agencies, the men were surprised by the swiftness with which they were themselves caught up in a new range of interests.

Irving S. Olds, in the course of the Second World War, had found himself bearing virtually sole responsibility for administering U. S. Steel's massive gifts to a variety of national and international welfare and emergency agencies. Speaking of this unaccustomed role to an interviewer in the course of the war, Olds had revealed a certain discomfort as to its scope, together with confidence that at the war's end the practice of company giving would return to "normal" levels and

[10] Officials of colleges and universities sought, and tried to justify, company gifts with most of the same arguments advanced by businessmen themselves. In addition, college presidents sometimes felt called upon to uphold educational independence from business control, on the one hand, and to reassure executives worried about "dangerous" and "radical" influences on the campus, on the other. See statements by Presidents White (of Haverford), "The Tuition Plan's Forum on Education and Industry," *School and Society*, LXX, 21 February 1953, 120–22; Griswold (of Yale), in A. H. Raskin, "The Corporation and the Campus," *New York Times Magazine*, 17 April 1955, 12ff.; and Hatcher (of Michigan), "Business, Congress, Education—Where Are We Going?" *Comm. Chron.*, CLXXXV (6 June 1957), 2618ff. Hatcher dwelt upon fears of federal aid to education. Speaking in the context of public alarm at the growing power of the Soviet Union, he said, "It is easier and more fun to solve this one [private support of higher education] than to learn Russian. And, as General Motors' Dr. Hofstad is alleged to have said, 'We will have to do one or the other.'"

See also Arthur S. Lord, Assistant Director of Development, Yale University, "Last Frontier. How Much Should Corporations Finance the Colleges?" *Barron's*, XXXII (18 August 1952), 5.

channels. By 1951, however, Olds had concluded that, since trained minds were a vital resource for American industry, education was a matter of prime economic significance. Business, he asserted, had "a direct obligation to support the free, independent, privately endowed colleges and universities to the limit of its financial and legal authority. And unless it . . . meets this obligation, I do not believe it is properly protecting the long range interests of its stockholders, its employees, and its customers." [11]

Frank W. Abrams, even after launching his career as a promoter of corporate aid to private education, continued to be surprised that he had actually done so. He found it "like being thrown into a Billy Sunday meeting . . . and getting converted. You didn't want to go in, but somebody pushed you—they thought you needed it." He added, "And it has been rather overwhelming and highly gratifying." Abrams denied that there was any distinction between the by now established practice of corporate giving to charities where no direct benefit could be shown and gifts to colleges and universities. Such contributions, he urged, were in the long-range interest both of a company's stockholders and of the nation. He tried both to put the positive case for aid to education before businessmen and to reduce the obstacles of tradition, habit, or law which stood in the way of its widespread acceptance. Receiving an award for outstanding service to education in 1952, Abrams asserted that, already, "increasing numbers of business managers . . . feel that corporations should not take substantial benefits from their membership in the economic community while avoiding the normally accepted obligations of citizenship in the social community." [12]

[11] "Interview with Irving S. Olds of the United States Steel Corporation," R. F. Duncan to John Price Jones, JPJC Papers, Case 4, "Giving—Corporations," Duncan quoted Olds: "If anyone had told me in 1938 that the Steel Corporation would be giving away $1,600,000 in 1944, I'd have laughed at him. Of course, this . . . will die out quickly when the war ends." U. S. Steel Corporation donations of over $10,000 required the approval of the board of directors.

Olds, "Should Business Support the College?" *Fortune*, XLIV (December, 1951), 74. See also "Needed: More Help for Colleges," *Management Review*, XLIII (September, 1954), 563–64, quoted from *Time*, LXIII (18 January 1954), 82. In this article A. A. Stambaugh, board chairman of Standard Oil of Ohio, was quoted to much the same effect: "Increasingly, corporation gifts are coming to be regarded as a blue-chip investment that will eventually pay heavy dividends."

[12] A. H. Raskin, "The Corporation and the Campus"; "The Tuition Plan's Forum on 'Education and Industry,'" *School and Society*, LXXVII (21 February 1953), 120–22; *Business Week*, 19 February 1949, 36.

Pointing to rising costs, Alfred P. Sloan, Jr., in the same year upheld contributions by business to higher education as infinitely preferable to federal subsidies. Sloan argued that, "in its own interest, corporate enterprise should support the sources from which fundamental knowledge flows"; and he compared such expenditures with payments for medical and welfare benefits for employees.[13]

Officials of the NAM as well as of other business organizations took up the cause. In 1951, the National Planning Association issued a general endorsement of company giving and published a pamphlet, "The Five Per Cent," by Beardsley Ruml and Theodore Geiger, which offered corporate officials an explanation of the tax advantages obtainable. The following year saw the creation of the Council on Financial Aid to Education, again sponsored by the heads of large corporations to act as a clearing house of information and to promote closer ties between the executive suites and the campuses.[14] An all-out effort on behalf of business support for higher education had been launched.

It was not only a talent for organization that executives such as Frank W. Abrams brought to business-educational relations. As professional managers and, frequently, as lawyers, officials of large corporations were conscious of the powers they wielded, as well as of the limitations—legal and other—which circumscribed their free exercise of those powers. Such sensitivity undoubtedly led them to desire clarification of the legal status of corporate philanthropy in the form of educational aid. Despite well-established practices in the welfare field, despite the encouragement offered by the federal tax laws, despite the rapid spread of enabling legislation at the state level, questions contin-

[13] Alfred P. Sloan, Jr., "Big Business Must Help Our Colleges," *Colliers*, CXXVII (2 June 1951), 13–15ff.

[14] Beardsley A. Ruml and Theodore Geiger, "The Five Per Cent," Planning Pamphlet No. 70, National Planning Association, 1951; "Colleges Turn to Industry," *Business Week*, 10 September 1949, 97; "Corporate Profits and Campus Budgets," *Fortune*, XLVI (December, 1952), 108. Ruml had earlier served as dean of the University of Chicago's Social Science Division.

See also "Support Without Control," *Collier's*, CXXVIII (15 September 1951), 82; "Save by Giving," *Business Week* (22 September 1951), 66–68; "What is Enough?" *ibid.* (20 September 1952), 104ff.; "Corporate Profits and Campus Budgets," *Fortune*, XLVI (December, 1952), 108; and "The N.A.M. Launches Campaign for Financial Support of Education," *School and Society*, LXXV (24 March 1952), 204. In December, 1951, the NAM's board of directors adopted a resolution asserting that "Business enterprises must find a way to support the whole educational program—effectively, regularly, and now." An Educational Advisory Committee of businessmen was established, together with a parallel Educational Advisory Council composed of educators. *Ibid.*

ued to be raised by corporate officers and legal staffs concerning the propriety of gifts to education.

The proponents of such contributions moved directly to meet this major remaining obstacle to the achievement of their goal. A test case was arranged by the NAM and Courtney Brown, assistant to Abrams at Standard Oil, between the A. P. Smith Manufacturing Company of New Jersey and one of its stockholders. Expenses of the case were shared by the Ford Foundation and the Standard Oil Company (New Jersey). The case produced the desired verdict. Judge Stein of the Newark, N.J., Superior Court held a gift by the Smith Company to Princeton University to be in keeping not only with the right but with the "solemn duty" of corporate officials to uphold private education. The future of education, Judge Stein asserted, involved "a cause intimately tied to the preservation of American business and the American way of life. Such giving may be called an incidental power, but when it is considered in its essential character, it may well be regarded as a major, though unwritten, corporate power." [15] The Smith decision, which was upheld by higher state and national courts, went a long way to end doubts and uncertainties, supporting a marked expansion of corporate contributions in the 1950s. Coupled with the rise of organized information and fund-raising efforts, both by business and by education, the resolution of the legal question cleared a new field for corporate philanthropy and social concern.

With the acceptance of higher education as an object of corporate philanthropy came a gradually broadening conception among interested business executives of the aims and scope of education. Again, Laird Bell's 1948 article had marked a turning point. Company support for research tied to the products or interests of the firm, Bell had pointed out, neglected the more general needs of the colleges and uni-

[15] A. P. Smith Manufacturing Company v. Barlow et al., 13 N. J. 145, 98 A. 2d 551 (1953). Interview with Frank W. Abrams, 2 December 1963; "Corporations May Be Good Citizens Too," *Christian Century*, LXX (2 June 1953), 653, quoted Judge Stein; "Corporate Profits and Campus Budgets," *Fortune*, XLVI (December, 1952), 108. Craig R. Smith, "The Banker's Part in the Rise of Business Aid to Education," *Banking*, XLVII (June, 1955), 120–21ff., also quoted Judge Stein: "Nothing that aids or promotes the growth and service of the American university or college . . . can possibly be anything short of direct benefit to every corporation in the land." For another reaction to the Smith case, see John Chamberlain, "Wanted: a Medici," *Barron's*, XXXIII (22 June 1953), 5–6, arguing in the name of individualism against collective, corporate philanthropy. "Pushed beyond a certain point, the idea of the corporation as a donor is a perversion of function made necessary by a bad tax system and inflationary economics."

versities that might also have a legitimate claim on business resources. As familiarity and understanding grew between executives and educators in the 1950s, there was a noticeable increase in aid for less specialized educational activities. Gifts to building funds and to general endowment and scholarship programs, unrestricted grants, and gifts earmarked specifically for basic research or the support of general education and the liberal arts won somewhat hesitant acceptance. Women's colleges met with significant, if limited, success in persuading company representatives to recognize their pressing needs. Although businessmen could hardly have been expected completely to abandon the "practical" emphasis which had so long governed their attitudes toward American education, the range, if not the proportions, of company giving moved markedly in the course of a decade to parallel the diverse interests and undertakings characteristic of higher learning in the United States.[16]

[16] The variety of forms of financial assistance winning business support testified to the ingenuity of educators and executives in devising a contributions plan for every taste. Among them were the matching plan (whereby a company agreed to match gifts by its employees to the institution of their choice), the National Merit Scholarship program (through which company scholarships were awarded to students selected by national examination), gifts to support programs in the liberal arts, scholarships for children of employees, support in the form both of financial and personnel assistance in curriculum planning and teaching, as well as open houses, lecture-demonstrations and the like made available to students. Many of these programs are discussed in the articles listed in note 17, below.

See also "Saturday's Children at Westinghouse Labs," *Business Week*, 20 May 1960, for a description of a program aimed at promising high school students. "Colleges Seek Aid from Industry," *Iron Age*, CLXXII (20 July 1953), 44–45, describes arrangements made by the Bethlehem Steel Company with over forty colleges and universities which provided grants averaging $3000 for each college graduate who enrolled in Bethlehem's management training program. Although presented in a context stressing industry's obligation to education as "the largest single consumer of college graduates in the world," the Bethlehem program was clearly conceived as an executive recruiting device.

Writing in 1955 of a contest among corporations to find "imaginative new ways to help get private colleges and universities out of the red," A. H. Raskin of the *New York Times* asserted, "Business executives who snort at the idea that Uncle Sam ought to provide 'a quart of milk for every Hottentot' are giving enthusiastic acceptance to the notion that a company is neglecting the obligations of 'corporate citizenship' if it fails to invest part of its profits in aid to higher education." ("The Corporation and the Campus"). See also "Twenty Business Men Set Out to Start a New Trend in Financing Education," *Business Week*, 13 September 1958, 78–80ff.; "Industry and the Liberal Arts," *Saturday Review of Literature*, XXXVI (21 November 1953), 31–46; "Our Corporations Become Patrons of the Liberal Arts," *Saturday Evening Post*, CCXXVII (5 March 1955), 10ff.

One of the most interesting developments in company support for higher

The diversity of educational programs which received company support revealed the growing sophistication of business leadership and a general willingness on its part to let educational authorities determine their own needs and priorities. At a time when an all-out attack upon academic freedom had been undertaken by Senator Joseph V. McCarthy and his followers, though, the entire business community was not prepared to defer without question to the colleges and universities. Instances of strong pressure on behalf of conservative economic and political positions were numerous in the 1950s. Yet, given the mood of the times, the caution and open-mindedness of the new corporate patrons compared favorably with the attitudes of their predecessors of the Twenties.

The basis upon which the interests of business and education might legitimately meet was defined clearly and eloquently by President A. Whitney Griswold of Yale University. "Private enterprise" in higher education, he argued, was important to the nation as well as to the schools:

> If we believe that a society in which authority is diffused and individual enterprise flourishes is preferable to one that is centralized and regimented on the totalitarian pattern; if we believe that within the society of our choice there are certain dominions of the human soul and the human mind in which the state trespasses at everyone's, including its own, ultimate peril; if we believe these fundamental articles of American democracy, then I think the welfare of Yale as a private institution of higher learning requires no special pleading; and I venture the opinion that our friends and colleagues in the public institutions are as solicitous of this welfare as our own alumni.[17]

education was the so-called Cleveland One Per Cent Plan, initiated by the leaders of a number of industries headquartered in Cleveland, including the Republic Steel Corporation, The Standard Oil Company (Ohio), and the Harris-Intertype Corporation. Under this plan companies pledged to contribute one per cent of income before taxes to aid education. See Clarence W. Hall, "America's Newest Partners: Corporations and Colleges," *The Reader's Digest*, LXXVIII (February, 1961), 99–102.

[17] Quoted in John A. Pollard, "Corporate Support of Higher Education, *HBR*, XXX (September–October, 1952), 111–26. For statements of parallel business views, see "Support Without Control," *Colliers*, CXXVIII (15 September 1951), 82; "What is Enough?" *Business Week*, 20 September 1952, 104ff.; H. A. Bullis, "Business and Higher Education," *Vital Speeches*, XXI (1 April 1955), 1144–47; F. S. Allis, Jr., "How Business Antagonized Some Teachers," *Fortune*, L (Sep-

On such broad principles, if not always on their specific applications, business and education moved toward recognition of a common interest and a common responsibility.

COMMUNITY RELATIONS

Concern for the strength and independence of higher education was but one dimension, albeit perhaps the most striking one, of American businessmen's widening social horizons in the years after the Second World War. In another area, that of community relations, equally significant ideas and practices were developing. Unlike education, community relations was by now a familiar field of company involvement and interest. From Lowell to Pullman to the community chest movement of the Twenties, business had faced the problems and conditions of the towns which housed its plants and its employees. The new community relations programs were distinguished from those of the past only by the degree of conscious commitment, initiative, organization, and sophistication which companies were now prepared to pour into them.

If depression and war had underlined the extent to which cities were influenced by the profits and progress of business, motives both of community loyalty and company interest encouraged fuller consideration of these ties by businessmen. Participation in community chest work, too, as we have seen, had led some business executives to a broader view of their environment. In the depths of the depression, Arthur Pound had suggested an alternative to employment and wage increases, at limited expense to the company: "the community

tember, 1954), 131ff. H. W. Prentis, Jr., believed, "There is probably nothing in the history of American philanthropy to equal the development, both in quality and in quantity, of giving to our colleges and universities by business concerns in the last five years." "New Goals for Business," *Saturday Review*, XL (19 January 1957), 14–15.

See also Merle Curti and Roderick Nash, *Philanthropy in the Shaping of American Higher Education* (New Brunswick, 1965); Alfred G. Larke, "How Corporations Aid Education," *Dun's Review and Modern Industry*, LXV (May, 1955), 47ff.; "Giving So That It Counts," *Business Week*, 18 August 1956, 46; "The Kind of Giving That Helps," *ibid.*, 7 July 1956, 144; Frank W. Abrams, "Growth of Corporation Giving to Education," *School and Society*, LXXXVI (18 July 1958), 28–30. For emphasis by an educator on the importance of academic freedom to criticize society, see L. P. Williams, "The Educational Consequences of Laissez-Faire," *ibid.*, LXXXV (2 February 1957), 38–39. Ben Morreel, "An Industrialist Views Industry-College Cooperation," *ibid.*, LXXXI (5 February 1955), 38–40.

interest . . . is often best served by the corporation's providing facilities for recreation, education and medical care which could hardly be maintained on a strictly individual basis." As war relief agencies and solicitations multiplied in 1943, *Management Review* had discussed the difficulties involved in balancing generous impulses toward community needs with the interests of company stockholders. Support for city welfare and recreation facilities used by company employees had become common practice; but nineteen of twenty companies queried by the National Industrial Conference Board in 1946 defended their gifts to local agencies on the broader basis of an obligation "to carry part of the community's burdens." This was one more than the number mentioning direct benefits to employees as a major consideration.[18]

Securing help from local chain store managers had proved difficult for community chest leaders throughout the 1920s and 1930s, but diligent and continuing effort along these lines produced significant results. The extent to which some chain store leaders embraced the idea of fuller participation in community projects was indicated, and probably exaggerated, in the response of the Illinois Chain Store Council, Inc., to a 1948 community chest solicitation campaign: "Cooperation of chain stores in Chest campaigns is one of the most important phases of a local manager's public relations program," the Council informed its members. "Your PROMPT, CHEERFUL, ADEQUATE support can gain GOOD WILL for you and your company; your FAILURE to act responsibly CAN and WILL draw CRITICISM and ILL WILL." [19]

As more systematic approaches to community relations spread, particularly on the part of large corporations with establishments in several cities, steps were taken to develop understanding and techniques suited to local needs. Peter F. Drucker's analysis of the General Motors Corporation, in 1946, noted such steps. Community relations programs had been attempted in a number of localities in which General Motors had installations, with responsibility clearly assigned to local management; but only in Dayton, Ohio, Drucker found, had the effort proved successful. There, a "plant-city committee" had been set up as a means of bringing company officials together with community leaders. Specific topics, such as housing, employment, traffic, city plan-

---

[18] Pound, *Industrial America*, 12–13; "When the Corporation Gives to Charity," *Management Review*, XXXII (February, 1943), 73–74; Helen A. Winselman, "Industry's Community Relations," NICB, Studies in Business Policy, No. 20 (New York, 1946).

[19] Illinois Chain Store Council, Inc., Bulletin, 16 August 1948, UCFCA File 77: Chain Stores—Joint National Committee.

ning, labor supply, and wages, were reviewed. Drucker noted that General Motors' overall public relations policy, which stressed the company's need to understand the public's problems first in order to relate itself effectively to the public, was supposed to apply to community relations as well. Even in the Dayton program, still in its formative stages, Drucker felt that practice did not fully measure up to principle. Indeed, despite the "two-way street" philosophy formally enunciated in policy statements, "it is perhaps not generally understood within General Motors' management that the main purpose of such a program is not to tell the public but to listen to it. . . ." [20]

Other corporations, too, were expanding their community relations commitments and staffs. In 1950 the Ford Motor Company established a community relations department, with a committee in each of the thirty-five cities in which the corporation operated. A departmental policy statement, issued in 1956, noted that

> . . . product preference and company preference go hand in hand because people naturally associate a company with its products. . . . We must create a character of good citizenship as a whole. . . . A company's reputation in town also affects its success in recruiting good personnel, in securing reputable vendors, in maintaining the morale of its employees, and in countless other ways.[21]

One of the most elaborate, and most elaborately rationalized, of the large corporation community relations programs was that of the Gen-

[20] Drucker, *Concept of the Corporation*, 94–97. General Motors' "Dayton Plan" is also discussed in "Industry's Community Relations," NICB, Studies in Business Policy, No. 2, 2, which emphasizes its origin as a countermeasure to "considerable agitation on the part of certain political and labor leaders to discredit big business in the eyes of the public." For other company public and community relations programs, see John H. Watson, III, "Public Relations in Industry," NICB, Studies in Business Policy, No. 80 (New York, 1956).

[21] Quoted in Form and Miller, *Industry, Labor, and Community*, 616–21. Other advantages listed by Form and Miller as accruing to companies with successful community relations programs included "*equitable tax rates*, assessments, and other municipal actions; *public support* in case of trouble, such as labor difficulties, lay-offs, and plant disasters; and increased employee *productivity*, since employees tend to reflect favorable community attitudes." "Ford's Good Neighbor Policy," Community Relations Department, Ford Motor Company (Dearborn, Michigan, 1956, 1959), was published as a handbook and guide for local company officials. To encourage individual initiative and contributions by its community relations personnel, the corporation established a Community Service Awards program to honor outstanding service.

eral Electric Company as it evolved under the guidance of Lemuel R. Boulware, vice-president for public and employee relations. Boulware, whose labor relations policy upheld the "right to manage" by refusal to bargain with union representatives once company officials had determined their own version of a "best offer," took an equally aggressive approach to the company's role in the communities in which it operated. Sensitive to the political implications of corporate public relations, Boulware stressed the principle that "businessmen must behave right, make sure no general complaints about business are justified, and make equally sure any exceptions to this are cleared up promptly and voluntarily." More than this, however, Boulware wanted the case for business to be presented regularly and persuasively; and he saw community relations as one part of a total effort to "make business politically important." To this end, he mounted a major effort to promote intimate ties between corporate offices and community institutions.[22] The very ambition of such a program, however, guaranteed its failure as a genuine expression of community interests.

[22] Lemuel R. Boulware, "Big Industry in the Community—General Electric Assesses Community Relations," *Journal of Educational Psychology*, XXVII (December, 1953), 152–60. The entire issue of this journal was devoted to consideration of industry-community relations. Boulware, "What Businessmen Can Do to Combat the Foes of Business," *Human Events*, XIV (2 February 1957); John T. McCarthy, *Community Relations for Business* (Washington, 1956); "Industry's Community Relations," NICB, Studies in Business Policies, No. 20, 3–4. General Electric, on occasion, demanded "Community Loyalty" to the company and its policies—a fact which Norton E. Long interpreted as a sign of corporate weakness rather than of strength. Norton E. Long, "Corporation Satellites," in Mason, *The Corporation in Modern Society*, 215–16.

For a comprehensive treatment of the subject, based upon a study of Syracuse, New York, and featuring the General Electric Company in particular, see Wayne Hodges, *Company and Community* (New York, 1959), *passim*. See also, "Looking Around," *HBR*, XXXIV (September–October, 1956), 135ff.; John W. Welcher, "The Community Relations Problem of Industrial Companies," *ibid.*, XXVII (November, 1949), 771–80.

The Timken Roller Bearing Company, of Canton, Ohio, had won a reputation for outspoken hostility to labor unions and government regulation. Herbert E. Markley, assistant to the company's president, expounded its philosophy of community relations in 1957: "We believe a company must be a citizen in the community—a good citizen. As a good citizen, he should speak up when anything threatens the best interests of the community, directly or indirectly. For many years in the newspapers, on the radio, and by direct mail to employees' homes, we have commented, among other subjects on the evils of communism, the impact of high taxes, the consequences of federal control of local projects, the need for good citizens to make their positions known to elected representatives, the obligation to register and vote, and the effects of union proposals." "Positive Employee Relations," *The Freeman*, August, 1957, 19–31.

One firm which, because of its far-flung consumer relationships, defined its community differently, was Sears, Roebuck and Co. Theodore V. Houser, Sears' president, held that the company's responsibility was "comparable to that of any private citizen's, and is not essentially altered by the fact of corporate rather than 'individual responsibility.'" Yet, with its size and resources, Houser conceded, Sears did have a special opportunity and responsibility "as a healthy combination of self-interest and public interest." To meet its widespread concerns constructively, Sears developed a variety of services. It supported 4-H clubs, reforestation projects, and other programs aimed at assisting American farmers. In 1947 it made strawberry plants available to Kentucky farmers, hoping thereby to promote the development of cash crops—an objective not entirely divorced from Sears' long-range interests. Joining with the American Medical Association, Sears offered loans for the purchase of medical equipment to young doctors in the hope of encouraging them to practice in small towns and rural areas. Such measures were in addition to substantial financial aid extended to a variety of educational programs.[23]

Other national corporations faced still different community conditions and evolved an ingenious array of devices to suit them. Some were openly paternalistic in their approach; others were conscious of the pitfalls of paternalism. The former outlook was exemplified, perhaps unconsciously, in a statement by the Allis-Chalmers Manufacturing Company: "A corporation must be more than just a neighbor in the community—it has to be a brother to the citizens of its plant and town—and often a big brother." Sylvania Electric Products, Inc., on the other hand, issued a promise: "We will not be paternal. . . . All we want to be is a neighbor who can be counted on to do his part when any need arises, the same as any other citizen."[24]

[23] Theodore V. Houser, *Big Business and Human Values* (New York, 1957), 48–55.

[24] "As Big Companies View Their Civic Responsibilities," *American City*, LXIV (June, 1949), 93–94; *ibid.*, LX (March, 1950), 118–20. See also "Civic Minded Executives," *Time*, 24 September 1956, 86; Giddens, *Standard Oil Company*, 667–71; Reuben B. Robertson, Jr. (President, The Champion Paper Company), "The Importance of Business and Businessmen's Participation in Local, State and National Governmental and Civic Affairs," Address at the General Electric Management Conference, Associate Island, July 2, 1954; Louis B. Lundberg, *Public Relations in the Local Community* (New York, 1950); Julian L. Woodward, "The Effective Public for Plant-Community Public Relations Efforts," *Public Opinion Quarterly*, XV (Winter, 1951–52), 624–34; Thomas C. Cochran, *The American Business System, A Historical Perspective, 1900–1955* (New York, 1957), 156.

The interests and resources of large corporations almost necessarily involved them in civic relations and issues; smaller companies, too, felt many similar pressures and attractions. The Ansul Chemical Company, of Marinette, Wisconsin, for example, had by 1956 developed a broad-gauged program including plant tours, a radio program making free civic and social announcements, provision of a community emergency rescue squad on a twenty-four-hour-per-day basis, demonstrations for Fire Prevention Week, and advertisements for a local "Go To Church" campaign, as well as the usual chamber of commerce activities. The Lehigh Standard Steel Corporation, of Allentown, Pennsylvania, equipped and backed a community playground in association with other companies of the city, while Lehigh's employees volunteered their labor. An unusual variation was offered by the South Line Material Company of Birmingham, Alabama, on Saturday, October 28, 1950. On that day employees of the company reported for work as usual and, in an extra five-hour day, earned nearly $5000 which was contributed to local charity. In still different circumstances, the Mobay Chemical Company and other employers of New Martinsville, West Virginia, were spurred by the need for trained technicians in their plants to join in an effort to upgrade the county's educational system.[25]

Such initiative by smaller companies and in smaller communities indicated that the factors which sustained "good neighborship" on the part of business firms were by no means limited to the corporate giants. Indeed, it seemed more likely that the opposite was true. Heads of small concerns in moderate-sized communities had always participated as individuals in civic affairs. The nineteenth-century company town had represented merely the extreme case of such involvement. In a society which interpreted business success as indicative of inherent virtue and talent, the community naturally looked to its independent middle-class and proprietor groups—together with some professionals—for its leaders. Industrialization, bringing large-scale organization and absentee ownership, had to a considerable degree undermined these traditional sources of guidance and initiative. In 1946 a United States Senate report had argued on the basis of supposedly objective criteria of economic and social welfare, that com-

---

[25] Form and Miller, *Industry, Labor, and Community,* 621ff.; T. R. Mullen, "Untapped Possibilities," *Recreation,* XXXIV (December, 1950), 356–58; *Business Week,* 11 November 1950, 126–27; "Schools to Fit Company's Needs," *ibid.,* 20 February 1960, 120ff. See also Francis K. Ballaine, "Businessmen and the Community Forum," *HBR,* XXV (Spring, 1947), 372–84.

munities "in which small business predominates have a higher level of civic welfare than comparable communities dominated by big business."[26] Since criteria of welfare are at least partially subjective, the point was debatable; but the community relations programs launched in force by large, national corporations were in part an effort to recapture the sense of identification and common interest of business with its neighbors associated with a somewhat idealized past.

In this light the preoccupation of company officials with their neighboring communities may have stemmed to a degree from nostalgia; but there were other respects in which it was plainly looking to the future. By mid-century the fate of the large American city—now characteristically the center of an even larger metropolitan complex crosshatched by a host of intricately intertwined human, social, and economic relationships—had become a subject of widespread speculation and concern. Urban renovation and renewal programs, burgeoning welfare and relief needs, efforts to modernize and upgrade educational facilities, racial segregation and conflict, housing, highways, air and water pollution, and a long list of other urban problems confronted and bewildered the nation. In moving to understand and meet these needs, business, scholarship, and local and national governments once again touched shoulders; but the record of achievement was, on the whole, disheartening. Nevertheless, instances of successful coping with some aspects of the frightening agenda of urban life could be found. Notably in cities such as Pittsburgh, Philadelphia, St. Louis, and New Haven, attacks upon urban blight achieved some success when business and political leadership united in cooperative efforts.

Even here, however, *Fortune* magazine, which devoted particular attention to urban renewal activities, was forced to concede that executives of national corporations had contributed little substantial leadership except in those cities in which their home offices were situated. Through its Civic Development Department, the U. S. Chamber of

---

[26] C. Wright Mills and Melville J. Ulmer, "Small Business and Civic Welfare," *Report of the Smaller War Plants Corporation to the Special Committee to Study Problems of American Small Business,* U.S. Senate, 79th Congress, 1st Session, Document No. 135 (Washington, D.C., 1946), vi, 14–22, *passim.* For other indications of large-corporation remoteness from local circumstances, see Norton E. Long, "The Corporation, Its Satellites, and the Local Community," in Mason, *The Corporation in Modern Society; Byington, Homestead;* and the "Yankee City" studies by W. Lloyd Warner. Arthur Morgan, "Little Industry in the Community," *Journal of Educational Sociology,* XXVII (December, 1953), 160–62, is an effort by an engineer, educator, and former chairman of the Tennessee Valley Authority to promote the small community on the basis of social health.

Commerce organized a number of national conferences after 1947 on aspects of urban development problems. The Committee on Economic Development, similarly, tried to prepare its members for more imaginative and understanding contributions to urban life. At least some business leaders had learned that their interests were too intimately bound up with the future of their communities for either indifference or flight to be a satisfactory response.[27]

That corporate leadership had only partially faced its civic role and responsibilities could be seen in relationship to such a fundamental problem as urban race relations. As the issue of equal opportunity in education, jobs, and housing moved to the forefront of the national consciousness in the late 1950s and early 1960s, business executives were noticeable by their absence from public discussion and action. Behind the scenes, undoubtedly, consideration was being given the issues involved. Some progress was being made, under heavy and insistent external pressures, in opening new areas of employment to qualified Negroes. Here, in some respects national companies—less deeply rooted in the circumstances of a single city—had greater freedom from local pressures and prejudices than did smaller firms. With regard, however, to community-wide problems such as education and housing, the business community—with some striking individual exceptions—often seemed intent primarily upon washing its hands of responsibility.

An example, exceptional primarily because of the national publicity it received, involved the Tennessee Coal and Iron Division of the United States Steel Corporation which was headquartered in Birmingham, Alabama. This city had by 1963 become a focus of racial conflict as southern Negro leadership pressed for expanded opportunities in a city long characterized by rigidly segregated social patterns. Roger M.

---

[27] "The Businessman's City," *Fortune*, LVII (February, 1958), 93–96. For a series of articles exploring aspects of urbanization, see The Editors of *Fortune*, *The Exploding Metropolis* (New York, 1957). See also Norton E. Long, "Businessmen's Stake in Regional Planning," *HBR*, XXXVI (July–August), 1958, 136–44. Chamber of Commerce of the United States, "Balanced Community Development," Community Development Series, No. 1, 1960; Arthur Van Buskirk (vice president of T. Mellon and Sons), "What Business Has Learned About Rebuilding a City," in "The 'Little' Economies, Problems of U.S. Area Development," Committee for Economic Development (New York, 1958). See also, the CED's "Guiding Metropolitan Growth" (New York, 1960). See Clarence B. Randall, *Over My Shoulder* (Boston, 1956), 34, for a comparison of the Chicago Community Fund with the small-town community spirit Randall had known in his youth.

Blough, chairman of U. S. Steel, rejected the suggestion of civil rights advocates that his company exercise initiative in bringing pressure to bear within the community in support of Negro demands. Blough acknowledged the company's responsibility to provide equal employment opportunities and asserted that it was, in fact, doing so. Beyond this, he noted that Arthur V. Wiebel, president of the local division, had participated in community efforts to improve opportunities for Negroes. Blough categorically denied corporate responsibility for further action:

> Any attempt by a private organization like U. S. Steel to impose its views, its beliefs and its will upon the community by resorting to economic compulsion or coercion would be repugnant to our American constitutional concepts, and . . . appropriate steps to correct this abuse of corporate power would be universally demanded by public opinion. . . .[28]

Thus during the late Fifties and early Sixties, the pattern of increasing business involvement in social problems was being repeated. A circumstance, racial prejudice and discrimination, called for a remedy. Americans looked to their established leadership, in which the business community was a major element, to indicate lines of direction toward resolution of the problem. Fumblingly and with many misgivings businessmen responded. A business leadership which claimed recognition for its social responsibility could not, however ingenuously, long avoid a commitment to lead in efforts to overcome the nation's racial conflicts.

In the postwar years many of the nation's larger corporations acquired interests and installations or subsidiaries overseas, thus extending into a new dimension the nature of their community interests. Much as recognition of their stake in the health and well-being of cities drew company officials in the United States into ever greater participation in civic affairs, so American firms operating in foreign lands found good reason to give high-priority consideration to their relationships to the communities, national and local, in which they operated. The interaction of foreign cultural and political pressures with Ameri-

---

[28] *New York Times,* 30 October 1963, 1. Mr. Blough's letter appeared in the *Times,* 7 November 1963. For further discussion of the issue, see Andrew Hacker, "Do Corporations Have a Social Duty?" *New York Times Magazine,* 17 November 1963, 21ff. For a report of the dismissal of a Bethlehem Steel Company executive for participation in a local civil rights organization, see the *New York Times,* 22 March 1964, 51.

can traditions and ideals had an effect upon the social policies of overseas firms which is beyond the scope of this study. It is nevertheless worth noting that the forces which supported a growing social consciousness among domestic corporations were also operative, perhaps even on an intensified level, with respect to companies engaged overseas.[29]

Given the wealth and power over which they presided, officials of large corporations were inevitably called upon by society in a variety of ways and in a multitude of circumstances to serve the public good. It appeared equally inevitable that this leadership would, however reluctantly and unevenly upon occasion, respond as the community expected it to. The stakes were too high for failure or resistance to prevail in the long run. Neither the community nor, for that matter, business itself could tolerate separation of such a major strand from the social fabric. As one observer pointed out, "The business community's acceptance of a vital share in planning for the metropolitan community's prosperity can be a major step in a program for re-creating a responsible citizenship transcending the lines of cleavage that now divide us." [30] The test of such ambitious sentiments and policies, however, would be years, if not decades, in the future.

BUSINESS AND THE ARTS

The growth of corporate support for intellectual and cultural activities was in one sense a logical consequence of an enlarged interest in community relations. It expressed, too, a new sophistication, spurred by the broadening effect of education and cultivation of popular tastes, in understanding the dimensions of personal and social wellbeing. For the boosters and promoters in the business ranks, the prestige and other presumed advantages of a city noted for its museums, libraries, theaters, or orchestras offered ample themes.

Support of the arts, though, however admirable in itself, was especially hard to justify in terms of any tangible return which managers and accountants could conclusively demonstrate. Participation in social welfare and educational ventures had led business officials to extend

[29] For some consideration of the community relations problems and policies of overseas corporations, see Clifton R. Wharton, Jr., "Aiding the Community: A New Philosophy for Foreign Operations," *HBR*, XXXII (March–April, 1954), 64–72; W. Jack Butler, "Public Relations for Industry in Underdeveloped Countries," *ibid.*, XXX (September–October, 1952), 63–71.

[30] Norton E. Long, "Businessmen's Stake in Regional Planning," 136–44.

the time perspective, as well as the range of interests, in terms of which they viewed company policies. But corporate support of cultural affairs seemed capable, at the extreme, of modifying the concept of business as a private profit-making activity. For such reasons, no doubt, corporate leadership approached the arts gingerly; yet there was every reason to expect that recognition of this sphere, too, as one appropriate for financial and other assistance would come with time.

There were strong pressures for the movement from beyond the business world. The support of culture, of the performing and representational arts, of literary activities, of museums and the like, had traditionally been the province of the wealthy. The advance of democracy had widened the interest and demand for such undertakings, increasing the cost of facilities. On the other hand, through taxation it had restricted the funds available in large fortunes for their support. Given the prevailing resistance to public subsidy, corporate treasuries offered a tempting source of funds for hard-pressed cultural institutions. Individual businessmen had, of course, long given leadership and dollars to such agencies. As the older generation of individual sponsors and donors retired and were replaced on the boards of directors by corporate managers or their wives, it was only natural that company funds should be tapped. The insistent needs of a host of cultural organizations pressing their claims thus opened still another area to corporate involvement.

One indicator of the coming of national business support for cultural programs had been the 1940 campaign for funds by the Metropolitan Opera Company of New York City. Although a local institution in one sense, the Metropolitan Opera had a national and indeed an international reputation as the chief American opera theater. Its performances were heard throughout the country in weekly radio broadcasts that were sponsored by the Texaco Company and thus were in themselves an important corporate cultural contribution. In a conscious effort to build national financial backing, George A. Sloan, who headed the fund drive, appealed to business leaders across the country through the drive's National Industrial Committee, referring to the "transition of the Metropolitan Opera from private sponsorship to a national civic enterprise. . . ." Contributions were solicited from corporations and firms, as well as from individual business executives.

The response was considerable, although Sloan conceded that it did not match expectations and hopes. Some $140,900, or about fifteen per cent of the total amount raised, came in 362 contributions from business organizations or individual executives. Fifty-two New York City firms gave $17,000, while an additional $1900 was secured from sixteen companies outside the New York metropolitan area. The remainder, nearly ninety per cent of the money raised by this committee, was presumably contributed by individual donors. Often such individual gifts were made specifically in lieu of a corporate contribution, since many companies were not prepared to consider the Metropolitan Opera as falling within their range of interests or responsibilities.[31]

In 1952, Beardsley Ruml's survey of corporate philanthropy called the attention of potential corporate donors to the rich opportunities open to them in the cultural field. Separate sections of Ruml's *Manual of Corporate Giving* dealt with museums, libraries, and music, indicating the kinds of company support which had thus far been proffered. There was discussion of company museums, of exhibits in public museums, of museum educational programs, and of the new industrial membership programs some institutions were developing. Cultural agencies and their advisors displayed an ingenuity in providing arguments for corporate contributions which rivaled that of the community chest leaders three decades earlier. The Chicago Art Institute, for example, in soliciting funds for a building program, advanced the

[31] The Metropolitan's fund-raising effort was planned by the John Price Jones Corporation, whose records provide the above information. In addition to the Industrial Committee, the organization of the drive provided for a Textile Division, a Retail Stores Division, and others. The Retail Stores Division was successful in securing contributions from many of the well-known New York department stores, such as Lord and Taylor, Bonwit Teller, Inc., B. Altman and Company, and R. H. Macy and Company. From outside New York City, gifts came from the Magnolia Petroleum Company, the Mercantile National Bank, and the Nieman-Marcus Company of Dallas, the Joseph Schlitz Brewing Company, the F. and M. Schaeffer Brewing Company, Joseph E. Seagram and Sons, Inc., the Southern Natural Gas Company, of Birmingham, Alabama, and the Warner Brothers Company, among others. See JPJC Papers, Casebooks 277, 278, and 299, The Metropolitan Opera Fund, 1940, especially a letter from George A. Sloan to Col. Joseph M. Patterson, 29 April 1940, Casebook 278. An earlier fund-raising campaign, managed by John Price Jones for the Theatre Guild, Inc., in 1923–25, had apparently involved no effort to approach business corporations as such. See Casebook 20.

Evidence that business organizations had shown some interest in local cultural conditions and institutions as early as the 1920s can be seen in the fact that the U.S. Chamber of Commerce's Civic Development Department was asked to survey the status of local symphony orchestras. John Ihlder, "The Movement for Symphony Orchestras in American Cities, Memorandum Prepared for Mr. Stanley C. Draper, Assistant Manager, Oklahoma City, Oklahoma, Chamber of Commerce" (New York, 1925).

following proposition: "A new concept of giving has arisen in many corporate circles, a concept that regards . . . contributions [to the arts] not merely as social obligations, but rather as opportunities for directly benefiting the business and its employees and for increased respect from its customers and its neighbors." The concept, clearly, was less new than the application now suggested.[32]

Symphony orchestras also were able to make appeals to corporations with growing success. Gifts from a number of companies in 1951 made possible the revival of the Detroit Symphony Orchestra, while orchestras in Pittsburgh, Washington, D.C., and other cities were also gaining business support. By 1954, the John Price Jones Corporation estimated that about four per cent of company giving was directed toward the fine arts, against two per cent three years earlier. By 1955 Dallas, Cleveland, Minneapolis, Atlanta, Buffalo, Rochester, Houston, and San Antonio had joined the list of cities whose orchestras received corporate gifts. In Minneapolis, business firms had given nearly fifty per cent of the more than $250,000 subscribed in 1954, while the corresponding figure in Atlanta had been forty-one per cent.[33]

In addition to company and community reputation and provision of cultural facilities for employees, other motives were appealed to in pleas for support of the fine arts. Thus an editorial in *Theatre Arts* which urged an employee-matching program of gifts to the theater arts similar to that of the General Electric Company in education emphasized international ideological competition: "Our survival and that of our friends abroad depends upon our ability to show them that we have a better way of life. . . . Here, surely, is a golden opportunity for enterprise to demonstrate [its] literal meaning . . . , on the very highest level." [34]

[32] Ruml, *Manual of Corporate Giving*, 117–29.

[33] *Ibid.*, 140–53; John Price Jones, *The American Giver: A Review of American Generosity* (New York, 1951), 84ff.; "Business Helps Foot the Bill," *Musical America*, LXXV (1 December 1955), 4; "The Orchestras Seek New Patterns of Support," *Musical America*, LXXII (February, 1952), 32. Response to the latter article, which included an account of the gifts by Detroit firms, included a letter from the manager of the Portland, Oregon, Symphony Orchestra, who complained that the General Motors Corporation refused contributions to orchestras in other cities where it had facilities; see *ibid.* (March, 1952), 14.

[34] *Theatre Arts*, XXXIX (March, 1955), 24–25. MacArthur's editorial was followed by another, detailing gifts to the American Shakespeare Festival Theatre by the International Business Machines Company, the Eli Lilly Foundation, and the Bridgeport Brass Foundation. Searching for still other points of contact and common interest between industry and the theater, the writer showed both

As the decade of the 1950s neared its end, a pattern of increasing company commitment to artistic and cultural ventures seemed well established. Studies showed that approximately three per cent of corporate contributions were directed toward activities classified as civic and cultural. If education had been added, the figure probably would have approached one-third of all company giving. One observer suggested that the field of corporate cultural contributions stood in 1958 about where giving to education had been five years earlier. It remained, of course, to be seen if the comparison would prove valid for the future.

One instance suggesting that the limits of support for the arts had not as yet been reached was the campaign for business contributions to the New York City Lincoln Center for the Performing Arts. The drive was under the general chairmanship of John D. Rockefeller, III, with Clarence Francis, former board chairman of General Foods, leading the appeal for corporate donations. Since the scope of the appeal, if not its general object, meant a break with tradition for many potential donors, personal contact between friendly business executives was planned; and arguments ranging from personal benefits to employees to presumed effects upon the nation's international prestige were prepared. By 1959, over $4,000,000 had been raised from business corporations, many of them national concerns with headquarters in New York City. Enough had been achieved to suggest the existence of still untapped possibilities for future growth in corporate ties to the artistic and cultural life of the nation.[35]

RELIGION AND POLITICS

Two additional fields of corporate social interest toward which managers found themselves drawn in the 1950s were religion and politics. In many ways each was a logical extension of business interest in a society anxiously reexamining traditional values in the face of rapidly accelerating change. Confrontation of communist and socialist expan-

---

ingenuity and a talent for exaggeration. The theater, he argued, trained actors for television, which, in turn, provided a major medium for the sale of commercial products. "What's good for acting is good for selling. And what's good for selling is certainly good for every producer of consumer goods and services in the land." *Ibid.*, XXXIX (April, 1955), 14.

[35] Helen Hill Miller, "American Culture in Search of Angels," *The New Republic*, CXXXVIII (14 April 1958), 8–9; John H. Watson, III, "Company Contributions, III. Policies and Procedures," NICB Studies in Business Policy, No. 89 (New York, 1958), 1. For the Lincoln Center campaign, see "Business Backs an Art Center," *Business Week*, 23 May 1959, 62ff.

sionism on a global stage was driving many Americans to search their history and their arsenals of argumentation for materials with which to fortify a distinctly American position. "Democracy" remained a word with dangerous overtones of radicalism to the cautious and defensive, many of whom felt that the nation had recently suffered from an overdose of that medicine under the New Deal. Like "democracy," "equality" was a word and a concept tainted in the sight of some by its incorporation into the communist lexicon with a meaning uncongenial to most Americans. Against the expropriation or distortion of familiar versions of "equality" and "democracy" by enemies, foreign or domestic, the rallying cries of "freedom," "individualism," or the even vaguer "Americanism" were sounded from many directions—from moderates concerned with reviewing and refurbishing the fundamental sources of the American faith to reactionaries whose aim was to divide and weaken the forces working for social change and reform. Against a threatening international communist enemy with twin standards of atheism and materialism, fearful Americans hastened to arm themselves with spiritual fervor and a renewed devotion to individualistic values. In such a climate of opinion, business management, conscious of its leadership status in the free enterprise system, was encouraged to reexamine the role of religious and moral values within the system.

It was plain that the American economic system, by whatever name it was called, could scarcely repudiate materialism. To do so would be to reject a central element of the national faith. But the dilemma stimulated thought, and not only in business circles, concerning the possibility that the American drive for material progress had been allowed to obscure more fundamental values which ultimately lent meaning to the effort. The times favored, if not a true religious revival, at least a quest for moral and spiritual reassurance at many social levels.

Nor could the spiritual malaise be dismissed by attributing it solely to an entrenched and aggressive conservatism, although this was certainly an exacerbating force. The scientific revolution made manifest by the explosion of the atomic bomb at Hiroshima posed still another set of questions and uncertainties. Thoughtful men and women, pondering the limits both of human capacity to control the powers unleashed by science and of human intelligence to probe the ultimate secrets of nature, sought comfort and support through a renewed religious faith. The interest, therefore, which executives showed in religion as a field of corporate concern reflected a climate of opinion which business shared with the nation.

It was not, however, an interest which, even under favorable circumstances, progressed very far. Some discussion of the relationship of business to religion, and vice versa, was generated. But tradition was on the side of noninvolvement by companies in religious issues and institutions, whatever the inclinations of individual businessmen. And, for once, tradition seemed to prove binding. A 1950 study of giving by 326 corporations revealed that 4.1 per cent of all donations had gone to religious agencies; and a separate study of the practices of companies with assets of over $50 million showed such agencies receiving 3.3 per cent of total gifts. Five years later, a report by the National Industrial Conference Board based upon the practices of 180 companies showed less than half of these companies giving and only 0.5 per cent of total company contributions going to religious agencies. While such limited statistics were scarcely conclusive, they indicated no increase in company giving in the field of religion over a five-year period. Considering the possibilities for controversy as well as the host of potential recipients which religion offered the socially minded corporation, management's prudence in shying away from the field was understandable.[36]

Although business practice with regard to the support of religious activities showed little change from the past, there was clearly a stirring of religious interest on the part of a number of executives. It was manifested chiefly in the idea that there was a spiritual side to business, which, usually neglected under the pressures of day-to-day material problems, was nevertheless real and deserving of recognition. James C. Worthy of Sears, for example, insisted that an ethical as well as an economic concern lay at the root of business thinking. A commitment to the dignity of the individual and to human welfare stemmed, ultimately, from religion, although this derivation had been obscured by secular influences. Business practice, Worthy felt sure, was better than business theory, with its exaggerated stress on self-in-

[36] Andrews, *Corporation Giving*, 70. Wartime company giving had shown greater inclination to support religious causes. Then, groups of corporations classified according to assets were found to be contributing between fifteen per cent and twenty-eight per cent of their giving to organizations categorized as religious. Yet a great many companies refused gifts to religious organizations (between thirty-eight per cent and sixty-five per cent by size category). NICB, "Company Policies on Donations," Studies in Business Policy, No. 7, 7; NICB, "Company Contributions, III. Policies and Procedures," Studies in Business Policy, No. 89, 11. See also "Corporation Giving and the Nation's Spiritual Life," *National Council Outlook*, III (February, 1953), 24, and the comments of James C. Worthy, vice president for public relations of Sears, Roebuck and Company, in Leo J. Shapiro and others, *Company Giving* (Chicago, 1960), xv.

terest as the touchstone of policy. Businessmen had been motivated not only by material gain but "by a desire to make goods and services more readily and more widely available to people in all walks of life." Exclusive emphasis upon the selfish motivations of business, Worthy believed, tended to alienate public opinion and prepare the way for public regulation. "Experience suggests that people are much more likely to put up with privation imposed in the name of public good than with plenty generated as a by-product of self interest."

The range of opinion in discussions of religion extended from the cautious concession that Christianity could be applied to business "without subjecting it [business] to undue risks" to more ambitious calls for a spiritual awakening among business leaders. Practical application of such viewpoints was, in the nature of things, difficult to discern. Very probably these expressions served more to show feelings than to guide concrete policies. But the attitudes and emotions they represented may have stimulated executive interest in other social issues and agencies for which their participation was solicited.[37]

The atmosphere of the 1950s was considerably better suited for ventures by businessmen and organizations into the arena of politics. Business and politics, to be sure, have never been so widely separated as businessmen like to believe. Indeed, intervention by business in the political process for the purpose of influencing legislation, administrative decisions, the choice of public officials, or other ends deemed necessary or desirable is probably as old as business and government themselves. Political movements and pressures both in the Progressive period and under the New Deal had played a part, as we have seen, in awakening American business to new conceptions of its role and responsibilities. Still, this much granted, the considerations which fostered political activism on the part of American business in the 1950s were very special ones.

Despite the generally conservative mood of the American people in the postwar years, national elections, with the exception of the congressional election of 1946 and the presidential contests of 1952 and

---

[37] James C. Worthy, "Religion and Its Role in the World of Business," *Journal of Business*, XXXI (October, 1958), 293–303. For response, see H. B. Arthur, "Religion and Its Role in the World of Business: A Comment," *ibid.*, XXXII (April, 1959), 183–84. Also, Harold L. Johnson, "Can the Businessman Apply Christianity?" *HBR*, XXXV (September–October, 1957), 68–76; O. A. Ohmann, " 'Skyhooks,' with Special Implications for Monday Through Friday," *ibid.*, XXXIII (May–June, 1955), 33–41; T. C. Campbell, Jr., "Capitalism and Christianity," *ibid.*, XXXV (July–August, 1957), 39–48; Benjamin F. Fairless, "Christian Vocation in Steel," *Christian Century*, LX (11 November 1953), 1293–94.

1956, consistently found the Democratic party retaining popular majorities. Even the landslide victory of President Eisenhower in 1956 failed to return control of Congress to the Republicans. Although the Democratic party in these years displayed a rather moderate version of progressivism, it was still associated with the New Deal. And for a majority of businessmen Republican victories were still seen as the only guarantee of "sound" governmental economic policies. The unexpected Republican reversals in the elections of 1948 and 1954 probably as much as any other single factor suggested to such men the desirability of efforts to strengthen the candidates, parties, and political policies they approved.

The prestige and respect regained by American industry in wartime encouraged efforts to attain political influence. The opportunity to secure business against a recurrence of public criticism and governmental regulation seemed promising. Richardson Wood, a staff member of Time, Inc., writing in the *Harvard Business Review* early in the war, noted that certain corporations—notably AT & T—had long enjoyed cordial governmental relations built upon a carefully formulated public relations program. The political benefits of this program to the company had been enormous and contrasted sharply with the experience of other firms which had failed to consider the political consequences of their policies. Now was the time, Wood argued, to anticipate future problems by preparing a groundwork of public understanding and acceptance. Holgar J. Johnson, president of the Institute of Life Insurance, similarly took advantage of the circumstances of the war to advise business corporations to anticipate reconversion to a peacetime economy. Business must be a good citizen as well as a good producer, Johnson warned. Having planned its own actions carefully, it should not hesitate to inform the public about them or to emphasize the importance of public and private policies aimed at restraining postwar inflation.[38]

The participation of businessmen and business organizations in the crucial postwar election of 1946 and in support of legislation before the Republican-controlled 80th Congress represented a first thrust into the field of political action. Passage of the Taft-Hartley Act in 1947, with its curbs upon union power, brought the first fruits of the new effort. But the harvest, when it came, was bitter: the upset election of 1948, returning the Truman administration to office, and the consistent

[38] Richardson Wood, "The Corporation Goes into Politics," *HBR*, XXI (Autumn, 1942), 60–70; "Warns Business Against Neglecting Basic Social Responsibilities," *Comm. Chron.*, XLIX (6 January 1944), 89ff.

failure of conservative Republicanism not only to win power but even to dominate its own party throughout the 1950s. The persistent frustration of conservatism, more than its uneasy triumphs, underlay efforts by a number of business corporations and groups to undertake programs in "political education."

The immediate response of *Business Week* to the Truman victory of 1948 was to call upon business to accept the verdict of the people, "to adjust their business thinking to the kind of community they actually work in, rather than to the kind they would like." Yet business, the editorial insisted, had a right to express its views, and to be heard on those matters for which it could claim special competence. The right and duty of business leadership to foster sound political and economic understanding and to encourage active political participation by responsible citizens provided the rationale for corporate ventures into political education and action.[39]

A detailed study of the motives, methods, and achievements of business-supported political activity in the 1950s, when it can be made, will undoubtedly be illuminating; but it seems unlikely to contain many surprises. Patterns of such political involvement are familiar and of long standing. Gifts by wealthy individuals to favored politicians and parties, the creation of organizations and pressure groups with patriotic-sounding titles, the use of "educational foundations" to cultivate popular support for approved policies—these were hardly new to American politics. Earlier versions had appeared in the American Liberty League and similar anti–New Deal organizations, "the American Plan" of the Progressive era, and the "educational" programs of such groups as the Edison Electric Institute in the 1920s. What was new, perhaps, was the scope of the later movement and the extent of direct corporate financial support granted it.

In a number of instances company funds financed company-sponsored schools of "practical politics." These were often directed specifically at employees who were more or less voluntarily enrolled, but sometimes they aimed at a wider audience. The programs of such firms as the Ford Motor Company, the General Electric Company, and the Gulf Oil Company won wide publicity. Officially nonpartisan, they were in all probability publicly subsidized under the tax laws. Often they utilized the services and knowledge of professional educa-

---

[39] *Business Week*, 6 November 1948, 124. *Fortune*, in the wake of the 1948 election, suggested to its readers that "the most important problem business faces today is the fact that business isn't out of the doghouse yet." *Fortune*, XXXIX (May, 1949), 67.

tors and political specialists. But to an impartial observer it was clear that their intent was to activate and strengthen conservative forces within both political parties, especially at the local level. In their franker moments, businessmen conceded that the programs were conceived, in part, to offset the political activities of the labor unions, especially the AFL-CIO's Committee on Political Education (COPE).[40]

The actual dimensions of business political activity were, in the nature of things, difficult to estimate. As usual, there was some reason to think that talk outstripped effective political action. A *Harvard Business Review* survey of its subscribers showed that nearly ninety per cent favored a more active political role for business; but less than half of the companies they represented actually had programs and an even smaller proportion of the individuals canvassed were themselves politically active. Forty-four per cent reported no activity whatsoever by their companies, although some seventy per cent of the larger firms had at least urged their employees to vote. About twenty per cent of the companies, it was indicated, took public stands on some political issues. To encourage the movement, the United States Chamber of Commerce undertook a long-range effort to foster more active political participation by businessmen, while the National Industrial Conference Board published an analysis of company policies and the legal limitations governing business in politics.[41]

Some executives strongly advocated the assumption of political leadership by business. Among them was John S. Coleman, president of

[40] Horace E. Sheldon, "Businessmen Must Get into Politics," *HBR*, XXXVII (March–April, 1959), 37–41. This article quoted a Gulf Oil vice president as believing, "Whether we want to be there or not, Gulf, and every other American corporation, is in politics, up to its ears in politics, and we must either start swimming or drown." See also Raymond Moley, "Gulf Good Citizenship," *Newsweek*, LIV (20 July 1959), 100.

[41] Dan H. Fenn, Jr., "Problems in Review: Business and Politics," *HBR*, XXXVII (May–June, 1959), 7ff.; Horace E. Sheldon, "Businessmen Must Get into Politics"; NICB, "Company Participation in the Political Process," *The Conference Recorder*, Vol. 7 (New York, 1961). A 1955 survey of 180 companies revealed that 2.1 per cent of their contributions went to "groups solely devoted to 'The American Way.'" This was four times the proportion donated to religious organizations, but about one per cent less than that given to civic and cultural activities. NICB, "Company Contributions. III. Policies and Procedures," Studies in Business Policy, No. 89, 11. A Russell Sage Foundation survey of 326 corporations found 4.5 per cent of total contributions going to "American Way" agencies in 1950. Andrews, *Corporation Giving*, 70. So-called American Way programs were ordinarily justified for corporate support as being educational in nature. Their inclusion here stems from the fact that their ultimate purpose was clearly to influence the climate within which political policy was forged. In any event, the data provided by such samples is only roughly indicative of actual practice.

the U. S. Chamber of Commerce and of the Burroughs Corporation. Political decisions at all levels of government had important implications for business, Coleman pointed out. The expression of business points of view on matters of policy was an entirely proper form of participation in these decisions: "We are not neglecting our business, but rather attending to it in its wider but no less important aspects. . . . Our function is no longer just business, it is rather if you like, the total business of America." [42] Yet it is clear that not all businessmen, and by no means all corporate boards of directors, favored more than a customary political role for their companies. Despite the numerous incentives for active political involvement, and despite instances of egregious misuse of corporate resources for partisan purposes, the limited and moderate character of many business political ventures in the 1950s calls for at least as much emphasis as do the more extreme examples. At the very least, the "political education" programs of some of the largest companies were sufficiently sophisticated and cautious to maintain a careful facade of nonpartisanship.

The effects of corporate political activity are even more difficult to assess than its scope. In terms of elections won by the presumably favored Republican party, the record by the end of the decade must have been discouraging. Still, the generally conservative tenor of American politics for a decade and a half probably owed something to the intensification of business efforts.

Seen from the viewpoint of social responsibility, the political adventures of business have additional significance. They raise the question of the extent to which acceptance by businessmen of a more comprehensive idea of social responsibility stemmed from expectations as to the political and public relations value of such a policy. They serve further as a reminder of the partial and gradual character of intellectual and institutional change. In politics, business leadership showed considerably less insight and forbearance than in such other social fields as welfare and education. Nor did its somewhat limited political successes seem to reinforce the lessons gradually being learned in those fields, of the danger and the ultimate futility of business efforts to impose on the public a one-sided interpretation of community needs. [43]

[42] John S. Coleman, "The New Dimensions of Business," *Comm. Chron.*, CLXXXV (17 January 1957), 222–23. See also Arthur B. Van Buskirk, "Responsibilities of Business Leadership," *Vital Speeches*, XXV (1 September 1959), 690–93.

[43] For debate within one company over the extent and advisability of political activity, see "Inland Steel Company—A Proposed Policy on Politics," a Harvard

Finally, in the political arena, as well as in the other social realms where their broadening interests were leading them, businessmen were encountering pressures and demands upon their resources which exceeded their capabilities. Hand in hand with the extension of their commitments to community betterment, therefore, went the need to organize and execute these commitments in a more orderly fashion.

Business School case study. The case materials showed that officials of the company decided in 1958 against holding a luncheon for Republican political candidates. Previously, the company had offered its employees time off for participation in election drives; and company officers had periodically met with congressmen and senators to discuss matters of mutual interest. In order to consider the company's political policy, Joseph Block, board chairman, had requested the formulation of a policy statement "related to our responsibility as a corporate citizen."

The legal limits of corporate political participation were discussed by businessmen, lawyers, and politicians in NICB, "Company Participation in the Political Process," *The Conference Recorder,* Vol. 7.

9 • WAYS AND MEANS: THE PRACTICE OF SOCIAL RESPONSIBILITY, 1945–1960

From the moment a company executive acknowledged that his firm had more than economic obligations to the groups with which it dealt, the problem of how properly to give concrete expression to these relations presented itself. The Pullman Land Company, the Railroad YMCA, and the planned communities of Waltham and Lowell were early efforts by company managements to provide social services to the employees of communities for which they felt some responsibility. Federated fund raising and the community chest movement had largely stemmed from a desire by businessmen to assess and simplify the many requests for help their offices were receiving. During the 1930s the difficulty of translating policy into practice had produced the "battle of standards," a search for appropriate yardsticks to measure the extent of corporate aid to welfare agencies. The impulse to organize and to systematize their social relations came naturally to men of business.

The extraordinary demands and opportunities of the Second World War intensified pressures for more orderly approaches to corporate social planning and philanthropy. The confusion which, despite the ef-

243

forts of community chest and some business officials, still characterized many company social programs found them ill-prepared to cope with wartime needs. When a company such as the United States Steel Corporation faced the communities and agencies which turned to it for help with no clear policy to guide its giving and with an apparently unending list of worthy causes to consider, the difficulties which confronted other firms can be imagined.[1]

Not all executives felt as free to exercise discretion in their giving as did Irving S. Olds at U. S. Steel. *The Management Review,* noting increasing pressure from national and international relief agencies in 1943, called for clearer definition of the limits of such responsibilities. It reminded readers that "the purse held by corporate directors belongs to the company's stockholders, whose interests must be considered."[2] Under these conditions businessmen turned for advice, as they had in the past, to agencies equipped to help them evaluate requests. Community chests, chambers of commerce, better business bureaus, as well as organizations such as the National Information Bureau, were called upon by hard-pressed executives. The limitations of spontaneous, haphazard giving were becoming increasingly clear. Contrary to Irving Olds's expectations, these difficulties did not disappear when peace returned.[3]

In effect, the question of standards for corporate responsibility and philanthropy was reemerging, this time in a context of prosperity and growth. Many of the familiar conflicts of interests and objectives characteristic of relationships between business and welfare officials in the Twenties and Thirties persisted but took on new dimensions suited to changing circumstances. Spurred by the challenges and opportunities of affluence, a host of new claimants upon the corporate conscience and pocketbook had appeared.

They were met by the enlargement of managerial staffs dealing with personnel, public, and community relations. New forms of organ-

[1] R. F. Duncan to John Price Jones, "Interview with Irving S. Olds of the U. S. Steel Corporation, "JPJC Papers, Case 4: "Giving . . . Corporations." Olds, confessing his difficulties, said, "We have no formula, and I doubt that a practical one can be evolved." Meanwhile each individual appeal was considered on its "merits." Yet, in 1943 the Steel Corporation and its subsidiaries contributed nearly $2,500,000 in major gifts. The total for the years 1940–43 was estimated at nearly $6,000,000. Confidential memorandum on U. S. Steel and subsidiaries' major contributions, *ibid.*

[2] "When the Corporation Gives to Charity," *Management Review,* XXXII (February, 1943), 73–74.

[3] NICB, *Management Record,* November, 1943, 352, quoted in *ibid.*

ization—company committees, company-sponsored foundations, community and industrial agencies, and special-interest associations—sprang into existence, reflecting the vitality of an expanding field. As efforts to satisfy the perennial demand for more effective evaluation, they meant that requests for corporate assistance were beginning to face closer scrutiny. As agencies for promoting and administering the community interests of business, these new institutions mediated between business leadership and the public, stimulating managerial initiative in the social field while at the same time winning widespread public acceptance for it.

Even so, the executives charged with this responsibility were often forced to face new and unfamiliar problems. As wartime enthusiasm waned and the repeal of the excess profits tax reduced financial incentives to giving, many companies undertook a reevaluation of their contributions policies. The harried merchants of Douglas, Georgia, even proclaimed a "Leave Us Alone Week" in response to numerous requests for aid. But, although corporate gifts fell sharply in 1946, they remained at levels far above those of the pre-war years. The practice of company donations had become too firmly fixed to be abandoned. "No one has yet thoroughly measured the stake that American business has in philanthropy," wrote *Fortune* in 1948. But one thing was already clear: "It's big, and getting bigger." Some companies had come to look upon philanthropy as "a part of the cost of doing business." This view implied greater stability over time, in good years as well as bad; and it called for more careful assessment of procedures as well as objectives.[4]

Landmarks in the evolution of more knowledgeable, orderly policies were Beardsley Ruml's and Theodore Geiger's "The Five Per Cent" and *The Manual of Corporate Giving*, published in 1951 and 1952, respectively, by the National Planning Association. The former, taking advantage of the renewed interest occasioned by the Korean War excess profits tax, stressed the benefits both to recipient agencies and donor companies offered by the five per cent tax deduction for philanthropy. Enthusiastic response to the pamphlet led to publication of

[4] "Pause for Inquiry," *Business Week*, 6 July 1946, 17–18; "The Business of Giving," *Fortune*, XXXVIII (December, 1948), 90–92; Herbert Fredman, "Solving the Donations Problem," *Commerce*, November, 1947, 21, reprinted in *Management Review*, XXXVII (January, 1948), 6–7. For the National Industrial Conference Board's survey reports of company donations policies, see NICB, "Company Policies on Donations," Studies in Business Policy, No. 7, and NICB, "Company Policies on Donations. II. Written Statements of Policy," Studies in Business Policy, No. 49. See also Laird Bell, "If Corporations Will Give."

the *Manual,* a guide for companies interested in building more systematic and suitable giving programs. Sections were devoted to the tax and legal aspects of contributions.

Ruml's suggestions for "Policy and Administration of a Five Percent Program" offered a framework for a carefully planned approach. Philanthropic expenditures, he noted, "must meet rigid tests of prudence and efficiency. There must be a reasonable belief on the part of management that the business under its trusteeship will be better off if the disbursement is made than if it is not made. . . . There must be an expectation that the business in the long run, directly or indirectly, will get back more than it gives." [5] He emphasized the importance of efficiency and clear designation of responsibility for decisions, as well as of wise and imaginative contributions programs. The *Manual* further pointed out the wide range of opportunities for company giving offered by such fields as education and cultural and community affairs.

Company giving reached new levels in the 1950s. Typical of the situation large corporations faced was the experience of the International Harvester Corporation. The company received over 5000 requests for funds each year. It carried on operations in 224 communities across the nation and recognized the desirability of maintaining its good name in each. By 1957, International Harvester was donating about $1,000,000 annually, both directly and indirectly through a company-sponsored foundation. It maintained a full-time staff member to work with a special contributions committee in developing overall policy and maintaining consistency in the practices of its many local offices.

Many firms, however, had not as yet adopted such a systematic approach. Smaller firms could not afford such elaborate procedures. Often the president, the top financial officer, or some other designated official exercised prime responsibility. In such cases, obviously, there was much less opportunity for a company to pursue a carefully worked-out program. One survey of companies of various sizes in the Chicago area indicated that, as late as 1960, only about ten per cent had formal policy statements to guide their giving. [6]

---

[5] Ruml, *Manual of Corporate Giving,* 17, *passim.;* Ruml and Geiger, "The Five Per Cent." For comment, see "It Doesn't Hurt Much to Give," *Business Week,* 18 August 1951, 28; "Save By Giving," *ibid.,* 22 September 1951, 66–68; "What Is Enough?" *ibid.,* 20 September 1952, 104ff.; "Support Without Control," *Collier's,* CXXVIII (15 September 1951), 82.

[6] Robert G. Dyment, "The Contributions Problem. How International Harvester Handles It," 28–30; Leo J. Shapiro and others, *Company Giving,* x–xv, 1–2, 18–19,

Although small companies were able to maintain some, at least, of the traditional personal flavor in their philanthropic undertakings, it was increasingly difficult to do so. The institutionalization of corporate external relations inevitably meant some loss of individuality, spontaneity, and freedom. In compensation, it offered more orderly, rational procedures in many instances. More accurate and detailed information about the size and scope of company community welfare programs became available, and better information stimulated more careful evaluation and criticism. Overall, better organization meant that, in the decade and a half following the Second World War, social relations had won acceptance as an integral part of business institutions and policy. The trend toward organization was too potent a force for corporate social and philanthropic programs to escape.

COMPANY FOUNDATIONS

As business organizations struggled to find means of regularizing their philanthropic interests a new institution, the company-sponsored foundation, emerged. Company foundations were tax-exempt and legally independent, although they received grants of money from the sponsoring company and, sometimes, from individuals closely associated with it. Despite its separate legal identity, a company foundation's board of trustees might be and often was composed of officers of

passim. See also "How Much Corporation Giving?" Steel, CXXXIII (30 November 1953), 58–59; John Price Jones, The American Giver, 103ff.; Gerard J. Eger, "Practical Standards for Corporation Giving," The Controller, November, 1952, 534, quoted in Management Review, XLII (January, 1953), 48–49; "Corporation Giving—a Survey," ibid., XL (May, 1951), 262; Lawrence Mehren, "To Give or Not to Give. A Study of Bank Contributions Policies," Financial Public Relations Associations (Chicago, 1960); John A. Pollard, "Emerging Pattern of Corporation Giving, HBR, XVIII (May-June, 1960), 103–12; Howard R. Dressner, "Business Can Assure Better Colleges," Nation's Business, XLVII (August, 1959), 84–86; "How to Gage Company Gifts," Business Week, 24 October 1959, 89.

As might be expected, some of the corporations with long traditions of involvement in social relations had systematized their programs well before the 1950s. General Electric had a contributions committee as early as 1925. F. Emerson Andrews, "This Business of Giving," The Atlantic Monthly, CXCI (February, 1953), 66. A number of companies had established donations policies or committees by the early Forties. "When the Corporation Gives to Charity," Management Review, XXXII (February, 1943), 73–74. Soon after the Second World War the Standard Oil Company (New Jersey) had a program similar to that of International Harvester, utilizing the services of a full-time executive, with systematic budgeting and investigating procedures. Business Week, 6 November 1948, 30–32; Claude L. Alexander, "Problems and Practices of Corporation Giving," Public Relations Journal, VI (December, 1950), 5ff.

the parent corporation. Its objective was to distribute funds received for "religious, charitable, scientific, literary, or educational purposes. . . ." Company foundations differed from the more familiar individually established foundations in being closely identified with a single firm, although occasionally more than one company was involved.

Initially, company-sponsored foundations centered their attention on philanthropies closely related to the parent firm. The Altman Foundation, for example, had been created by Benjamin Altman in 1913 to promote the welfare of his company's employees, but with the additional charge to "aid charitable, benevolent, or educational institutions within the state of New York." Another motive for the creation of such foundations was the promotion of industry-related research. From such beginnings, company foundations were gradually drawn outward into more general community and philanthropic interests.[7]

The relatively high tax rates of the 1940s and 1950s promoted a rapid increase in the number of company foundations. The corporate excess profits tax in particular, which between 1950 and 1953 took eighty-two per cent of the largest corporate incomes, caused company officials to consider the advantages of creating foundations. A study of corporation-sponsored foundations in the Chicago area noted in 1957 that nearly three-quarters of those surveyed had been created since 1950. Of the same group, only six per cent had been in existence before 1945. The rapid growth in numbers did not mean that the company-sponsored foundation had become common; fewer than five per cent of the companies studied had them. But since, as might be expected, these were usually the larger, wealthier corporations, the importance and influence of the company foundation was indeed far-reaching.[8]

Many of the major American industrial corporations, among them the General Electric Company, U. S. Steel, Procter and Gamble, the Shell Oil Company, the Parker Pen Company, the Union Pacific Railroad Company, the Bulova Watch Company, and the Inland Steel

[7] F. Emerson Andrews, *Corporation Giving*, 101–3; Frank M. Andrews, *A Study of Company Sponsored Foundations* (New York, 1960), 1–2, 20–21.

[8] Other survey findings indicated that manufacturing, financial, and communications companies were more likely to sponsor foundations than were those engaged in retail or wholesale selling or services. Rapidly growing companies and those with geographically distributed facilities were also characterized by a higher proportion of foundations. *Ibid.*, 23–26. For specific consideration of the tax aspects of foundations, see J. K. Lasser, "Why Do So Many Businessmen Start Foundations?" *Dun's Review*, LVII (February, 1949), 15ff.

Company, had set up company foundations by 1953. By the end of the decade, the larger of these foundations were receiving annual contributions in the neighborhood of one million dollars and had obviously become a potent force in the philanthropic field. Some were supporting imaginative and far-ranging programs. The Bulova Foundation, for example, developed a training program for the physically handicapped which prepared them to become self-supporting watch repairmen.

The program of the United States Steel Foundation, as outlined by President Roger M. Blough in 1957, encompassed a host of activities and needs. In addition to aiding national agencies, such as the Community Chest, the Boy Scouts, and the Red Cross, it assisted medical research and education, slum clearance and urban renewal, vocational and liberal education, scholarships, libraries, research in the physical and social sciences, art museums, and symphony orchestras. The education of engineers in India, television classes to improve the teaching of science in schools, and the independence of the Greek Orthodox Church in America were among the causes receiving Steel Foundation funds. The scope of its philanthropies reflected the parent corporation's international interests.[9]

The company foundation, however, was not exclusively a device of the large national corporations. The Lehigh Structural Steel Company, of Allentown, Pennsylvania, had its own foundation with funds contributed by the company, by its officers, and even by employee organizations. Giving was largely concentrated on the local community, although national health agencies and the like were also assisted. Sometimes a number of small companies arranged to pool their contributions through a foundation for more effective charitable, civic, or educational giving. Still another variation was the industry-wide foundation, such as the Nutrition Foundation, which assisted basic research in nutrition with funds supplied by many food industry companies.[10]

[9] For the U. S. Steel Foundation, see Roger M. Blough, *Free Man and the Corporation* (New York, 1959), 114–20. The Bulova Foundation is described in Andrews, "This Business of Giving," 63–66. See also Pollard, "Emerging Pattern of Corporate Giving"; Frank G. Dickinson, ed., *Philanthropy and Public Policy* (New York, 1962), 105–7, for the cautious procedure of the Union Pacific Railroad in establishing its foundation. Also, "But It's Not Easy to Give Money Away," *Business Week*, 12 January 1952, 66ff.; "The Business of Giving," *Fortune*, XXXVIII, 90–92.

[10] Thomas R. Mullen, "Smaller Companies Can Give Wisely," *Philanthropy*, II (Fall, 1953), 14–15, described the Robert L. Kift–Thomas R. Mullen, Jr., Memorial Foundation of the Lehigh Steel Company. See also NICB, "Company

Tax avoidance provided a powerful stimulus for the creation of many company foundations, but it would be inaccurate to interpret them simply as a tax dodge. True, company officials who worried about their accountability to their stockholders could and did stress the tax benefits involved, but other justifications and advantages soon became apparent. Among those cited the most impressive was the ability of company foundations to stabilize corporate giving. Whereas profits and ability to give varied considerably from year to year, a foundation was able to plan its contributions program over a longer time span. It could receive large gifts in prosperous years and, by holding them on a tax-free basis, could maintain reserves adequate to compensate for the years in which company receipts might fall. A carefully managed company foundation, thus, could commit support to projects of several years' duration where the parent company might otherwise have hesitated to do so. Conversely, a foundation was under no pressure to give hastily without adequate investigation of projects, while the corporation might find itself pressed to give on short notice at the year's end in order to optimize its tax position.

Other advantages sometimes cited for company foundations included the ability to employ persons knowledgeable in fields of special philanthropic interest as paid staff members, consultants, or trustees; provision of time and resources for better administration and more careful review of requests for help; an escape from "pressure" on the parent company by clients, friends, or customers; diversion from company management of criticism for specific contributions; increased capacity to give, both as a result of tax advantages and through income earned on investment of foundation reserves; and the ability to assume the initiative in planning comprehensive contributions policies, rather than merely responding to haphazard requests.

In some instances, the creation of company foundations involved losses as well as gains. Loss of control by management over the disposition of company funds might mean stockholder criticism. Occasionally, infringements upon the initiative and responsibility of company branch managers occurred. And, contrary to the hopes and expectations of executives, pressures upon the parent corporation were sometimes increased rather than alleviated by the creation of a foundation, as the firm's reputation for philanthropic activity gained wider recognition. Such considerations presumably account for the fact that companies which had created foundations often continued the practice of

Sponsored Foundations," Studies in Business Policy, No. 73 (New York, 1955), 70–74, passim. Andrews, Corporate Giving, 107–12, gives other illustrations.

making direct contributions themselves to certain causes or agencies in which their officers felt a special interest.[11]

Essentially, what the company foundation offered was a formal means for more systematic corporate philanthropy. The spread of the new device both paralleled and extended the broadening social interests of American business. By making corporate contributions more rational, it offered, in the opinion of many executives, a "scientific approach" to the management of giving. Clearly, too, it represented another step in the institutionalization of national welfare practices.[12]

BUSINESS ORGANIZATIONS AND COMMUNITY NEEDS

Long before most corporations had seriously considered the creation of contributions committees or foundations, businessmen had sought advice and evaluation of requests for funds from chambers of commerce, trade associations, and other business organizations. One result of this kind of consultation was the studies of welfare agencies and their needs undertaken by the Cleveland Chamber of Commerce in the first decade of the century. The national chamber's Civic Development Division, inaugurated in the 1920s, and its journal, *Nation's Business*, which publicized and otherwise offered encouragement to company participation in philanthropic and civic undertakings, were others. The U. S. Chamber of Commerce also sponsored summer institutes in community relations in the 1950s and even proposed the development

[11] The most complete analysis of company foundations is NICB, "Company Sponsored Foundations," *Studies in Business Policy*, No. 73, based upon an analysis of 141 companies with foundations. Despite the possibility which the foundation offered of broadening the approach to philanthropy through reliance upon the experience and advice of non-business experts, few foundations in fact did so. Directors and staffs of the company foundations were almost invariably employees of the parent firm, using company time and equipment to carry on foundation business. The divorce of company from foundation was, thus, largely a legal fiction. *Ibid.*, 19–20, 47.

For other discussions of the company foundation, see the sources cited in note 9, above. Also, "The Company Foundation—A Solution to the Donations Problem," *Mangement Review*, XLI (May, 1952), 323–34; Dickinson, *Philanthropy and Public Policy*, 108–18; Geneva Seybold, "Company Giving Through Foundations," *Conference Board Management Record*, XIV (January, 1952), 2–5ff.; *Proceedings of the Fifth Biennial Conference on Charitable Foundations* (New York, 1961).

[12] NICB, "Company Sponsored Foundations," 58. A 1960 report of company foundations in the Chicago area revealed that only one of the forty-two foundations studied published an annual report for circulation outside the sponsoring corporation. Andrews, *Company Sponsored Foundations*, 28.

of a college curriculum leading to a B.C.C. degree (Bachelor of Chamber of Commerce Work) for community organization specialists. As for trade associations, in 1940 the motion picture industry, for example, had created its own Permanent Charities Committee to develop standards and quotas for the industry's members.[13]

As philanthropic expenditures grew after the Second World War, other business organizations undertook studies of company donations and their recipients. In 1946, the National Information Bureau, Inc., was serving as advisor to community chests, foundations, and individual companies such as Sears, General Electric, General Mills, A & P, and Standard Brands. The National Industrial Conference Board in 1945 created its own Council of Executives on Company Contributions to wrestle with the question "What is our fair share?" In the same year the conference board began to report on corporation donations programs and policies and on community and public relations as part of its Studies in Business Policy. These publications offered descriptions of representative contributions and community relations programs, statistical analyses, and samples of executive opinion to aid companies searching for ideas and examples.[14]

One new organization which sprang into existence in the early 1950s to provide still further opportunities for businessmen to meet and discuss their donations problems was the National Conference on Solicitations. This conference was an outgrowth of the long and active interest displayed by the Cleveland Chamber of Commerce in the solicitations problem. The chamber had maintained its own Solicitations Department for many years under the supervision of a twenty-five-man committee; by 1957 the department's annual budget was $30,000. Meanwhile, the growth of business interest in the field led to communication between cities and firms and, eventually in 1953, to the formation of the national conference. Representatives of interested business concerns and organizations met annually thereafter for exploratory conferences and exchange of views and experiences. Subjects

[13] Form and Miller, *Industry, Labor, and Community*, 630ff.; Leo Shapiro and others, 47–48; "The Business of Giving," *Fortune*, XXXVIII, 90–92; *Business Week*, 6 July 1957, 77. In Beloit, Wisconsin, the Commercial Club received contributions from fifty firms in 1947 and allocated them among local institutions. In this case, the object apparently was to control the rate of giving, since it was reported that companies were contributing only about fifty per cent of the amount of their gifts in 1937. *Sales Management*, 15 June 1947, 115, JPJC Papers, Case 4: "Giving . . . Corporations."

[14] John A. Pollard, "Emerging Pattern of Corporate Giving," 107. The NICB studies have either been cited previously or are listed in the bibliography.

considered ranged from methods of accounting and evaluation to broad considerations of corporate philanthropy and public policy.[15]

Still other established business groups undertook to promote or evaluate the status of corporate philanthropy in these years. The National Planning Association's publication of Beardsley Ruml's and Theodore Geiger's "The Five Percent" and *The Manual of Corporate Giving* has already been noted as an important mobilizing factor. At the local level, the Harvard Business School Club of Cleveland, an association of alumni, issued an analysis in 1953 of the practices, policies, and problems of local corporations.[16]

Quite different from such efforts by business groups to promote, organize, systematize, and justify corporate philanthropy as an expression of the new sense of interdependence between the company and the public was the activity of another kind of business organization, the Committee for Economic Development. The committee had been conceived in the early 1940s by Paul Hoffman, president of The Studebaker Company, William Benton, of Benton and Bowles, an advertising agency, and President Robert M. Hutchins of the University of Chicago. It aimed to serve as a means of bringing together businessmen and academicians for discussion and exchange of views on matters of national policy. Inherent in the idea was recognition of a gap of understanding between the two groups and the conviction that each could learn from the other. Another clear assumption was that, for many large companies at least, national conditions and problems were demanding as much attention as local ones, if not more.

According to the committee's historian, Karl Schriftgeisser, Secretary of Commerce Jesse Jones suggested that Owen D. Young become the group's first chairman—a proposal which, had it been carried out, would have tied the growing interest in corporate social relations in the Fifties even more directly to its historic roots in the 1920s. Among the other early members of the group were Clarence Francis of General Mills and Thomas McCabe of the Scott Paper Company.

After much discussion, Paul Hoffman was named the CED's first chairman and its general purpose was set forth: "To conduct itself strictly as a business group dedicated to improving the performance of business in carrying out its own organic public duties: namely, the supply of goods to our families and jobs to our citizens." As this state-

[15] *Proceedings of the Fourth National Conference on Solicitations* (Cleveland, 1957), 18, 21, 34–37, *passim*.

[16] "Corporate Giving in Cleveland," A Survey by the Harvard Business School Club of Cleveland, Inc. (Cleveland, 1953).

ment made clear, the new group was consciously rejecting the concepts of social responsibility symbolized in the Twenties by Owen D. Young and following instead the rival tradition of Henry Ford and E. A. Filene. Hoffman insisted, in terms reminiscent of these predecessors, that "the primary responsibility of a businessman is to operate his business profitably." [17]

To focus business attention upon important economic problems, the CED evolved an interesting procedure. It began with the selection of a problem, followed by the preparation of an analysis and recommendations for action by a research group composed largely of academicians. A thorough examination and discussion of the analysis, participated in jointly by businessmen and scholars, followed. It was in this process of confrontation, disagreement, debate, and resolution of differences that the CED offered a different approach to the social relations of business. The reports it issued over the years, by reason of their quality and the nature of their authorship, commanded wide respect. The topics covered ranged widely among the major issues of national and international economic policy, including inflation, taxation, full employment, and agricultural problems. One of the first issues it undertook to study was that of conversion from a wartime economy to one of peace.

Despite its pledge to focus strictly upon business problems, the CED's agenda made clear that it could not resist a broad definition of business's "own organic public duties." In a very real sense, the CED became a latter-day heir of E. A. Filene. As Filene himself had dedicated his Twentieth Century Fund to research on fundamental economic problems, so the CED carried further his belief that the busi-

---

[17] Karl Schriftgeisser, *Business Comes of Age: The Story of the Committee on Economic Development and Its Impact Upon the Economic Policies of the United States, 1942–60* (New York, 1960), 6–9, 25–30, 70, 136–37, *passim*. According to Schriftgeisser, Jones and Young disagreed over whether or not to include representatives from other groups. Young may have conceived of the organization as a potential descendant of the Swope Plan for private national economic planning; see Chap. 6.

When the CED first attracted public notice, it was criticized for representing big business interests. To some degree this was true of the founders; but Ralph Flanders of the Jones and Lamson Machine Company was named director of its Research Committee and special efforts were undertaken to include small businesses. Local CED branches, over 3,000 of them, eventually came into being; *ibid.*, 30–41. The claim later made, however, that the CED was responsible for originating the ideology of "managerialism," was clearly in error. R. Joseph Monsen, Jr., "Can Anyone Explain Capitalism?" *The Saturday Review*, XLVI (14 December 1963), 14.

nessman's greatest contribution to society lay in the more effective discharge of his own distinctive function and the gift of his knowledge and experience for a more productive society.[18]

The outbreak of World War II brought into existence still another business organization, which was later to be described by Evans Clark of the Twentieth Century Fund as "the most striking recognition which American business has ever given of its responsibility for the public welfare." This was the Advertising Council, which emerged from efforts by the advertising industry to counteract public criticism and the simultaneous need of the federal government for help in promoting public support and understanding of the war effort. Converted to peacetime activities after 1945, the council contributed the skills and channels of its membership to "projects serving the public interest, both governmental and nongovernmental." Among the civilian causes it championed were forest fire prevention, soil conservation, world trade, accident prevention, and the sale of United States Savings Bonds.

Typical of the work of the council was a national campaign mounted to rally support for public school needs in 1947. The council's help was requested by interested public and private agencies, the Citizens' Federal Committee on Education, the American Association of University Women, and the U. S. Office of Education. Funds were supplied by the American Textbook Publishers, Inc.; and a national advertising campaign was launched around the general theme, "Our Teachers Mold the Future." Local school officials and boards thus were able to approach their constituencies for funds against the background of nationwide publicity.[19]

As corporation executives set about the task of organizing their own companies, their trade associations, and their peers for more efficient philanthropy, they could hardly have failed to cast an organizational eye upon the activities of those who sought their financial aid. Almost from the beginning, requests for donations directed to business firms had produced counterpressures upon the welfare agencies to organize

[18] For Filene, see Chap. IV, note 4.

[19] Harold B. Thomas, "The Background and Beginning of the Advertising Council," in C. H. Sandage, ed., *The Promise of Advertising* (Homewood, Illinois, 1961), 28–35, *passim.;* Advertising Council, *Newsletter,* 1942 and after. For Clark's evaluation of the council, see the report of the first meeting of its Public Advisory Committee, *ibid.,* II, 10 July 1946. See also The Advertising Council, "Report of a Discussion 'Basic Elements of a Free, Dynamic Society'" (New York, 1951); "Commercial Agencies Campaign for Better Schools," *Elementary School Journal,* XLVIII (November, 1947), 123–24.

and consolidate their efforts. Now, at the century's midpoint, the broadening horizons both of givers and receivers led to a drive for organization by those hoping to solicit more business support. In almost every field in which corporate giving grew, new and consolidated agencies came into being to accommodate the process.

The first of the younger generation of federated organizations was the United Negro College Fund, created in 1944 with help from the Julius Rosenwald Foundation and the General Education Board. Twenty-seven private Negro colleges participated in the original fund-raising venture. The Rockefeller interest and influence were strongly behind the new program, with John D. Rockefeller, Jr., giving his name as well, presumably, as his money in the capacity of chairman of the National Campaign Advisory Committee. Winthrop W. Aldrich, Rockefeller's brother-in-law, was appointed national treasurer. Walter Hoving, president of the Lord and Taylor department store, who had served as national chairman of the United Services Organization, became chairman of the first UNCF campaign. General chairman for New York City solicitations was W. E. S. Griswold of W. & J. Sloane and Company. Corporate contributions were from the beginning a UNCF objective. Nearly a decade later, the fund served as a model for other private colleges and universities, as they too moved to win business support.[20]

Cooperative fund raising, especially on the part of the smaller liberal arts colleges, became common practice in the 1950s. The swarms of requests for business assistance created bewilderment and resistance among company officers similar to that which the charity drives of the years following the First World War had encountered. Business insistence upon orderly procedures and evaluation quickly led educators to see the advantages which joint solicitation promised. In this instance, too, President Truman's Commission on Higher Education had offered a nudge, while college officials grasped at means to reduce the costs and increase the returns of solicitations. Regional groupings offered the most popular, if not the only, basis for joint efforts by the schools. The New England College Fund, Inc., and the Ohio Foundation of Independent Colleges, both created in 1951, were pioneers of

[20] See Chap. VIII for the 1948 President's Commission on Higher Education report, citing the UNCF as a model. See also the *New York Times*, 2 March, 18, 6 March, 11, 9 March, 19, and 21 March 1944, 15, for the organization of the UNCF. Of the $765,000 raised by the UNCF in 1944, thirty per cent came from corporations; and corporate gifts kept pace with the Fund's subsequent growth. Andrews, *Corporation Giving*, 216.

the new approach. The latter in its first six months was able to secure eighty-six corporate contributions totaling $197,165. By pressure and by example, the leaders of industrial and business organizations were teaching better methods of planning to their educational counterparts.[21]

On occasion, universities were able to turn the tables on business-men by inducing them, in turn, to organize into affiliated "Industrial Associates" groups. These plans offered participating companies oppor-tunities for consulting with faculty specialists, the possibility of early access to research results, and other intangible if not entirely invisible benefits in exchange for pledges of regular contributions. The appeal of such programs was necessarily limited primarily to the larger uni-versities and institutes of science and technology.[22]

At the national level, the Council on Financial Aid to Education was probably the most influential promotional agency. A product of the collaborative efforts of Frank W. Abrams, Irving S. Olds, and Alfred P. Sloan, Jr., this council became a major influence in fostering interest and support for education among business executives. It spon-sored conferences and speeches and made available literature aimed at educating company officials about the conditions and needs of private colleges and universities. The council itself did not solicit or re-ceive contributions; it defined its role as educational and informative. Among other objectives, it worked to overcome resistance to corpo-rate philanthropy, to promote broad principles of "corporate citizen-ship," and to relax restrictions imposed by companies upon the objec-tives for which their gifts might be used.[23]

[21] Virginia Roller Batdorff, "Big Business' Little Brother," *American Mercury*, LXXX (Fall, 1955), 107–10; Pollard, "Corporation Support of Higher Education," 121–22. Geography did not provide the only basis for cooperative solicitation: the National Fund for Medical Education, created in 1951, indicated another possi-bility. Andrews, *Corporation Giving*, 216–18.

In 1949, the Association of American Universities created a Commission on College and Industry to interest business leaders in the financial problems of higher education. Frank Sparks, a businessman who had assumed the presidency of Wabash College, served as the commission's chairman between 1953 and 1958. Curti and Nash, *Philanthropy in the Shaping of American Higher Education*, 246.

[22] Jones, *The American Giver*, 106.

[23] Alfred G. Larke, "How Corporations Aid Education," *Dun's Review and Modern Industry*, LXV (May, 1955), 47ff.; Raskin, "The Corporation and the Campus."

The close relationship which the CFAE established between business and educa-tion was symbolized by the membership of Everett N. Case on its board of

Business pressures for unified solicitations were by no means confined to education. As the number of agencies seeking contributions
continued to grow, particularly in the large metropolitan centers,
health and welfare drives again faced the demand that they unify and
systematize their activities. The older community chest structure no
longer was adequate to comprehend the enlarged demands of national
as well as local agencies. The United Funds, which began in 1949, enlarged the old circle of the community chest agencies and joined them
with national health drives. This new approach stemmed from combined corporate and public resistance to another round of solicitations. As part of their unified, community-wide fund-raising program,
the United Funds often included solicitation of workers as well as of
companies themselves; payroll deduction plans and—on more than
one occasion—considerable pressure by company officials and union
leaders upon individual donors contributed to its success. Despite resistance by some agencies, especially national ones such as the Red
Cross and some health agencies, the United Fund approach gained
widespread public acceptance. Through it, the institutionalization and
coordination of private welfare programs were carried to new levels.
Both individual and corporate givers now participated in a truly national structure of public and private welfare. Short of full-fledged nationalization, the transition from the personal charity of the nineteenth century to the organized philanthropy of the twentieth seemed
to have gone about as far as it could go.[24]

directors. Case, the president of Colgate University until 1961 and thereafter president of the Alfred P. Sloan Foundation, had served as assistant to Owen D.
Young of the General Electric Company and had married Young's daughter. In
1954–55, Case served as chairman of the Empire State Foundation of Independent
Liberal Arts Colleges.

[24] Detroit, in 1949, saw the first metropolitan United Fund Campaign, in which
the automobile industry (management and unions) played a leading role. Andrews,
Corporation Giving, 168–72. "When Charity Drives Collide," *Business Week*, 16
May 1957, 78, reported that the recent Pittsburgh United Fund campaign had
reached its goal for the first time since 1944. Two-thirds of the 36,000 volunteers
participating were company employees working on company time. Eleven executives had given some 3,644 hours of their time, with one man's time for seven
weeks contributed by his company. The contributions of a large number of firms
were reported to have increased by between seventy per cent and one hundred
per cent over former levels.

The newer fields of cultural interest quickly mirrored the practices of better-
established agencies. One of the attractions of the New York City Lincoln Center
for the Performing Arts for corporate donors was that it enabled them to carry
out their cultural donations on a "once-for-all" basis. "Business Backs an Art
Center," *Business Week*, 23 May 1959, 62ff.

THE DIMENSIONS OF CORPORATE PHILANTHROPY

The organizing and rationalizing process which, in the course of the 1950s, brought business, welfare, educational, and cultural institutions into increasingly close contact led also to more voluminous record-keeping and statistical reporting and analysis than had ever before been possible. Consequently, the objective results of what was, in fact, a major social movement were relatively clear and accessible. Studies of different communities, as well as of different trades and industries, underlined again the fundamental fact of variety in corporate philanthropy. Personalities, traditions, local and regional variations, and specific trade or company circumstances all were the elements of an intricate institutional pattern. If national trends and averages should be allowed to obscure these underlying diversities, a significant dimension of the picture would be lost. In no small part, the efforts, which this chapter has summarized, to impose order and regularity were attempts to counterbalance the confusion and near-anarchy of corporate welfare and philanthropic policies.

With these reservations and limitations in mind, a number of significant general patterns can be noted. Fundamental, of course, was the fact of steadily increasing commitment by American business to the practice of philanthropic contributions. Measured both by the number of firms participating and the amounts contributed, the results were impressive. Treasury Department figures (see Table 4) gave clear indication of the nature and dimensions of the advance.[25]

Economic fluctuations, war-born profits, and tax incentives had played a part in encouraging corporation giving. The percentage of net corporate profits represented by donations had climbed perceptibly, if not spectacularly, toward the deductible five per cent in the quarter-century after 1935. The experience of the 1950s gave no clear indication as to how much further the advance might go, but it did suggest that philanthropy could expect to share the profits of American business at at least the one per cent rate for the foreseeable future.

Formal monetary contributions, of course, were by no means the only form of corporate assistance to community and philanthropic agencies. Loans of company personnel, gifts in kind and services, use of company clerical and other facilities, payroll deduction plans, sponsorship of community activities, advertising, and a host of similar

[25] NICB, "Company Contributions," Studies in Business Policy, No. 89, 9; U.S. Treasury Department, Internal Revenue Service, Statistics of Income, 1955–60.

Table 4—Corporate Contributions
Amount and Per Cent of Net Profit, Before Taxes
1936–1960

(Dollar amounts in millions)

| Year | Net Profit | Contributions | |
		Amount	Per Cent
1936	$ 7,771	$ 30	0.39
1937	7,830	33	0.42
1938	4,131	27	0.66
1939	7,178	31	0.43
1940	9,348	38	0.41
1941	16,675	58	0.35
1942	23,389	98	0.42
1943	28,126	159	0.57
1944	26,547	234	0.88
1945	21,345	266	1.24
1946	25,399	214	0.84
1947	31,615	241	0.76
1948	34,588	239	0.69
1949	28,387	223	0.78
1950	42,613	252	0.50
1951	43,495	341	0.78
1952	38,735	399	1.03
1953 *	39,801	495	1.24
1954	36,538	311	0.85
1955	47,949	415	0.87
1956	47,413	418	0.88
1957	45,073	417	0.93
1958	39,224	395	1.01
1959	47,655	482	1.01
1960	44,499	482	1.08

* Final year of excess profits tax

services added untold amounts to the values actually contributed by business firms. The cost of such gifts of time and talent was incalculable—an accountant's nightmare. Estimates ranged widely, up to several full man-years for a large corporation. Roger M. Blough estimated in 1959 that more than one million management people were serving civic activities of all kinds, not all of them necessarily on company time. An extreme example was that of the Humble Oil Company, which lent a full-time staff of one hundred people to organize the United Fund drive in Houston, Texas, in 1956. And the Boeing Airplane Company contributed the time of six executives for three months to manage plant solicitation for the Seattle United Fund.

Larger corporations, of course, were better able to afford such contributions; but a study of Chicago companies of all sizes indicated that nearly half of those employing over one hundred men did lend some executive time. Considerations of profit and loss, theoretically still the motive force behind corporate behavior, were difficult to relate to such undertakings. An estimate which placed their value as roughly equal to that of actual financial donations appeared reasonable. By such a standard, an annual outlay for corporate philanthropy of roughly one billion dollars a year had been reached by 1960.[26]

Analyses of the percentage of income contributed to philanthropy in relation to the size of the donor corporation produced significant and often surprising results. From the very beginning of corporate philanthropy, the leadership in public discussions of the role and responsibilities of the business corporation had been assumed by men associated with large national companies; and at almost every subsequent stage in its development, from the railroad YMCAs to the Council on Financial Aid to Education, executives of large corporations had appeared to take the lead. The chief exception to this pattern had occurred in the 1920s and 1930s, when the community chests experienced difficulty in persuading some national companies to support local welfare drives. Yet statistical analyses indicated that the largest corporations did *not* in fact contribute in proportion to their capacity. Both governmental and private surveys of company giving, with few exceptions, supported this conclusion. A Russell Sage Foundation study in 1950 produced the following data: [27]

[26] NICB, "Company Contributions," Studies in Business Policy, No. 89, 7–10; Dickinson, *Philanthropy and Public Policy*, 114–17; "Civic-Minded Executives," *Time*, LXVIII (24 September 1956), 86; Blough, *Free Man and the Corporation*, 113; Shapiro and others, *Company Giving*, 42ff.; Hodges, *Company and Community*, 2. One estimate put total corporate philanthropy at twice the amount reported in income tax returns; Dickinson, *Philanthropy and Public Policy*, 114. Cf. Cutlip, *Fund Raising*, 319.

[27] Andrews, *Corporation Giving*, 44–48. The chief departure from the pattern which showed smaller companies giving a larger share of their income was Leo J. Shapiro's study of companies in the Chicago area. Shapiro and his associates found that medium-sized firms, those in the 500–999 employee class, gave a

Table 5—Contributions of 326 Surveyed Corporations: Amount, Per Cent of Net Income, and Amount per Employee, by Number of Employees, 1950 *

| Employee class | Corporations returning questionnaire | Net income (thousands) | Contributions | | Number of employees | Contribution per employee |
			Amount (thousands)	Per cent of net income		
Under 50	35	$ 16,054	$ 41	0.3	1,145	$36
50 under 100	46	5,459	66	1.2	3,460	19
100 under 250	73	16,454	165	1.0	10,998	15
250 under 500	63	43,164	334	0.8	22,368	15
500 under 1,000	34	64,875	530	0.8	23,389	23
1,000 under 5,000	49	225,730	1,580	0.7	116,729	14
5,000 under 10,000	9	135,833	820	0.6	63,493	13
10,000 under 20,000	8	113,084	819	0.7	106,587	8
20,000 and over	9	704,071	2,434	0.3	314,165	8
Total	326	$1,324,724	$6,789	0.5	662,334	$10

* Russell Sage Foundation Survey. Computations made from nonrounded figures.

Certainly, there was little here to support the frequently heard view that big business exceeded the norm in its philanthropic interests. The officers of national corporations might be more prominently associated with national philanthropic and cultural ventures, but a number of observers of business at the level of the local community were persuaded that small enterprise was more deeply committed to civic improvement.[28]

Variations in giving patterns between different trade and industrial groups were also considerable, as shown in Table 6: [29]

Table 6—Contributions of 326 Surveyed Corporations:
Amount and Per Cent of Net Income, by
Major Industrial Groups, 1950 *

(Dollar figures in thousands)

Industrial group	Corpora-tions	Net income	Contributions		
			Amount	Per cent of total	Per cent of net income
Manufacturing	182	$ 512,255	$3,159	47	0.6
Public utilities	46	242,485	979	14	0.4
Trade	33	45,863	787	11	1.7
Finance, insurance, real estate, lessors of real property	41	198,162	853	13	0.4
Other groups **	24	325,959	1,011	15	0.3
Total	326	$1,324,724	$6,789	100	0.5

* Russell Sage Foundation Survey.
** Mining and quarrying, service, construction, agriculture, forestry, and fishery.

greater percentage of their incomes than either their bigger or their smaller brothers. *Company Giving*, x-xiv, 38–39, 99. This finding was further corroborated by an NICB survey of 163 companies reported in NICB, "Company Contributions," Studies in Business Policy, No. 89, 6–7. Shapiro and his associates speculated that companies of this size were vulnerable to requests in that they had seldom developed the systematic evaluation and budgeting procedures which were becoming more customary among the giants.

[28] Norton E. Long, "The Corporation, Its Satellites, and the Community"; Wilensky and Lebeaux, *Industrial Society and Social Welfare*, 278–79; Frederic B. Greene, "Social Work and the Philistines."

[29] Andrews, *Corporation Giving*, 48–60. See also NICB, "Company Contributions," Studies in Business Policy, No. 89, 11–15; and Mehren, "To Give or Not to Give."

Differences in the nature of the industry, number and character of employees, legal position, and similar factors, of course, helped to account for the diversity of practices illustrated.

That variety characterized the recipients as well as the donors of corporate philanthropy is already apparent. The extent of this variety is partly demonstrated by Table 7, which, however, by reflecting overall practice, fails to indicate the differential giving patterns of industries and individual companies: [30]

Table 7—Percentage Distribution of $38,260,198 by
Areas of Support, 1955—180 Companies

Area of Support		Per cent
Social welfare		40.1
Community chests/United Funds	21.9	
Red Cross	4.5	
Youth work	3.1	
Other agencies	10.6	
Medicine and health		10.6
Hospitals	8.6	
National health agencies	1.3	
Other	0.7	
Education		31.3
Civic and cultural		3.2
Religious causes		0.5
Groups devoted solely to "The American Way"		2.1
International gifts		0.3
All other		4.6
		92.7
Unidentified		7.3
		100.0

The broad outlines of corporate philanthropic activity seemed clear at mid-century, although its future dimensions, prospects, and meaning remained in doubt. A set of ideas and institutions significantly different from traditional business patterns had won general acceptance. It remained to assess their implications.

[30] NICB, "Company Contributions," Studies in Business Policy, No. 89, 11. For estimates based upon other studies, see Andrews, Corporation Giving, 68–71; "Corporation Giving in Greater Cleveland," 42–50.

CORPORATE PHILANTHROPY AND PUBLIC OPINION

The practice of corporate philanthropy had won widespread acceptance not only in the managerial offices of business corporations but
also among the American people generally. Not only did judicial sanction come with the A. P. Smith Company case of 1952; other branches
of government signified their formal and informal approval. In 1954,
the United States Congress further encouraged company giving by
modifying the Revenue Code to permit deductions to exceed five per
cent in any one year if the excess was absorbed within the succeeding
two-year period. And by 1956, three-quarters of the states had adopted
legislation permitting corporate philanthropic donations.[31]

Still further encouragement came from the President of the United
States himself. In September, 1953, Harold R. Harris, president of
Northwest Orient Airlines, wrote President Eisenhower to ask whether
the five per cent deduction which Congress had provided was intended to encourage corporate giving on more than a local scale. Mr.
Harris, who seemed to be under the impression that the new Republican administration was about to repeal the preceding twenty years,
inquired if the President expected corporations to give to medical,
educational, and similar programs "until such time as private income
can again take over that burden." The Eisenhower reply was couched
in general terms. It noted that Congress had provided for the five per
cent deduction to foster private alternatives to governmental assistance and added an endorsement of them: "By joining in the effort, it
seems to me that American corporations will properly and legally be
assisting in the propagation of our American faith." [32] The publication of this exchange rounded out the atmosphere of governmental acceptance and approval within which corporate philanthropy flourished.

Official sanction was not the only sign that the new corporate role
was well established. Studies of public opinion revealed little evidence
of resistance to the spread of business community and philanthropic

[31] Richard Eells, *Corporate Giving in a Free Society* (New York, 1956), 17ff.;
NICB, "Company Sponsored Foundations," Studies in Business Policy, No. 73, 4,
9–14. Wilber G. Katz ("The Philosophy of Midcentury Corporation Statutes," *Law
and Contemporary Problems*, XXIII [Spring, 1958], 177–92) held, however, that
corporation law provided little or no basis for theories of corporate social responsibility.

[32] Jones, *The American Giver*, 101–3; "Company Gifts: Bars Go Down," *U.S.
News and World Report*, XXV (13 November 1953), 104–7.

services. On the contrary, considerable approval was registered. A 1951 survey by the Public Opinion Index for Industry found eighty per cent of those interviewed, including stockholders, favoring the practice of company contributions; sixty-two per cent of those who owned stock approved giving by their own companies. This finding corroborated the fact that corporations which did pursue philanthropy found little criticism or objection to their policies on the part of their shareholders.

At the same time, there were other signs that indifference or vague acceptance, rather than enthusiastic approval, characterized public opinion and that the public was not particularly well-informed about the nature and purposes of corporate giving. Stockholders generally tended to see corporation giving as a sign of management confidence in the company's financial status. Among the public at large, as well as among business specialists, there appeared to be a tendency to equate corporate philanthropy with a growing, progressive, and well-intentioned company. Most stockholders seemed to worry considerably less than their managements about the respective claims and merits of potential recipients. "At the present, then," one report concluded, "with certain exceptions, we find companies relatively free to pursue whatever direction of philanthropy they desire and still have their giving fit into and support their public relations program[s]." [33]

Public attitudes toward business, though not always based upon sound information or interest, were generally friendly in the 1950s. And the initiative of business leadership in promoting a favorable "image" of the socially conscious and progressive corporation had played a part in the creation of the public's mood of approval. A University of Michigan study of "Big Business as the People See It," sponsored by the General Motors Corporation in 1951, indicated some of the dimensions of this mood; but, at the same time, it suggested that

[33] Pollard, "Corporate Support of Higher Education," 12; Shapiro and others, *Company Giving*, xvi, 90–97. Philip D. Reed, board chairman of the General Electric Company, stated that his company had received during 1953–54 only one letter from a stockholder criticizing its donations policies. Many letters of approval had been sent. Larke, "How Corporations Aid Education," *Dun's Review and Modern Industry*, LXV (May, 1955), 47ff. A letter sent in 1954 to 118,000 stockholders of the Standard Oil Company (Indiana) explaining the company's gifts to liberal arts colleges in its marketing area produced only one critical reply. Raskin, "The Corporation and the Campus." The annual stockholders' meeting of the Standard Oil Company (New Jersey) heard some discussion of corporate philanthropy; a resolution opposing the practice was overwhelmingly defeated. See the company's *Annual Report* for 1961 and 1962.

there were real if not clear limits to the public's confidence. Americans, the survey found, credited business firms and their managers for the rising living standards and other economic benefits which they enjoyed. Their approval, consequently, was based overwhelmingly upon the role of business as a producer and employer—in other words, upon economic performance. There was a rather strong suggestion, too, that it was conditioned very heavily upon the continuation of that performance. Fringe activities of companies, such as community and philanthropic programs, were mentioned as one of the desirable contributions of the business system by only six per cent of those surveyed. Furthermore, there were clear signs that many Americans still questioned business concerns for the profits they earned as well as for their real or potential power in labor-management relations. Suspicion of the motives and objectives of corporate leadership remained present, if dormant, among the American people.[34]

One example, not widely publicized in the 1950s, of the way in which abuse of the new forms of philanthropy might ultimately discredit them involved a number of the company-related foundations. As these tax-exempt institutions grew in number (from 12,295 in 1952 to 45,124 in 1960) and wealth, their economic power alarmed those who feared they were being used for improper purposes. A series of congressional inquiries between 1948 and 1964 into the activities of tax-exempt foundations revealed a number of serious abuses as well as lax enforcement of the tax laws by the Internal Revenue Service.

Chairman Wright Patman of the House of Representatives' Small Business Committee, who led the investigation in 1962, compared the charitable trusts and foundations to the holding companies of an earlier era, through which control over complex corporate empires might be exercised. Some foundations owned large blocks of stock in major corporations—occasionally as much as one hundred per cent—and thus avoided the payment of taxes on company dividends. There were frequent instances of inadequate reporting of the foundations' economic status regarding investments, income, expenses, and contributions. Some foundations appeared to have been created as means by which individuals or families could maintain large and complicated economic holdings while minimizing their taxes—in effect benefiting from a public subsidy based upon tax exemptions. Some were lending

[34] B. R. Fisher and Stephen B. Withey, "Big Business as the People See It," Survey Research Center, Institute for Social Research, University of Michigan, 1951, xiii, 20–21, 34, *passim.*; Elmo Roper, "The Public Looks at Business," *HBR*, XXVII (March, 1949), 165–74.

funds, providing services and even competing with commercial firms under the privileged conditions afforded them by their tax-exempt status.

Congressman Patman's recommendations for reform included limiting the life span permitted foundations, prohibiting their engaging either directly or indirectly in commercial operations, requiring "armslength relations" between foundations and the companies they controlled, limiting the amount of stock a foundation could hold in any corporation, withdrawing tax-exempt status from contributions to foundations until such time as they were actually channeled to philanthropic agencies, and tightening governmental scrutiny and reporting procedures.[35]

Most of the abuses reported had been practiced by foundations created by individuals or families rather than by corporations; but there were exceptions. In any case, the line between a company foundation and an individual or family foundation which held sufficient stock to influence corporation policies was not always clear. While few companies whose shares were widely held and which had created philanthropic foundations were subjected to criticism, the fact that there were abuses was disturbing and seemed to call for further consideration and legislation. The abuses to which company-related foundations were prone might, unless remedial action were undertaken, outweigh the benefits they offered to corporations bent upon meeting their social obligations.[36]

Despite inevitable abuses, uncertainties, and disagreements, the fact remained that corporate philanthropy had by mid-century become an established and growing practice. As a proportion of total company commitments and expenditures, it was small. Indeed, for the sake of perspective it is important to remember what an extremely small share

[35] "Tax-Exempt Foundations and Charitable Trusts: Their Impact on Our Economy," Chairman's Report to the Select Committee on Small Business, House of Representatives, 87 Congress, 31 December 1962. See also the second and third installments of this report and investigation, Subcommittee Chairman's Report to Subcommittee No. 1, Select Committee on Small Business, dated 16 October 1963 and 20 March 1964. An Advisory Committee on Foundations created by the Treasury Department in response to Congressman Patman's criticism was shown to be heavily weighted with men closely associated with the foundations themselves. *Ibid.*, iv.

[36] Congressman Patman's charges aroused relatively little immediate public outcry. See Fred J. Cook, "Foundations as a Tax Dodge," *The Nation*, CXCVI (20 April 1963), 321–25; and "Uncharitable," *Newsweek*, LVIII (21 August 1961), 71.

of the objectives and activities of American business—less than two per cent in all probability—philanthropy represented. For the fact was that, at modest expense to themselves, business corporations were exercising a significant impact upon American society. Not only its agencies of public and private welfare but its educational system, its cultural and civic life, and its ideological commitments and foundations were affected. From the perspective of the corporate balance sheets the sums involved appeared almost inconsequential, but those who took them seriously were right after all. Not only the social environment, but the institutions of business itself were involved in what was proving to be a basic modification of long-accepted ways.

As the organization of business philanthropy continued to grow, old distinctions began to blur. Sharp divisions between public and private enterprise, between work and welfare, between corporations, colleges, and governments seemed suddenly somehow less sharp. Without conscious planning on the part of the participants, certainly without anything that could reasonably be considered coercion, the economic and social system was developing a new dimension. The shift was so slight as to win only passing mention. Its direction seemed clear, but its significance could only be assessed in the light of the future.

10 · THE THEORY OF CORPORATE SOCIAL RESPONSIBILITY, 1945–1960

Differing views of the scope and propriety of corporate philanthropy reflected basic questions concerning the role of the business corporation as a social institution. Initially, interest had centered on the powers of management in relation to the rights and interests of stockholders or employees. As time went on the arena of debate had widened to include such issues as the responsibility of the corporation for social welfare, education, the arts, and even government itself. Although the precincts claimed for corporate "good citizenship" had been steadily enlarged, the rationale for such claims remained ill-defined and subject to challenge.

Although controversy could still be generated in some quarters as late as 1946 over the justification and feasibility of corporate philanthropy, the most influential leaders of business opinion were pushing ahead toward a definition of corporate—and therefore of managerial —responsibilities which left few if any areas of society outside the circle of business interests. That business and society were essentially coterminous was implicit in the view expressed by Frank W. Abrams in 1948 and by others with increasing frequency in the 1950s that "the long-term interests of the shareholders cannot run counter to the long-term interests of the American people." By the end of the decade, Roger M. Blough felt able to dismiss opposition to company giving as "impractical" since stockholders had come to accept it; he conceded, however, that "they might not be able to explain why" they felt it justifiable. Blough himself was by now more concerned to demonstrate that corporate philanthropy was one aspect of a broader phenomenon which he described as "the voluntary corporate way" and which he considered essential to the preservation of a free society.[1] Business leadership and responsibility had become identified, for Blough and others who accepted this position, with the preservation and progress of democratic society itself.

Such an ambitious, confident conception of corporate powers and responsibilities strongly supported the growth of business involvement in community affairs during the Fifties. Sweeping claims of social leadership by and for the executives of large corporations were not, however, universally welcomed even within the business community itself. Indeed, they provoked a considerable amount of doubt and resentment, although criticism was muffled in a climate of opinion generally friendly to business leadership. The debate over the proper social role of corporate enterprise did not break fully into the open until the 1960s, when a more critical assessment of business achievements and pretensions became possible. In the meantime, doubtful businessmen and other observers of the business system were laying the foundations for a reassessment of both the ideology and the practice of corporate social responsibility.

THE "MANAGERIAL" WORLD VIEW

Among the most thoughtful advocates of the enlarged view of corporate responsibilities was Richard Eells, a General Electric Company staff member. Eells's studies of the changing role of the corporation brought him into contact with the faculty of Columbia University's Graduate School of Business, where he eventually became Adjunct Professor. Keenly sensitive to shifting social patterns, Eells developed a position which justified corporate philanthropy in very broad terms, while avoiding the pitfalls—for businessmen—of "do-goodism." "A properly planned program of giving," Eells held, "is not an irrelevant diversion of corporate assets. Instead it is a contribution to society as one means of strengthening the donor's own position in society."

In a small volume entitled *Corporate Giving in a Free Society*, Eells in 1956 elaborated a theory of philanthropy and responsibility for

[1] Abrams is quoted in "College Aid," *Business Week*, 19 February 1949, 36; Blough, *Free Man and the Corporation*, 120–23; *Forbes*, 15 August 1946, 14.

business. The objective should "always be to strengthen a balanced multi-group social structure" and thus to hold government's role to a minimum. This would not only benefit business, Eells argued, but society as well, since it would lend "vitality to American values of individual freedom and human dignity. . . ." The good will which business might garner from its philanthropies was, for Eells, desirable but of strictly secondary importance. "The aim is to protect and preserve the donor's autonomy by protecting and preserving those conditions within the greater society which ensure the continuity of a system of free, competitive enterprise." Through taxation business helped to maintain "an indispensable structure of public government." Corporate giving should enable business *to preserve and maintain the vital private sectors in the corporate environment.*" [2]

The idea that American business had a responsibility to defend private initiative and voluntary institutions on all fronts had many sources. It derived in part from the nation's historic faith in its mission to uphold the ideals of liberty and democracy before the world. It was intensified, clearly, by the threats to those ideals which businessmen and other Americans perceived in the growth of governmental regulatory power at home and in the spread of antidemocratic forces abroad. And it was made specific by the prosperity and prestige enjoyed by corporate management after the Second World War.

Eells's formulation of the concept and his relation of it to the practice of corporate philanthropy were by no means the first, although they were more systematically worked out than most. Resistance to government intervention into the previously private precincts of charity, education, the arts, and other voluntary activities had, indeed, long provided an effective basis for appeals to corporate philanthropy. In the 1950s, however, business leadership at times almost seemed intent upon socializing itself in its zeal to avoid the threat of public socialization.

It received much encouragement in this attitude, to be sure, from spokesmen for other private sectors. At the eighteenth annual conference of the Harvard Business School Alumni Association in 1948, for example, Dean Donald David urged that, in view of the businessman's power and influence, he had special responsibility to do "what he can to strengthen the social structure of his community, local or national." And Clarence Francis, speaking before the same group, held that business represented a free system in opposition to totalitarianism. The

[2] Eells, *Corporate Giving in a Free Society,* 7, 111, 136–37, *passim.* Italics Eells's.

system must be shown to work and businessmen must exercise the leadership: "[these] are the men who have the *will* to define and meet responsibilities." [3]

Other influential businessmen and publications took up the same theme. Notable among these was Clarence J. Randall, who retired in 1952 from the chairmanship of the Inland Steel Company to enter upon a new career as elder industrial statesman and public servant. In a widely read book, which he called *A Creed for Free Enterprise,* Randall summed up the ideas he had gained from long experience as a business and civic leader. Calling for a militant spirit of responsibility on the part of business, Randall argued that this should not be thought of as charity. Rather, "the meeting of the social needs of the community is a proper charge to the cost of production." For its own sake and for that of democratic society, Randall believed, business should cultivate "a new tradition of public service, a new habit of mind by which business-men actively seek participation in public affairs at every level. . . ." [4]

The belief that freedom of enterprise was inextricably tied to the independence of other private activities and interests, that "freedom is indivisible," stretched the bounds of managerial trusteeship. Never-theless, some corporation executives, public relations specialists, and others concerned with the social environment of business seemed pre-pared to accept the challenge. Beardsley Ruml's argument for corpo-rate philanthropy rested in part upon its potential for preserving "the decentralized and private character of the decision-making process in all phases of our national life." Peter F. Drucker, although skeptical of extreme claims made in the name of corporate social responsibility, ac-knowledged the "social character and the public existence of even the most private of enterprises." A. T. Collier, writing in the *Harvard*

[3] David's and Francis's addresses are contained in Harwood F. Merrill, ed., *Responsibilities of Business Leadership* (Cambridge, Massachusetts, 1948), xi–xii, 4–5, *passim.*, a compilation of talks given at the conference. For another state-ment, by a University of Chicago business school faculty member, of corporate social responsibility as a defense of freedom against government encroachment, see Edward A. Duddy, "The Moral Implications of Business as a Profession," *Journal of Business,* XVIII (April, 1945) 63–72. Also Gras, *Development of Business History Up to 1950,* 65; R. F. Wilkins, "Business Ethics and World Conflict," *Dun's Review* (September, 1951), 15ff.; and Frank W. Abrams, "Credo," *Satur-day Review of Literature,* XXXVII (23 January 1954), 26.

[4] Clarence B. Randall, *A Creed for Free Enterprise* (Boston, 1952), 66–68, 80–81. John Knox Jessup, in "A Political Role for the Corporation," *Fortune,* XLVI (August, 1952), 112ff., analyzed the corporation as a "force of economic power" capable of checking government power in defense of individual "self-government."

Business Review, called for a new ideology of business—one which would emphasize individuality, diversity, and creativity within industry and, at the same time, would recognize the increasingly "public" character of private enterprise. "The Chinese Wall between business and the home, the community, the school, and the church has long since been stormed," Collier asserted.[5]

The widening horizons of managerial trusteeship did not obscure the continuing interest and responsibility of corporate executives toward those groups directly involved in enterprise. The concept of management as the balancer and coordinator of the interests of stockholders, employees, customers, suppliers, and similar groups was elaborated beyond the rather rudimentary notions which had appeared in the 1920s. A generation of experience, as well as the results of intensive research and scrutiny into all aspects of managerial activity, had produced a new sophistication as to the ends and means of corporate behavior.

Business executives set forth their understanding of these relationships in a variety of ways, but they agreed in assigning to management a formidable list of responsibilities. Oswald W. Knauth, drawing upon his own business career, contrasted the realities of managerial enterprise with the traditions and principles of a now-outmoded free enterprise system. The old concepts were no longer valid, Knauth insisted. Profits were only one, and not necessarily the most important, objective of corporate management. The function of a "wise management is to keep all its operations in equilibrium." "Managerial enterprise," Knauth wrote, "is a system of production and distribution, uni-

---

[5] Ruml, *Manual of Corporate Giving,* 12; Peter F. Drucker, *The Practice of Management* (New York, 1954), 381; A. T. Collier, "Business Leadership and a Creative Society," *HBR,* XXXI (January, 1953), 29–38. See also John Price Jones, ed., *Philanthropy Today* (New York, 1949).

Donald K. David's interpretation of managerial responsibilities was equally wide-ranging. Profits were earned by business, David held, "by serving the public and by achieving a proper balance among the real long-term interests of employees, stockholders, suppliers, customers, and all the others directly affected by the activities of business. . . . I maintain that in an industrial civilization business leaders must assume the responsibility for increasing all the human satisfactions of the groups with which they are associated." Quoted in Merrill, *Responsibilities of Business Leadership,* xv.

Leila A. Sussman, in "The Personnel and Ideology of Public Relations," *Public Opinion Quarterly,* XII (Winter, 1948–49); 704ff., reported that eleven out of twelve of the thousands of works on the subject of public relations since the New Deal which she had examined stressed the trusteeship concept of management's role.

fied by policies and controlled by managers, whose main idea is to administer the business that concerns them in the interest of continuity." W. T. Gossett, vice president and general counsel of the Ford Motor Company, also saw corporation management as coordinating related participant groups and developing "a variety of devices and procedures to assure that its dealings with other groups are fair and just." The responsibility to deal justly stemmed, Gossett acknowledged, from the fact that in many relationships management's "power is preponderant and not subject to ready control or review by others." [6]

Influenced by the growing popularity of psychology and "human relations," philosophers and practitioners of management were beginning to replace the notion of trusteeship with that of "team leadership." In cynical hands, this approach could readily mask manipulation of subordinates behind a screen of democratic participation. But there was no mistaking the sincerity of a man such as Frank W. Abrams, who combined the older values with modern phraseology in discussing the responsibilities and dilemmas of management:

> We have a stewardship in a company like Jersey Standard and a personal pride. We would like to leave the company in a sounder and more assured position than when we took it over. We are not looking to the company just to support us; we want to make it healthy for future generations and for the employees who will come along. We like to feel that it is a good place for people to work. We have equal responsibilities to other groups: stockholders, customers, and the public generally, including government.

Striking a proper balance between these forces and instilling a due sense of responsibility for them were among the most important duties of management, Abrams held. Properly discharged, they gave to all members of the organization "a sense of belonging, of knowing what [the managers] are after. The company then is a kind of team that they want to belong to; it is a great moral drive of many persons." [7]

---

[6] Oswald K. Knauth, *Managerial Enterprise: Its Growth and Methods of Operation* (New York, 1948), 11, 79, *passim.*; William T. Gossett, *Corporate Citizenship*, The John Randolph Tucker Lectures, Vol. II (Washington and Lee University, 1957), 177–187. See also Courtney C. Brown, "Toward a New Business Philosophy," *Saturday Review of Literature*, XXXVI (24 January 1953), 11–12ff.

[7] Quoted in Maurer, *Great Enterprise*, 75–76. See also Frank W. Abrams, "Management's Responsibilities in a Complex World," *HBR*, XXIX (May, 1951), 29–34; Drucker, *The Practice of Management*, 138, *passim.*; and Andrew Hacker, "Utopia, Inc.," *The Commonwealth*, LXV (8 February 1957), 479–51.

In adding national, if not global, commitments to their immediate company responsibilities, business leaders were undertaking a heavy burden. True, many—perhaps most—of them did not follow the doctrine of universal trusteeship for freedom to its logical conclusion. Consciously or unconsciously, words raced far ahead of real or intended actions. Even so, the implications and consequences of many assertions of social responsibility by corporate officials and their advisors were such as to stagger the imagination. Charles E. Wilson, president of the General Motors Corporation, aroused a public furor in 1953 by testifying before a Senate committee investigating his suitability for the office of Secretary of Defense in terms which suggested that he understood the national welfare to be little more than that of General Motors writ large. Outrage and surprise might have been lessened—or, perhaps, they might have been increased—had there been more general understanding that Wilson's was simply one of the more awkwardly formulated versions of the managerial "creed." [8]

Efforts to work out in company practice the implications of social responsibility led, as we have seen, to a considerable expansion of corporate philanthropy. They led in many other directions, too. Internally, many companies intensified their measures to improve working conditions, industrial relations and personnel policies, and customer and stockholder relations. Externally oriented activities, efforts to control inflation by holding the line on price increases, and executive and company contributions to civic affairs have already been discussed. The list of corporate ventures into social welfare was exceeded in length only by the number of social problems and needs. Not every new program was wise, appropriate, or successful; but the mere fact of the constant creation of new programs demonstrated a growing sensitivity on the part of management toward new dimensions of corporate interest.[9]

[8] From Benjamin F. Fairless's statement, "I know of no way by which any large enterprise can survive today unless it is managed in the long-range public interest," to that mistakenly attributed to Wilson, "What's good for General Motors is good for the country," was a short step for an unsubtle mind. Fairless, "Christian Vocation in Steel." Wilson's actual remark was quite different from the widely publicized version of it: ". . . for years I thought what was good for our country was good for General Motors and vice versa," *New York Times*, 24 January 1953, 8.

[9] For some examples of activities undertaken in the name of corporate social responsibility, see A. T. Collier, "Social Responsibility of the Businessman," *Management Review*, XLVI (July, 1957), 62–70; George B. Hurff, *Social Aspects of Enterprise in the Large Corporation* (Philadelphia, 1950), 114–16; and many

With such a list of social activities, obligations, and opportunities for which their leadership and resources were solicited, it was little wonder that executives were sometimes tempted to conclude that they, almost alone, must shoulder the burdens of Atlas. Thus Theodore V. Houser of Sears could assert that no other group held such "broad responsibilities to the people as a whole" as did corporate management; and an article in *Fortune* could argue that of all interest groups management had "the best claim to disinterestedness and foresight." No one, perhaps, put the case more ambitiously than Frank W. Abrams. As a "good citizen, and because it cannot properly function in an acrimonious and contentious atmosphere," Abrams wrote, management had "the positive duty to work for peaceful relations and understanding among men—for a restoration of faith of men in each other in all walks of life." [10]

Whatever the merit of such claims, there was little doubt about their implications for the role and training of managers. The concept of management as a profession, requiring special training and analytical skills as well as broad social understanding and high ethical standards, had grown steadily since the 1920s. New techniques and concepts in the social sciences, the continued increase in the number of business executives with postgraduate training, and the parallel expansion of corporate bureaucracies offering specialized managerial skills all combined to emphasize the professional ideal for business executives. Doubts might linger over the old question of whether management could truly become a profession, but there was little doubt that it constantly required more technical skill and broader social horizons. "It takes professional judgment, experience, and knowledge of the consequences of specific decisions," Frank W. Abrams noted, "to resolve all the claims and to keep all the groups in cooperative support of the joint enterprise." [11]

---

other sources previously cited. Clarence B. Randall offered a long list of social problems which company officials, in his opinion, might well take into their consideration. These included equal employment opportunities, air and water pollution, traffic, housing, noise, and similar urban-industrial conditions. *A Creed for Free Enterprise*, 69–75.

[10] Theodore V. Houser, *Big Business and Human Values*, 62; Merrill, *Responsibilities of Business Leadership*, xi–xii; John Knox Jessup, "A Political Role for the Corporation." Abrams is quoted in J. D. Glover, *The Attack on Big Business* (Boston, 1954), 338–39.

[11] Abrams, "Management's Responsibilities in a Complex World." For the development of management as a profession, see Chap. III; also, Gordon and Howell, *Higher Education for Business;* Pierson, *Education of American Business-*

The university schools of business administration, a training ground for successive generations of corporate officials, played a crucial role in exposing their students to the standards, techniques, and ideals of modern management. Among these, as Howard R. Bowen, dean of the University of Illinois College of Commerce and Business Administration, emphasized in 1948, was the responsibility "to promote good human relations within the enterprise and with its customers and the public, and . . . to be a civic leader and an economic statesman." James B. Conant, Harvard's president, told potential contributors to its Graduate School of Business Administration that business, more than ever before, needed men who recognized their responsibility equally to business itself and to a free society. "Such men must understand the practical workings of business organizations," Conant held, "but also the economic and social climate in which business operates. . . ." The statement that business managers should be men with "a responsibility to the nation, as well as to themselves, to reestablish themselves in the public mind as objective thinkers and seekers of the public interest" represented the ultimate aspiration of professionalism.[12]

That business leadership, from the vantage point of its knowledge and experience, had an obligation to inform the public and the public's servants on matters of public interest was a point frequently stressed in the management literature of the 1950s. What was more difficult was to define precisely those areas for which businessmen had special competence to advise. Under the circumstances, as we have seen, the tendency was to extend the boundaries indefinitely. As one writer to the *Harvard Business Review* argued, "Management cannot be held responsible for the total welfare of the enterprise unless it has the authority to seek the social conditions most conducive to that welfare." Cleo F. Craig, board chairman of the American Telephone and Telegraph Company, underlined the idea of the inseparability of business and public interests:

men; and Paul Meadows, "Professional Behavior and Industrial Society," *Journal of Business*, XIX (July, 1946), 145–50.

[12] A. A. Berle paid tribute to the Harvard Business School's contribution to the professionalization of management in Mason, *The Corporation in Modern Society*, xiii. Dean Bowen's remarks, at a ceremony celebrating the fiftieth year of the University of Chicago's business school, appear in "The Challenge of Business Education," University of Chicago, Graduate School of Business (Chicago, 1949), 36ff. See also "Education for Business Responsibility," Harvard University, The Graduate School of Business Administration (Cambridge, Massachusetts, 1947); Edward Duddy, "The Moral Implications of Business as a Profession," *Journal of Business*, XVIII (April, 1945), 63–72. Abrams, "Management's Responsibilities in a Complex World."

No one can accept responsibility in the world unless he takes it first on his own doorstep. So for us in industry, I can see only one sure course to follow. Call it common sense, call it policy, call it anything you like. To my mind industry must aim for, exist for, and everlastingly operate for the good of the community. The community can't ride one track and business another. The two are inseparable, interactive, and interdependent.[13]

However persuasive this argument might seem, it had troublesome implications for corporations and their managements. Both idealism and realistic analysis might contribute to managerial assertions that the machine age had "caused all of us to become our brothers' keepers"; but critics feared that they might also point in dangerous directions. "The fact is," wrote one observer, "that the corporation promises to become a sort of welfare community." In a thoughtful discussion of corporate philanthropy, Edward Littlejohn, director of public relations for the Burroughs Corporation, spelled out some of the consequences of corporate assumption of responsibility for the entire private sector. Such responsibility would inevitably involve control, he believed, through the sheer necessity of choice between alternative recipients of corporate support. Management might prefer it otherwise, but the fact could not be avoided. Still further, if company donations were ever to achieve the five per cent level, "a new theory of business enterprise" which modified traditional profit objectives would have to win acceptance.

It seemed to Littlejohn that the theory and fact of corporate enter-

13 Gras, "Shifts in Public Relations," 120–22; letter from Leland Hazard, Professor of Law at Carnegie Institute of Technology, in "From the Thoughtful Businessmen," *HBR*, XXXVII (November–December, 1959), 15–16ff. Cleo F. Craig's statement, from *Think*, April, 1957, is quoted in A. T. Collier, "Social Responsibility of the Businessman."

Not only the business corporation, but all the key institutions of a highly collectivized, industrial society share this deep involvement in the general welfare, one economist pointed out. "Big organization, both in industry and labor, carries responsibility for its internal integrity and its external power. Industry has responsibilities—in which we all share—for what it does to the products, to the quality of our activities in leisure and in work, for equitable distribution of incomes, for security, for employment opportunities, for avoiding inflation, and for good citizenship generally, in taking care of the ramifying effects and social by-products of the industry." Clark, *Economic Institutions and Human Welfare*, 198.

The view that managerial responsibility extended to efforts to influence or control the environment within which business operated led directly to the political interests and activities discussed in Chap. VIII.

prise stood on the verge of transformation. "Those who built the corporation did so in order to accomplish business objectives," but in the process they had managed also to transform "the economic fauna and flora of our society . . . [so that] the health and strength of the private sector . . . has become increasingly dependent upon corporate action." The problem was to find a basis in principle for the exercise of such corporate power. It was one thing, he felt, to interpret the self-interest of the corporation more broadly, and quite another to assert "a close relationship between corporate objectives and the total health of the private sector."

That the threat of government intervention was enough to justify "the defense of private enterprise strictly understood," Littlejohn had no doubt.

> What must be shown is that all private sectors of the economy stand and fall together. Schools, colleges, churches, research institutions—all are part of private as against governmental enterprise. And not only institutions but ideas are important in this regard. The private sector of our society will be weak indeed if it does not include the opportunity to pursue creative work in art, literature and music.[14]

What he failed to add, although it did indeed seem to be at the back of his mind, was the question of whether such an assumption of corporate responsibility might not end by obliterating all distinctions between public and private sectors.

CRITICS OF SOCIAL RESPONSIBILITY

Not all American businessmen hesitated at the awe-inspiring prospects opened by the enlarged concept of managerial trusteeship. Nor did all grasp at them eagerly. Some, in fact, rejected them out of hand. Loyalty to custom, a sense of the limitations of management's capacities, and allegiance to democratic values kept many executives from wholehearted acceptance of the new theories. True, the themes of "managerialism" dominated business literature, speeches, and con-

[14] Jessup, "A Political Role for the Corporation"; Abrams, "Management's Responsibilities in a Complex World." Edward Littlejohn, "Should Corporations Give?" *Proceedings of the Fourth National Conference on Solicitations* (Cleveland, 1957), 34–37. See Knauth, *Managerial Enterprise*, 197, for acknowledgement that many of the functions being undertaken by corporate officials were "quasi-governmental" in character.

ferences; but some voices expressed resistance or criticism, while others remained silent altogether.

From the founding of the Committee for Economic Development in 1942, at least one influential group had spoken strongly and effectively for the view that business responsibility was primarily economic. While not denying that modern industrial enterprise had broad social consequences, the committee and its leaders held that what business executives could best contribute to society were those qualities which they possessed in greatest measure, strictly economic experience and insight.

Paul Hoffman, one of the CED's founders, set forth his ideas of how businessmen could best defend a free society in 1946. They could, in the first place, promote economic dynamism through research and the development of new products, new methods, and new ways of stimulating people. Secondly, business could promote economic stability through profitable and equitable operations and through cooperation with government in the regularization of employment. Finally, Hoffman felt that business could contribute to public affairs through efforts to promote economic literacy and understanding. Another early CED leader, Ralph Flanders, similarly emphasized economic issues—prices, production, economic stability, and economic legislation—as those toward which management had special responsibilities.[15]

Hoffman and Flanders, as successors of E. A. Filene, were joined—appropriately enough—by the grandson of Henry Ford. "It is *work*, not theories of social responsibility," wrote Henry Ford, II, "which is basic to the success of all of us." To a group of Catholic laymen in 1957, Ford elaborated the idea, pointing to the difficulties of other countries in achieving economic development. "Apart from the overriding obligation to serve God and to look to his eternal destiny, the primary responsibility of the businessman is, of course, to keep his business solvent," Ford argued. "In those countries where social gain has been placed ahead of individual incentive and the right of private property, they have discovered that it is extremely difficult to get their economies moving. . . ."[16]

[15] Paul G. Hoffman, "The Survival of Free Enterprise," *HBR*, XXV (Autumn, 1946), 21–27; Ralph Flanders, "The Moral Dilemma of an Industrialist," *ibid.*, XXIII (Summer, 1945), 433–41; Flanders, *"The Function of Management in American Life."*

[16] Henry Ford, II, "Leadership—Obligation of Management," *Comm. Chron.*, CLXV (1 May 1947), 2338ff. (italics Ford's); Ford, II, "Business Welfare Concepts for the Benefit of All," *ibid.*, CLXXXV (4 April 1957), 1589.

Neither Ford nor others who questioned the assumption of broad and nebulous social obligations by business meant, however, to exclude all forms of corporate social participation. The substantial civic activities and political education programs of the Ford Motor Company, for one, made this fact unmistakably clear. The problem was where to draw the line between justifiable and excessive social activities; and the answer was not self-evident. Leland I. Doan, president of the Dow Chemical Company, put it in a perspective that would have commanded widespread approval:

> Some of the things we do, the policies we follow, can hardly be reduced to accounting. We would be hard put to identify for our stockholders the dollars of profit that have resulted from any particular program or practice. . . . We have learned, sometimes the hard way, that business, if it is to be successful and enduring, must be operated *within the framework* of public interest. And a pretty large framework it is. But I hope we never kid ourselves that we are operating for the public interest *per se*.
>
> Our function is an economic one, and we have a very direct responsibility to carry out the function just as ably as we possibly can. Our social responsibilities are part of the package, but they are indirect.[17]

Arguments for a more traditional approach to managerial responsibilities and corporate social relations came also from outsiders. Journalists, professors of business administration, economists, lawyers, and other business consultants and observers—although as a group they had done much to foster the concept of social responsibility—were far from unanimous in approving it. One of the most widely read and re-

---

[17] Leland I. Doan, "Fundamental Role of Business Is to Operate Profitably," *Comm. Chron.*, CLXXXVI (18 July 1957), 286 (italics Doan's); Alfred P. Sloan, Jr., "Road to Serfdom Blocked," *ibid.*, CLXXXVII (22 January 1953), 295ff.

The editors of *Fortune* also held that the broad concept of managerial responsibility, which they associated with the Harvard Business School, was unjustified. Most company presidents and executives were primarily interested in their companies; they were "primarily men who get things done, fast and with results. . . ." Frequently they disliked civic work, which entailed "a diffusion of their energies," and participated with interest only when they could see a direct relationship to their own companies or careers. *The Executive Life*, 67–72, 226.

spected, Peter F. Drucker, took a distinctly cool view of the lengths to which corporate social responsibility was sometimes pushed. In his *The Concept of the Corporation* (1946) and *The New Society* (1950), Drucker had argued that the corporation was, in many respects, the key institution of modern industrial society, whose influence radiated far beyond its own immediate affairs. Nevertheless, by 1954, he was counseling caution in drawing sweeping conclusions from what he continued to recognize as the "social character and the public existence of the most private enterprises."

Management's responsibilities, Drucker insisted, began with the enterprise: "everything else arises out of this trust." "Business enterprise must not become the 'welfare corporation' and attempt to embrace all phases of the individual's life," he thought. Furthermore, social responsibilities could never justify actions contrary to the corporation's own best interests. Instead a corporation "should be so organized as to fulfill automatically its social obligations in the very act of seeking its own best self-interest." Drucker feared, too, that the expansion of corporate responsibilities would necessarily bring with it control or authority over the areas taken under the corporate wing. Drucker preferred a wide field for managerial discretion, but he emphasized that the first duty of the corporation was to survive. Profit, not philanthropy, was the test of performance.[18]

Drucker's position was midway between traditionalist views of corporate enterprise and those of the "managerialists"; but it was a difficult position to maintain. A widely respected writer on business problems, J. A. Livingston, could argue straightforwardly for the orthodox interpretation of the rights and powers of the legal owners of the corporation. In a book entitled *The American Stockholder,* written in 1958, Livingston insisted that management's discretionary powers should be circumscribed and scorned talk of "corporate good citizenship." Others were equally insistent. But John Knox Jessup, who began with the simple assertion that management's function was "to make [its] corporation successful," moved from such apparently solid ground directly into a quicksand of responsibilities and powers. Corporate success, as Jessup saw it, depended upon realization of the fact that the enterprise had become "a new, vital kind of commonwealth, within which individual citizens can work to produce wealth in harmony and to share rewards in a spirit of practical justice." Hence, the manager's role, after all, was an ambitious one: "As chief of this little

[18] Drucker, *The Practice of Management,* 14, 38, 46, 82, 269, 381–84.

commonwealth, . . . [he] has the political job of keeping all his constituents happy in that part of their lives which relates to work." [19]

In earlier decades critics of American business leadership had, justly in many cases, called for greater attention to the social consequences of company policies. Now, with even-handed cheerfulness, they attacked corporate assertions of social responsibility. Many, though by no means all, took up the supposedly old-fashioned idea that the objective of business was profit alone and found in it hitherto undiscovered virtues. Businessmen moving slowly toward acceptance of broader conceptions of their social role might well have been bewildered at the sight of academic and other critics of business behavior racing swiftly past them—in the opposite direction. The business corporation, its managers might have concluded, could not win the approval of the intellectual community whichever way it turned.

Yet there was point to the latter-day doubts expressed by those who had come to fear the implications of total corporate social responsibility. Criticism centered about three closely related points: the power wielded by corporate managements; the uncertain quality of the standards by which such power was guided and governed; and possibilities for authoritarian paternalism inherent in unlimited corporate power.

That the management of large corporations had a considerable area of freedom, within broad limits, to define and direct company policy was a fact by now largely agreed upon. Businessmen themselves, ever since the Twenties, had made much of management's role as balancer and adjuster of competing interests in the publicly owned corporation. The idea of trusteeship implied that no single interest, even that of ownership, could hold managers solely accountable to it. On the contrary, management involved discretion, judgment, and sensitivity to long-range considerations. None of these was meaningful without freedom.

Furthermore, although businessmen might disagree, economists in-

[19] Jessup, "A Political Role for the Corporation." For similar views see Cole, *Business Enterprise in its Social Setting*, 123; and Glover, *The Attack on Big Business*, 327–40.

For the stricter traditionalist position, see J. A. Livingston, *The American Stockholder* (New York, 1958); Louis D. Kelso and Mortimer J. Adler, *The Capitalist Manifesto* (New York, 1958); and Milton Friedman's remarks in *Social Science Reporter, Eighth Social Science Seminar on "Three Major Factors in Business Management: Leadership, Decision-Making and Social Responsibility"* (San Francisco, March 19, 1958), 4–5, summarized in Eells's *The Meaning of Modern Business*, 77–87.

sisted that large corporations enjoyed a degree of freedom from market pressures without which company officials would have hardly been in a position to dispense charity and assume the roles of statesmen. Freedom from domination by stockholders or by the market was the necessary prerequisite for managerial social involvement. When the enormous power of national corporations was directed under circumstances of substantial freedom by a small group of corporate leaders there was cause for concern. When, still further, these leaders were essentially self-selected the concern was heightened.

Talk of managerial social responsibility, then, appeared to many of its critics to be little more than a "mask for privilege," a rationalization for freedom from effective social control. "No direct responsibility, made effective by formal and functioning machinery of control, exists," wrote the economist Carl Kaysen. "No matter how responsible managers strive to be, they remain in the fundamental sense irresponsible oligarchs in the context of the modern corporate system." [20]

Apart from the fact of sheer power were the issues of the qualifications of those who exercised it and the standards by which they judged. Despite the spread of business education and claims of managerial professionalization, it was not clear that professional considerations did or, indeed, could guide all executive decision-making. To Ernest Dale, long a student of management behavior, talk of professionalism was in large part window-dressing. Clear standards of managerial behavior, effectively enforced and subject to independent criticism, were lacking in many aspects of corporate activity and not least in those areas involving broad social considerations. For the clear test of immediate profit, managerialism had substituted executive discretion and vaguely defined objectives of long-run profitability and social responsibility. Even a sympathetic student of the new management conceded that, "The often-expressed notion of a 'balance of interests' actually conceals the company-centered behavior of managers themselves." [21]

[20] Carl Kaysen, "The Social Significance of the Modern Corporation," *The American Economic Review*, Supplement, XLVII (May, 1957), 311–19. Ernest Dale, *The Great Organizers*, 176ff., agreed that the trend in management was toward "increasing power by internal managers and the lessening or elimination of their accountability." See also Mason, *The Corporation in Modern Society*, 5, 56, *passim*.

[21] Maurer, *Great Enterprise*, 169. See also Ernest Dale, "Executives Who Can't Manage," *Atlantic Monthly*, CCX (July, 1962), 58–64, and *The Great Organizers*, 195ff.; Leonard Silk, "The Education of Businessmen," 9; Benjamin M. Selekman, "Is Management Creating a Class Society?" *HBR*, XXXVI (January–February,

The exercise of power by an undemocratically selected minority without clearly defined and accepted standards was the essence of authoritarianism. To critics of corporate enterprise it was no answer at all to say that managerial discretion and judgment were guided by a new sense of social responsibility. "It is much easier to dispense justice, to be benevolent, than it is to share power—especially with those who have the means to compel such sharing," wrote Benjamin M. Selekman in 1958. As their critics saw it, corporation executives were assuming unwarranted authority and influence over matters of public concern. A party to the social contract was, in effect, threatening to become its sole interpreter. Both from the point of view of society and from that of management itself, it was dangerous for responsibility for all aspects of social welfare to be concentrated in the business corporation. Such welfare capitalism, one economist argued, provided an ideology "which embraces the aims of the New and Fair Deal but proposes (and sometimes in concrete detail) to give business the responsibility for the materializing of these aims." [22]

Not only did welfare capitalism threaten to rival the welfare state. In the minds of a number of observers, it was increasingly difficult to tell where one left off and the other began. According to Carl Kaysen,

> The soulful corporation becomes less and less distinguishable, except in the matter of formal control and management responsibility, from the socialist enterprise if the latter operates under instructions to serve the public welfare but not to rely on the public treasury. They share common structural features: market power and a very long decision horizon—although the socialist enterprise as observable to date excels in both directions.

Theodore Levitt similarly attacked what he termed "The New Federalism," which threatened to "turn the corporation into a twentieth cen-

1958), 37–46; Howard R. Bowen, *Social Responsibilities of the Businessman* (New York, 1953), 49; Eugene V. Rostow, "To Whom and for What Ends is Corporate Management Responsible?" in Mason, *The Corporation in Modern Society*, 47–71; A. H. Cole, "The Evolving Perspective of Businessmen," *HBR*, XXVII (January, 1949), 123–28; Edward S. Mason, "The Apologetics of Managerialism," *Journal of Business*, XXXI (January, 1958), 1–11; "Have Corporations a Higher Duty than Profits?" *Fortune*, LXI (August, 1960), 108ff.; and A. T. Mason, "Business Organized as Power," *Am. Pol. Sci. Review*, XLIV (June, 1950), 323–42.

[22] Selekman, "Is Management Creating a Class Society?" 37–46; Robert E. Lane, *The Regulation of Businessmen: Social Conditions of Economic Control* (New Haven, 1954), 24. Also, Ernest Dale, "Management Must Be Made Accountable," *HBR*, XXXVIII (March–April 1960), 49–59.

tury equivalent of the medieval Church." The danger, Levitt thought, was that "the corporation would eventually invest itself with all-embracing duties, obligations, and finally powers—ministering to the whole man and molding him and society in the image of the corporation's narrow ambitions and essentially unsocial ends." Like others who called for a return to traditionalist corporation theory, Levitt rejected the theory of corporate social responsibilities. "We do not want a pervasive welfare state in government, and we do not want it in unions. And for the same reasons we should not want it in corporations," he insisted. "There is a name for this kind of encircling business ministry, and it pains me to use it. The name is fascism." Levitt believed business should occupy itself with improving production and increasing profits, leaving to government the role of caring for the general welfare. "In the end business has only two responsibilities—to obey the elementary canons of everyday face-to-face civility (honesty, good faith, and so on) and to seek material gain." [23]

If some critics of the new managerialism feared that it might ultimately lead to the welfare state, others saw it as a mere sham—a device by which business leadership had effectively bought off public regulation. Organized labor had from the outset charged that corporate philanthropy was an effort to win friends for its opposition to regulatory legislation and union demands. That such suspicions were not without foundation could be seen in the statements of some business leaders themselves, as well as in episodes such as the "Boulwarism" phase of the General Electric Company's program. The political activism of corporate leadership was likewise attacked by labor spokesmen; businessmen replied that they were simply countering the successful political methods of the unions.

Critics of business "statesmanship" attacked on two somewhat contradictory fronts. John K. Galbraith, the Harvard economist, held that corporation giving to education was "inequitable and inadequate." He proposed a payroll tax as an alternative, to assure adequate funds for the education of those upon whom business relied so heavily. Corporate philanthropy, Galbraith implied, was a stop-gap measure—in ef-

[23] Kaysen, "The Social Significance of the Modern Corporation," 311–19; Theodore Levitt, "The Dangers of Social Responsibility," *HBR*, XXXVI (September–October, 1958), 41–50. For an early critique of the idea of social responsibility as a front for fascism, see Brady, *Business as a System of Power*, 1943.

For the suggestion that corporate philanthropy was reducing voluntarism in private giving, see Dickinson, *Philanthropy and Public Policy*, 135. Others held, however, that the very impersonality of corporate giving made it more acceptable —because less patronizing—than personal charity. Richard S. Eells and Clarence C. Walton, *Conceptual Foundations of Business* (Homewood, Illinois, 1961), 456.

fect, an avoidance of the real issue of tax-supported higher education. The sociologist, C. Wright Mills, however, saw talk of the "corporate soul" as a screen for the growing domination of American society by an industrial-military elite. And T. K. Quinn, an outspoken individualist who quit "Monster Business" where he had risen high in the executive ranks of the General Electric Company, was almost equally suspicious. Public regulation and dismemberment of the corporate giants was essential for the preservation of democracy, in his view.[24]

THE TESTING OF CORPORATE RESPONSIBILITY

The moral and psychological perils to which the doctrine of corporate social responsibility exposed its adherents were clearly indicated by the economist Charles E. Lindblom. "We are never so reprehensible as when righteous, never so unjust as when being just," Lindblom wrote in 1957. "The enlargement of corporate personality . . . encompasses . . . the capacity to do confidently in the name of industrial statesmanship what the soulless corporation would hesitate to do under the stigma of monopoly." Instead of a clearer definition of the socially responsible enterprise, events were producing greater confusion. Lindblom found it increasingly difficult "to distinguish between the contribution of emerging codes of corporation conduct to corporate responsibility, on the one hand, and the contribution of emerging corporate self-righteousness to misconduct, on the other." [25] Not only on these grounds but on economic and political grounds as well it appeared that the case for the corporation as chief agent and prop of the general welfare was far from closed. Indeed, as the decade of the 1950s approached its end, spokesmen for a broad conception of corporate social responsibilities were forced on more than one occasion into a defensive stance.

[24] Raskin, "The Corporation and the Campus"; John K. Galbraith, "Men and Capital," *The Saturday Evening Post*, CCXXXII (5 March 1960), 32ff.; C. Wright Mills, *The Power Elite* (New York, 1956), 126; Brady, *Business as a System of Power*, 272; T. K. Quinn, *Giant Business: Threat to Democracy* (New York, 1953), *passim*. Quinn referred to Alfred P. Sloan, Jr., as a "believer in the divine right of capital," with no interest in the equitable division of its fruits. " 'Survival of the fittest,' was Mr. Sloan's law, but he would temper it by a degree of humanity and by acknowledged gifts. . . ." *Ibid.*, 99. See also Quinn's *I Quit Monster Business* (New York, 1948).

[25] In "The Monopoly Problem—Discussion," *American Economic Review*, XLVII (May, 1957), 326–27. See also James L. Cullather, "The Corporation Acquires a Soul," *America*, XCVIII (25 July 1958), 483–84.

Two kinds of business activity in particular, involving both individual behavior and company policy, focused attention on questions about the ability of corporations to govern their undertakings by standards of public rather than private interest. The areas in question were those of illegal behavior by company personnel and of conflict between corporate and public policy. Many examples of each might be cited, serving only to document the point that in a highly specialized society conflicts of interest are inevitable. Individuals and groups can always be found using institutional opportunities and screens for their own special advantage. Organized interest groups sufficiently powerful and free to do so will inevitably be tempted to place private advantage ahead of public good. There was nothing unusual about the fact that such goings-on occurred in the Fifties. What was striking, however, and incongruous was the fact that they often involved executives and corporations well known as leaders in the assertion of social responsibilities for business.

Perhaps the most notorious and widely publicized incident of this kind was the conviction in 1961 of a number of executives of major electrical appliance companies for violation of the antitrust laws in conspiring to set prices and allocate sales during the 1950s. The trial exposed a series of secret meetings between representatives of supposedly competing companies. Especially revealing was the involvement of the General Electric Company, whose association and sponsorship of corporate trusteeship, philanthropy, and civic welfare was of long standing. Ralph Cordiner, General Electric's chairman, had been an outspoken advocate of managerial professionalism and responsibility. His denial of knowledge of the illegal activities of his subordinates was scarcely satisfactory either to friends or critics of the company.[26]

[26] For discussion of the case, see John Brooks, "The Impacted Philosophers," *The New Yorker*, XXXVIII (26 May 1962), 45–86; and Richard Austin Smith, "Incredible Electrical Conspiracy," *Fortune*, LXIII (April, 1961), 132ff., and (May, 1961), 161ff. Smith termed the General Electric story one of "cynicism, arrogance and irresponsibility." See also an address by Henry Ford, II, to the Minneapolis Junior Chamber of Commerce, discussing the implications of the case. Ford was a member of GE's board of directors. *New York Times*, 21 April 1961, 16. Ralph Cordiner's *New Frontiers for Professional Managers* (New York, 1956), had constituted the first in the McKinney Foundation Lecture Series.

Indication of the interest aroused by the electrical price fixing case was provided by Peter Bart, "Ethics Issue Stirs Business Colleges," *New York Times*, 12 March 1961, F–1ff. Bart quoted Dean Karl Hill of Dartmouth's Amos Tuck School of Business Administration: "Many of our students are quite disturbed about this case. The affair has sparked a great deal of discussion about the whole question of the business executive's social responsibilities."

The General Electric Company, of course, was not unique in having been found in violation of antitrust laws, although it did have a long history of such violations. Among the large national corporations noted for their assertions of social responsibility, as a matter of fact, there was a rather impressive record of antitrust difficulties—a fact calling for careful evaluation when a final assessment of such companies and their claims was made.[27]

There were other situations in which company behavior, although not illegal, seemed to conflict with the public interest. A prolonged strike in the steel industry in 1959, for example, found both management and union spokesmen arguing their respective positions in the name of the national interest, while the public, in fact, was caught in the middle. When peace talks were arranged in Washington, a government official was said to have suggested that they be held at the Arlington Cemetery, at the "Tomb of the Forgotten Public." The conflict led George Romney, president of American Motors Corporation, to suggest that the concentration of union and of industrial power which the strike involved was excessive and contrary to the public interest.[28] A later union-management settlement in the steel industry, one which did not produce a strike, provoked intervention on the highest level by President John F. Kennedy in 1962. In this instance, the President held that the steel companies had violated a tacit agreement to hold the line on prices. Invoking the public interest and threatening antitrust investigations, he managed to force a rescinding of the increases. In their pursuit of group interest, neither labor nor management gave evidence of genuine concern for the public's welfare.[29]

[27] Corwin D. Edwards, *Big Business and the Policy of Competition* (Cleveland, 1956), 133ff., presented the anti-trust records of the fifty largest industrial companies based on 1948 figures. The violations included Sherman Act, Clayton Act, and Federal Trade Commission cases. General Electric led the list of convictions or pleas of *nolo contendere* with 14 (in completed cases); General Motors had 10; Standard Oil (New Jersey), 4; U. S. Steel, 4; Republic Steel, 5; A & P, 9; Aluminum Company of America, 5; Firestone, 5; Goodyear, 7; etc. DuPont, which rivaled General Electric with 12 violations, had not notably participated in discussions of corporate social responsibility or philanthropy. John K. Galbraith's comment, though pertinent, was apparently only partially true: "An anti-trust suit can destroy the most laboriously constructed reputation for economic and social virtue." "The Defense of Business: A Strategic Appraisal," *HBR*, XXXII (March–April, 1954), 37–43.

[28] A. H. Raskin, "A Question of Principle," *New York Times*, 3 September 1959, 18. For Romney's comments, see *ibid.*, 16 September 1959.

[29] Some broader implications of President Kennedy's controversy with the steel industry were considered in A. A. Berle, "Unwritten Constitution for Our

Such issues as price fixing and labor-management collusion were, of course, controversial. They revealed wide discrepancies of opinion as to the interest of corporate leadership in, and its ability to direct its efforts toward, the public welfare. If the doctrine of social responsibility did not clearly govern company economic policies which so closely affected the public, the alternative seemed to be a kind of corporate schizophrenia.

REEVALUATING SOCIAL RESPONSIBILITY

In the face of criticism and doubt concerning the ramifications of the social responsibility doctrine, some hesitancy and resistance to further applications of it appeared in business circles. Not only did the rate of corporate giving tend to settle roughly at the one per cent level during the 1950s, as indicated in Chapter IX, but there were even signs that it had declined as a per cent of total philanthropic giving by the end of the decade.[30] The accusation that corporate welfarism threatened to become as all-embracing as that of the state gave pause to those businessmen who still fancied themselves rugged individualists. It also troubled those more seriously concerned for the maintenance of individuality and spontaneity in an increasingly organized society. Yet, there was no denying the facts of organization and interdependence. The operations and policies of business did af-

---

Economy," *New York Times Magazine*, 29 April 1962, 7ff. See also Grant McConnell, *Steel and the Presidency* (New York, 1963).

In addition to Owen D. Young, as noted in Chapter IV, other early business leaders who had championed the idea of managerial trusteeship had at one time or another been involved in investigations or trials which threw doubt upon their business integrity or responsibility. These included: George W. Perkins (the Armstrong committee investigation of life insurance practices); John D. Rockefeller, Jr. (the Colorado Fuel and Iron Company strike); Robert E. Stewart, of Standard Oil (Indiana), (the Teapot Dome affair). Such instances suggested the existence of a considerable gap between theory and practice in the thinking of even the most advanced managerial philosophers.

[30] Company giving to Community Chest and United Fund campaigns fell from 40.2 per cent to 33.2 per cent of total giving between 1950 and 1964, despite the fact that the dollar value of corporate contributions had more than doubled, from $78 million to $182 million, during the same years. "The Case for National Corporation Giving to United Campaigns," United Community Funds and Councils of America, Inc., 1964. Much of the decline was accounted for by the great increase in employee giving after 1955, a program sponsored and supported by corporations through executive leadership and payroll deduction plans. See Vaughn Davis Bornet, *Welfare in America* (Norman, Oklahoma, 1960), 176–80.

fect the lives of individuals and the health of communities in many ways of which traditional economic theories failed to take cognizance. What seemed to be needed was a more balanced approach, a concept of business enterprise which recognized its social dimensions on the one hand while avoiding arrogant and absurd, or dangerous, extensions of its functions on the other.

One effort to strike such a balance between past practice and current reality was that of Richard Eells, who had already worked out a rationale for corporate philanthropy based on the principle of freedom of association. Eells had joined the spokesmen for a broadened view of the corporate role; but he was sensitive to the criticism that view had attracted. He also felt the need for a firmer footing on which to base a theory of the modern corporation.

In a book entitled *The Meaning of Modern Business,* published in 1960, Eells advanced the concept of the "well-tempered corporation." This he contrasted with the traditional profit-oriented corporation and the "metro-corporation," defined as one which

> . . . does not confine its activities to business purposes in any narrowly defined sense. It has broad social goals and assumes large social responsibilities. It holds itself accountable to many different sectors of society. Its managers regard themselves as arbiters, adjusters, or balancers of many diverse interests.[31]

Officials of the traditional corporation might talk of social responsibility; but for them, Eells wrote, it means "little more than a verbal commitment to abstract principles of justice." The broad social responsibilities claimed for the metro-corporate model, on the other hand, obviously involved new and forbidding difficulties. What was needed was a more systematic approach, free from charges and counter-charges, to an understanding of the functions, structure, and objectives of modern business.

As it emerged from his scrutiny of the elements involved in corporate behavior, Eells's well-tempered corporation seemed little, if any, more sharply defined than the metro-corporate idea he had rejected. He dismissed as unrealistic the notion of the corporation as simply and solely an economic institution. Eells argued that there were "many legitimate claimants on the fruits of enterprise; and one insistent claim is that it maintain its viability and growth as an institution, quite aside from the rate of return or productivity." Allied with this

[31] Eells, *The Meaning of Modern Business,* 53.

claim was the responsibility at least for "certain well-established companies . . . to participate *continuously* in the coordinate economic, political, and social processes of a free society." Such companies were no longer "free to act as though they were just small, private businessmen operating in a classical market situation." [32]

Among these coordinate responsibilities, Eells clearly gave high priority to the maintenance of free centers of private social activity in the face of government encroachment. Yet he could offer no definitive list of corporate obligations, nor did he succeed in developing clear boundaries within which the assertion of responsibilities could be confined. Much more detailed analysis both of corporate and social procedures, objectives, and relationships would be needed, he said with some justice, before such ends could be achieved. Eells recognized that social change inevitably would affect corporate interests and responsibilities, as it had in the past. On one point he was explicit: as a vital participant in social change, the business corporation must share responsibility for the directions change took.

Whatever its shortcomings, Eells's approach to the sociology of the business corporation had the advantage of clearly setting the institution in a total social environment. He even projected this environment onto a global stage. "There is a sense in which the corporation tempered to these times cannot be neutral," Eells wrote; "it must subscribe [to] a kind of economic brotherhood of man. This is only remotely an ideological alignment, however, and it has nothing to do with religious and political crusades." Nevertheless, Eells conceived of "secular business enterprise" as a "revolutionary force." Its development, therefore, might parallel that of similar social forces such as the universal religious or proletarian movements. "They all have sought new and wider concepts of community; yet may it not be that the present moves toward economic integration—in which corporate enterprise will figure prominently—will be a more effective means of establishing a world community than the cross, the sword, the clenched fist, and the hammer and sickle?" [33] Certainly this was an ambitious agenda for an institution traditionally conceived simply as a money-making proposition!

Implicit in Eells's recognition that the business corporation was deeply and inextricably involved in the life of society was acknowledgment of the fact that democracy had a stake in the treatment of its citizens by private as well as public institutions. The corporation was,

[32] *Ibid.*, 337. Italics Eells's.

[33] *Ibid.*, 334–35.

in fact, a kind of private government. Its managers conceded that they exercised quasi-judicial responsibilities, allocating rewards and rights among the groups it comprised. Their power in relationship to these groups joined in the corporate enterprise was plainly controlling. Unions, to be sure, had secured checks upon unrestrained managerial power in the course of the twentieth century. A system of "industrial jurisprudence" and corporate constitutionalism had grown up, elements of which had won recognition among economists, political scientists, and other students of business enterprise. Despite both internal and external checks, however, managerial power and initiative remained great. Some observers of corporate policy questioned whether the existence of such concentrated private power could be reconciled with democratic principles. To make matters worse, as Peter F. Drucker acknowledged, the status and power of management could not be legitimized on traditional grounds. Within the corporation, Americans were governed by rulers in whose selection they had no voice and over whose actions they exercised relatively little influence. To project this situation, too, onto a global stage, security from corporate authoritarianism seemed as basic as defense against foreign dictatorship.[34]

It was against this background of self-acknowledged managerial power and responsibility, on the one hand, and of concern for the preservation of democratic procedures, on the other, that debate arose during the 1950s over the internal constitution of the corporation. It was not sufficient, critics of the managerial philosophy argued, to rely upon the conscience, the responsibility, or the sense of trusteeship of business management to safeguard the rights and opportunities of American citizens. If the corporation was, indeed, a private government, why should not the constitutional safeguards which shielded Americans from the abuses of governmental power apply within its borders?

Among those raising the question was A. A. Berle, Jr., who for more than a quarter-century had observed the transformation of corporate enterprise and pondered its meaning. Berle believed that corporate managements had exercised their awesome powers with considerably greater responsibility than he had anticipated when he and Gardiner

---

[34] Sumner Slichter, *Union Policies and Industrial Management* (Washington, D.C., 1941), discusses the concept of industrial jurisprudence with relation to the emergence of jointly established collective bargaining and grievance procedures in the field of industrial relations. Peter F. Drucker's *The New Society*, 99–106, *passim.*, considers the problem of managerial legitimacy.

Means had noted the emergence of this power in *The Modern Corporation and Private Enterprise;* but he was not entirely satisfied.

A student of constitutional law, Berle questioned how long the "conscience" of the corporation could remain unregulated by government. In theory, it was the creature of the state and its operations were both "sanctioned and in measure aided by any state in which it . . . [was] authorized to do business." Thus, Berle thought, the corporation could be brought under the operation of the Fourteenth Amendment, which forbade "any state government (or anyone acting for such a government) from taking life, liberty, or property from any individual without due process." Accepting the argument that corporate economic power inevitably involved political interests and power as well, Berle thought it only a matter of time until this power would be clearly subordinated by the courts to constitutional guarantees.[35]

A series of essays and analyses sponsored by the Fund for the Republic and its Center for the Study of Democratic Institutions took up and expanded upon Berle's notion. In addition to the protections possible under the Bill of Rights and the Fourteenth Amendment, it was suggested that the constitutional guarantee of a republican form of government might be applied to the corporation—despite the fact that this right was one which the courts had seldom effectively applied to the states themselves. The corporate system was, in effect, seen as a kind of economic federalism subject to constitutional checks and guarantees. In a very real sense it was proposed that the large business corporations be incorporated into the political structure and theory of twentieth-century democracy.[36]

[35] A. A. Berle, Jr., *The Twentieth Century Capitalist Revolution* (Harvest Books, 1954), 104–5. In the 1932 election campaign, Berle and Rexford G. Tugwell had drafted a speech given by Franklin D. Roosevelt before the Commonwealth Club of San Francisco. Here Roosevelt, discussing the accumulation of power in private hands through the agency of the great corporation, had called for business and government to collaborate in "an economic declaration of rights, an economic constitutional order." After the demise of the NRA, little was heard of the idea in business literature until it reemerged in the 1950s. See R. S. Kirkendall, "A. A. Berle, Jr., Student of the Corporation, 1917–1932," *Business History Review,* XXXV (Spring, 1961), 43–58.

[36] See Scott Buchanan, "The Corporation and the Republic," The Fund for the Republic, 1958. Also, A. A. Berle, Jr., "Economic Power and the Free Society" (1957), W. H. Ferry, "The Economy Under Law" (1960), Arthur S. Miller, "Private Governments and the Constitution" (1959), and "The Corporation and the Economy" (1959), all published by the Center for the Study of Democratic Institutions. For a parallel view, see Kingman Brewster, Jr., "The Corporation and Economic Federalism," in Mason, *The Corporation in Modern Society,* 72–84.

These proposals for a constitutionalization of corporate power served notice that ultimately those who wielded that power would be held accountable, however "soulful" or conscience-guided its exercise, to the nation at large. For the moment, there was no apparent threat to managerial initiative. No perceptible popular demand arose for the immediate implementation of a larger system of checks and balances. Yet it appeared that in its present form the doctrine of corporate social responsibility might serve merely to postpone and not to avert governmental intervention. Richard Eells, among others, had taken note of this possibility. Indeed, his model of the well-tempered corporation was at least in part an effort to offset it. Eells doubted that the courts could effectively deal with such an unprecedented area of constitutional law. "The proper forum for working out norms of corporate constitutionalism," he wrote, "is the corporation itself, though this is not to say that statutory guidance should be precluded." Essentially, the alternative he offered was corporate initiative in self-generated constitutional principles. This left the question of managerial legitimacy unanswered, however, and government still in the background, should private efforts fall short.[37]

Nearly two decades of discussion and elaboration, then, had not brought the doctrine of corporate social responsibility much closer to clear definition and acceptance. True, more activities than ever before were undertaken in its name and more words were devoted to probing its implications. Its role in winning public support for business appeared to be substantial also. But as an adequate guide either for corporate or for public policy the concept still left much to be desired. Broadening experience, more careful study, and new opportunities beckoning ahead might shape it as a foundation stone in a mixed system of public and private enterprise. Or they might lead to its rejection in favor of some more unitary concept of public control and responsibility. One conclusion seemed plain amid the prevailing confusion and uncertainty. By no stretch of the imagination or the will could the corporation which served the technological and human com-

[37] Eells, *The Meaning of Modern Business*, 322–25, 336. Others recognized that the treatment which business accorded those within its control provided a major test of responsibility. Theodore V. Houser, discussing Sears' personnel policies, acknowledged a responsibility "to make sure that people have an opportunity to grow and develop." In view of the role of big business in society, Houser said, this had to happen in business or it might not happen at all. *Big Business and Human Values*, 4. For a similar comment, but one more critical of business performance, see Bernard W. Dempsey, "The Roots of Social Responsibility," *HBR*, XXVII (July, 1949), 393–404.

plexities of the twentieth century's closing decades return to the simple patterns from which it had evolved. Society was on the move and was remaking its institutions as it traveled. Business, to retain its position of leadership and influence, would have continually to reassess its responsibilities and methods.

11 ▪ CONCLUSION: THE ASSESSMENT OF RESPONSIBILITY

That business enterprise, especially when ordered through a large national corporation, had become an agency for social organization as well as for economic production could scarcely be questioned after the middle of the twentieth century. Even critics of the idea of corporate social responsibility, in effect, conceded the point. When they spoke of long-run profit maximization or profitability, when they justified corporate philanthropy only to the extent that a reasonable expectation of return existed, or even when they attacked the seemingly unwarranted accumulation of power in business hierarchies, they were recognizing as a simple fact of modern life the extent to which corporate policies and practices influenced every aspect of society. "Modern industry makes more than the objects that come off its assembly lines: it makes living conditions for human beings," wrote Eugene Staley in 1941.[1] Twenty years later the point was obvious, beyond dispute, although its implications were still far from fully understood. Not only had business corporations transformed the American economy, they had changed the structure of American society and were now modifying themselves and being modified by the societal changes they had helped to bring about.

[1] Eugene Staley, ed., *Creating an Industrial Civilization; A Report of the Corning Conference, held under the Auspices of the American Council of Learned Societies and the Corning Glass Works, May 17–19, 1941, Corning, New York* (New York, 1942), xi.

298

In one sense, the corporate revolution might be seen as the leading edge of the relentless collectivizing and bureaucratizing apparently required by an industrial order. Government, labor, science, education, and, indeed, philanthropy had felt and responded to many of the same pressures. The rise of the welfare state reflected this general tendency. What was different about business was simply the fact that it had long professed to be concerned merely with the production of goods and services. From the vantage point of the 1960s, however, it appeared doubtful that this had ever been a realistic assessment. "Can you point to one responsibility that lies with management today that management, as such, didn't have fifty years ago?" asked Thomas Roy Jones, a business school graduate and company president. "Haven't these responsibilities that loom so large today always been there? Has management ever had the moral right to act in such a way as to endanger the welfare of her [sic] people?" [2]

Yet, perennial though they might be, managerial responsibilities clearly had been forced more to the forefront of consciousness by the experiences of half a century. Governmental policies had greatly stimulated corporate community relations and philanthropic activities, yet private initiative had established both long before public sanction was secured. In an era of drastic and sudden change their growth had been surprisingly steady through times of war and peace, of depression and prosperity. They had flourished despite criticism and opposition both from within and outside the circle of business. Recognition of the social dimensions and responsibilities of private corporate enterprise thus appeared, in every respect, a central feature of the evolution of modern business institutions and thought. Only their scope and significance remained controversial.

In the 1960s, they were to become increasingly so. A reawakened sensitivity to a long agenda of social ills, ranging from the quality of urban life to racial injustice, poverty, and the uncertainties of international economic development, led many Americans to view the social performance of business as far from adequately responsible. From this perspective, the achievements of business philanthopy were dwarfed if not discredited by their evident inadequacy to the needs of modern society. In such a climate it was easy for some to become cynical about assertions of corporate social responsibility, to suspect that they had merely promoted a myth while obscuring the power- and profit-oriented motives still guiding management. Undoubtedly, there was

[2] Thomas Roy Jones, "Obligations of Leadership in an Evolving Society," *Dun's Review*, LVII (March, 1949), 11–13ff.

some truth in such criticisms; still, a final evaluation seemed premature. What could be asserted with greater confidence was that, in the friendlier climate of the Fifties, business leadership had asserted and exercised a responsibility on behalf of community welfare more sweeping and ambitious than ever before and that its performance in pursuit of that responsibility had failed to satisfy not only its critics but even thoughtful members of its own ranks.[3]

SOURCES OF SOCIAL RESPONSIBILITY

As early as 1926 John Maynard Keynes, the British economist, had commented upon the "tendency of big enterprise to socialize itself." Donaldson Brown, reviewing his career in the DuPont and General Motors complexes, put the same point in a somewhat different perspective when he wrote in 1957 of an emerging "awareness by enlightened leaders in industry of the absolute interdependence between the welfare of business and the common welfare of society." Still another observer, writing a year later in the *Journal of Business*, suggested that American capitalism was gradually becoming "collectivized without nationalization, democratized without revolution, not via universal common-stock ownership a la Merrill Lynch, Pierce, Fenner and Smith, but via the disfranchisement of the stockholder and

---

[3] Among the many discussions of the social dimensions of business during the 1960s were "Is Business Abandoning the Big City?" *HBR*, XXXIX (January–February, 1961), 7ff. (urban problems); Peter F. Drucker, "Big Business and the National Purpose," *HBR*, XL (March–April, 1962), 49ff. (automation, metropolitan problems); Benjamin M. Selekman, "Conservative Labor/Radical Business," *HBR*, XL (March–April, 1962), 80ff. (anti-communism, technological unemployment, education); Dan H. Fenn, Jr., *Business Responsibility in Action* (New York, 1960) (urban revitalization, business overseas); Paul W. Cook, Jr., and George A. von Peterfly, *Problems of Corporate Power* (Homewood, Illinois, 1966) (race relations, urban problems, automation, international affairs); H. K. Nason, "Management's Changing Responsibilities," *Mechanical Engineering*, LXXXI (October, 1959), 42–43; and George Champion, "Private Enterprise and Public Responsibility in a Free Economy," *Conference Board Record*, III (June, 1966), 18–22. To these, many more might be added asserting managerial responsibility across a wide spectrum of social problems.

Critics of corporate social policy found, on the other hand, considerably more support in the literature than they had a decade earlier. Cf. David Finn, "The Price of Corporate Variety," *HBR*, XXXIX (July–August, 1961) 135–43; Paul G. Kaponya, letter to the editor, *HBR*, XL (July–August, 1962), 7–8; John K. Galbraith, *The New Industrial State* (Boston, 1967); Paul T. Heyne, *Private Keepers of the Public Interest* (New York, 1969).

the rise of the professional manager, on the one hand, and the transformation in the role of the government on the other." [4]

Some critics saw the concept of corporate social responsibility as a mere propaganda device of business to conceal selfish motives and objectives. But the record showed that, at many times and under widely varying circumstances, the idea had been pressed upon a dubious or reluctant business leadership by spokesmen for welfare agencies, for academic and cultural institutions, for government, and for others. Businessmen could not in all honesty claim full credit for its achievement, nor could they be accorded full blame for its deficiencies. Selfish and unselfish motives had combined to open managerial minds to ideas about social obligations and relationships. The desire to forestall government intervention and regulation and to preserve corporate freedom and initiative was obviously strong. Yet the concept of managerial trusteeship had taken shape and found its first concrete expression in an era, the 1920s, when government posed little threat to free-wheeling enterprise.

Other factors, too, were at work. The need to justify and dignify a new status could be seen in the idea of the manager as a professional or as a trustee for the interests of other, less powerful groups. The continuing vitality of democratic values undoubtedly exercised powerful, if intangible, lines of force limiting the assertion of unrestrained power. Social scientists studying the behavior of American executives abroad noted the influence of the equalitarian tradition in generating suspicion of authority even among those in top positions: "We often find U. S. executives behaving as if they felt somewhat guilty about being in authority and being greatly concerned about winning the support of their subordinates." [5] Overseas, external restraints on corporate power were often weaker than at home. Circumstances in the United States were probably calculated to stimulate even more strongly whatever feelings of guilt or insecurity lay deep in managerial psyches.

[4] Keynes's comment appears in "The End of Laissez-Faire," published in his *Essays in Persuasion* (London, 1931), 314–15. Donaldson Brown, *Some Reminiscences of an Industrialist*, 2; Robert C. Turner, " 'The Apologetics of Managerialism': Comment," *Journal of Business*, XXXI (July, 1958), 243–48. For a similar interpretation, see Gossett, *Corporate Citizenship*, 157.

[5] William F. Whyte and Allan R. Holmberg, "Human Problems of U. S. Enterprise in Latin America," *Human Organization*, XV (Fall, 1956), 7. A. A. Berle, *Power Without Property*, New York, 1959, 114–16, noted the limiting effects of what he termed the "public consensus." See also James C. Worthy, *Big Business and Free Men* (New York, 1959), 44–45.

Without searching far for hidden motives, certain obvious though seldom commented-upon influences could be noted. A simple concern for social conditions and problems aroused many sympathetic businessmen to utilize whatever resources and facilities were at hand. The spirit of charity and service did not die with the rise of the business corporation, although institutionalization and talk of return on investment may have obscured the fact. Success in business no more fully satisfied the demands of this spirit among corporate managers than it had among the tycoon philanthropists of an earlier generation. The need for personal satisfaction, for a sense of contribution to society as a whole, could seldom in the nature of things be fully met within business as business. That some executives derived sheer personal pleasure from feeling that they could make a useful social contribution beyond the limits of their business lives by helping philanthropic and community activities was apparent. Some company officials and their public relations personnel capitalized on the fact, recognizing that executive morale and identification with corporate objectives were often strengthened by a corporate reputation for good citizenship.[6] Even fur-

[6] Julian W. Woodward and Elmo Roper, "The Effective Public for Plant-Community Relations Effort," *Public Opinion Quarterly*, XV (Winter, 1951–52), 624–34. Shapiro and others, *Company Giving*, 18, reported that twenty-five per cent of the company officials interviewed stressed personal satisfaction as a motive for giving, while only fifteen per cent cited the factor of corporate responsibility.

Kenneth Boulding, in *The Organizational Revolution: A Study in the Ethics of Economic Organization*, 141–42, noted the businessman's need "to make his business something which yields rich and satisfactory relationships and which is in itself a creative and satisfying experience, and yet something which can survive in a market economy." Unions provided something of this feeling for some of their members, Boulding felt; but for businessmen organizations such as Rotary, trade associations, and the like did not quite suit the need. A. T. Collier, vice president of the John Hancock Mutual Life Insurance Company, agreed: "Men in business, quite properly, do not want to risk the charge of selling piety in the sky, but more and more they are coming to realize, without fanfare or drum beating, that their work has significance and purpose only to the extent that it is a fulfillment of their own, and others', inner lives." "Faith in a Creative Society," *HBR*, XXXV (May–June, 1957), 35–41.

The popularity of the "human-relations" emphasis in managerial ideology was explained by the sociologist Reinhard Bendix on the basis that it offered a rationale and justification for careers in bureaucratic structures where the traditional values of hard work and individual effort were no longer entirely applicable. He noted that the new ideology was far from completely accepted in managerial practice, especially by those at the top. Bendix, *Work and Authority in Industry*, 331–33. That corporate philanthropic and social activities offered a means whereby young executives could test themselves, and be tested, for advancement within the organization was suggested by Aileen D. Ross, "Organized Philanthropy in an

ther than this, American missionary zeal and idealism were evident in the determination to vindicate the economic and social system in which the business corporation flourished, to demonstrate before a world in turmoil the virtues and achievements of the "American Way."

Idealistic and charitable considerations moved many businessmen, but practical motives were at least equally important. The value of public approval of business and its policies had grown increasingly apparent and tangible. The conviction that successful marketing of the products of enterprise could be enhanced by the projection of a favorable public "image" had become widespread. Both the Progressive movement and the New Deal had shown, further, that the long-run price for private neglect of responsibility for the social consequences of business was likely to be public regulation. The tax advantage accorded corporate philanthropy further encouraged its growth during and after the Second World War. Business had seen the possibilities of such a provision early in the Twenties and had pressed hard to secure them. Even so, companies remained hesitant to utilize the five per cent deduction fully in the absence of overwhelming pressures to do so. In this as in other phases of its development the idea of corporate social responsibility had been both strengthened and limited by the extent to which it related to specific business needs.

Management often felt constrained to show that activities undertaken in the name of social responsibility were justifiable on more orthodox economic grounds. Even when a strong case could be made, there were difficulties; the dollar return for such expenditures could seldom be demonstrated with any precision. Sometimes the arguments used to demonstrate fiscal responsibility stretched the bounds of credibility. On some occasions, the belief in the justification of expenditures may not have been well-grounded. Contributions to community chests by no means ended the need for substantial public welfare programs, nor did aid to higher education bring a halt to the growth of federal expenditures in this field. Community relations programs and plant visits failed to stem the advance of international communism, as enthusiasts at times seemed almost to think that they might.

Still, each of these programs did have perceptible effects; and on balance their results probably favored business objectives. For the truth was that, behind the rhetoric of moralism and idealism in which the discussion of social responsibility was couched, the movement was

Urban Community," *Canadian Journal of Economics and Political Science,* XVIII (November, 1952), 474–86.

an essentially pragmatic one. It was a recognition of needs arising from changing circumstances both within and beyond the business corporation. The responses which collectively emerged as a theory and practice of social obligation were efforts to deal with substantial issues and pressures. If there were businessmen who escaped from reality and "practicality," they were not those who accepted a social role for enterprise.

Yet, beyond motivation lay the test of performance; and for business performance must finally be the measure of achievement. Social responsibility, in the end, must stand or fall on the basis of the actual accomplishments achieved in its name. The difficulty was, as businessmen and others had discovered, that standards for measuring social responsibility, its accomplishments, and proposals to extend it into new areas were not clear. From the very beginning the concept had floundered in a sea of confusion, conflict, and uncertainty, both within the business community itself and between businessmen and other social groups. While experience had broadened the territory claimed for corporate responsibility, it had done little if anything to define the boundaries more precisely.

Spokesmen for American business could make a strong case in its behalf. Externally, business resources and leadership had strengthened community health and welfare agencies, supported private educational institutions, supplemented government domestic and international policies, and met the needs of a higher proportion of the population at a higher standard of living than any other major industrial society enjoyed. Internally, more humane and understanding personnel policies provided comfort as well as opportunity for many employees; generally favorable wages and conditions of labor—arrived at through collective bargaining with representatives of the workers—prevailed throughout large segments of the economy; continuous pressure for more efficient and technologically progressive methods of production and service characterized large segments of business. In such a record of economic and social achievement lay evidence to support a claim of social obligations successfully, almost triumphantly, discharged.

The concurrent list of complaints, however, nearly equalled that of achievements. Did corporate philanthropy deal with fundamental causes or merely allay effects? Did it foster or discourage alertness to opportunities for more effective—and therefore more socially beneficial—economic performance? Did it serve, or divert attention from, efforts to increase and stabilize employment opportunities? Did support for inadequate voluntary social programs conceal opposition to necessary public welfare measures? Did "enlightened" personnel policies cover up for the subtle manipulation and destruction of individual self-reliance and initiative? Was corporate "good citizenship" simply a cheap form of political persuasion and pressure? Or was it an effort to undermine the effective power of organized labor? Did the theory of social responsibility merely hide the naked fact of relatively unrestrained market power and enable large corporations to charge unjustifiably high prices while claiming public credit for contributions of a very small part of those profits? Could responsibility and power to affect public ends be permitted to rest with undemocratically selected leaders, however conscientious? [7]

[7] Most of the questions raised here have been previously considered in the context in which they arose. One, the nature of management's exercise of the pricing power in imperfectly competitive markets, has been omitted as not having directly contributed to the development of the idea of corporate social responsibility. Considering E. A. Filene's insistence, however, that true social responsibility lay in the most efficient and economical utilization of resources, charges such as those of Gardiner Means that large corporations had pursued irresponsible pricing policies deserve consideration.

In studies dealing with the steel industry and with the General Motors Corporation, Means argued that administered prices had been set at unduly high levels, and thus production had been limited and economic fluctuations aggravated.

> . . . when the businessman has the power to affect industrial [industry-wide] policy, he almost necessarily makes wrong industrial decisions. The very position, experience and training of the businessman which leads him to make the correct decisions on business [company] policy tend to force him to make the wrong decisions in industrial policy in spite of the utmost public spirit which he, as an individual, may seek to exercise. The fact that his decisions are wrong from the point of view of the public interest is no necessary reflection on either his character or his intelligence, but arises from the nature of the situation within which he operates and the functions he performs.

Means, *The Corporate Revolution in America*, 92, 169–73; see also his *Pricing Power and the Public Interest* (New York, 1962), 45, 154–58, *passim.*, for a study of the steel industry.

The Means analysis asserts, in effect, that corporations enjoying significant ability to set their own price levels and utilizing some form of the target pricing technique—and these would presumably include the major companies in every line of trade where perfectly competitive market conditions do not prevail—practice essentially irresponsible pricing policies from the point of view of society as a whole. By holding prices at artificially high levels, they restrict production and consumption. This, in turn, hampers the achievement of full employment and thereby increases demands upon public and private welfare agencies.

The fact that such pricing techniques developed in the 1920s, almost simultaneously with the spread of the idea of corporate social responsibility among the

The roll of questions was apparently interminable. And the answers were not necessarily clear, depending as they did upon the judgment and perspective of individuals. One man's social responsibility was obviously another's privilege. Nor could answers be satisfactorily reached until agreement was arrived at upon two necessarily preceding queries: Where did responsibility properly lie? And how was it to be determined?

RESPONSIBILITY AND LEGITIMACY

"Corporations are not accepted in public opinion as the institutions through which society makes its educational policy, its foreign policy, or its national policy." So wrote Eugene V. Rostow, Dean of the Yale Law School in 1959,[8] and the heart of the issue of social responsibility seemed to lie precisely here. So long as the legitimacy of managerial

---

leaders of the same companies, suggests that the two departures from orthodox economic theory and practice were, in fact, related. They stemmed from, and were, indeed, made possible by, a common source. This was the achievement of power over the market by firms sufficiently large to withstand short-run competitive pressures. The combination movement which, by the Twenties, had extended through many sectors of the economy permitted systematic pricing at the same time that it encouraged companies to look elsewhere—to advertising, public and human relations, service, and research—for acceptable areas of competition. Similar—if less systematic—manipulation of prices by business interests able to do so, and similar attacks upon them as antisocial in character, of course, had provided a central issue of economic and political controversy at least from the beginning of the Industrial Revolution. What Means was asserting, however, was that the conditions of modern business made such behavior an integral and continuing part of business planning rather than a response to more or less casual or occasional opportunities.

Many observers of business have commented, from the 1920s on, on the diminished pressure for short-run profits characterizing large-scale enterprise. Lengthened time-horizons made possible by a degree of market security, in turn, encouraged managers to think in broader terms of the whole range of factors and relationships upon which the long-range success of their companies depended.

For discussion of the changing attitude toward profit in executive circles, see Gordon, *Business Leadership in the Large Corporation*, 336; Maurer, *Great Enterprise*, 134–44; Cochran, *American Business System*, 180, 189; Clark, *Economic Institutions and Human Welfare*, 206–7; and Worthy, *Big Business and Free Men*, 36–39. For the contribution of General Motors' management to the refinement of corporate financial controls and "target pricing" techniques, see Alfred P. Sloan, Jr., *My Years with General Motors* (New York, 1964), 139–43. Also, Donaldson Brown, *Some Reminiscences of an Industrialist*.

[8] In Mason, *The Corporation in Modern Society*, 68. See also Means, *Pricing Power and the Public Interest*, 294.

social policies remained in doubt, their content and the forces that motivated them could not be clarified or evaluated. The issues of legitimacy and acceptance, in the end, would determine the nature—and the future—of the social responsibility of business.

They were issues, too, which both business executives and their critics had sensed from the beginning. Implicit in the ideas of trusteeship, professionalism, and service had been the assumption that economic power must be guided in the general interest by those qualified, through training, experience, or ethical concern, to define that interest. In this view, managerial legitimacy rested upon the superior knowledge and understanding of those in control. Yet such a foundation was clearly not adequate to changing circumstances. As early as 1908, George W. Perkins had conceded that the large business corporation had become in fact a semipublic institution calling for some form of public regulation or supervision.

The dimensions of private trusteeship and governmental regulation had been further explored in the 1920s and 1930s before a new trial balance emerged at the end of the Second World War. Despite the increased role of governmental initiative and supervision, this was a balance which left large areas of social and economic activity essentially free for private decision making. As Russell Davenport pointed out, "This is unique in America: the development in private hands of the social goals which elsewhere people have turned over to the state."[9] It was within this private sector that the idea and practice of corporate social responsibility had flourished. Yet given the scope of corporate power, the question of how much real privacy remained called for careful consideration. If neither position, talent, nor method of selection could assure that corporate policies would be determined by a socially responsible management, what alternatives were there?

In a 1956 *Harvard Business Review* article, Thomas C. Cochran, a long-time student of business leadership, pointed to the conflict between the democratic tradition of government by consent and the inevitably hierarchical and authoritarian procedures of business.[10] Top management seldom had the experience of dealing with others on a basis of equality. Businessmen had long feared and resented outside

[9] "Report of Discussion on 'Basic Elements of a Free, Dynamic Society,'" The Advertising Council (New York, 1951), 21.

[10] Thomas C. Cochran, "Business and the Democratic Tradition," *HBR*, XXXIV (May, 1956), 39–48, and his *The American Business System*, 194–201. See also Worthy, *Big Business and Free Men*, 3–8, for essentially the same argument as that presented here.

criticism. Their persistent cries for a "favorable business climate" were primarily a demand that the public accept business on its own terms. Their resistance to government regulation and their publicly expressed contempt for intellectuals and other nonbusiness groups—which often screened a deep-seated insecurity—were expressions of this attitude. Even in their association with union leadership, the executives of large corporations only occasionally approached common problems in an atmosphere of true mutuality and respect. Although they might not like it, they were forced in effect to work toward agreement with the representatives of employees. No other private interest group shared even to this extent with the business decision makers in the determinations which affected its members' lives.

Executives often recognized the value of freedom for criticism and exchange of ideas within their companies more readily than in their dealings with the outside world. The reluctance or inability of many to participate in the give-and-take discussion of social issues unquestionably bred suspicion and hostility on the part of the public. It encouraged, too, a snobbish paternalism on the part of some businessmen. And it contributed, as the most perceptive among them recognized, to the frequent failures of business leadership accurately to assess public opinion and social issues.

The value of participation in the exchange of ideas and in cooperative efforts in the solution of problems had been recognized in principle—and to some degree in practice—by many corporation managements. It had provided an incidental objective for the public and personnel relations programs which constituted such an important interest of the large business enterprises. It had entered into the ill-fated employee-representation plans of the 1920s, as well as into the more elaborate and sophisticated community relations programs of the 1950s. The difficulty was that management had seldom appreciated the validity of its own assertions that communication was a "two-way street." Despite occasional exceptions, the prevailing tendency had been to try to "sell" business ideas and practices to the public rather than to work toward mutual understanding and respect. The truth of the matter was that the thinking of business leadership tended to develop in substantial isolation and ignorance of the needs and interests of others.

Occasionally, businessmen themselves recognized this fact and attempted to deal with it, usually without conspicuous success. Owen D. Young, sensitive to the power of public opinion, had suggested in 1932, "It would be well if we could step outside the industries and look at them as a whole from the standpoint of the outsider, for the purpose of seeing whether or not from the social and community point of view we are doing all we can." [11] Three decades later, the need to do so remained unfilled. Clarence B. Randall noted with concern the isolation and "intellectual divorcement from the tumult of thought" of many executives who found themselves at the top of the corporate pyramids. "Preoccupied with the complex affairs of their own corporations, they cut themselves off from the sources of facts and ideas by which mass judgments are formed in our country," Randall wrote. "Their thinking on the great questions is borrowed and the opinions they hold are seldom tested by controversy." For such men, Randall prescribed "the sort of grilling a congressman must take when he has to stand up in succession before each unit in his constituency and justify his every vote and conviction."

Businessmen needed "to be more appreciative of the virtues of dissent and criticism, not only from the outside but from within their own organizations as well," agreed James C. Worthy of Sears, Roebuck and Company. "They need to recognize the role of dissent in a free society, and they need to understand what would happen to such a society if any important institution within it should ever be effectively insulated from criticism." So long as corporate leadership was unable or unwilling to work *with*, rather than merely for, others, it could not achieve a full measure of social responsibility.[12]

[11] Tarbell, *Owen D. Young*, 224. *The New Republic* had commented acidly upon Young's concept of managerial trusteeship, however. Executives needed special training and exposure to the "world of ideas" and must be made to report to autonomous representatives of employees and the public. Otherwise, the concept of a professional management would be little but "a sentimental smoke-screen" covering the penetration of society by "market values." *The New Republic*, LI (15 June 1927), 84–85.

A Harvard Business School survey of executives of large corporations in 1962 still found them saying that ways of "selling business to the public" should be the subject of a course for business students. "From the Thoughtful Businessman," *HBR*, XI (March–April, 1962), 38–43. See also "Research Topics Suggested by Sixty Prominent Businessmen," Harvard University Graduate School of Business Administration, 1962 (mimeographed). William H. Whyte, Jr., dealt with aspects of this situation in two studies of business public and personnel relations programs: *Is Anybody Listening?* (New York, 1952), and *The Organization Man* (New York, 1956).

[12] Clarence B. Randall, "Business, Too, Has Its Ivory Towers," *New York Times Magazine*, 8 July 1962, 5ff.; Randall, *A Creed for Free Enterprise*, 63–65; Worthy, *Big Business and Free Men*, 7; Drucker, *Concept of the Corporation*, 88–93; Theodore Levitt, "The Changing Character of Capitalism," *HBR*, XXXIV (July–

"The social responsibilities of business, large or small, are existent because the public says they are," acknowledged Harry A. Bullis, chairman of General Mills, in 1955. But how were business executives to know what responsibilities the public expected them to discharge without channels for communicating this information short of government fiat? It might be true that most companies and their leadership wished neither to dominate nor paternalize the other social groups and institutions with which they dealt. But how was this to be avoided unless provision were made for frank and open discussion, on a basis of equality, between participants? [13]

In the period of readjustment and reevaluation immediately following the Second World War, a number of leading executives had considered the possibility of more adequate representation of the public in the councils of business. Both Ernest R. Breech and Henry Ford, II, had seen a need to develop closer contact between business leadership, the public, and government. They emphasized that this contact should be constructive and in a spirit of real partnership and mutual understanding, but they offered no concrete plan. Gerard Swope had recommended the appointment and remuneration of directors from outside the corporation as recognition in some degree of its quasi-public character. Beardsley Ruml had disagreed, rejecting the idea of public representation on corporate directorates because the "true general public interest in the company's management . . . is expressed in the laws of the state, of the city, and of the nation." Yet Ruml, too, felt the need of extra-legal checks, for he had suggested a management-appointed "director-trustee." He conceded, "Today the obvious

---

August, 1956), 37–47; Max Wolff, "Industry in Partnership. An Interpretation of Case Histories," and Joseph Monserrat, "Industry and Community—a Profitable Partnership," *Journal of Educational Sociology*, XXVII (December, 1953), 162–70, 171–81; O. A. Ohmann, "Search for Managerial Philosophy," *HBR*, XXXV (September–October, 1957), 41–51. Andrew Carnegie's cultivation of leaders of the non-business world seems to have reflected a similar belief. Hendrick, *Carnegie*, II, 36–37. Benjamin M. Selekman, "Cynicism and Managerial Morality," *HBR*, XXXVI (September–October, 1958), 61–71, interpreted "Boulwarism" as an example of cynical manipulation based upon the assumption of managerial superiority.

[13] That some businessmen were conscious of the potential for domination and paternalism inherent in corporate philanthropy was indicated by John A. Pollard, "Emerging Pattern of Corporate Giving," 103; H. W. Prentis, Jr. (chairman of the Armstrong Cork Company and former president of the NAM), "New Goals for Business," *Saturday Review of Literature*, XL (19 January 1957), 14–15; and Raphael Demos, "Business and the Good Society," *HBR*, XXXIII (July–August, 1955), 33–34.

interests of the several parties subject to business government are not properly safeguarded under the present form of control of business power." Both business and other interest groups would profit from the creation of such safeguards, Ruml thought.[14] Little effort, however, was made to give concrete expression to these gropings, except insofar as the burgeoning of corporate social and community activities may have been considered to meet the need.

Where businessmen stopped, others also encountered difficulties. Robert A. Gordon, in a careful study of corporate leadership and structure, concluded that the board of directors was the best place to look for, or to create, an independent check upon management's authority. "Executives need the advice of outside directors," he concluded, "and, what is even more important, we must rely on the board as an independent body to provide the link between executives and those outside groups whose welfare the company exists to serve." Others, less sanguine that management-dominated boards could act effectively, nevertheless acknowledged the need to establish an independent review of corporate policies. Richard Eells, anxious to avoid further public intervention, suggested a "voluntary system of public accountability," especially with regard to corporate philanthropic policies. This would consist, as Eells sketched it, primarily of reports to stockholders and the general public "on the objectives, the programs, and the achievements of . . . corporate giving." He agreed that corporations had "much to gain through the initiation of procedures for squaring their philanthropic designs with generally accepted community values;" but, aside from suggesting an exchange of information between companies, he proposed only a vaguely formulated "organized collaboration" with other groups.[15]

[14] Ernest R. Breech, "The Challenge to Leadership," *Comm. Chron.*, CLXIV (21 November 1946), 2602ff. Henry Ford, II, "Leadership—Obligation of Management"; Beardsley Ruml, *Tomorrow's Business*, 87–91. Gerard Swope, "Some Aspects of Corporate Management," *HBR*, XXIII (Spring, 1945), 314–22.

[15] Gordon, *Business Leadership in the Large Corporation*, 146, *passim.*; Dale, "Management Must Be Made Accountable," 49–59; Dale, *The Great Organizers*, 189–214; Eells, *Corporate Giving in a Free Society*, 68ff. Dean David of the Harvard Business School suggested in 1949 the appointment of a "major officer" of the corporation to serve as its "conscience" in respect both to internal and to external policies. Donald K. David, "Business Responsibilities in an Uncertain World," *HBR*, XXVII, Supplement (May, 1949), 1–8. James W. Culliton, "Business and Religion," *ibid.*, 265–71, offered further discussion of David's proposal in the light of the managerial responsibilities and attitudes which it attempted to reconcile.

There was, of course, no certain magic in the idea of consultation and collaboration between management and others having an interest in the making of corporate social policies. Labor-management relations, again, were solid evidence of this truth. Collective bargaining had offered a basis for mutual graft, crime, and extortion from the public, as well as for industrial cooperation and statesmanship. Yet, whatever its shortcomings, few would deny that collective bargaining had laid a foundation for healthier labor-management relations. There was every reason to expect similar results from the growth of consultative techniques in the field of social relations.

PROSPECTS FOR PARTNERSHIP

In 1952 an industrial relations consultant, Frederick H. Blum, discussed an investigation of the personnel policies of a number of Philadelphia companies. The study, sponsored by the Philadelphia Friends Social Order Committee, amounted to a "social audit" of companies' policies and their execution.[16] Although Blum did not suggest it, the extension of this approach to the evaluation of a wider range of company programs offered interesting possibilities. In effect, some way of achieving an audit such as Blum proposed was what the situation seemed to call for; but his idea fell on deaf ears. The means for institutionalizing it were difficult to conceive, public pressure on its behalf was virtually nonexistent, and corporation officials—naturally—were not eager to impose new limitations on their freedom of action.

Ironically, the participation of business corporations in philanthropic and community activities pointed, at least potentially, in the same direction as the social audit idea. For over twenty-five years business leadership had been increasing the scope of its involvement and interest in civic, social, and educational planning. And in many areas it had at least made a start at doing so on the basis of mutual respect and consent. Company support of the community chest movement had survived the debacle of depression because it helped to meet real needs, defined by professional welfare leaders, clarified and accepted through the give-and-take of the conference table. Corporate gifts to education in the 1920s, on the other hand, had produced scandalous results because the underlying motive was to dominate, rather than to contribute intelligent support and understanding of educational needs.

[16] Frederick H. Blum, "Social Audit of the Enterprise," *HBR*, XXXVI (March–April, 1952), 77–86. The idea of a social audit had previously been advanced by Howard R. Bowen in *Social Responsibilities of the Businessman*, 155.

The rapid growth of corporate support for the nation's colleges and universities in the 1950s, fortunately, had taken place on a firmer foundation. With few exceptions, corporate donors had recognized and respected the independence and competence of the recipients. Businessmen had been guided to a considerable degree by the educators' definitions of their needs—by respect, in other words, for the judgment and integrity of the leaders of another interest group. Out of this recognition and respect had emerged, indeed, a significant change in the basis of company giving. Unrestricted gifts, support for general and liberal education, and support for women's education, for example, were concessions and departures from traditional business interests made possible by deeper understanding of the role of education. Business and educational leaders had even joined in creating new intermediary agencies to provide for the giving and allocation of funds in such fashion as to assure that undue influence or pressure could not be exerted. The system, as it evolved, was far from adequate; but it represented a significant step forward both for business and for education.[17]

Other examples could be cited. The Committee for Economic Development commanded widespread respect and influence precisely because its reports resulted from real and meaningful exchanges between groups with common interests but different viewpoints. Clarence B. Randall testified to the eye-opening effects of his own experience in community chest and civic work. Close association with "men from other forms of business activity, and particularly with those who come from fields totally unrelated to business, all in pursuit of a public cause," had a broadening effect. It provided "a most salutary corrective on the extremes of our opinions. We gain a new perspective, a new humility, and a suspicion that perhaps we are not quite as right as we thought."[18]

There was nothing either miraculous or inevitable about the educative effect of such social interaction. Face-to-face contact between spokesmen for different groups might produce superficial, if not positively harmful, understandings rather than genuinely useful ones. Many who sat on the boards or the fund-raising committees of community agencies served in a routine and unimaginative fashion. Often

[17] Pollard, "Emerging Pattern of Corporate Giving," 108ff.

[18] Randall, A Creed for Free Enterprise, 65–66. Gerard Swope's earlier Hull House experience provided another case in point, as did that of Edward L. Ryerson, also of the Inland Steel Corporation, at Graham Taylor's Chicago Commons. Clarke A. Chambers, Seedtime of Reform, American Social Service and Social Action, 1918–1933 (Minneapolis, 1963), 199.

such jobs were turned over by top management to young executives who filled them routinely, with one eye cocked on their primary business careers. Randall recognized that such delegation of responsibility might be self-defeating. "When we tell ourselves that we are too busy and too important to the enterprise to do these things personally, and when we ask someone . . . to do them for us, that man knows we have ducked. He will then duck, too, doing just as little as he can. . . . Actions still speak louder than words." [19]

Participation in the work of social, educational, and cultural agencies was not the only way in which business executives might meet, test, and learn from others. Through their own creation, the company foundation, they had developed another potential channel for bringing representative ideas and men from other segments of society into closer contact with business. This possibility had been sensed by some foundation officials but never fully exploited. Preoccupation with financial, tax, and administrative problems had diverted attention from other purposes. The appointment of outside consultants and the addition of other community leaders to the foundation boards, already heavily staffed with company representatives, might provide the basis for a forum of analysis and criticism enlightening to the corporation and to the community alike. The sponsorship by company foundations or other business organizations of conferences consciously designed to bring together representatives from various walks of life and interest groups might carry further the tentative first steps by which corporate officials had begun to respond to the common life. Richard Eells's suggestion that company foundations issue public reports offered still another avenue for discussion and debate.

Business leadership might well hesitate, on several grounds, before undertaking such additional commitments. The expenditure of executive time and talent involved would be considerable; but, given the lengthened time span upon which decisions involving large corporate enterprises were based, this was not an insuperable problem—especially if results in added company understanding and acceptance could be shown. The argument that managerial performance and responsibility were best tested and demonstrated in the marketplace, although weakened where markets were shown to be less than perfectly competitive, remained strong. But it had little application to the social dimensions of corporate behavior; and it was social, rather than purely economic, performance which was in question. Participation

19 *A Creed for Free Enterprise*, 66–67; Long, "The Corporation, Its Satellites, and the Local Community."

and partnership might challenge the splendid isolation and security of managerial status, but they offered at least a partial answer to the nagging issue of managerial legitimacy. Ultimate responsibility for corporate social policies would necessarily remain with management, whatever provisions might be made for consultation in policy making.

The concept and the practice of corporate social responsibility had arisen out of a basically sound, pragmatic analysis of the changing realities of social and industrial life. That they had strengthened and sustained important institutions threatened by the gales of change was as undeniable as that they had thus far failed to resolve the problems of standards and legitimacy. So long as corporate leadership accepted the notion that good public relations could be bought or "sold," it seemed unlikely that these problems would vanish.

True partnership, through joint participation in determining social needs and responsibilities, might offer a sounder approach. Rather than a futile search for absolute standards of business social responsibility, it might provide the basis for continuing explorations of mutual needs and resources. One student of corporation and constitutional law noted that the framers of the Constitution had relied more heavily upon representative institutions than upon clear delineation and definition of authority to check abuses of political power.[20] To what extent might this experience offer lessons for the twentieth-century effort to manage social and economic power?

Institutions which assured that the social responsibilities of business

[20] Abram Chayes, "The Modern Corporation and the Rule of Law," in Mason, *The Corporation in Modern Society*, 25–45. A. A. Berle's concept of a "public consensus," which somehow emerged from the contributions of journalists, professors, and politicians and which indirectly influenced the politics of large corporations, suggested that an unstructured form of representation was already emerging. In the long run, however, such informal techniques could scarcely prove adequate. Berle, *Power Without Property*, 110–13.

A parallel situation is presented in a provocative essay by John William Ward, "The Ideal of Individualism and the Reality of Organization," in Earl F. Cheit, ed., *The Business Establishment* (New York, 1964), 37–76. In an analysis which somewhat resembles that presented here, Ward considers the problem of reconciling democratic values—in his case primarily the values of individualism—to the life of an organized interdependent society. He cites the example of a Public Review Board established by the United Auto Workers to provide an independent channel for dealing with individual members' complaints and differences with leadership policies. For a fuller analysis, see Jack Stieber, Walter E. Oberer, and Michael Harrington, *Democracy and Public Review: An Analysis of the UAW Public Review Board*, A Report to the Center for the Study of Democratic Institutions (Santa Barbara, California, 1960).

were fulfilled on a basis of mutual understanding and interest could offer a significant step toward the democratic goal of government by consent. Long ago, Edmund Burke had defined society as "a partnership in all science; a partnership in all art; a partnership in every virtue, and in all perfection." Probably no human society could approach very near to that ideal. But reason and representation were signposts which the American democracy had erected along the way. No sector of society, however powerful, could long avoid fulfilling the terms of the partnership. For half a century business had been exploring them. All signs pointed to the conclusion that its commitment would continue to grow.

APPENDIX

LETTER FROM RALPH H. BLANCHARD, MANAGER,
NIAGARA FALLS, NEW YORK, COMMUNITY CHEST

December 29, 1927

Mr. A. A. MacLean,
U. S. L. Battery Corp.,
Niagara Falls, New York.

Dear Mr. MacLean:

I am sorry that we have been so delayed in gathering material regarding services rendered U. S. L. employees by Chest agencies. This fall and early winter has been very heavy in its demands on all of us and this has without question made the material much more difficult to gather.

As I told you when Miss Kellogg and I were in your office, this letter is sent with reservations. In the first place it is manifestly impossible to reckon the value of service on a dollar and cent basis. It is impossible to tell how much value there is to your company in having better schools, a better health department, better hospitals, better agencies for the care of those who are in need of the particular services for the simple reason that so many of the benefits are indirect. However, they all go to make a civilized community and if Niagara Falls is to be the city we all want it to be increasing attention will have to be paid to these features. I am sure that you agree with all this because your work in these various fields indicates it. Incidentally there is no question but that they make the city a better place in which to do business and there is thus a very substantial return to your plant as well as all others.

317

In the second place it is impossible to figure service rendered by some of our agencies. For instance, the Y. W. C. A. suggests but does not require membership for use of its facilities. Any woman in Niagara Falls can take advantage of these facilities without the membership and no doubt many of the members of U. S. L. families make use of them. It is impossible to tell how many of them do use it and it is even more impossible to estimate the value of these services. The same thing is true of the Travelers Aid Society. No one doubts the value of the service, I believe, but it is impossible to tell how travelers who later became identified with the U. S. L. have been helped by that organization. In the same way it is also impossible to estimate service rendered by the Catholic Daughters of America. Thus three of the Chest agencies are immediately put in the class where it would be most difficult, if not impossible, to gauge the value of service rendered to your employees.

We are informed that there are no past employees of the U. S. L. in Locust Haven Home for the Aged. And Commandant Cook of the Salvation Army tells me that his records do not indicate direct service from that agency. No doubt some of their holiday or other relief work or the value of some of their other activities has been felt by your people but the records are not clear enough to cover the point. We know that the Red Cross bedside nurses have done some work for your employees also but this service is so young that we are not counting that agency either.

Of the remaining eight organizations we have secured data as follows:

It is estimated that there are 40 Boy Scouts, members of whose families work in the U. S. L. The average cost to the community per Boy Scout year is $11.44. This would mean that the Boy Scouts give service to U. S. L. employees amounting to $457.60.

Miss Kellogg showed you a list of families which have been helped during the past year by the Charity Organization Society. These number 10 and the direct relief given to these families totals $672.36. This is exclusive of services rendered by paid employees of that organization, which is an important factor when it is considered that over half of its cases do not need material relief but do need and receive trained assistance in untangling family troubles of all kinds.

There are 6 Girl Scouts whose parents work in the U. S. L., and one Girl Scout leader herself works at the U. S. L. The average cost to the community per Girl Scout year is $12.36 which makes total $74.16 aside from the leader.

In the case of the Niagara Falls Memorial Hospital we find that 46 employees of yours spent a total of 439 days in the hospital. They paid an average of $4.15 per day and the cost last year averaged $5.04 per patient day. There would therefore be a loss of $390.71 on this group.

In addition to this, 21 patients related to employees of the U. S. L. spent a total of 165 days in the hospital but they apparently used private rooms almost entirely which were considered self-supporting.

In addition there were 237 outside cases of laboratory work which were paid for. There is therefore no further cost to be considered in that connection.

Sister Bernice informs us that there were a total of about 10 employees who used St. Mary's Hospital in ward beds. There were also 12 who used the out patient clinic. We are estimating the total loss on these patients at $250.00 which we consider conservative.

We find also that 2 children of U. S. L. employees are in Wyndham Lawn Home for children. The Chest pays approximately $50.00 per year for each Niagara Falls child in that institution. This is over and above the amount of board paid by parents or the county and is supplemented by further gifts received in Lockport and other parts of the county.

We find that there are 64 senior members of the Y. M. C. A. in your organization who pay dues averaging about $12.00. The Y. M. C. A. figures the cost of senior membership at $24.41 which means that there is a loss of $12.41 each or a total of $794.24 on that group. In addition there are 8 boys' memberships where the fathers work in the U. S. L. These membership dues average $6.00 and the cost is $28.51. There is therefore a loss of $180.08 on this group or a total of $974.32 on the two classes of memberships. It would be very difficult to make estimate of further services rendered to your employees. For instance, plant nights use practically all the facilities of the association and the industrial basket ball work takes a great deal of the time of the physical department instructors. No figures are put in for these services and any that were stated would have to be purely arbitrary.

The direct charges above stated, aside from any general services which are rendered and aside from the five agencies for which no charge is stated, total $3,115.65. This does not take into account at all the Community Chest itself. I think perhaps we had better leave the matter of judging that question entirely to you.

Personally I like to look at the whole situation this way. All of us do not agree as to the relative merits of organizations in the Chest but I think that all will agree that the tendency of all is to make the city a better place in which to live and to [sic] business. Therefore we should assume that they are all good. Chest agencies this year will spend approximately $556,000. Of this amount earnings will take care of all except the amounts appearing in the Chest Budget. The total of these together with Chest administration [,] etc. was about $203,000. Figuring your average number of employees as 1,000 and the average U. S. L. family at 4 you have about one-twentieth of the city's population closely allied with you. One twentieth of our budget would be a little over $10,000 and it seems to me that the U. S. L. as a corporation plus the individuals working in the plant should look forward to carrying approximately this $10,000 item. We have been very glad to see the total pledges from your plant approaching this figure and know that it is due to the earnest efforts of yourself and others in the organization. Is it too much to hope that the 1928 campaign will see an even greater total from corporation and employees pledges than the $6,200 pledged in 1927?

Please do not hesitate to call upon me for any assistance which you may desire in working out the situation to your complete satisfaction.

With kind personal regards and best wishes for the coming year, I am

Sincerely yours,
Ralph H. Blanchard
Manager

RHB:M

P. S. I find that one agency has been omitted in the above statement. Mount Garmel [sic] Guild assisted 5 families last year with a total relief cost of $196.50. As in the case of the Charity Organization Society this is exclusive of service cost which is not so pronounced in the case of this agency since the work is done by volunteers. The above figure for Mount Carmel Guild is included in the total stated, namely, $3,115.65.

R. H. B.

BIBLIOGRAPHICAL NOTE

MANUSCRIPT SOURCES

Source materials for the history of business in America are voluminous; and, despite the rapid growth of business history, many remain untapped. This is even more true when, as in the present case, the subject is one usually considered tangential to the central purposes of business. The two manuscript collections upon which I have relied heavily are not themselves primarily business materials. The archives of the United Community Funds and Councils of America, Inc., in New York City, contain materials relating to a major national welfare fund-raising organization, one which played a crucial role in the mobilization of both individual and corporate philanthropy. Businessmen were active leaders at every stage of the organization's growth; corporations were important targets and benefactors of its activities from the beginning. As the national headquarters of a federation of local agencies, the UCFCA communicated regularly with the local branches. Its archives, therefore, contain much that reveals the conditions and problems of specific cities, as regards both welfare and business.

The John Price Jones Corporation Papers, deposited at the Baker Library of the Harvard Graduate School of Business Administration, contain the records of one of the first and largest fund-raising agencies. These include detailed summaries, reports, and analyses of fund-raising campaigns carried out on behalf of educational, welfare, artistic, and other philanthropic organizations. Although business organizations as such were not an object of many solicitations in which the

Jones agency engaged before the 1940s, there are occasional indications of company contributions even in the earlier period. Overall, the collection provides a comprehensive basis for understanding the problems and techniques involved in the growth and spread of organized solicitation.

The records of many other health, welfare, educational, and fund-raising institutions could undoubtedly supply a wealth of additional data. So could the records of national and local business organizations, chambers of commerce, trade associations, and management and public relations organizations. Of these, I have used only the papers of the Boston Chamber of Commerce, deposited at the Baker Library, which cover the early years of the century, and those of the Cleveland Chamber of Commerce. Close scrutiny of the records of any of these organizations will surely bring to light much more detailed information concerning business social policies and ideas.

Company records and papers of individual businessmen provide still another source of information, which I have tapped only indirectly through reliance upon company histories. The number, diversity, and difficulty of access to these materials has limited their further use. But the growth of business history, the new appreciation of the significant part played by business leadership in many phases of national development, and the growing sophistication and self-confidence of business leadership are rapidly increasing their availability. The cultivation of these sources through monographic studies has already added greatly to our understanding of business thought and behavior. Much remains to be done, however, in reexamining these materials for the light they throw on the social dimensions of business. No final assessment of business institutions and leadership will be possible until this basic work has been undertaken.

BOOKS

Books treating the general social and economic background of the period under consideration are numerous. I have consulted, and profited, from many; but I list here only those which have proved most useful. Others will be found in the footnotes relating to specific topics for which they contributed material. Three volumes in The Economic History of the United States series are relevant: Harold U. Faulkner, *The Decline of Laissez-Faire, 1897–1917*, New York, 1951; George Soule, *Prosperity Decade, 1917–1929*, New York, 1947; and Broadus Mitchell, *Depression Decade, 1929–1941*, New York, 1947. Thomas C.

Cochran and William Miller, *The Age of Enterprise: a Social History of Industrial America,* New York, 1942, is a landmark interpretation, integrating business into the history of American development. Thomas C. Cochran, *The American Business System: A Historical Perspective, 1900–55,* Cambridge, Massachusetts, 1957, ably summarizes the major developments of the period. Two scholarly interpretations of the social significance of business and its leaders are A. H. Cole, *Business Enterprise in Its Social Setting,* Cambridge, Massachusetts, 1959, and Sigmund Diamond, *The Reputation of the American Businessman,* Cambridge, Massachusetts, 1955. Frederick Lewis Allen, *The Big Change: America Transforms Itself, 1900–1950,* New York, 1952, is a somewhat overly enthusiastic popular interpretation.

The key study of the evolution of big business remains A. A. Berle and Gardiner C. Means, *The Modern Corporation and Private Property,* New York, 1933. Thorstein Veblen, *The Theory of Business Enterprise,* 1904, is a brilliant, opinionated predecessor. A. A. Berle has brought his study of business institutions up to date in *The Twentieth Century Capitalist Revolution,* New York, 1954, and *Power Without Property,* New York, 1959. Less concerned with the external relations of business but equally perceptive is Kenneth Boulding, *The Organizational Revolution: A Study in the Ethics of Organization,* New York, 1953. Another student of economic institutions whose work spans the years during which the social dimensions of business won recognition is John M. Clark, whose *Social Control of Business,* Chicago, 1926, and *Economic Institutions and Private Property,* New York, 1957, are important contributions to analysis. Robert A. Gordon, *Business Leadership in the Large Corporation,* Washington, D.C., 1945, deals with the changing status of management and other parties involved in corporate enterprise but pays relatively little attention to community relations. This gap is partly filled by Howard Bowen, *Social Responsibilities of the Businessman,* New York, 1953, a thoughtful exposition.

The Progressive era produced some of the sharpest critiques, as well as some of the first constructive formulations, of the new implications of business. W. J. Ghent, *Our Benevolent Feudalism,* New York, 1902, although less familiar than Veblen, is equally trenchant. A socialist, Ghent nevertheless conceded a growing deference to public opinion on the part of business. Louis D. Brandeis, whose *Other People's Money and How the Bankers Use It,* New York, 1913, attacked the financial irresponsibility of investment bankers, offered a partial solution in "Business, the New Profession," an essay published in *Business—A*

Profession, Boston, 1914. Arthur J. Eddy, in *The New Competition,* New York, 1912, defended big business from the point of view of the public interest. Ida M. Tarbell, *New Ideals in Business: An Account of Their Effects Upon Men and Profits,* New York, 1916, is a laudatory treatment of business personnel policies. William Lyon MacKenzie King, *Industry and Humanity,* Boston and New York, 1918, reflects the Progressive spirit at its best and is particularly significant because of its author's influence with the Rockefellers. Robert W. Wiebe, *Businessmen and Reform: A Study of the Progressive Movement,* Cambridge, Massachusetts, 1962, deals primarily with government but reveals a sensitivity on the part of businessmen to public opinion and social relations which parallels my findings.

Books about business in the 1920s, whether written then or since, have seldom achieved objectivity. Arundel Cotter, *United States Steel: A Corporation with a Soul,* New York, 1921, reflects the boosterism of the day, the compulsive drive of business to win friends by self-praise. It reveals by its very superficiality a strong need for public acceptance. A more scholarly study of business thought in the same decade, James Warren Prothro, *The Dollar Decade: Business Ideas in the 1920s,* Baton Rouge, 1954, errs in the opposite direction, by failing to recognize the social and organizational context of business thinking and by presenting too limited a range of business thought.

Apart from politics, the histories of individual companies, and the special field of labor-management relations, business in the 1930s has attracted little scholarly interest. Attention has centered on the New Deal, with the business community and its leaders cast in the role of not-so-loyal opposition. No period of business history deserves more careful scrutiny, or has received so little.

The literature of business since the Great Depression, on the other hand, is bountiful. A number of its outstanding contributions have been cited previously. James Burnham, *The Managerial Revolution: What is Happening in the World,* New York, 1941, marks the recovery from the Depression with renewed appreciation of the importance of managerial leadership. Peter F. Drucker's volumes, *The Concept of the Corporation,* New York, 1946; *The New Society,* New York, 1952; and *The Practice of Management,* New York, 1954, have done much to win recognition and understanding for the social implications of business institutions and policies, although Drucker has resisted the more ambitious formulations of corporate social responsibility. Wayne Hodges, *Company and Community,* New York, 1959, focuses on the General Electric Company's community relations program in Syracuse, New York. Karl Schriftgeisser, *Business Comes of Age: The Story of the Committee for Economic Development and Its Impact upon the Economic Policies of the United States, 1942–60,* New York, 1960, deals with an important new business agency. More general in scope is William G. Scott, *The Social Ethic in Management Literature,* Georgia State College of Business Administration, Bureau of Business and Economic Research, Studies in Business and Economics, No. 4, Atlanta, 1959, a useful survey.

Richard Eells has made two attempts to formulate a theoretical foundation for the socially conscious corporation: *The Meaning of Modern Business,* New York, 1960, and *Conceptual Foundations of Business,* Homewood, Illinois, 1961, co-authored by Clarence Walton. Of these, the former is more significant. Corwin D. Edwards, *Big Business and the Policy of Competition,* Cleveland, 1956, offers a needed corrective to excessive claims of social responsibility—as do other studies of antitrust policy. Gardiner C. Means has criticized the pricing policies of large corporations such as General Motors as inherently socially irresponsible in *The Corporate Revolution in America,* New York, 1962. Edward S. Mason has edited a remarkable volume of essays on many aspects of modern corporate affairs, *The Corporation in Modern Society,* Cambridge, Massachusetts, 1960. Francis X. Sutton and others, *The American Business Creed,* Cambridge, Massachusetts, 1956, is a careful study of changing ideologies.

Analysis of the characteristics of business leadership began with F. W. Taussig and C. S. Joslyn, *American Business Leaders,* New York, 1932, reflecting the interest of the 1920s. Subsequent studies have extended the time span over which changes in recruitment patterns and leadership characteristics can be studied. They include W. Lloyd Warner and James C. Abegglen, *Big Business Leaders in America,* New York, 1955; Mabel Newcomer, *The Big Business Executive,* New York, 1955; the Editors of *Fortune, The Executive Life,* Garden City, 1956; and William Miller, ed., *Men in Business: Essays in the History of Entrepreneurship,* Cambridge, Massachusetts, 1952. C. Wright Mills, *The Power Elite,* New York, 1956, includes data from another study, Suzanne I. Keller, "Social Origins and Career Lines of Three Generations of American Business Leaders," Columbia University unpublished Ph.D. thesis, 1954. Ernest Dale, *The Great Organizers,* New York, 1960, discusses the business lives and contributions of a number of outstanding executives. Seymour Martin Lipset and Reinhard Bendix survey the literature dealing with the social origins of business leadership in *Social Mobility and Industrial Society,* Berkeley, 1959.

The growth and range of corporate philanthropy can be followed in Pierce Williams and Frederick E. Croxton, *Corporation Contributions to Organized Community Welfare Services,* New York, 1930, a pioneer study sponsored by the community chests; F. Emerson Andrews, *Corporation Giving,* New York, 1952; Leo J. Shapiro and others, *Company Giving,* Chicago, 1960, based on a survey of giving practices of companies in the Chicago area; Beardsley A. Ruml and Theodore Geiger, "The Five Per Cent," Planning Pamphlet No. 70, The National Planning Association, 1952; Beardsley A. Ruml and Theodore Geiger, *Manual of Corporate Giving,* National Planning Association, 1952, and three studies sponsored by the National Industrial Conference Board, "Company Policies on Donations," No. 7; "Company Policies on Donations. II. Written Statements of Policy," No. 49; and "Company Contributions. III. Policies and Procedures," No. 89, in its Studies in Business Policy series, New York, 1945, 1950, and 1958, respectively. Frank W. Andrews, *A Study of Company Sponsored Foundations,* New York, 1960, deals with an important new instrument. Richard Eells, *Corporate Giving in a Free Society,* New York, 1956, sees an essential role for corporate philanthropy in a free, diversified society. Scott M. Cutlip, *Fund Raising in the United States,* New Brunswick, 1965, is a comprehensive survey. Floyd Hunter, *Community Power Structure: A Study of Decision Makers,* Chapel Hill, 1953, treats the influence of business leadership on community welfare organizations.

Books by or about business leaders provide an obvious source of information concerning the ideas and conditions influencing business behavior. Only the most pertinent and revealing can be listed here. Others cited in the footnotes under the appropriate sections are helpful for rounding out the picture but are not essential to the delineation of its chief features.

Individual business leaders, by virtue of the power they wield in their organizations and the respect in which they are held by the business community and—to only a somewhat lesser degree—by society at large, have strongly influenced the development of policy and attitudes. This is true despite the fact that the bureaucratization of business has provided top executives with staffs and "ghost writers" whose contributions cannot be overlooked. Whatever the source of his ideas and pronouncements, the businessman gives them new life and significance by presenting them under his name. He may not be able to claim credit for their formulation but neither can he escape responsibility for their presentation.

Many nineteenth-century businessmen were concerned with social conditions and with their own relationship to, and responsibility for, them; but Andrew Carnegie stands out as one who most dramatically exemplified and stated these concerns. Carnegie's writings, especially his essays "Wealth" and "The Best Fields for Philanthropy," are major statements. The essays are contained in *The Gospel of Wealth,* edited by Edward C. Kirkland, Cambridge, Massachusetts, 1962. Burton J. Hendrick, *The Life of Andrew Carnegie,* 2 volumes, New York, 1932, is also helpful. Almont Lindsey, *The Pullman Strike: The Story of a Unique Experiment and of a Great Labor Upheaval,* Chicago, 1942, is a detailed study.

As socially conscious industrialists, the Rockefeller family outshone even Carnegie. In this case, the ideas were put forward in speeches by John D. Rockefeller, Jr., in *The Personal Relation in Industry,* New York, 1923, where the interest centers on industrial and personnel relations. The younger Rockefeller represented a second generation of business leadership as well as a period of transition from individual to corporate social consciousness. Rockefeller drew heavily on the ideas and advice of the publicist Ivy Lee and of William Lyon MacKenzie King, whose *Industry and Humanity* has been referred to above. His life and philanthropic interests are treated in Raymond B. Fosdick, *John D. Rockefeller, Jr.: A Portrait,* New York, 1956. Another transitional figure was George W. Perkins, whose role is well treated in John A. Garraty, *Right Hand Man: The Life of George W. Perkins,* New York, 1957. Ida M. Tarbell, *The Life of Elbert W. Gary: The Story of Steel,* New York, 1925, presents a more representative and influential figure in a less scholarly and effective way.

The 1920s saw the doctrines of managerial trusteeship and of the social responsibility of business enterprise put forward by businessmen themselves for the first time. A number of corporation executives made important contributions to the dissemination and discussion of the new viewpoints. Ida M. Tarbell, *Owen D. Young: A New Type of Industrial Leader,* New York, 1932, is revealing but uncritical. David Loth, *Swope of G.E.,* New York, 1958, deals with Young's partner in the leadership of the General Electric Company with greater insight. Even the leading critics of the idea of social responsibility recognized the growing interdependence of business and society. Henry Ford, by far the most famous although not the most effective of these, contributed two volumes in collaboration with Samuel Crowther, *My Life and Work,* New York, 1922, and *Moving Forward,* Garden City, 1930. Ford's own particular contributions to the understanding of the implications of mass production and consumption and to industrial relations are judiciously treated in Allen Nevins and Frank Ernest Hill, *Ford: the Times, the Man, the Company,* New York, 1954, and *Ford: Expansion and Challenge, 1915–1933,* New York, 1957. More articulate and sensitive than Ford was Edward A. Filene, whose *The Way Out: A Forecast of Coming Changes in American Business and Industry,* Garden City, 1924, and *Successful Living in the Machine Age,* New York, 1931, written in collaboration with Charles W. Wood, entitle him to be considered a major interpreter of the promise of mass production and distribution, as well as a major critic of the idea of business social responsibility divorced from emphasis upon economic performance. Gerald W. Johnson, *Liberal's Progress,* New York, 1948, is a popular biography of Filene.

The evolution of the General Motors Corporation under the leadership of Alfred P. Sloan, Jr., during and after the 1920s was a crucial contribution to the theory and practice of managerial control and responsibility. Sloan has discussed this experience in two autobiographical volumes, *Adventures of a White Collar Man,* written in collaboration with Boyden Sparkes, New York, 1941, and *My Years with General Motors,* New York, 1964. Donaldson Brown, *Some Reminiscences of an Industrialist,* privately printed at Pt. Deposit, Maryland, 1957, also deals with General Motors.

Not until the 1950s did business leaders again find time and incentive for discussions of the social responsibilities of their companies. Then, however, a flood of books, articles, and speeches appeared. Among the most serious and perceptive were those by Clarence H. Randall. His widely read *A Creed for Free Enterprise,* Boston, 1952, reflects business's ideological offensive during these years but was considerably more thoughtful than most. Randall's *Over My Shoulder,* Boston, 1956, contains personal reminiscences as well as reflections on the changing nature of business organization and relationships. The McKinney Lecture series of Columbia University provided an opportunity for some of the major business figures to formulate their positions on the nature of modern business and its place in the community. Published in book form, these statements provide insight into the ideas and policies of some of the most influential leaders and their companies. Of particular importance are Roger M. Blough, *Free Man and the Corporation,* New York, 1959; Theodore V. Houser, *Big Business and Human Values,* New York, 1957; and James C. Worthy, *Big Business and Free Men,* New York, 1959.

The development of business education is analyzed in Robert A. Gordon and James S. Howell, *Higher Education for Business,* New

York, 1959; and Frank C. Pierson and others, *The Education of American Businessmen*, New York, 1959.

As with business, so with welfare and philanthropy: the history of these institutions has won growing attention in recent years. The standard history is Robert G. Bremner, *American Philanthropy*, Chicago, 1960. The conditions and institutions of welfare are surveyed in Harold L. Wilensky and Charles N. Lebeaux, *Industrial Society and Social Welfare*, New York, 1958; Vaughn Davis Bornet, *Welfare in America*, Norman, Oklahoma, 1960; Alfred de Grazia and Ted Gurr, *American Welfare*, New York, 1961; and John Price Jones, *The American Giver: A Review of American Generosity*, New York, 1954. More specialized are Clarke A. Chambers, *Seedtime of Reform: American Social Service and Social Action, 1918–1933*, Minneapolis, 1963; Merle Curti and Roderick Nash, *Philanthropy in the Shaping of American Higher Education*, New Brunswick, 1965; C. Howard Hopkins, *History of the Y.M.C.A. in North America*, New York, 1951; Sherwood Eddy, *A Century with Youth: a History of the Y.M.C.A. from 1844 to 1944*, New York, 1944; and John F. Moore, *The Story of the Railroad "Y"*, New York, 1930; and John R. Seeley and others, *Community Chest: A Case Study in Philanthropy*, Toronto, 1957, a sociological analysis.

JOURNALS

This study depends heavily upon the periodical literature of business, of which there is a great deal. Specific journals, both of individual industries and of broader business organizations such as chambers of commerce, the National Association of Manufacturers, and the American Management Association, provide a wealth of information not only about business and economic problems but about business thought concerning social and political issues as well. It is a source which still remains largely untapped. House organs, annual reports, and other publications of individual companies also deserve more attention than they have thus far received. The problem of interpreting the representative character of such materials, as well as their influence upon the thinking of their readers, is not easy. Its existence does not eliminate the value of such materials for research.

A number of scholarly journals devoted to business and business history have come into existence, testifying to the expansion of interest in the field. Most have been associated with one of the university schools of business: for example, the *Journal of Business* with Chicago, and the *Business History Review* with Harvard. *Explorations in Entrepreneurial History* was also a Harvard product. The *Harvard Business Review,* not strictly speaking a scholarly publication, presents articles by both scholars and business leaders. It has been one of the most influential forces promoting and discussing the new concepts of managerial and corporate social responsibility. *Fortune,* a popular journal for and about managers, has glamorized business and its leadership and occasionally criticized their performance.

These journals and many others are repeatedly cited in the footnotes where they provide materials for the discussion of specific ideas and events. It would be supererogatory to list them all again here.

INDEX

Abrams, Frank W.: on education and business, 212 n; leads effort to secure business support of higher education, 216–17; on company and national interest, 271; on stewardship of management, 275; on professional judgment of management, 277

Addams, Jane: on George M. Pullman, 8–9; at Hull House, 23; sees business as a public trust, 28

Advertising Council, The: public affairs program of, 255

Allen, Frederick Lewis: evaluates business leadership in the 1920s, 110–11

American Association of Community Organizations: founded 1918, 117–18

Americanization Movement: business support of, 38

American Management Association: created, 1923, to promote professionalism, 64

American Rolling Mill Company: community relations policy, 37

American Telephone and Telegraph Company: owners' control replaced by executive leadership, 1925, 58

Appleton, Nathan: and founding of Lowell Textile industry, 4; questions effectiveness of hired management, 57

Arts, the: as objects of business contributions, Carnegie's view, 18–19

Association of Community Chests and Councils: AACO renamed, 1927, 131

Associations, Business: involvement in public and community relations, 91–93

Baker, Newton D.: at Washington Conference, 1928, 132; reports increases in company contributions, 151–52; heads 1932 drive for business community chest contributions, 154; heads 1933 Mobilization for Human Needs, 155 n; testifies before Senate Committee in favor of 5% charitable deduction, 169–70

Barnard, Chester: analyzes roles of business management, 199–200

Bell, Laird: calls business attention to needs of higher education, 212–13; argues for broad conception of business interest in education, 218–19

Benevolence: of business motives, 2; as a business motive, 5; Robert Owen's concept of management, 4 n; G. M. Pullman's, 8

Birdseye, Clarence F.: on corporate morality, 47–48

Blanchard, Ralph H.: manager, Niagara Falls Community Chest, 123 n; at AACO, 1928, 124; at Washington Conference, 133; appointed assistant director, Community Chest and Councils, Inc., 156 n

Blough, Roger M.: on company responsibility for racial segregation, 228–29; estimates one million management people working for civic

331